STATISTICS WITH R FOR DATA ANALYSIS

Mohsen Nady

ARCLER
PRESS

www.arclerpress.com

Statistics with R for Data Analysis

Mohsen Nady

Arcler Press
4164 Lakeshore Road
Burlington, ON L7L 1A4
Canada
www.arclerpress.com
Email: orders@arclereducation.com

ISBN: 978-1-77956-353-8 (Hardcover)

STATISTICS WITH R FOR DATA ANALYSIS

ABOUT THE AUTHOR

Mohsen Nady is a pharmacist with a M.D. in Microbiology and a Diploma in Industrial Pharmacy. Besides, Mohsen has more than 10 years of experience in Statistics and Data Analytics. Mohsen has applied his skills to different projects related to Genomics, Microbiology, Biostatistics, Six Sigma, Data Analytics, Data Visualization, Building Apps, Geography, Market Analysis, Business Analysis, Machine Learning, etc. Mohsen also published his thesis in a high-impact journal that attracted many citations, where all the statistical analyses were performed by him in addition to the methodological part. Furthermore, Mohsen has earned different certificates, from top universities (Harvard, Johns Hopkins, Denmark, etc) in Statistics, Data Analytics, Data Visualization, and Machine Learning that highlight his outstanding diverse skills.

TABLE OF CONTENTS

LIST OF TABLES

PREFACE

This book covers the use of the R programming language for data analysis. Data analysis is a broad term that includes exploratory data analysis by calculating summary statistics and plotting summary plots, and inferential data analysis by conducting statistical tests to infer population characteristics from the data samples we have. The two types of data analysis, whether exploratory or inferential, can be done perfectly using R programming.

R has many useful packages that can not only perform all the previous data analysis steps but also has additional packages that were developed by different scientists specifically for creating specific analyses for various fields like genomics, geography, environmental sciences, marketing, etc. Furthermore, R is free software and can run on all major platforms: Windows, Mac OS, and UNIX/Linux.

This book covers the different types of data analysis that can be performed on the main two types of data, categorical and continuous. As such, it is divided into 5 chapters that demonstrate these analyses with different real-world datasets.

Chapters 1 and 2 were designed for univariate analysis of continuous and categorical variables, respectively. Different datasets were used to illustrate how to calculate summary statistics, create summary plots, and conduct statistical tests on these variables.

Chapter 3 is designed to demonstrate how to examine the relationship between two continuous variables using summary statistics of different correlation coefficients, various summary plots like scatter plots or correlation matrices, and finally some statistical tests for the significance of these correlations.

Chapter 4 shows how to examine the relationship between one categorical and one continuous variable using summary statistics of location or spread, different summary plots like box plots, histograms, etc., and some statistical tests.

Finally, Chapter 5 demonstrates how to examine the relationship between two categorical variables using summary statistics of counts and proportions, summary plots like bar and line plots, and some statistical tests.

In all these chapters, different datasets per chapter were used so each chapter can be viewed as a separate entity for the interested researcher in any of the five chapter topics. All the data analysis steps were done using the R programming language with several code chunks to demonstrate these complex analyses. I hope that this book, covering the main five types of data analysis, will be a valuable addition to your journey in data analysis.

–Author

CHAPTER 1

UNIVARIATE ANALYSIS OF CONTINUOUS DATA

Contents

1.1. DATA USED IN THIS CHAPTER

1.1.1. The Economics Data

The US economic time series data is available from https://fred.stlouisfed.org/ and is part of the ggplot2 package under the name "economics." To load this data into our R session, we will load the tidyverse package (which contains the ggplot2 package) using the library function. Then, we will load the economics data using the data function.

```
library(tidyverse)

data("economics")
```

Then, to see the data structure, we will use the glimpse function.

```
glimpse(economics)
## Rows: 574
## Columns: 6
## $ date     <date> 1967-07-01, 1967-08-01, 1967-09-01, 1967-10-01, 1967-11-01, …
## $ pce      <dbl> 506.7, 509.8, 515.6, 512.2, 517.4, 525.1, 530.9, 533.6, 544.3…
## $ pop      <dbl> 198712, 198911, 199113, 199311, 199498, 199657, 199808, 19992…
## $ psavert <dbl> 12.6, 12.6, 11.9, 12.9, 12.8, 11.8, 11.7, 12.3, 11.7, 12.3, 1…
## $ uempmed <dbl> 4.5, 4.7, 4.6, 4.9, 4.7, 4.8, 5.1, 4.5, 4.1, 4.6, 4.4, 4.4, 4…
## $ unemploy <dbl> 2944, 2945, 2958, 3143, 3066, 3018, 2878, 3001, 2877, 2709, 2…
```

The glimpse function gives the number of rows, the number of columns in the data followed by the column names (with a dollar sign prefix), the column classes (within parentheses), and the first values of each column. We see that the economics data contains 574 rows and 6 columns:

1. date: the month of data collection. It is a date column.
2. pce: the personal consumption expenditures, in billions of dollars. It is a double or numeric column with decimals.
3. pop: the total population, in thousands. It is a double or numeric column.
4. psavert: the personal savings rate. It is a double or numeric column with decimals.
5. uempmed: the median duration of unemployment, in weeks. It is a double or numeric column with decimals.
6. unemploy: the number of unemployed in thousands. It is a double or numeric column.

1.1.2. The Midwest Data

The midwest data frame contains demographic information of midwest counties from the 2000 US census. As before, we load the "midwest" data frame using the data function. Finally, we explore the data using the glimpse function.

```
data("midwest")
glimpse(midwest)
## Rows: 437
## Columns: 28
## $ PID                <int> 561, 562, 563, 564, 565, 566, 567, 568, 569, 570,…
## $ county             <chr> "ADAMS," "ALEXANDER," "BOND," "BOONE," "BROWN," "…
## $ state              <chr> "IL," "IL," "IL," "IL," "IL," "IL," "IL," "IL," "…
## $ area               <dbl> 0.052, 0.014, 0.022, 0.017, 0.018, 0.050, 0.017, …
## $ poptotal           <int> 66090, 10626, 14991, 30806, 5836, 35688, 5322, 16…
## $ popdensity         <dbl> 1270.9615, 759.0000, 681.4091, 1812.1176, 324.222…
## $ popwhite           <int> 63917, 7054, 14477, 29344, 5264, 35157, 5298, 165…
## $ popblack           <int> 1702, 3496, 429, 127, 547, 50, 1, 111, 16, 16559,…
## $ popamerindian      <int> 98, 19, 35, 46, 14, 65, 8, 30, 8, 331, 51, 26, 17…
## $ popasian           <int> 249, 48, 16, 150, 5, 195, 15, 61, 23, 8033, 89, 3…
## $ popother           <int> 124, 9, 34, 1139, 6, 221, 0, 84, 6, 1596, 20, 7, …
## $ percwhite          <dbl> 96.71206, 66.38434, 96.57128, 95.25417, 90.19877,…
## $ percblack          <dbl> 2.57527614, 32.90043290, 2.86171703, 0.41225735, …
## $ percamerindan      <dbl> 0.14828264, 0.17880670, 0.23347342, 0.14932156, 0…
## $ percasian          <dbl> 0.37675897, 0.45172219, 0.10673071, 0.48691813, 0…
## $ percother          <dbl> 0.18762294, 0.08469791, 0.22680275, 3.69733169, 0…
## $ popadults          <int> 43298, 6724, 9669, 19272, 3979, 23444, 3583, 1132…
## $ perchsd            <dbl> 75.10740, 59.72635, 69.33499, 75.47219, 68.86152,…
## $ percollege         <dbl> 19.63139, 11.24331, 17.03382, 17.27895, 14.47600,…
## $ percprof           <dbl> 4.355859, 2.870315, 4.488572, 4.197800, 3.367680,…
## $ poppovertyknown    <int> 63628, 10529, 14235, 30337, 4815, 35107, 5241, 16…
## $ percpovertyknown   <dbl> 96.27478, 99.08714, 94.95697, 98.47757, 82.50514,…
## $ percbelowpoverty   <dbl> 13.151443, 32.244278, 12.068844, 7.209019, 13.520…
## $ percchildbelowpovert <dbl> 18.011717, 45.826514, 14.036061, 11.179536, 13.02…
## $ percadultpoverty   <dbl> 11.009776, 27.385647, 10.852090, 5.536013, 11.143…
## $ percelderlypoverty <dbl> 12.443812, 25.228976, 12.697410, 6.217047, 19.200…
## $ inmetro            <int> 0, 0, 0, 1, 0, 0, 0, 0, 0, 1, 0, 0, 0, 1, 0, 1, 0…
## $ category           <chr> "AAR," "LHR," "AAR," "ALU," "AAR," "AAR," "LAR," …
```

The midwest is a data frame with 437 rows and 28 variables:

1. PID: Unique county identifier and its class is integer or numeric.
2. county: County name and its class is character.
3. state: State to which county belongs and its class is character.
4. area: The area of the county and its class is double with decimal places or numeric.
5. poptotal: Total population and its class is integer or numeric.
6. popdensity: Population density (person/unit area) and its class is double or numeric.
7. popwhite: Number of whites and its class is integer or numeric.
8. popblack: Number of blacks and its class is integer or numeric.
9. popamerindian: Number of American Indians and its class is integer or numeric.
10. popasian: Number of Asians and its class is integer or numeric.
11. popother: Number of other races and its class is integer or numeric.
12. percwhite: Percent white and its class is double or numeric.
13. percblack: Percent black and its class is double or numeric.
14. percamerindan: Percent American Indian and its class is double or numeric.
15. percasian: Percent Asian and its class is double or numeric.
16. percother: Percent other races and its class is double or numeric.
17. popadults: Number of adults and its class is integer or numeric.
18. perchsd: Percent with high school diploma and its class is double or numeric.
19. percollege: Percent college educated and its class is double or numeric.
20. percprof: Percent with professional degree and its class is double or numeric.
21. poppovertyknown: Population with known poverty status and its class is integer or numeric.
22. percpovertyknown: Percent of population with known poverty status and its class is double or numeric.
23. percbelowpoverty: Percent of people below the poverty line and its class is double or numeric.

24. percchildbelowpovert: Percent of children below poverty line and its class is double or numeric.
25. percadultpoverty: Percent of adults below poverty line and its class is double or numeric.
26. percelderlypoverty: Percent of elderly below poverty line and its class is double or numeric.
27. inmetro: County considered in a metro area and its class is integer or numeric. This column has 2 values only, 1 for counties in a metro area and 0 for counties not in a metro area.
28. category: Miscellaneous column and its class is a character.

1.2. SUMMARY STATISTICS FOR LOCATION

There are different measures of the central tendency (central location) of numerical data. A measure of central tendency is a single value that describes the numerical data by identifying its central position. The measures of central tendency are also called summary statistics because they try to summarize numerical data with a single number. The mean, median and mode are all measures of central tendency, but under certain conditions, some measures of central tendency become more suitable to use than others.

1.2.1. The Mean

The (arithmetic) mean is calculated by summing all data values and dividing them by the number of these data values. For the numbers (1,2,3), their mean would be=(1+2+3)/3= 2.

The mean is sensitive to extreme values in small samples. For a sample of two observations, each observation will affect the mean by 50% while for a sample of 100 observations, each observation will affect the mean by 1%. So, increasing the sample size will lead to a more stable sample mean.

For the numbers (1,2,10), their mean = (1+2+10)/3 = 4.333. The mean has doubled compared to the previous example although we still have three values. With more outliers in your data, the mean loses its ability to provide the central location for the data because the outlier values are dragging the mean away from the central position.

1.2.1.1. The Mean of Economics Data Columns

In the economics data, we can see the mean of every numeric column in our data using the functions:

1. The get_summary_stats function, from the rstatix package, using the argument, show = c("mean"), to show the mean of every numeric column in the economics data.
2. The flextable package functions, flextable, theme_box, and set_caption, to convert the result to a table with a caption.

All these functions were applied in sequence using the "%>%" operator. Because we are using functions from the rstatix and flextable packages, so we must first load these packages into our R session using the library function.

```
library(rstatix)
library(flextable)
economics %>% get_summary_stats( show = c("mean")) %>%
 flextable() %>% theme_box() %>%
 set_caption(caption = "Mean of every numeric column in the economics data")
```

Table 1.1. *Mean of Every Numeric Column in the Economics Data*

Variable	n	Mean
pce	574	4,820.093
pop	574	257,159.653
psavert	574	8.567
uempmed	574	8.609
unemploy	574	7,771.310

The mean has the same unit of the numerical data, so:

1. The mean of pce column (personal consumption expenditures) is 4,820.093 billion dollars.
2. The mean of pop column or population is 257,159.653 thousand.
3. The mean of psavert column (personal savings rate) is 8.567.
4. The mean of the uempmed column (median duration of unemployment) is 8.609 weeks.
5. The mean of the unemploy column (number of unemployed) is 7,771.310 thousand.

In addition, we see that the sample size for every column is 574 which is the number of rows in our data, meaning that no numeric column has any missing data.

1.2.1.2. The Mean of Midwest Data Columns

Similarly, we can use the same functions to get the mean value of each numeric column of the midwest data.

```
midwest %>% get_summary_stats( show = c("mean")) %>%
 flextable() %>% theme_box() %>%
 set_caption(caption = "Mean of every numeric column in the midwest data")
```

Table 1.2. *Mean of Every Numeric Column in the Midwest Data*

Variable	n	Mean
PID	437	1,437.339
area	437	0.033
poptotal	437	96,130.302
popdensity	437	3,097.743
popwhite	437	81,839.915
popblack	437	11,023.881
popamerindian	437	343.110
popasian	437	1,310.465
popother	437	1,612.931
percwhite	437	95.558
percblack	437	2.676
percamerindan	437	0.799
percasian	437	0.487
percother	437	0.479
popadults	437	60,972.613
perchsd	437	73.966
percollege	437	18.273
percprof	437	4.447
poppovertyknown	437	93,642.284
percpovertyknown	437	97.110
percbelowpoverty	437	12.511
percchildbelowpovert	437	16.447
percadultpoverty	437	10.919
percelderlypoverty	437	11.389
inmetro	437	0.343

We get the mean of every numeric column of the midwest data:

1. The first column is PID or the Unique county identifier and it is a meaningless mean.

2. By looking at the means of similar columns, we can get the interesting properties of midwest counties. Because the mean of percent white in these counties is 95.558% compared to 2.676% of percent black, 0.799% of percent American Indian, 0.487% Asians, and 0.479% of other races, we conclude that these counties have mostly white races.
3. The sample size for every column is 437 which is the number of rows in our data, meaning that no numeric column has any missing data.

1.2.2. The Median

The median is the value that halves a set of data values equally. In other words, it is the middle value of a data set and so it is called the 50th percentile. For an odd number of data points, it is the central data point after arranging them. For an even number of data points, it is the average of the two central data points.

When the data is evenly spaced (or evenly distributed), the mean and median are nearly the same. When there are large outliers in our data, the mean is pulled by them to the right and will be larger than the median. This data is called right-skewed data.

When there are small outliers in our data, the mean is pulled by them to the left and will be smaller than the median. This data is called left-skewed data.

The median gives the data center without being affected by the extreme values or outliers in the data. Median is a type of robust statistics because of this.

1.2.2.1. The Median for Economics Data

In the economics data, we can see the median (and the mean) of every numeric column in our data using the functions:

1. The get_summary_stats function, from the rstatix package, using the argument, show = c("mean," "median"), to show the mean and median of every numeric column in the economics data.
2. The flextable package functions, flextable, theme_box, and set_caption, to convert the result to a table with a caption.

```
economics %>% get_summary_stats( show = c("mean," "median")) %>%
 flextable() %>% theme_box() %>%
 set_caption(caption = "Mean and median of every numeric column in the economics data")
```

Table 1.3. Mean and Median of Every Numeric Column in the Economics Data

Variable	n	Mean	Median
pce	574	4,820.093	3,936.85
pop	574	257,159.653	253,060.00
psavert	574	8.567	8.40
uempmed	574	8.609	7.50
unemploy	574	7,771.310	7,494.00

We see that:

1. When the mean is larger than the median, this indicates right-skewed data for the pce, pop, uempmed, and unemploy columns. We will also see that in the subsequent summary plots.
2. When the mean is nearly equal to the median, this indicates evenly-spaced or normally distributed data as for the psavert column. The normal distribution with a bell shape can be checked using summary plots and statistical tests as described below.
3. Because for each column we have 574 data points, we can arrange these values for a certain column to check if the median is calculated correctly. To arrange the values of psavert column, we will use the sort function with the argument, economics$psavert to extract that column.

```
sort(economics$psavert)
##   [1] 2.2 2.7 2.7 2.9 3.1 3.1 3.1 3.4 3.4 3.4 3.4 3.4 3.4 3.5 3.5
##  [16] 3.5 3.6 3.6 3.6 3.6 3.6 3.7 3.7 3.7 3.7 3.7 3.7 3.8 3.8 3.8
##  [31] 3.9 4.0 4.0 4.0 4.0 4.1 4.1 4.1 4.1 4.2 4.2 4.2 4.2 4.2 4.2
##  [46] 4.4 4.4 4.4 4.5 4.5 4.5 4.5 4.5 4.5 4.5 4.5 4.6 4.6 4.6 4.7
##  [61] 4.7 4.8 4.8 4.8 4.8 4.8 4.9 4.9 4.9 4.9 4.9 4.9 5.0 5.0 5.0
##  [76] 5.0 5.2 5.2 5.2 5.2 5.2 5.3 5.3 5.3 5.3 5.3 5.3 5.3 5.4 5.4
##  [91] 5.4 5.4 5.4 5.5 5.5 5.5 5.5 5.5 5.5 5.6 5.6 5.6 5.7 5.7 5.7
## [106] 5.7 5.7 5.8 5.8 5.8 5.8 5.8 5.8 5.8 5.9 5.9 5.9 5.9 5.9 5.9
## [121] 5.9 6.0 6.0 6.0 6.1 6.1 6.1 6.1 6.2 6.2 6.2 6.2 6.2 6.2 6.2
## [136] 6.2 6.3 6.3 6.3 6.3 6.3 6.3 6.4 6.4 6.4 6.4 6.4 6.4 6.4 6.4
## [151] 6.4 6.4 6.4 6.4 6.4 6.4 6.4 6.5 6.5 6.5 6.5 6.6 6.6 6.6 6.6
## [166] 6.6 6.6 6.6 6.7 6.7 6.7 6.7 6.7 6.7 6.7 6.7 6.7 6.7 6.7 6.8
## [181] 6.8 6.8 6.8 6.8 6.8 6.8 6.8 6.8 6.8 6.8 6.8 6.8 6.9 6.9 6.9
## [196] 6.9 6.9 6.9 6.9 6.9 6.9 6.9 7.0 7.0 7.0 7.0 7.0 7.0 7.0 7.1
## [211] 7.1 7.1 7.1 7.1 7.1 7.1 7.1 7.2 7.2 7.2 7.2 7.2 7.2 7.2 7.2
## [226] 7.3 7.3 7.3 7.3 7.4 7.4 7.4 7.4 7.4 7.4 7.4 7.4 7.4 7.5 7.5
```

```
## [241] 7.5 7.5 7.5 7.6 7.6 7.6 7.6 7.6 7.6 7.6 7.7 7.7 7.7 7.8 7.8
## [256] 7.8 7.8 7.8 7.8 7.9 7.9 8.0 8.0 8.0 8.0 8.0 8.0 8.0 8.1 8.1
## [271] 8.1 8.1 8.1 8.2 8.2 8.2 8.2 8.2 8.2 8.2 8.2 8.2 8.3 8.3 8.3
## [286] 8.3 8.4 8.4 8.4 8.4 8.4 8.4 8.4 8.5 8.5 8.5 8.5 8.5 8.5 8.6
## [301] 8.6 8.6 8.6 8.6 8.6 8.6 8.6 8.6 8.6 8.6 8.7 8.7 8.7 8.7 8.7
## [316] 8.7 8.7 8.8 8.8 8.8 8.8 8.8 8.8 8.8 8.8 8.9 8.9 8.9 8.9 9.0
## [331] 9.0 9.0 9.0 9.1 9.1 9.1 9.1 9.1 9.1 9.2 9.3 9.3 9.3 9.3 9.3
## [346] 9.3 9.4 9.4 9.4 9.5 9.6 9.6 9.6 9.6 9.7 9.7 9.7 9.7 9.7 9.7
## [361] 9.7 9.7 9.7 9.7 9.7 9.7 9.8 9.9 9.9 9.9 9.9 9.9 9.9 9.9 10.0
## [376] 10.0 10.1 10.1 10.1 10.1 10.1 10.2 10.2 10.3 10.3 10.3 10.3 10.3 10.3
10.3
## [391] 10.4 10.5 10.5 10.5 10.5 10.5 10.5 10.6 10.6 10.6 10.6 10.6 10.6 10.6
10.6
## [406] 10.6 10.7 10.7 10.8 10.8 10.8 10.8 10.8 10.9 10.9 10.9 10.9 10.9 10.9
10.9
## [421] 11.0 11.0 11.0 11.0 11.1 11.1 11.1 11.1 11.1 11.1 11.1 11.1 11.1 11.1
11.1
## [436] 11.1 11.2 11.2 11.2 11.2 11.3 11.3 11.3 11.3 11.3 11.4 11.4 11.4 11.4
11.4
## [451] 11.4 11.4 11.5 11.5 11.5 11.5 11.6 11.6 11.6 11.6 11.7 11.7 11.7 11.7
11.7
## [466] 11.7 11.7 11.7 11.7 11.7 11.7 11.7 11.7 11.7 11.8 11.8 11.8 11.8 11.8
11.8
## [481] 11.8 11.8 11.9 11.9 12.0 12.0 12.0 12.0 12.0 12.1 12.1 12.2 12.2 12.2
12.3
## [496] 12.3 12.3 12.3 12.3 12.3 12.3 12.3 12.4 12.4 12.4 12.4 12.5 12.5 12.5
12.5
## [511] 12.5 12.6 12.6 12.6 12.6 12.7 12.7 12.7 12.7 12.8 12.8 12.8 12.8 12.8
12.9
## [526] 12.9 12.9 12.9 13.0 13.0 13.0 13.0 13.0 13.1 13.1 13.1 13.1 13.2 13.2
13.2
## [541] 13.2 13.2 13.2 13.2 13.3 13.3 13.3 13.3 13.3 13.4 13.4 13.4 13.4 13.5
13.5
## [556] 13.6 13.6 13.6 13.6 13.6 13.7 13.8 13.8 13.9 14.0 14.2 14.2 14.3 14.3
14.4
## [571] 14.4 14.7 14.8 17.3
```

The indices in the square brackets indicate the value rank. For example, the value of 8.2 has a rank of [281] and the value of 8.5 has a rank of [295]. The 2 central points are 287th and 288th values and both have a value of 8.4 so the median = (8.4+8.4)/2 = 8.4.

We can also see that using the following functions:

1. The arrange function with the psavert argument to arrange the rows according to the psavert value in ascending order.

2. The select function to select only the psavert column.
3. The slice column with the argument, 287 and 288, to select the 287th and 288th rows.

```
economics %>% arrange(psavert) %>% select(psavert) %>% slice(287,288)
## # A tibble: 2 × 1
##   psavert
##     <dbl>
## 1     8.4
## 2     8.4
```

Again, we see that the 287th and 288th values are both 8.4 so the median = (8.4+8.4)/2 = 8.4. We can also use the same functions for the uempmed column.

```
economics %>% arrange(uempmed) %>% select(uempmed) %>% slice(287,288)
## # A tibble: 2 × 1
##   uempmed
##     <dbl>
## 1     7.5
## 2     7.5
```

We see that the 287th and 288th values, of median duration of unemployment column, are both 7.5 so the median = (7.5+7.5)/2 = 7.5.

1.2.2.2. The Median for Midwest Data

We can use the same functions for the midwest data with 437 data points to get the median and mean for every numeric column.

```
midwest %>% get_summary_stats( show = c("mean," "median")) %>%
 flextable() %>% theme_box() %>%
 set_caption(caption = "Mean and median of every numeric column in the midwest data")
```

Table 1.4. *Mean and Median of Every Numeric Column in the Midwest Data*

Variable	n	Mean	Median
PID	437	1,437.339	1,221.000
area	437	0.033	0.030
poptotal	437	96,130.302	35,324.000
popdensity	437	3,097.743	1,156.208
popwhite	437	81,839.915	34,471.000
popblack	437	11,023.881	201.000
popamerindian	437	343.110	94.000

popasian	437	1,310.465	102.000
popother	437	1,612.931	66.000
percwhite	437	95.558	98.033
percblack	437	2.676	0.539
percamerindan	437	0.799	0.215
percasian	437	0.487	0.297
percother	437	0.479	0.178
popadults	437	60,972.613	22,188.000
perchsd	437	73.966	74.247
percollege	437	18.273	16.798
percprof	437	4.447	3.814
poppovertyknown	437	93,642.284	33,788.000
percpovertyknown	437	97.110	98.170
percbelowpoverty	437	12.511	11.822
percchildbelowpovert	437	16.447	15.270
percadultpoverty	437	10.919	10.008
percelderlypoverty	437	11.389	10.869
inmetro	437	0.343	0.000

We see that:

1. When the mean is larger than the median, this indicates right-skewed data for the poptotal, popdensity, and popwhite columns. We will also see that in the subsequent summary plots.
2. When the mean is nearly equal to the median, this indicates evenly-spaced or normally distributed data for the area column. The normal distribution with a bell shape can be checked using summary plots and statistical tests as described below.
3. When the mean is smaller than the median, this indicates left-skewed data for the percwhite column. We will also see that in the subsequent summary plots.
4. Because each column has 437 data points, we can arrange these values for a certain column, using the sort function, to check if the median is calculated correctly. For the area column.

```
sort(midwest$area)
##  [1] 0.005 0.009 0.009 0.010 0.010 0.010 0.011 0.011 0.012 0.012 0.013 0.013
## [13] 0.013 0.014 0.014 0.014 0.014 0.014 0.015 0.015 0.015 0.016 0.016 0.016
```

```
## [25] 0.016 0.016 0.017 0.017 0.017 0.017 0.018 0.018 0.018 0.018 0.018 0.019
## [37] 0.019 0.019 0.019 0.020 0.020 0.020 0.020 0.020 0.020 0.020 0.020 0.020
## [49] 0.021 0.021 0.021 0.021 0.021 0.021 0.021 0.021 0.021 0.021 0.021 0.021
## [61] 0.021 0.021 0.022 0.022 0.022 0.022 0.022 0.022 0.022 0.022 0.022 0.022
## [73] 0.022 0.022 0.022 0.022 0.022 0.022 0.023 0.023 0.023 0.023 0.023 0.023
## [85] 0.023 0.023 0.023 0.023 0.023 0.023 0.023 0.023 0.023 0.023 0.023 0.023
## [97] 0.023 0.023 0.024 0.024 0.024 0.024 0.024 0.024 0.024 0.024 0.024 0.024
## [109] 0.024 0.024 0.024 0.024 0.024 0.024 0.024 0.024 0.024 0.024 0.024 0.024
## [121] 0.024 0.024 0.024 0.024 0.024 0.024 0.024 0.024 0.024 0.024 0.024 0.024
## [133] 0.024 0.024 0.025 0.025 0.025 0.025 0.025 0.025 0.025 0.025 0.025 0.025
## [145] 0.025 0.025 0.025 0.025 0.025 0.025 0.025 0.025 0.025 0.025 0.025 0.025
## [157] 0.025 0.025 0.026 0.026 0.026 0.026 0.026 0.026 0.026 0.026 0.026 0.026
## [169] 0.026 0.026 0.026 0.026 0.026 0.026 0.026 0.026 0.026 0.026 0.027 0.027
## [181] 0.027 0.027 0.027 0.027 0.027 0.027 0.027 0.027 0.028 0.028 0.028 0.028
## [193] 0.028 0.028 0.028 0.028 0.028 0.028 0.028 0.028 0.028 0.028 0.028 0.029
## [205] 0.029 0.029 0.029 0.029 0.029 0.029 0.029 0.029 0.029 0.029 0.029 0.029
## [217] 0.030 0.030 0.030 0.030 0.030 0.030 0.030 0.030 0.030 0.030 0.030 0.030
## [229] 0.030 0.030 0.030 0.030 0.030 0.030 0.030 0.031 0.031 0.031 0.031 0.031
## [241] 0.031 0.031 0.031 0.031 0.032 0.032 0.032 0.032 0.032 0.032 0.032 0.032
## [253] 0.033 0.033 0.033 0.033 0.033 0.033 0.033 0.033 0.033 0.033 0.033 0.033
## [265] 0.033 0.033 0.033 0.033 0.033 0.033 0.033 0.033 0.033 0.034 0.034 0.034
## [277] 0.034 0.034 0.034 0.034 0.034 0.034 0.034 0.034 0.034 0.034 0.034 0.034
## [289] 0.034 0.034 0.034 0.034 0.034 0.034 0.034 0.034 0.034 0.034 0.034 0.035
## [301] 0.035 0.035 0.035 0.035 0.035 0.035 0.035 0.035 0.035 0.036 0.036 0.036
## [313] 0.036 0.036 0.036 0.036 0.036 0.037 0.037 0.037 0.037 0.037 0.037 0.037
## [325] 0.038 0.038 0.038 0.038 0.038 0.039 0.039 0.040 0.040 0.040 0.040 0.041
## [337] 0.041 0.041 0.041 0.041 0.041 0.041 0.041 0.041 0.042 0.042 0.042 0.042
## [349] 0.042 0.042 0.042 0.043 0.043 0.043 0.043 0.044 0.044 0.044 0.044 0.045
## [361] 0.045 0.045 0.046 0.046 0.046 0.047 0.047 0.047 0.048 0.048 0.048 0.048
## [373] 0.048 0.048 0.049 0.049 0.050 0.050 0.050 0.050 0.050 0.050 0.050 0.051
## [385] 0.051 0.051 0.051 0.052 0.052 0.052 0.052 0.052 0.053 0.053 0.053 0.054
## [397] 0.054 0.054 0.054 0.054 0.055 0.055 0.055 0.055 0.056 0.057 0.058 0.058
## [409] 0.059 0.060 0.060 0.060 0.060 0.060 0.062 0.063 0.064 0.067 0.068 0.068
## [421] 0.068 0.069 0.069 0.070 0.071 0.072 0.073 0.075 0.075 0.078 0.078 0.078
## [433] 0.079 0.082 0.089 0.094 0.110
```

The central point is the 219th point and has a value of 0.03 so the median = 0.03. We can also see that using the arrange, select, and slice functions as described above.

```
midwest %>% arrange(area) %>% select(area) %>% slice(219)
## # A tibble: 1 × 1
##   area
##   <dbl>
## 1 0.03
```

We see that the median = 0.03. For the poptotal column.

```
midwest %>% arrange(poptotal) %>% select(poptotal) %>% slice(219)
## # A tibble: 1 × 1
##   poptotal
##     <int>
## 1   35324
```

The median = 35324.

1.2.3. The percentiles

The pth sample percentile is the data point such that p% of data points are below that value and (100-p) % of data points are larger than that value. For example, the median or 50th percentile is that data point that nearly 50% of data is below that value and 50% are larger than that value, while the 75th percentile is that data point that nearly 75% of data points are below that value and 25% are larger than that value.

The 25th percentile is also known as the first quartile or Q1, the 50th percentile is known as the second quartile, Q2, or the median, and the 75th percentile is known as the third quartile or Q3. The percentiles including the median are not affected by the extreme values or outliers in the data so they are robust statistics.

Percentiles are used to understand values such as test scores or health indicators. For example, if a student has a score of 90 out of 100 on a certain test. That score has no meaning unless he knows what percentile he falls into. If his score (90 out of 100) is the 95th percentile. This means that his score is better than 95% of the test takers in his class. If his score is the 20th percentile. This means that only his score is better than 20% of the test takers.

1.2.3.1. The Percentiles for Economics Data

In the economics data, we can see the percentiles (and the median) of every numeric column in our data using the functions:

1. The get_summary_stats function, from the rstatix package, using the argument, type = "quantile," to show the 0% (minimum),25% (Q1), 50% (median), 75% (Q3), and 100% (maximum) percentiles of every numeric column in the economics data.

2. The flextable package functions, flextable, theme_box, and set_caption, to convert the result to a table with a caption.

```
economics %>% get_summary_stats(type = "quantile") %>%

 flextable() %>% theme_box() %>%

 set_caption(caption = "The 0, 25, 50, 75, 100%of every numeric column in the economics data")
```

Table 1.5. *The 0, 25, 50, 75, 100%of Every Numeric Column in the Economics Data*

Variable	n	0%	25%	50%	75%	100%
pce	574	506.7	1,578.3	3,936.85	7,626.325	12,193.8
pop	574	198,712.0	224,896.0	253,060.00	290,290.750	320,402.3
psavert	574	2.2	6.4	8.40	11.100	17.3
uempmed	574	4.0	6.0	7.50	9.100	25.2
unemploy	574	2,685.0	6,284.0	7,494.00	8,685.500	15,352.0

The default result will give the 0% (minimum),25% (Q1), 50% (median), 75% (Q3), and 100% (maximum) percentiles. We see that the 50% is the same as the median calculated above.

We can get any required percentiles using the probs argument with proportion numbers. For example, we can get the 30% and 60%of every column using the probs = c(0.3,0.6) argument for 30% and 60%respectively.

```
economics %>% get_summary_stats(type = "quantile," probs = c(0.3,0.6)) %>%

 flextable() %>% theme_box() %>%

 set_caption(caption = "The 30% and 60%of every numeric column in the econom-
ics data")
```

Table 1.6. *The 30% and 60%of Every Numeric Column in the Economics Data*

Variable	n	30%	60%
pce	574	1,970.2	5,165.2
pop	574	230,803.9	268,548.8
psavert	574	6.7	9.3
uempmed	574	6.3	8.3
unemploy	574	6,590.0	8,048.0

1.2.3.2. The Percentiles for Midwest Data

We can use the same functions to get the same percentiles for every numeric column in the midwest data.

```
midwest %>% get_summary_stats(type = "quantile") %>%

 flextable() %>% theme_box() %>%

 set_caption(caption = "The 0, 25, 50, 75, 100%of every numeric column in the midwest data")
```

Table 1.7. *The 0, 25, 50, 75, 100%of Every Numeric Column in the Midwest Data*

Variable	n	0%	25%	50%	75%	100%
PID	437	561.000	670.000	1,221.000	2,059.000	3,052.000
area	437	0.005	0.024	0.030	0.038	0.110
poptotal	437	1,701.000	18,840.000	35,324.000	75,651.000	5,105,067.000
popdensity	437	85.050	622.407	1,156.208	2,330.000	88,018.397
popwhite	437	416.000	18,630.000	34,471.000	72,968.000	3,204,947.000
popblack	437	0.000	29.000	201.000	1,291.000	1,317,147.000
popamerindian	437	4.000	44.000	94.000	288.000	10,289.000
popasian	437	0.000	35.000	102.000	401.000	188,565.000
popother	437	0.000	20.000	66.000	345.000	384,119.000
percwhite	437	10.694	94.886	98.033	99.075	99.823
percblack	437	0.000	0.116	0.539	2.601	40.210
percamerindan	437	0.056	0.158	0.215	0.384	89.177
percasian	437	0.000	0.174	0.297	0.521	5.070
percother	437	0.000	0.091	0.178	0.481	7.524
popadults	437	1,287.000	12,271.000	22,188.000	47,541.000	3,291,995.000
perchsd	437	46.912	71.325	74.247	77.195	88.899
percollege	437	7.336	14.114	16.798	20.550	48.079
percprof	437	0.520	2.998	3.814	4.949	20.791
poppovertyknown	437	1,696.000	18,364.000	33,788.000	72,840.000	5,023,523.000
percpovertyknown	437	80.902	96.895	98.170	98.599	99.860
percbelowpoverty	437	2.180	9.199	11.822	15.133	48.691
percchildbelowpovert	437	1.919	11.624	15.270	20.352	64.308
percadultpoverty	437	1.939	7.668	10.008	13.182	43.312
percelderlypoverty	437	3.547	8.912	10.869	13.412	31.162
inmetro	437	0.000	0.000	0.000	1.000	1.000

We see that:

1. The percent white has 10.694 as 0% or minimum, 94.886 as 25% or Q1, 98.033 as 50% or median, 99.075 as 75% or Q3, and 99.823 as 100% or maximum. According to these numbers, about 75% of the 437 midwest counties have a percent white equal to 94.886 (Q1) or more.
2. The percent black has 0.000 as 0% or minimum, 0.116 as 25% or Q1, 0.539 as 50% or median, 2.601 as 75% or Q3, and 40.210 as 100% or maximum. According to these numbers, only 25% of the 437 midwest counties have percent black equals 2.601 (Q3) or more.

1.2.4. The Mode

The mode is the data point that appears most frequently in a set of data points. The mode is not necessarily unique to a given data, since certain numbers or categories may occur the same maximum value. In that case, the data is called multimodal data as opposed to unimodal data with only one unique mode.

1.2.4.1. The Mode of Economics Data

To see the mode of any numeric column, we can use the count function with the argument, sort = TRUE to sort the frequency of different values in descending order. Then, we will use the head function to get the top 6 most frequent values of every column. Finally, we convert the result to a table as above. For the pce column.

```
economics %>% count(pce, sort = TRUE) %>% head() %>%

 flextable() %>% theme_box() %>%

 set_caption(caption = "The top 6 most frequent values of the pce column from
economics data")
```

Table 1.8. *The Top 6 Most Frequent Values of the pce Column from Economics Data*

pce	n
506.7	1
509.8	1
512.2	1
515.6	1
517.4	1
525.1	1

We see that all values have a count of 1 so there is no mode in this column. For the pop column.

```
economics %>% count(pop, sort = TRUE) %>% head() %>%
 flextable() %>% theme_box() %>%

 set_caption(caption = "The top 6 most frequent values of the pop column from
economics data")
```

Table 1.9. *The Top 6 Most Frequent Values of the Pop Column from Economics Data*

Pop	n
198,712	1
198,911	1
199,113	1
199,311	1
199,498	1
199,657	1

Similarly, we see that all values have a count of 1 so there is no mode in this column. For the psavert column.

```
economics %>% count(psavert, sort = TRUE) %>% head() %>%
 flextable() %>% theme_box() %>%
 set_caption(caption = "The top 6 most frequent values of the psavert column
from economics data")
```

Table 1.10. *The top 6 Most Frequent Values of the Psavert column from Economics Data*

Psavert	n
6.4	15
11.7	14
6.8	13
9.7	12
11.1	12
6.7	11

We see that 6.4 has the top frequency of 15 so psavert is an example of unimodal data with a mode = 6.4. For the uempmed column.

```
economics %>% count(uempmed, sort = TRUE) %>% head() %>%

 flextable() %>% theme_box() %>%

 set_caption(caption = "The top 6 most frequent values of the uempmed column
from economics data")
```

Table 1.11. *The Top 6 Most Frequent Values of the Uempmed Column from Economics Data*

Uempmed	n
8.3	22
6.9	15
6.8	14
7.1	14
5.7	13
5.8	13

We see that 8.3 has the top frequency of 22 so uempmed is an example of unimodal data with a mode = 8.3. For the unemploy column.

```
economics %>% count(unemploy, sort = TRUE) %>% head() %>%
 flextable() %>% theme_box() %>%
 set_caption(caption = "The top 6 most frequent values of the unemploy column
from economics data")
```

Table 1.12. *The Top 6 Most Frequent Values of the Unemploy Column from Economics Data*

Unemploy	n
2,856	2
4,305	2
4,959	2
6,109	2
6,590	2
6,655	2

We see that many values have the top frequency of 2 so unemploy is an example of multi-modal data.

1.2.4.2. The Mode of Midwest Data

To get the mode of all numeric columns in the midwest data, we will use the following functions:

1. The select function with the argument, area:percelderlypoverty, to select the 23 columns from the area column to percelderlypoverty column. The resulting data will be 437 rows and 23 columns.

```
midwest %>% select(area:percelderlypoverty)
## # A tibble: 437 × 23
##    area poptotal popdensity popwhite popblack popamerindian popasian popother
##   <dbl>    <int>      <dbl>    <int>    <int>         <int>    <int>    <int>
## 1 0.052    66090      1271.    63917     1702            98      249      124
## 2 0.014    10626       759      7054     3496            19       48        9
## 3 0.022    14991       681.    14477      429            35       16       34
## 4 0.017    30806      1812.    29344      127            46      150     1139
## 5 0.018     5836       324.     5264      547            14        5        6
## 6 0.05     35688       714.    35157       50            65      195      221
## 7 0.017     5322       313.     5298        1             8       15        0
## 8 0.027    16805       622.    16519      111            30       61       84
## 9 0.024    13437       560.    13384       16             8       23        6
## 10 0.058  173025      2983.   146506    16559           331     8033     1596
## # i 427 more rows
## # i 15 more variables: percwhite <dbl>, percblack <dbl>, percamerindan <dbl>,
## #   percasian <dbl>, percother <dbl>, popadults <int>, perchsd <dbl>,
## #   percollege <dbl>, percprof <dbl>, poppovertyknown <int>,
## #  percpovertyknown <dbl>, percbelowpoverty <dbl>, percchildbelowpovert <dbl>,
## #   percadultpoverty <dbl>, percelderlypoverty <dbl>
```

2. The pivot_longer function with the argument, cols = area:percelderlypoverty, collapses all 23 columns into 2 columns, the name and value columns. The resulting data will be 10051 rows and 2 columns.

```
midwest %>% select(area:percelderlypoverty) %>%
 pivot_longer(cols = area:percelderlypoverty)
## # A tibble: 10,051 × 2
##   name          value
##   <chr>         <dbl>
## 1 area          0.052
## 2 poptotal      66090
## 3 popdensity     1271.
## 4 popwhite      63917
## 5 popblack       1702
## 6 popamerindian   98
## 7 popasian       249
## 8 popother       124
## 9 percwhite       96.7
## 10 percblack       2.58
## # i 10,041 more rows
```

3. The group_by function with the argument name to split the data frame or tibble into multiple data frames each containing a single name or column.
4. The count function with the arguments, value, sort = TRUE, to count the values of each name (column) and sort them in descending order.
5. The slice_head function with the argument, n=6, to get the top 6 most frequent values of each column. Then we convert the result to a table as before.

```
midwest %>% select(area:percelderlypoverty) %>%
 pivot_longer(cols = area:percelderlypoverty) %>%
 group_by(name) %>% count(value, sort = TRUE) %>%
 slice_head(n = 6) %>% flextable() %>% theme_box() %>%
 set_caption(caption = "The top 6 most frequent values of every numeric column
from the midwest data")
```

Table 1.13. *The Top 6 Most Frequent Values of Every Numeric Column from the Midwest Data*

Name	Value	n
area	0.02400000	36
area	0.03400000	26
area	0.02500000	24
area	0.03300000	21
area	0.02300000	20
area	0.02600000	20
percadultpoverty	1.93850430	1
percadultpoverty	2.35504872	1
percadultpoverty	2.39906403	1
percadultpoverty	2.58450033	1
percadultpoverty	2.59006144	1
percadultpoverty	2.84384454	1
percamerindan	0.05623243	1
percamerindan	0.05953710	1
percamerindan	0.07306158	1
percamerindan	0.08007779	1
percamerindan	0.08035525	1

percamerindan	0.08193140	1
percasian	0.00000000	1
percasian	0.01059210	1
percasian	0.01594981	1
percasian	0.02703190	1
percasian	0.03250447	1
percasian	0.05315379	1
percbelowpoverty	2.18016760	1
percbelowpoverty	2.71473392	1
percbelowpoverty	3.12105990	1
percbelowpoverty	3.23762786	1
percbelowpoverty	3.38529044	1
percbelowpoverty	3.49159858	1
percblack	0.00000000	1
percblack	0.00859660	1
percblack	0.00942596	1
percblack	0.01058145	1
percblack	0.01119069	1
percblack	0.01223092	1
percchildbelowpovert	1.91895478	1
percchildbelowpovert	2.94525227	1
percchildbelowpovert	3.78581963	1
percchildbelowpovert	4.06964667	1
percchildbelowpovert	4.06985404	1
percchildbelowpovert	4.22803082	1
percelderlypoverty	16.78004540	2
percelderlypoverty	3.54706685	1
percelderlypoverty	3.83824912	1
percelderlypoverty	4.08547929	1
percelderlypoverty	4.28088917	1
percelderlypoverty	4.90623387	1
perchsd	46.91226100	1
perchsd	56.65217390	1

perchsd	58.38525270	1
perchsd	58.41880340	1
perchsd	58.69596440	1
perchsd	59.56804830	1
percollege	7.33610822	1
percollege	7.91325578	1
percollege	8.54375099	1
percollege	8.74173036	1
percollege	8.84588804	1
percollege	9.33070866	1
percother	0.00000000	3
percother	0.00824776	1
percother	0.01347648	1
percother	0.01530456	1
percother	0.01598849	1
percother	0.01935859	1
percpovertyknown	80.90244120	1
percpovertyknown	81.77562140	1
percpovertyknown	82.50514050	1
percpovertyknown	85.20980230	1
percpovertyknown	85.64711410	1
percpovertyknown	85.97423330	1
percprof	0.52029136	1
percprof	1.56541721	1
percprof	1.57567381	1
percprof	1.72665917	1
percprof	1.79346254	1
percprof	1.94520548	1
percwhite	10.69408740	1
percwhite	57.39520110	1
percwhite	62.77972450	1
percwhite	66.38434030	1
percwhite	66.88820950	1

percwhite	70.27065100	1
popadults	17,369.00000000	2
popadults	1,287.00000000	1
popadults	1,922.00000000	1
popadults	2,821.00000000	1
popadults	3,057.00000000	1
popadults	3,457.00000000	1
popamerindian	26.00000000	7
popamerindian	8.00000000	6
popamerindian	16.00000000	6
popamerindian	37.00000000	6
popamerindian	49.00000000	6
popamerindian	31.00000000	5
popasian	15.00000000	7
popasian	38.00000000	7
popasian	21.00000000	6
popasian	24.00000000	6
popasian	19.00000000	5
popasian	41.00000000	5
popblack	1.00000000	7
popblack	8.00000000	7
popblack	9.00000000	7
popblack	10.00000000	7
popblack	2.00000000	6
popblack	4.00000000	6
popdensity	1,156.20833000	2
popdensity	85.05000000	1
popdensity	104.78181800	1
popdensity	110.69333300	1
popdensity	113.51282100	1
popdensity	130.91489400	1
popother	6.00000000	10
popother	10.00000000	10

popother	13.00000000	9
popother	2.00000000	7
popother	14.00000000	7
popother	7.00000000	6
poppovertyknown	34,833.00000000	2
poppovertyknown	1,696.00000000	1
poppovertyknown	3,820.00000000	1
poppovertyknown	4,160.00000000	1
poppovertyknown	4,513.00000000	1
poppovertyknown	4,815.00000000	1
poptotal	19,464.00000000	2
poptotal	35,427.00000000	2
poptotal	1,701.00000000	1
poptotal	3,890.00000000	1
poptotal	4,373.00000000	1
poptotal	4,590.00000000	1
popwhite	416.00000000	1
popwhite	1,688.00000000	1
popwhite	4,072.00000000	1
popwhite	4,562.00000000	1
popwhite	5,032.00000000	1
popwhite	5,062.00000000	1

We see that:

1. Some columns are unimodal with 1 mode as for the area column (mode = 0.024), and the percother column (mode = 0.00).
2. Some columns are multimodal with 2 modes or more as for the popasian column (mode = 15.0,38.0) and the popblack column (mode = 1.00, 8.00, 9.00, 10.00).
3. Other columns have no mode because all values have a frequency of 1 as for the percadultpoverty and percamerindan columns.

1.3. SUMMARY STATISTICS FOR SPREAD

In some cases, we see that two samples have the same mean. However, this does not indicate that the two samples are identical. In fact, the data sample spread may differ between the two samples, so to better describe any sample, we should report a combination of location and spread measures.

1.3.1. The Range

The simplest measure of spread is the range. The range is the difference between the largest and smallest observations in a sample.

The disadvantages of the range as a spread measure are:

1. The range is very sensitive to extreme values or outliers.
2. The range depends on the sample size. The larger the sample size, the larger the range tends to be. This makes it difficult to compare ranges from samples of differing sizes.

1.3.1.1. The Range of the Economics Data

To get the range of every numeric column in the economics data, we will use the functions:

1. The get_summary_stats function with the argument, show = c("min," "max"), to get the minimum and maximum value of every column.
2. The mutate function creates a new column (range) by subtracting the minimum value from the maximum value.
3. The flextable, theme_box, and set_caption to convert the result to a table.

```
economics %>% get_summary_stats(show = c("min,""max")) %>%

mutate(range = max-min) %>%

flextable() %>% theme_box() %>%

set_caption(caption = "The minimum, maximum, and range of every numeric column
in the economics data")
```

Table 1.14. *The Minimum, Maximum, and Range of Every Numeric Column in the Economics Data*

Variable	n	Min	Max	Range
pce	574	506.7	12,193.8	11,687.1
pop	574	198,712.0	320,402.3	121,690.3
psavert	574	2.2	17.3	15.1
uempmed	574	4.0	25.2	21.2
unemploy	574	2,685.0	15,352.0	12,667.0

We see that:

1. The highest range was for the pop column with a range = 121,690.3.
2. The lowest range was for the psavert column with a range = 15.1.
3. We conclude that the pop values are more spread than the psavert values.

1.3.1.2. The Range of the Midwest Data

Using the same functions, we can get the range of every numeric column in the midwest data.

```
midwest %>% get_summary_stats(show = c("min,""max")) %>%
 mutate(range = max-min) %>%
 flextable() %>% theme_box() %>%
 set_caption(caption = "The minimum, maximum, and range of every numeric column
in the midwest data")
```

Table 1.15. *The Minimum, Maximum, and Range of Every Numeric Column in the Midwest Data*

Variable	n	Min	Max	Range
PID	437	561.000	3,052.000	2,491.000
area	437	0.005	0.110	0.105
poptotal	437	1,701.000	5,105,067.000	5,103,366.000
popdensity	437	85.050	88,018.397	87,933.347
popwhite	437	416.000	3,204,947.000	3,204,531.000
popblack	437	0.000	1,317,147.000	1,317,147.000
popamerindian	437	4.000	10,289.000	10,285.000
popasian	437	0.000	188,565.000	188,565.000
popother	437	0.000	384,119.000	384,119.000
percwhite	437	10.694	99.823	89.129
percblack	437	0.000	40.210	40.210
percamerindan	437	0.056	89.177	89.121
percasian	437	0.000	5.070	5.070
percother	437	0.000	7.524	7.524
popadults	437	1,287.000	3,291,995.000	3,290,708.000
perchsd	437	46.912	88.899	41.987
percollege	437	7.336	48.079	40.743

percprof	437	0.520	20.791	20.271
poppovertyknown	437	1,696.000	5,023,523.000	5,021,827.000
percpovertyknown	437	80.902	99.860	18.958
percbelowpoverty	437	2.180	48.691	46.511
percchildbelowpovert	437	1.919	64.308	62.389
percadultpoverty	437	1.939	43.312	41.373
percelderlypoverty	437	3.547	31.162	27.615
inmetro	437	0.000	1.000	1.000

We see that:

1. The highest range was for the poptotal column with a range = 5,103,366.000.
2. The lowest range was for the area column with a range = 0.105 only.
3. The highest range in percent columns was for the percent white column (range = 89.129) and the lowest range was for the percent asian column (5.07). This means that the percent white values are more spread across these 437 counties than the percent asian values.

1.3.2. The Variance

The variance is the average of the squared differences from the sample mean. As such, it has the squared unit of the data points and can be calculated from the formula:

$$s^2 = \frac{\sum_{i=1}^{n}\left(x_i - \bar{x}\right)^2}{n-1}$$

Where;

Where s^2 is the sample variance.

x is the sample mean.

n is the sample size.

$\sum_{i=1}^{n}\left(x_i - \bar{x}\right)^2$ means sum the squared difference between every element of our sample (from x_1 to x_n) and the sample mean x. Every element of our sample is denoted as x with a subscript to indicate its position in our sample.

We divide by n-1 when calculating the sample variance (and not by n as any average) to make the sample variance a good estimator of the true population variance. If we have population data, we will divide by N (where N is the population size) to get the variance.

1.3.2.1. Variance Interpretation

A large variance indicates that data points in your sample are far from the mean and far from each other, while a small variance indicates the opposite. A zero variance indicates that all values within our data are identical.

Variance is important in investment where stock price variance (as a measure of spread or variability) can be used as a measure of risk. Also, in the industrial machines, the products produced from these machines are with high variance. This indicates that these machines need adjustment.

1.3.2.2. Disadvantages of Variance

1. Variance is affected by outliers. Squaring the differences between these numbers and the mean can skew the variance.
2. Not easily interpreted because the variance has the squared unit of the data.

1.3.3. The Standard Deviation

The standard deviation is the square root of the variance. As such, it has the same unit of data and is more easily interpreted. It can be calculated from the square root of the variance formula:

$$s = \sqrt{\frac{\sum_{i=1}^{n}\left(x_i - \bar{x}\right)^2}{n-1}}$$

As before, we divide by n-1 when calculating the standard deviation (and not by n as any average) to make the sample standard deviation a good estimator of the true population standard deviation. If we have the population data, we will divide by N (where N is the population size) to get the standard deviation.

1.3.3.1. Interpretation of the Standard Deviation

They are the same as variance.

1.3.3.2. Disadvantages of Standard Deviation

1. The standard deviation is affected by outliers, and so it is not one of the **robust statistics**.

1.3.3.3. The Variance and Standard Deviation of Economics Data

Similarly, we can calculate the standard deviation of every numeric column in the economics data using the get_summary_stats function with the argument, show = c("sd). Then, we use the mutate function to create a new column (variance) by raising the standard deviation to the power of 2.

```
economics %>% get_summary_stats(show = c("sd")) %>%
 mutate(variance = sd^2) %>%
 flextable() %>% theme_box() %>%
 set_caption(caption = "The standard deviation and variance of every numeric column in the economics data")
```

Table 1.16. *The Standard Deviation and Variance of Every Numeric Column in the Economics Data*

Variable	n	sd	Variance
pce	574	3,556.804	12,650,854.694416
pop	574	36,682.399	1,345,598,396.395201
psavert	574	2.964	8.785296
uempmed	574	4.107	16.867449
unemploy	574	2,641.959	6,979,947.357681

We see that:

1. The standard deviation of the pce column is 3,556.804 billion dollars, while the variance is 12,650,854.694416 billion dollars^2.
2. The highest standard deviation (and variance) was for the pop column with a value of 36,682.399. So the population values are more spread than other column values in the economics data. However, the columns in the economics data are not on the same scale. For example, the population column is in thousands while the pce is in billions which makes comparing the standard deviation between them difficult.

1.3.3.4. The Variance and Standard Deviation of Midwest Data

Using the same functions, we can obtain the standard deviation and variance of every numeric column in the midwest data. In addition, we can arrange the standard deviation values in descending order using the arrange and desc functions on the sd column.

```
midwest %>% get_summary_stats(show = c("sd")) %>%
 mutate(variance = sd^2) %>% arrange(desc(sd)) %>%
 flextable() %>% theme_box() %>%
 set_caption(caption = "The standard deviation and variance of every numeric column in the midwest data in descending order")
```

Table 1.17. The Standard Deviation and Variance of Every Numeric Column in the Midwest Data in Descending Order

Variable	n	sd	Variance
poptotal	437	298,170.540	88,905,670,923.891586
poppovertyknown	437	293,235.058	85,986,799,240.263382
popwhite	437	200,196.648	40,078,697,870.435898
popadults	437	191,644.862	36,727,753,130.999039
popblack	437	78,958.267	6,234,407,927.643291
popother	437	18,526.541	343,232,721.424681
popasian	437	9,518.394	90,599,824.339236
popdensity	437	7,664.752	58,748,423.221504
PID	437	876.390	768,059.432100
popamerindian	437	868.927	755,034.131329
percchildbelow-povert	437	7.229	52.258441
percwhite	437	7.087	50.225569
percollege	437	6.262	39.212644
perchsd	437	5.843	34.140649
percbelowpoverty	437	5.150	26.522500
percblack	437	5.136	26.378496
percadultpoverty	437	5.109	26.101881
percamerindan	437	4.536	20.575296
percelderlypoverty	437	3.661	13.402921
percpovertyknown	437	2.750	7.562500
percprof	437	2.408	5.798464
percother	437	0.838	0.702244
percasian	437	0.628	0.394384

inmetro	437	0.475	0.225625
area	437	0.015	0.000225

We see that:

1. In the population columns, the highest standard deviation or spread was for the poptotal column (298,170.540). So the poptotal column values are more spread than other population count columns (popwhite, popblack, etc).
2. In the percent columns, the highest standard deviation or spread was for the percchildbelowpovert column (7.229). So the percent child below poverty line column values are more spread than other percentage columns (percwhite, percblack, etc).

1.3.4. The Coefficient of Variation (CV)

The coefficient of variation is used to relate the mean and the standard deviation to each other. It is calculated using the formula:

$ CV = (s/{x}) X 100$

Where:

CV = coefficient of variation.

s = standard deviation.

x = the mean.

The CV remains the same regardless of the scale of the different samples (columns) used, so the CV is more useful in comparing the variability of different samples (columns) with different means than using the standard deviation.

1.3.4.1. The CV of Economics Data

We can get the CV for all numeric columns of the economics data using the functions:

1. The get_summary_stats function with the arguments, show = c("sd," "mean"), to calculate the standard deviation and mean for each column respectively.
2. The mutate function to create a new column, CV, is calculated by the above formula.
3. The flextable, theme_box, and set_caption functions create a table from the resulting data frame as described above.

```
economics %>% get_summary_stats(show = c("sd,""mean")) %>%
 mutate(CV = (sd/mean)*100) %>%
```

```
flextable() %>% theme_box() %>%
set_caption(caption = "The standard deviation, mean, and coefficient of variation
for all columns of the economics data")
```

Table 1.18. The Standard Deviation, Mean, and Coefficient of Variation for All Columns of the Economics Data

Variable	n	sd	Mean	CV
pce	574	3,556.804	4,820.093	73.79119
pop	574	36,682.399	257,159.653	14.26445
psavert	574	2.964	8.567	34.59788
uempmed	574	4.107	8.609	47.70589
unemploy	574	2,641.959	7,771.310	33.99631

We see that the highest variability was for the pce column with 73.79119 CV and 3,556.804 standard deviation and not the pop column with 14.26445 CV and 36,682.399 standard deviation.

1.3.4.2. The CV of Midwest Data

Similarly, we can get the CV for all numeric columns of the midwest data. In addition, we use the arrange and desc functions to order the columns according to their CV values in descending order.

```
midwest %>% get_summary_stats(show = c("sd,""mean")) %>%
 mutate(CV = (sd/mean)*100) %>% arrange(desc(CV)) %>%
 flextable() %>% theme_box() %>%
 set_caption(caption = "The standard deviation, mean, and coefficient of variation
for all columns of the midwest data in descending order of CV value")
```

Table 1.19. The Standard Deviation, Mean, and Coefficient of Variation for All Columns of the Midwest Data in Descending Order of CV Value

Variable	n	sd	Mean	CV
popother	437	18,526.541	1,612.931	1,148.625763
popasian	437	9,518.394	1,310.465	726.337140
popblack	437	78,958.267	11,023.881	716.247454
percamerindan	437	4.536	0.799	567.709637
popadults	437	191,644.862	60,972.613	314.313021
poppovertyknown	437	293,235.058	93,642.284	313.143855
poptotal	437	298,170.540	96,130.302	310.173310

popamerindian	437	868.927	343.110	253.250270
popdensity	437	7,664.752	3,097.743	247.430210
popwhite	437	200,196.648	81,839.915	244.619814
percblack	437	5.136	2.676	191.928251
percother	437	0.838	0.479	174.947808
inmetro	437	0.475	0.343	138.483965
percasian	437	0.628	0.487	128.952772
PID	437	876.390	1,437.339	60.973090
percprof	437	2.408	4.447	54.148864
percadultpoverty	437	5.109	10.919	46.789999
area	437	0.015	0.033	45.454545
percchildbelowpovert	437	7.229	16.447	43.953305
percbelowpoverty	437	5.150	12.511	41.163776
percollege	437	6.262	18.273	34.269140
percelderlypoverty	437	3.661	11.389	32.145052
perchsd	437	5.843	73.966	7.899575
percwhite	437	7.087	95.558	7.416438
percpovertyknown	437	2.750	97.110	2.831840

We see that the highest variability was for the popother column with 1,148.625763 CV and 18,526.541 standard deviation and not the poptotal column with 310.173310 CV and 298,170.540 standard deviation.

1.3.5. The Interquartile Range (IQR)

The interquartile range (IQR) is the difference between the first and third quartiles (Q3-Q1) and provides an estimate of the data spread. The IQR contains the middle 50% of our data. If the median or Q2 is closer to Q1 than Q3, this means that our data is **right-skewed** with a low frequency of large values. On the other hand, if the median or Q2 is closer to Q3 than Q1, this means that our data is **left-skewed** with a low frequency of small values. This will be seen from the summary plots described below. Finally, if the median is nearly in the center between Q1 and Q3, this means that our data is nearly normally distributed.

1.3.5.1. Advantages of Interquartile Range

1. The interquartile range is less sensitive to outliers than standard deviation, variance, or range so it is a **robust statistic**.

2. The interquartile range is less affected by the sample size than the range.

1.3.5.2. IQR of economics Data

Using the get_summary_stats function with the argument, show = c("median," "q1," "q3," "iqr"), we will get the median, Q1, Q3, and IQR values, respectively, of all numeric columns in the economics data. In addition, we will arrange the columns by their IQR value in descending order.

```
economics %>% get_summary_stats(show = c("median,""q1,""q3,""iqr")) %>%

arrange(desc(iqr)) %>%

 flextable() %>% theme_box() %>%

 set_caption(caption = "The median, Q1, Q3, and IQR for all columns of the
economics data in descending order by IQR value")
```

Table 1.20. The Median, Q1, Q3, and IQR for All Columns of the Economics Data in Descending Order by IQR Value

Variable	n	Median	Q1	Q3	IQR
pop	574	253,060.00	224,896.0	290,290.750	65,394.750
pce	574	3,936.85	1,578.3	7,626.325	6,048.025
unemploy	574	7,494.00	6,284.0	8,685.500	2,401.500
psavert	574	8.40	6.4	11.100	4.700
uempmed	574	7.50	6.0	9.100	3.100

We see that:

1. The highest variability was for the pop column with IQR = 65,394.750.
2. The IQR is calculated as Q3-Q1 for each column.
3. The median is nearly in the center between Q1 and Q3 for the unemploy column indicating a nearly normal distribution. On the other hand, the median is closer to Q1 than Q3 for the pce and uempmed columns indicating right-skewed data. This will be more clearly seen in the summary plots described below.

1.3.5.3. IQR of Midwest Data

Using the get_summary_stats function, we will get the median, Q1, Q3, and IQR values of all numeric columns in the midwest data. In addition, we will arrange the columns by their IQR value in descending order.

```
midwest %>% get_summary_stats(show = c("median,""q1,""q3,""iqr")) %>%
arrange(desc(iqr)) %>%
 flextable() %>% theme_box() %>%
  set_caption(caption = "The median, Q1, Q3, and IQR for all columns of the
midwest data in descending order by IQR value")
```

Table 1.21. The Median, Q1, Q3, and IQR for All Columns of the Midwest Data in Descending Order by IQR Value

Variable	n	Median	Q1	Q3	IQR
poptotal	437	35,324.000	18,840.000	75,651.000	56,811.000
poppover-tyknown	437	33,788.000	18,364.000	72,840.000	54,476.000
popwhite	437	34,471.000	18,630.000	72,968.000	54,338.000
popadults	437	22,188.000	12,271.000	47,541.000	35,270.000
popdensity	437	1,156.208	622.407	2,330.000	1,707.593
PID	437	1,221.000	670.000	2,059.000	1,389.000
popblack	437	201.000	29.000	1,291.000	1,262.000
popasian	437	102.000	35.000	401.000	366.000
popother	437	66.000	20.000	345.000	325.000
popamerin-dian	437	94.000	44.000	288.000	244.000
percchildbe-lowpovert	437	15.270	11.624	20.352	8.728
percollege	437	16.798	14.114	20.550	6.436
percbelow-poverty	437	11.822	9.199	15.133	5.935
perchsd	437	74.247	71.325	77.195	5.870
percadult-poverty	437	10.008	7.668	13.182	5.514
percelderly-poverty	437	10.869	8.912	13.412	4.500
percwhite	437	98.033	94.886	99.075	4.189
percblack	437	0.539	0.116	2.601	2.486
percprof	437	3.814	2.998	4.949	1.951
percpover-tyknown	437	98.170	96.895	98.599	1.704

inmetro	437	0.000	0.000	1.000	1.000
percother	437	0.178	0.091	0.481	0.389
percasian	437	0.297	0.174	0.521	0.347
percamerin-dan	437	0.215	0.158	0.384	0.226
area	437	0.030	0.024	0.038	0.014

We see that:

1. The highest variability was for the poptotal column with IQR = 56,811.0.
2. The median is nearly in the center between Q1 and Q3 for the perchsd column indicating a nearly normal distribution. On the other hand, the median is closer to Q1 than Q3 for the popblack and percblack columns indicating right-skewed data. Finally, the median is closer to Q3 than Q1 for the percwhite column indicating left-skewed data. This will be more clearly seen in the summary plots described below.

1.3.6. Median Absolute Deviation (MAD)

The MAD is another robust statistic for measuring the variability of numeric data. MAD is the median absolute distance that the data points are from the median. So it is calculated using the formula:

$$MAD = median\left(\left|x_i - \overset{\blacklozenge}{x}\right|\right)$$

Where:

$\left|x_i - \overset{\blacklozenge}{x}\right|$ is the absolute difference between every element in our sample (from x_1 to x_n where n is the sample size or the number of rows in our data) and the sample mean x.

1.3.6.1. MAD of Economics Data

Using the get_summary_stats function with the argument, show = c("mad), we will get the MAD value of all numeric columns in the economics data. In addition, we will arrange the columns by their MAD value in descending order.

```
economics %>% get_summary_stats(show = c("mad")) %>%
arrange(desc(mad)) %>%
 flextable() %>% theme_box() %>%
```

```
set_caption(caption = "The median absolute deviation (MAD) for all columns of the economics data in descending order by MAD value")
```

Table 1.22. *The Median Absolute Deviation (MAD) for All Columns of the Economics Data in Descending Order by MAD Value*

Variable	n	MAD
pop	574	48,097.027
pce	574	4,139.123
unemploy	574	1,788.016
psavert	574	3.558
uempmed	574	2.224

We see that the highest variability was for the pop column with MAD = 48,097.027.

1.3.6.2. MAD of Midwest Data

Using similar functions, we can get the MAD value for all numeric columns of the midwest data.

```
midwest %>% get_summary_stats(show = c("mad")) %>%
arrange(desc(mad)) %>%
 flextable() %>% theme_box() %>%
 set_caption(caption = "The median absolute deviation (MAD) for all columns of the midwest data in descending order by MAD value")
```

Table 1.23. *The Median Absolute Deviation (MAD) for All Columns of the Midwest Data in Descending Order by MAD Value*

Variable	n	MAD
poptotal	437	29,662.378
popwhite	437	28,525.224
poppovertyknown	437	27,826.919
popadults	437	17,779.339
popdensity	437	948.537
PID	437	892.525
popblack	437	286.142
popasian	437	121.573
popamerindian	437	100.817

popother	437	84.508
percchildbelowpovert	437	6.282
percollege	437	4.543
perchsd	437	4.371
percbelowpoverty	437	4.204
percadultpoverty	437	4.175
percelderlypoverty	437	3.359
percwhite	437	1.962
percprof	437	1.311
percpovertyknown	437	0.902
percblack	437	0.722
percasian	437	0.207
percother	437	0.166
percamerindan	437	0.110
area	437	0.009
inmetro	437	0.000

We see that the highest variability was for the poptotal column with MAD = 29,662.378.

1.4. SUMMARY PLOTS FOR CONTINUOUS UNIVARIATE ANALYSIS

The measures of location (mean, median, mode) and spread (standard deviation, IQR, MAD) do not tell the whole story of the data distribution or the distribution shape. Instead, we can use different plots to quickly look at the different data distributions. The ggplot2 package (a member of the tidyverse package) allows us to quickly visualize and explore data and we will heavily use it in this chapter and subsequent chapters.

1.4.1. Introduction to ggplot2

In ggplot2, it is recommended that everything you want to plot is included in a data frame (a tabular R object) as a column.

The basic steps to create a plot with the ggplot2 package are:

1. Create an object of the ggplot class using the ggplot() function.
2. Add geoms and other elements to create and customize the plot using +.

1.4.1.1. Create a ggplot Object

The ggplot() function will create a blank plot without anything in it. It has 2 main arguments:

1. The data argument specifies the data frame you want to use.
2. The aes() argument specifies which columns of that data frame are mapped to which aesthetics. Common plot aesthetics include:
3. x: Position on x-axis.
4. y: Position on the y-axis.
5. shape: Shape.
6. color: Color of the border of elements.
7. fill: Color of the inside of elements.
8. size: Size.
9. alpha: Transparency (1: opaque; 0: transparent).
10. linetype: Type of line (e.g., solid, dashed).

To plot the psavert (personal savings rate) values from the economics data on the x-axis, we use the ggplot function with 2 arguments:

1. data = economics which is our data frame containing the psavert column.
2. aes with the argument x = psavert to plot psavert values on the x-axis. Then, we add a title using the labs function with the title argument to further customize this plot.

```
ggplot(data = economics, aes(x = psavert))+
 labs(title = "Blank plot using ggplot function")
```

A blank plot is produced because the exact geom (plot type) has not been specified yet. The x-axis has a title of "psavert" and no title appears for the y-axis.

Another way of producing this plot is using the "%>%" function after the economics data and using only the aes argument inside the ggplot function.

```
economics %>% ggplot(aes(x = psavert))+
 labs(title = "Another blank plot using ggplot function")
```

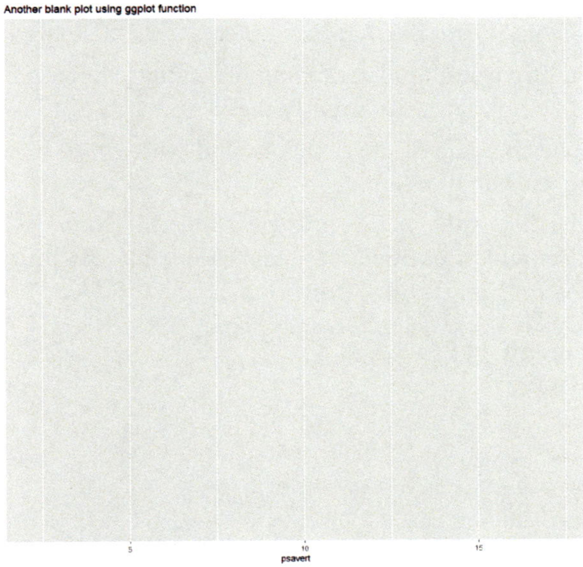

The aesthetics required for a plot depend on the geoms (plot types).

1.4.1.2. Adding Geoms

The geom functions add the graphical elements to the plot (e.g. histogram, boxplot, scatterplot). When you run the code to create a plot in RStudio, the plot will be shown in the "Plots" tab in one of the RStudio panels. If you would like to save the plot, you can do so using the "Export" button in this tab.

The aesthetics required for a geom type (plot type) can be found in the "Aesthetics" section of the geom's help file (e.g., ?geom_histogram). Required aesthetics are in bold in this section of the help file and optional ones are not.

1.4.2. Histograms

Histograms show the distribution of a continuous variable by dividing the x-axis into bins, counting the number of observations in each bin, and displaying the counts with bars. The geom_histogram() function requires only one aesthetic (x) or the continuous variable you want to visualize.

To plot a histogram of the psavert column, we will:

1. Create a blank plot using the ggplot function as before.
2. Add geom_histogram function to create the histogram plot.
3. Add a title using the labs function with the title argument. Also, the x and y arguments can modify the x- and y-axis titles.
4. Remove the default gray background with white lines by using the theme_classic function.
5. Put the plot title in the top center of the graph using the theme function with plot.title argument = element_text(hjust = 0.5) where hjust is for horizontal justification.

```
ggplot(data = economics, aes(x = psavert))+ geom_histogram()+
  labs(title = "Histogram of personal saving rate in economics data," x =
"Personal Saving Rate,"
    y = "Count")+
 theme_classic()+
 theme(plot.title = element_text(hjust = 0.5))
```

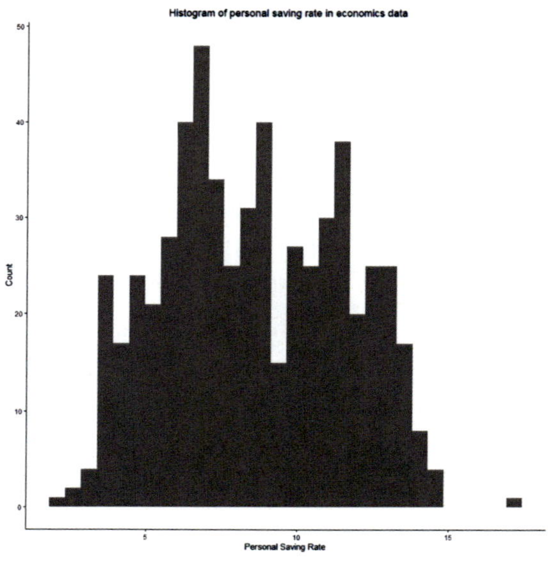

The peak count of observations (> 40 rows) appears between 5 and 10. The personal saving rate values appear normally distributed with a high frequency of values in the center and a low frequency at the tails.

1.4.2.1. Coloring the Bar Borders

The default histogram has a black color with difficult-to-see bar borders. We can add an extra argument, color = "red," to the geom_histogram function to see the bars more clearly.

```
ggplot(data = economics, aes(x = psavert))+
 geom_histogram(color = "red")+
  labs(title = "Histogram of personal saving rate in economics data with red borders," x = "Personal Saving Rate,"
y = "Count")+
theme_classic()+
 theme(plot.title = element_text(hjust = 0.5))
```

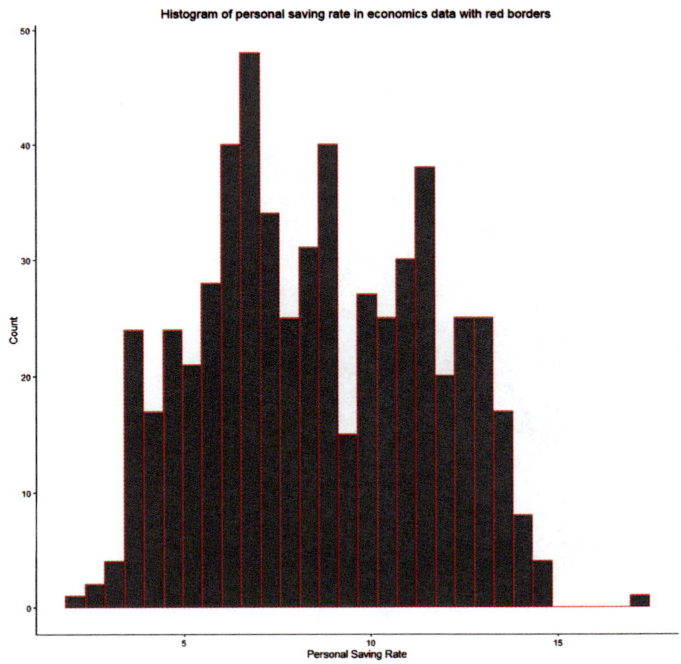

The bars are now more clearly seen.

1.4.2.2. Bins

The bins argument controls the number of bins into which the numeric variable is divided (i.e., the number of bars in the plot). The default is 30, but it is helpful to try smaller and larger numbers to get a better impression of the distribution shape. For example, using 20 bins for the personal saving rate column.

```
ggplot(data = economics, aes(x = psavert))+
 geom_histogram(color = "red," bins = 20)+
 labs(title = "Histogram of personal saving rate in economics data using 20 bins,"
x = "Personal Saving Rate,"
y = "Count")+
theme_classic()+
 theme(plot.title = element_text(hjust = 0.5))
```

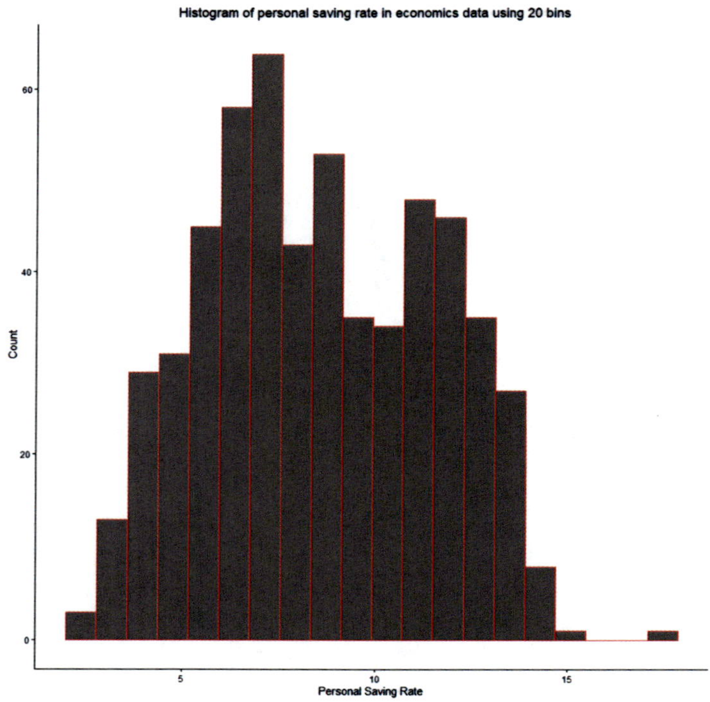

For example, using 40 bins for the personal saving rate column.

```
ggplot(data = economics, aes(x = psavert))+
 geom_histogram(color = "red," bins = 40)+
 labs(title = "Histogram of personal saving rate in economics data using 40 bins,"
```

```
x = "Personal Saving Rate,"
y = "Count")+
 theme_classic()+
 theme(plot.title = element_text(hjust = 0.5))
```

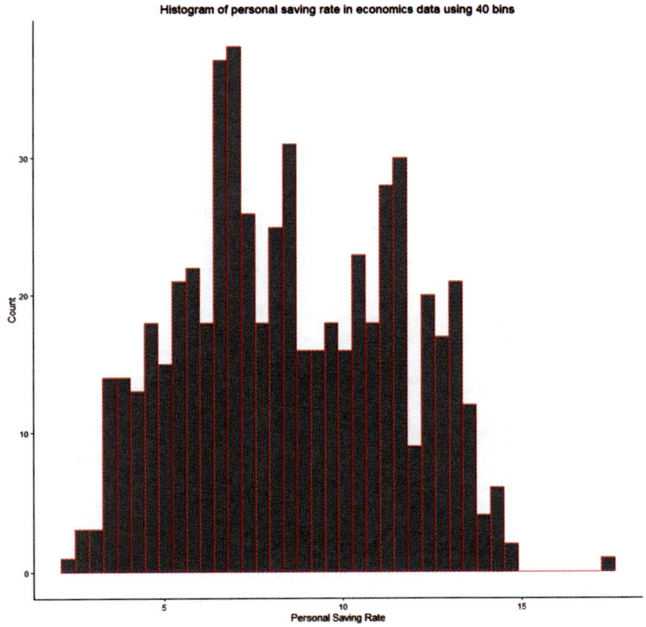

We see that the personal saving rate is still a normally distributed variable.

1.4.2.3. Binwidth

In some of the above plots, we see that the bin boundaries are not integer numbers. If we want integer bin boundaries, we can use the binwidth argument with an integer value within the geom_histogram function. For example, using binwidth = 1 for the personal saving rate column. In addition, we will use the scale_x_continuous function with the argument, breaks = seq(0,20,1), to break the x-axis in 1 point value interval.

```
ggplot(data = economics, aes(x = psavert))+
 geom_histogram(color = "red," binwidth = 1)+
  labs(title = "Histogram of personal saving rate in economics data using 1 binwidth,"
    x = "Personal Saving Rate,"
    y = "Count")+ scale_x_continuous(breaks = seq(0,20,1))+
```

```
theme_classic()+
theme(plot.title = element_text(hjust = 0.5))
```

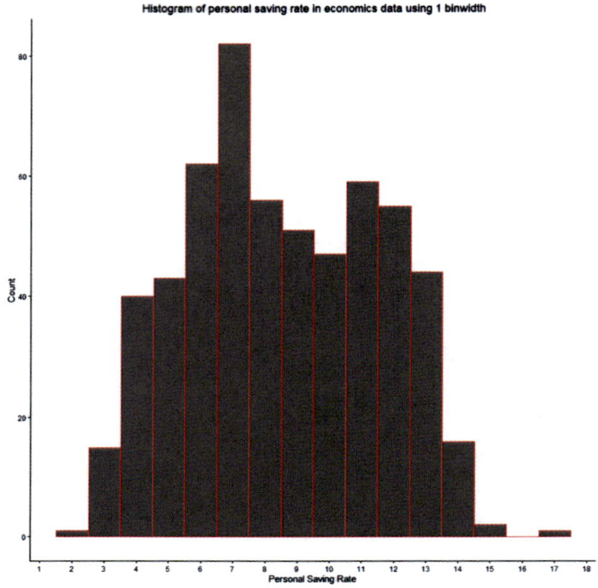

We see that each bar now corresponds to a single integer value.

1.4.2.4. Histograms with Reference Lines

A more informative histogram can be obtained by using reference lines indicating certain summary statistics like mean, median, etc. In that case, we will see if the data is right-skewed (median < mean), left-skewed (median > mean), or normally distributed (median nearly = mean).

For the economics data, we will generate a data frame containing the desired summary statistics in a long format using the functions:

1. The get_summary_stats function with the argument, show = c("mean," "median"), to get the mean and median value for each column in the economics data in a separate column.
2. The pivot_longer function with the arguments:
   2.1. cols = c(mean, median) to convert the 2 numeric columns of mean and median into 2 columns.
   2.2. names_to = "Statistics" which is the first character column holding the statistic name, mean, or median.

2.3. values_to = "value" which is the 2nd numeric column holding the mean and median value for each column.

3. The resulting data frame "df" is converted to a table as before.

```
df<-economics %>% get_summary_stats(show = c("mean," "median")) %>%
 pivot_longer(cols = c(mean,median), names_to = "Statistics,"
values_to = "value")
df %>% flextable() %>% theme_box() %>%
 set_caption(caption = "Mean and Median value for every numeric column in the
economics data in long format")
```

Table 1.24. Mean and Median Value for Every Numeric Column in the Economics Data in Long Format

Variable	n	Statistics	Value
pce	574	mean	4,820.093
pce	574	median	3,936.850
pop	574	mean	257,159.653
pop	574	median	253,060.000
psavert	574	mean	8.567
psavert	574	median	8.400
uempmed	574	mean	8.609
uempmed	574	median	7.500
unemploy	574	mean	7,771.310
unemploy	574	median	7,494.000

As shown above, the right-skewed columns are the pce, pop, uempmed, and unemploy columns because the mean is greater than the median. On the other hand, the psavert column is an evenly-spaced or normally distributed data because the mean is nearly equal to the median.

To plot a histogram of the psavert column with mean and median reference lines, we will use the same above functions with an additional geom_vline function to plot vertical lines with the arguments:

1. data = df %>% filter(variable=="psavert") to filter for only rows containing the psavert column.
2. aes(xintercept = value, color = Statistics) so it will plot 2 vertical lines one for the mean and one for the median with a different color. We also use the "\n" in the title to break the long title into 2 lines.

```
ggplot(data = economics, aes(x = psavert))+
 geom_histogram(color = "red")+
```

```
geom_vline(data = df %>% filter(variable=="psavert"),
aes(xintercept = value, color = Statistics))+
labs(title = "Histogram of personal saving rate in economics data\n with mean and median reference lines,"
x = "Personal Saving Rate,"
y = "Count")+
theme_classic()+
theme(plot.title = element_text(hjust = 0.5))
```

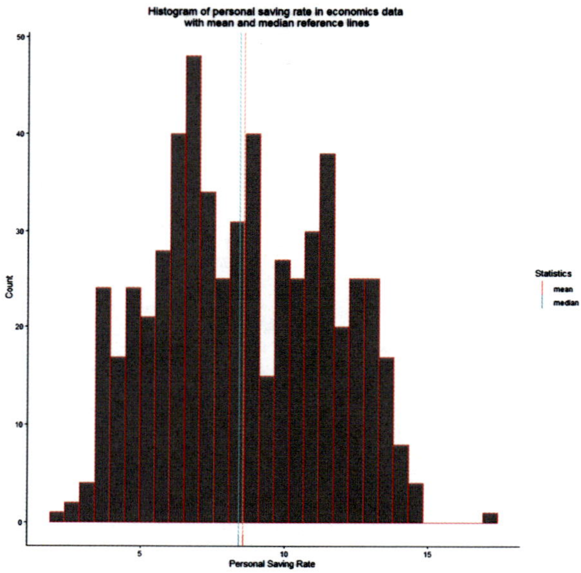

We see that the mean is plotted as a red vertical line while the median is plotted as a blue vertical line. The 2 lines are near to each other or nearly equal indicating a normally distributed variable. Similarly, we can plot the pce column with 2 reference lines.

```
ggplot(data = economics, aes(x = pce))+
geom_histogram(color = "red")+
geom_vline(data = df %>% filter(variable=="pce"),
aes(xintercept = value, color = Statistics))+
labs(title = "Histogram of personal consumption expenditures \n with mean and median reference lines,"
x = "personal consumption expenditures (billions of dollars),"
y = "Count")+
theme_classic()+
theme(plot.title = element_text(hjust = 0.5))
```

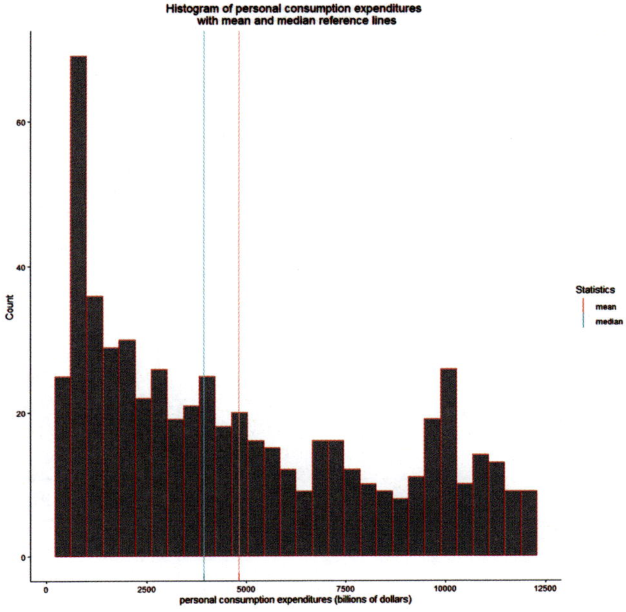

The mean is plotted as a red vertical line while the median is plotted as a blue vertical line. The mean line is greater than the median line indicating a right-skewed variable or a low frequency of large values.

For the midwest data, we will generate a data fame "df" containing the desired summary statistics in the long format using the same functions.

```
df<-midwest %>% get_summary_stats(show = c("mean," "median")) %>%
 pivot_longer(cols = c(mean,median), names_to = "Statistics,"
values_to = "value")
df %>% flextable() %>% theme_box() %>%
 set_caption(caption = "Mean and Median value for every numeric column of the
midwest data in long format")
```

Table 1.25. Mean and Median Value for Every Numeric Column of the Midwest Data in Long Format

Variable	n	Statistics	Value
PID	437	mean	1,437.339
PID	437	median	1,221.000
area	437	mean	0.033

area	437	median	0.030
poptotal	437	mean	96,130.302
poptotal	437	median	35,324.000
popdensity	437	mean	3,097.743
popdensity	437	median	1,156.208
popwhite	437	mean	81,839.915
popwhite	437	median	34,471.000
popblack	437	mean	11,023.881
popblack	437	median	201.000
popamerindian	437	mean	343.110
popamerindian	437	median	94.000
popasian	437	mean	1,310.465
popasian	437	median	102.000
popother	437	mean	1,612.931
popother	437	median	66.000
percwhite	437	mean	95.558
percwhite	437	median	98.033
percblack	437	mean	2.676
percblack	437	median	0.539
percamerindan	437	mean	0.799
percamerindan	437	median	0.215
percasian	437	mean	0.487
percasian	437	median	0.297
percother	437	mean	0.479
percother	437	median	0.178
popadults	437	mean	60,972.613
popadults	437	median	22,188.000
perchsd	437	mean	73.966
perchsd	437	median	74.247
percollege	437	mean	18.273
percollege	437	median	16.798
percprof	437	mean	4.447
percprof	437	median	3.814

poppovertyknown	437	mean	93,642.284
poppovertyknown	437	median	33,788.000
percpovertyknown	437	mean	97.110
percpovertyknown	437	median	98.170
percbelowpoverty	437	mean	12.511
percbelowpoverty	437	median	11.822
percchildbelowpov-ert	437	mean	16.447
percchildbelowpov-ert	437	median	15.270
percadultpoverty	437	mean	10.919
percadultpoverty	437	median	10.008
percelderlypoverty	437	mean	11.389
percelderlypoverty	437	median	10.869
inmetro	437	mean	0.343
inmetro	437	median	0.000

When the mean is larger than the median, this indicates right-skewed data as for the poptotal, popdensity, and popwhite columns. When the mean is nearly equal to the median, this indicates evenly-spaced or normally distributed data as for the area column. Finally, when the mean is smaller than the median, this indicates left-skewed data as for the percwhite column.

To plot a histogram of the poptotal column with mean and median reference lines, we will use the same above functions with an additional geom_vline function.

```
ggplot(data = midwest, aes(x = poptotal))+
 geom_histogram(color = "red")+
 geom_vline(data = df %>% filter(variable=="poptotal"),
aes(xintercept = value, color = Statistics))+
labs(title = "Histogram of total population from midwest data\n with mean and median reference lines,"
x = "Total Population,"
y = "Count")+
theme_classic()+
theme(plot.title = element_text(hjust = 0.5))
```

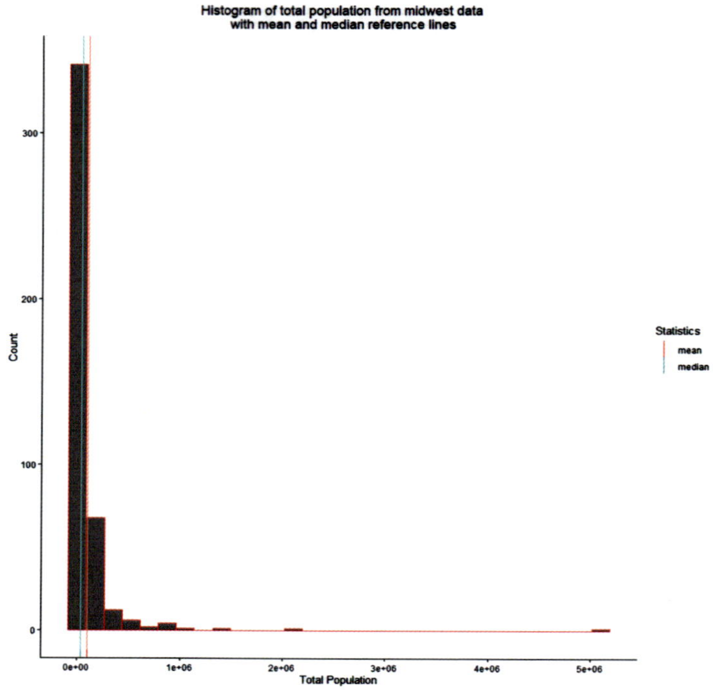

We see that the mean (red vertical line) is greater than the median (blue vertical line) indicating right-skewed data. Although the 2 lines are near to each other, they have great differences because the scale of the x-axis is in millions.

Similarly, we can plot the area column with 2 reference lines.

```
ggplot(data = midwest, aes(x = area))+
 geom_histogram(color = "red")+
 geom_vline(data = df %>% filter(variable=="area"),
aes(xintercept = value, color = Statistics))+
labs(title = "Histogram of county area from the midwest data \n with mean and median reference lines,"
x = "County Area,"
 y = "Count")+
 theme_classic()+
 theme(plot.title = element_text(hjust = 0.5))
```

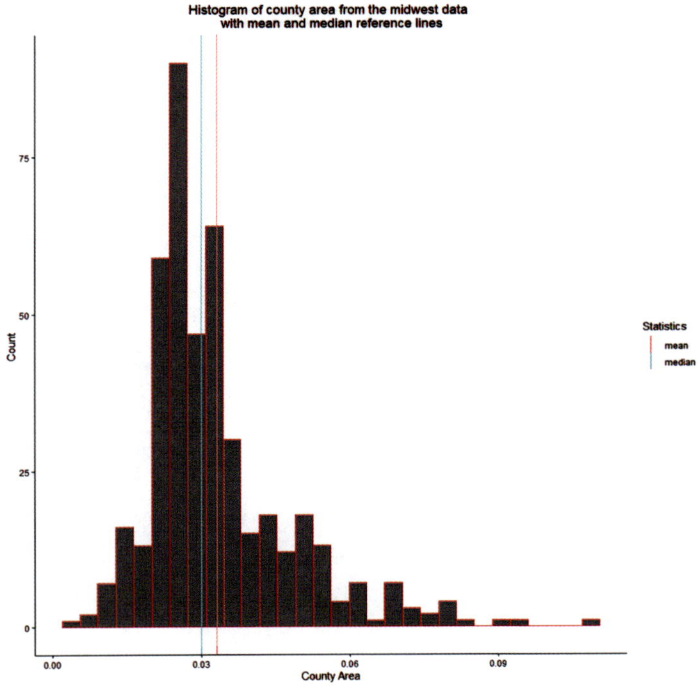

The mean line is near the median line (with a difference of 0.003) indicating a normally-distributed variable.

Finally, we can plot the percwhite column with 2 reference lines.

```
ggplot(data = midwest, aes(x = percwhite))+
 geom_histogram(color = "red")+
 geom_vline(data = df %>% filter(variable=="percwhite"),
aes(xintercept = value, color = Statistics))+
labs(title = "Histogram of White percentage from the midwest data \n with mean and median reference lines,"
x = "White Percentage,"
y = "Count")+
 theme_classic()+
 theme(plot.title = element_text(hjust = 0.5))
```

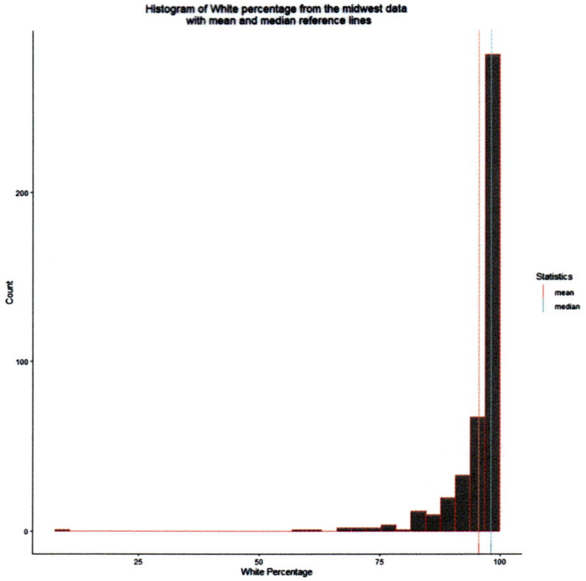

We see that the mean (red vertical line) is smaller than the median (blue vertical line) indicating left-skewed data with low frequency of small values.

1.4.3. Box Plots

The box plot displays the distribution of a continuous variable. It visualizes five summary statistics (the median, two hinges, and two whiskers), and all outliers individually. The lower and upper hinges correspond to the first and third quartiles (Q1 and Q3)respectively.

The upper whisker extends from Q3 to the largest value no further than 1.5 X IQR from Q3. The lower whisker extends from Q1 to the smallest value at most 1.5 X IQR from Q1. Data beyond the end of the whiskers are called "outlying" points and are plotted individually.

The median (central line in the box), the upper quartile, and the lower quartile be used to determine the symmetry of the distribution:

1. If the distribution is symmetric, then the upper and lower quartiles should be nearly equally spaced from the median. This can be seen in the psavert column of the economics data.
2. If the median is closer to the 1st quartile than to the 3rd quartile, then the distribution is right-skewed. This can be seen in the pce column from the economics data.

3. If the median is closer to the 3rd quartile than to the 1st quartile, then the distribution is left-skewed. This can be seen in the percent white column from the midwest data.

1.4.3.1. Box plots for Symmetric Distribution

The geom_boxplot function is used to plot a box plot by providing the x or y value as the continuous variable you want to plot. To plot a box plot of the psavert column from economics data on the x-axis, we will use the following functions:

1. The ggplot function with arguments:
    1.1. data = economics which is the data frame containing the psavert column.
    1.2. aes(x = psavert) to plot personal saving rate values on the x-axis.
2. The geom_boxplot function to create the box plot.
3. The labs, theme_classic, and theme functions as described above.

```
ggplot(data= economics, aes(x = psavert))+ geom_boxplot()+
 labs(title = "Boxplot of personal saving rate on the x-axis from economics data,"
 x = "Personal Saving Rate")+
 theme_classic()+
 theme(plot.title = element_text(hjust = 0.5))
```

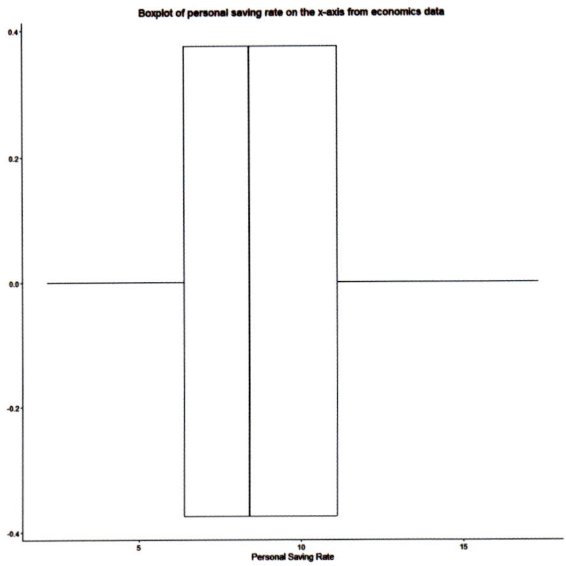

The box plot shows no outliers and the personal saving rate is plotted on the x-axis. Because the median is equally spaced from the 1st and 3rd quartiles, so the personal saving rate has a symmetric distribution.

Alternatively, we can plot the personal saving rate values on the y-axis using the argument, aes(y = psavert), and adjust the labs function accordingly.

```
ggplot(data= economics, aes(y = psavert))+ geom_boxplot()+
 labs(title = "Boxplot of personal saving rate on the y-axis from economics data,"
y = "Personal Saving Rate")+
 theme_classic()+

 theme(plot.title = element_text(hjust = 0.5))
```

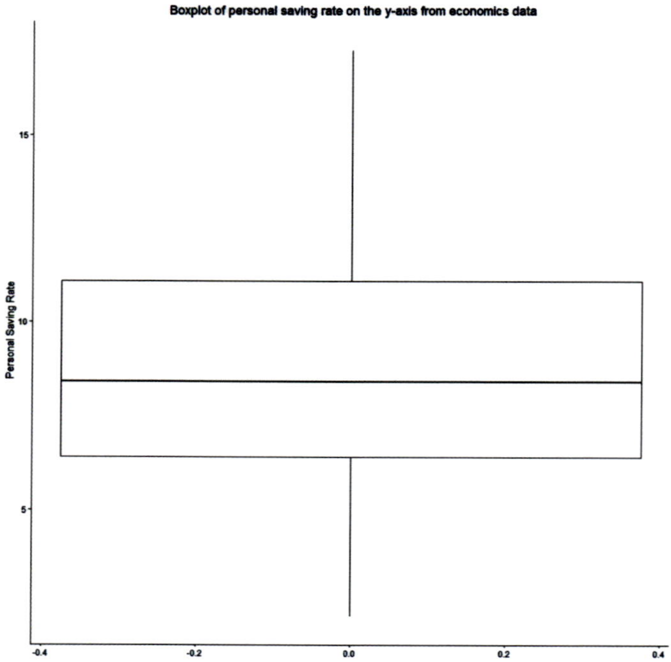

1.4.3.2. Box Plots for Right-Skewed Distribution

Using the same functions, we can plot the pce column values on the x-axis.

```
ggplot(data= economics, aes(x = pce))+ geom_boxplot()+
 labs(title = "Boxplot of personal consumption expenditures on the x-axis from economics data,"
```

```
x = "Personal Consumption Expenditures (billions of dollars)")+
 theme_classic()+
 theme(plot.title = element_text(hjust = 0.5))
```

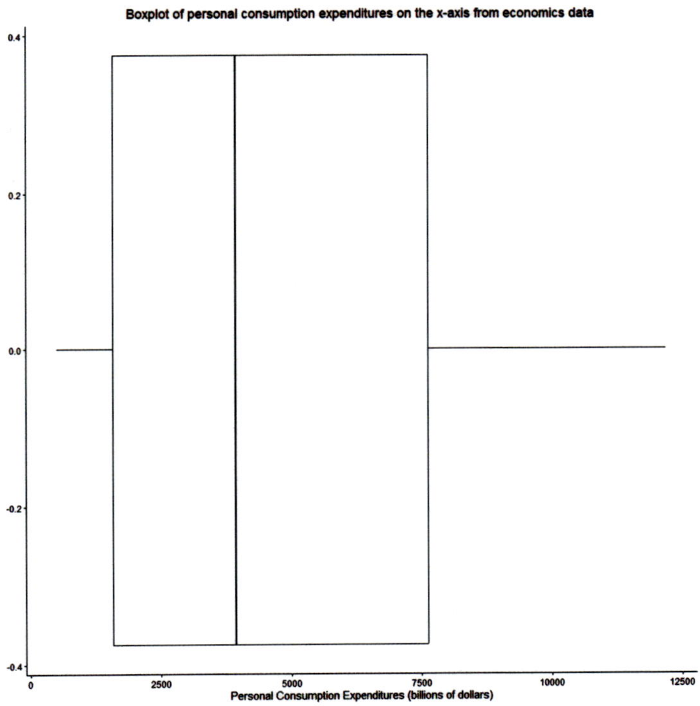

The box plot shows no outliers. Because the median is closer to the 1st quartile than to the 3rd quartile, the personal consumption expenditures have a right-skewed distribution.

Using the same functions, we can plot the poptotal column values from the midwest data on the x-axis.

```
ggplot(data= midwest, aes(x = poptotal))+ geom_boxplot()+
 labs(title = "Boxplot of total population on the x-axis from midwest data,"
x = "Total Population")+
 theme_classic()+
 theme(plot.title = element_text(hjust = 0.5))
```

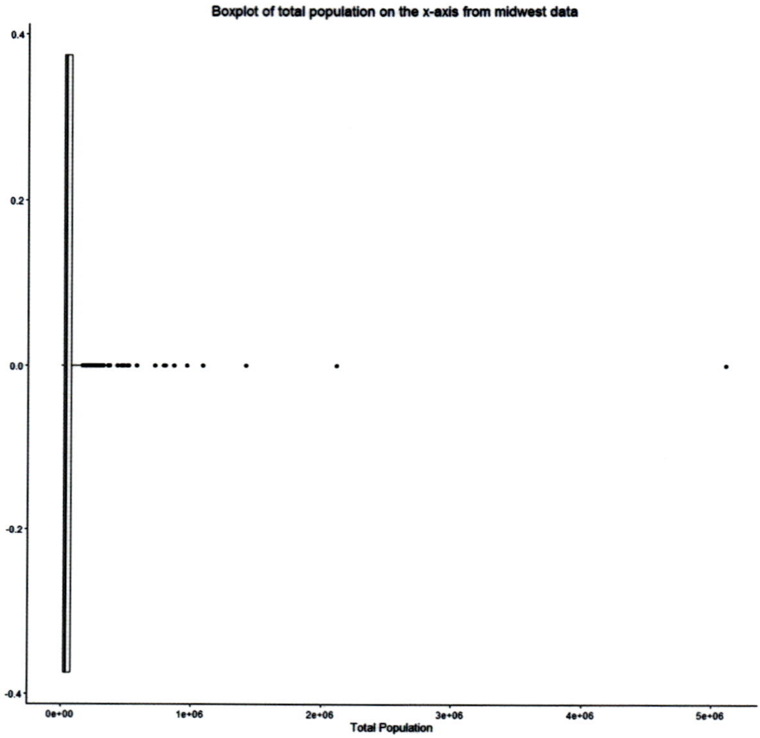

The box plot shows some large outliers as black points. Because the median is closer to the 1st quartile than to the 3rd quartile, the total population has a right-skewed distribution.

1.4.3.3. Box Plots for Left-Skewed Distribution

Using the same functions, we can plot the percent white column values on the x-axis from the midwest data.

```
ggplot(data= midwest, aes(x = percwhite))+ geom_boxplot()+
 labs(title = "Boxplot of White percentage on the x-axis from midwest data,"
 x = "White Percentage")+
 theme_classic()+
 theme(plot.title = element_text(hjust = 0.5))
```

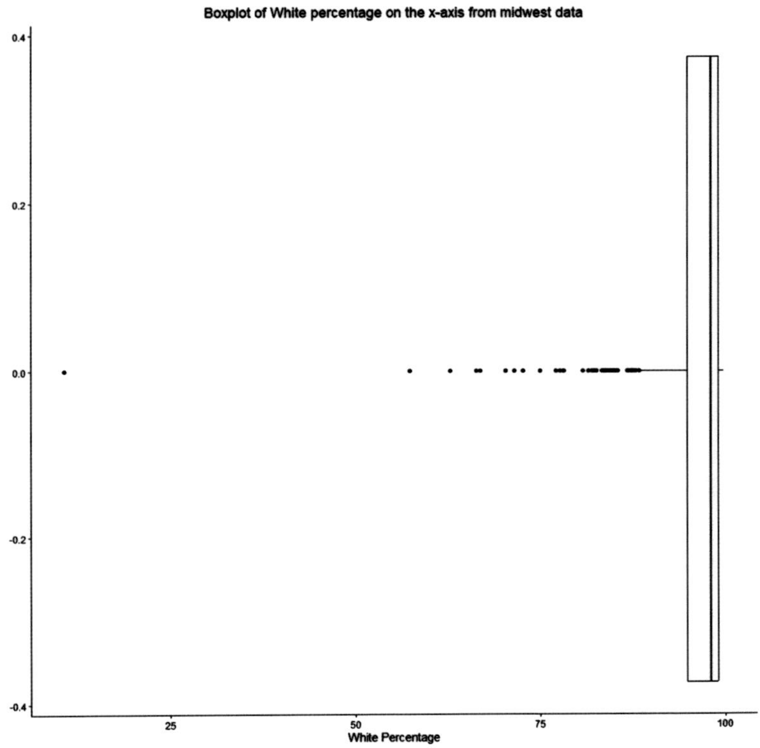

The box plot shows small outlier values as black points. Because the median is closer to the 3rd quartile than to the 1st quartile, the percentage white has a left-skewed distribution.

1.4.3.4. Box Plots with Reference Points

A more informative box plot can be plotted with a reference point for the mean value. Because the median is plotted as a central black line, the mean point can be compared to the median to deduce the data distribution as discussed in the above sections.

In R, there are many point shapes that can be supplied by their numbers.

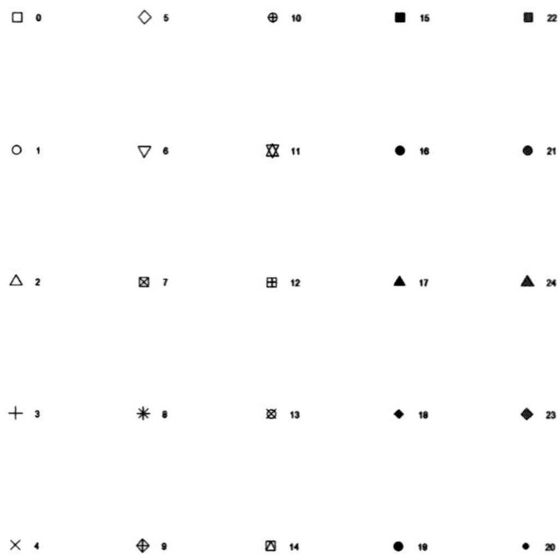

Or can be supplied by their names.

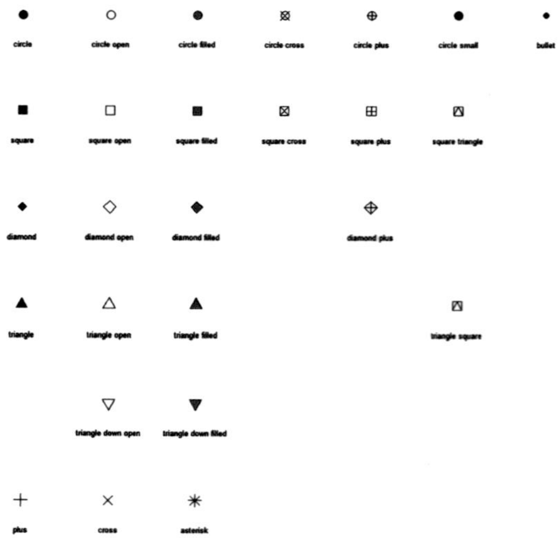

For example, we can plot a box plot of the psavert column from economics data on the y-axis with a plus mean reference point, we will use the following functions:

1. The ggplot function with arguments:
   i. data = economics which is the data frame containing the psavert column.

  ii. aes(y = psavert, x = 0) to plot personal saving rate values on the y-axis. The whiskers will have an x-axis position at 0 as well as the reference point.

2. The geom_boxplot function to create the box plot.
3. The stat_summary function with the arguments:
   i. geom = "point" to plot a point.
   ii. fun = "mean" the point plotted is for the mean value of personal saving rate.
   iii. shape = "plus" which is the point shape.
   iv. color = "red" which is the point color.
   v. size = 2 which is the point size.
4. The labs, theme_classic, and theme functions as described above.

```
ggplot(data= economics, aes(y = psavert, x = 0))+ geom_boxplot()+
 stat_summary(geom = "point," fun = "mean," shape = "plus,"
color = "red," size = 2)+
labs(title = "Boxplot of personal saving rate on the y-axis with
a plus mean reference point,"
x = "Personal Saving Rate")+
 theme_classic()+
 theme(plot.title = element_text(hjust = 0.5))
```

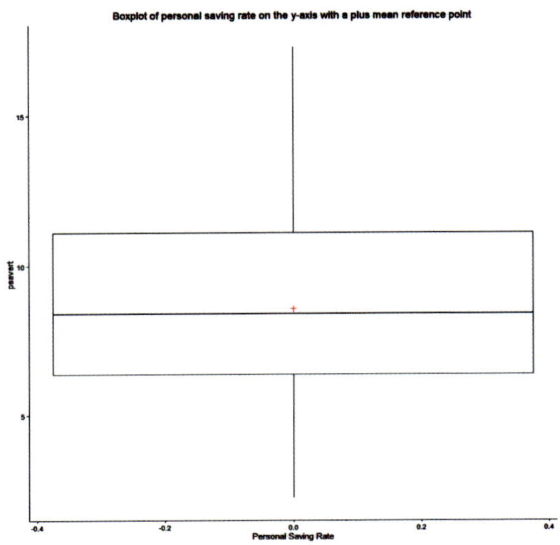

Alternatively, we can plot this reference point as an asterisk.

```
ggplot(data= economics, aes(y = psavert, x = 0))+ geom_boxplot()+
 stat_summary(geom = "point," fun = "mean," shape = "asterisk,"
color = "red," size = 2)+
labs(title = "Boxplot of personal saving rate on the y-axis with an asterisk
mean reference point,"
 y = "Personal Saving Rate")+
theme_classic()+
 theme(plot.title = element_text(hjust = 0.5))
```

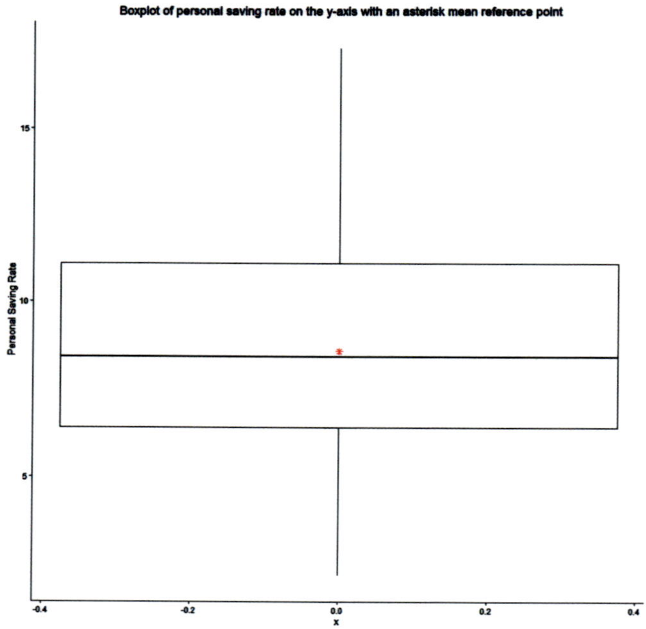

We see that the mean reference point is near the median central line of the box indicating a symmetrical distribution.

In a second example, we can plot the popwhite column from the midwest data with a diamond mean reference point.

```
ggplot(data= midwest, aes(y = popwhite, x = 0))+ geom_boxplot()+
 stat_summary(geom = "point," fun = "mean," shape = "diamond,"
color = "red," size = 2)+
 labs(title = "Boxplot of White population on the y-axis with a diamond mean
reference point,"
y = "White population")+
 theme_classic()+
```

```
theme(plot.title = element_text(hjust = 0.5))
```

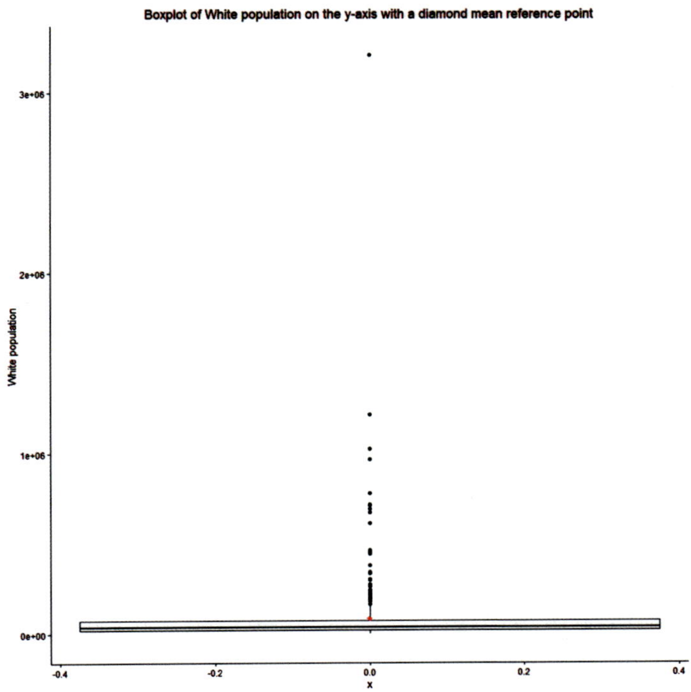

We see that the red mean reference point is above (greater than) the median central line of the box indicating a right-skewed distribution.

In a third example, we can plot the percwhite column from the midwest data with a cross mean reference point.

```
ggplot(data= midwest, aes(y = percwhite, x = 0))+ geom_boxplot()+
 stat_summary(geom = "point," fun = "mean," shape = "cross,"
color = "red," size = 2)+
  labs(title = "Boxplot of White percentage on the y-axis with a cross mean reference point,"
y = "White Percentage")+
theme_classic()+
theme(plot.title = element_text(hjust = 0.5))
```

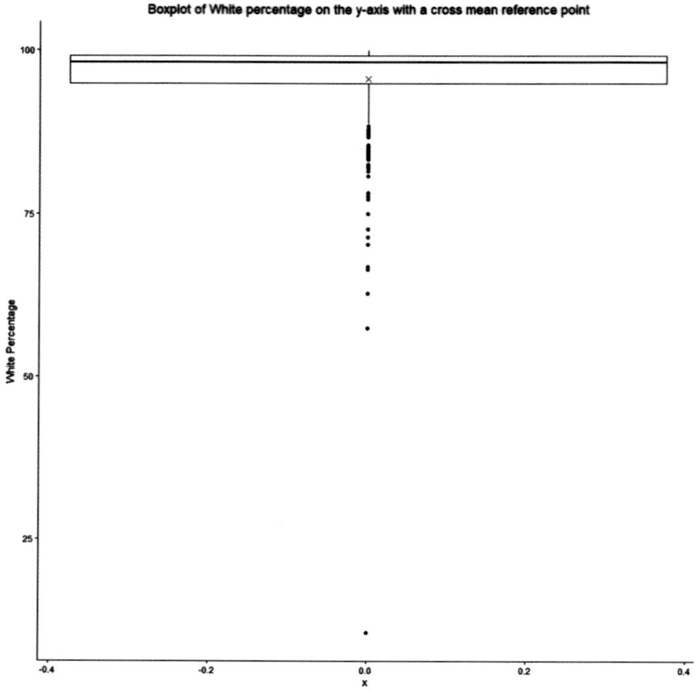

We see that the red mean reference point is below (smaller than) the median central line of the box indicating a left-skewed distribution.

1.4.4. Density Plots

The density plot is a kernel density estimate of the data (or a smoothed version of the histogram). Kernel density estimation is a method for estimating the probability density function of a continuous variable.

For the continuous variables, the probability distribution is known as the probability density function or PDF. The probability distribution for any variable describes how the probabilities are distributed over the different values of this variable. The density plot quickly shows the distribution shape of any variable.

1.4.4.1. Density Plot for a Symmetric Distribution

The geom_density function plots a kernel density plot of your continuous variable on the x or y-axis. To plot a density plot of the psavert column from the economics data on the x-axis, we will use the following functions:

1. The ggplot function with arguments:
   i. data = economics which is the data frame containing the psavert column.
   ii. aes(x = psavert) to plot personal saving rate values on the x-axis.
2. The geom_density function to create the density plot.
3. The labs, theme_classic, and theme functions as described above.

```
ggplot(data= economics, aes(x = psavert))+ geom_density()+
 labs(title = "Kernel density plot of personal saving rates in economics data,"
x = "Personal Saving Rate," y = "Density")+
 theme_classic()+
 theme(plot.title = element_text(hjust = 0.5))
```

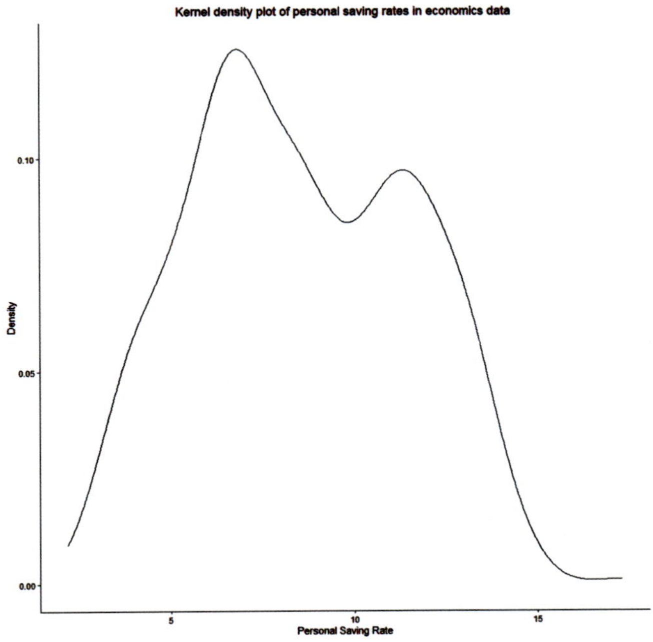

We see that the peak density appears between 5 and 10. The personal saving rate values appear nearly normally distributed with a high frequency of values in the center and a low frequency at the tails. There is also another density peak at a value greater than 10. To look at the exact location of these peaks, we can look at section 1.2.4.1. for calculating the mode of economics data. The table for the psavert column shows that the highest frequency (probability) was for

6.4 value (1st density peak) and the 2nd most frequent value was for 11.7 value (the second peak).

1.4.4.2. Density Plot for Right-Skewed Distribution

Using the same functions, we can plot a density plot for the pce column.

```
ggplot(data= economics, aes(x = pce))+ geom_density()+
 labs(title = "Density plot of personal consumption expenditures from the economics data,"
 x = "Personal Consumption Expenditures (billions of dollars),"
y = "Density")+
 theme_classic()+
 theme(plot.title = element_text(hjust = 0.5))
```

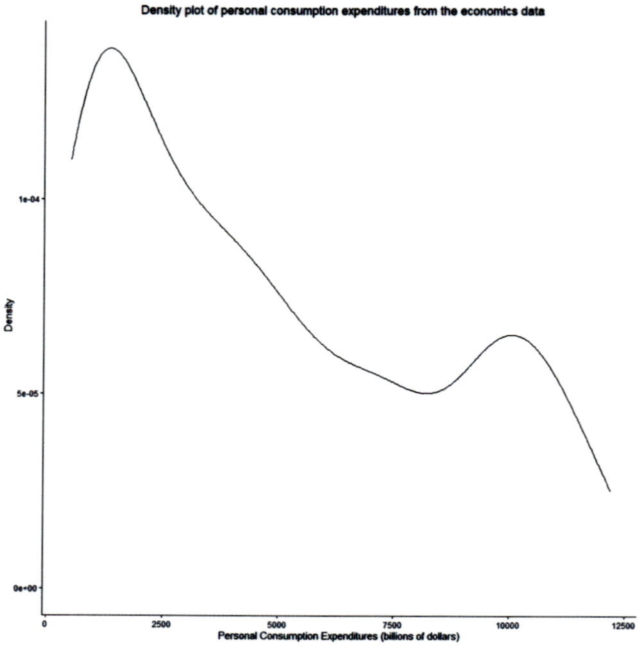

We see that the highest density was at low values (< 2500) and larger values have much lower density. This indicates that the personal consumption expenditures have a right-skewed distribution. Using the same functions, we can plot a density plot for the poptotal column values from the midwest data on the x-axis.

```
ggplot(data= midwest, aes(x = poptotal))+ geom_density()+
 labs(title = "Density plot of total population from the midwest data,"
```

```
 x = "Total Population," y = "Density")+
theme_classic()+
theme(plot.title = element_text(hjust = 0.5))
```

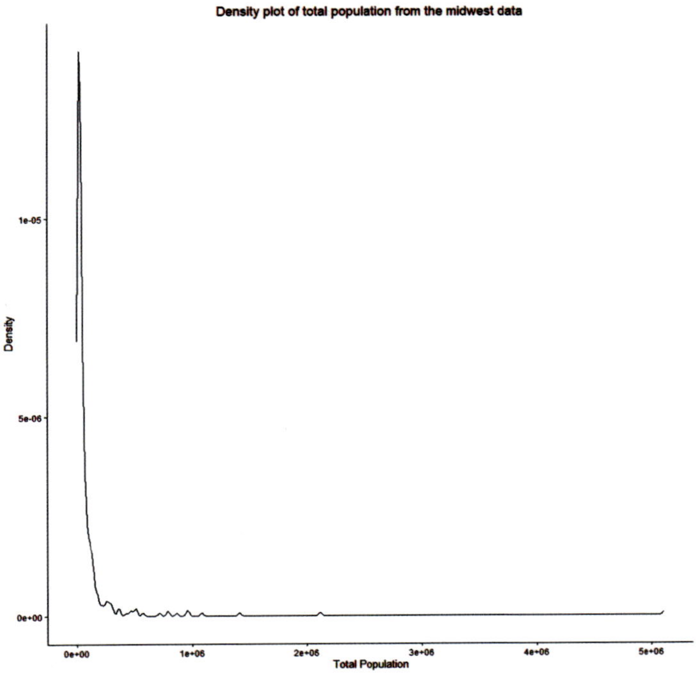

We see that the highest density was at low values (< 1000000) and larger values have a much lower density, so the total population has a right-skewed distribution.

1.4.4.3. Density Plot for left-Skewed Distribution

Using the same functions, we can plot a density plot of the percent white column values on the x-axis from the midwest data.

```
ggplot(data= midwest, aes(x = percwhite))+ geom_density()+
 labs(title = "Density plot of White percentage from midwest data,"
x = "White Percentage," y = "Density")+
theme_classic()+
 theme(plot.title = element_text(hjust = 0.5))
```

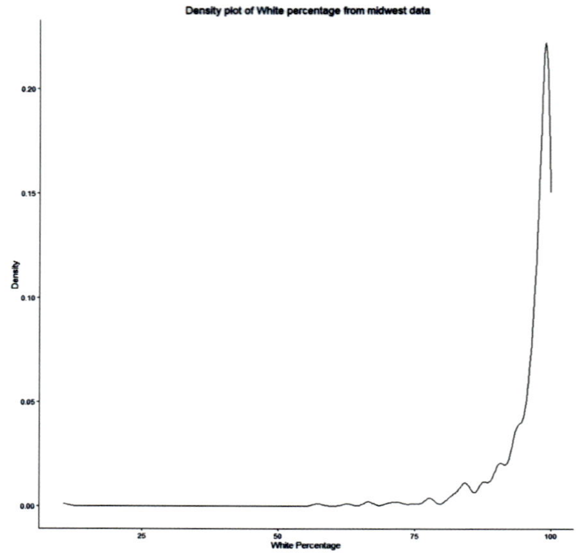

We see that the highest density was at high values (at < 100) and smaller values have a much lower density, so the percentage white has a left-skewed distribution.

1.4.4.4. Bandwidth

The degree of density plot smoothness is controlled by the bandwidth parameter bw. To find the default value for a particular variable, use the bw.nrd0 function. For example, to find the default value of the personal saving rate of economics data.

```
bw.nrd0(economics$psavert)
## [1] 0.7487979
```

The default bandwidth value is 0.75. Larger values will result in more smoothing, while smaller values will produce less smoothing.

Example using bw = 0.01.

```
ggplot(data= economics, aes(x = psavert))+ geom_density(bw = 0.01)+
 labs(title = "Kernel density plot of personal saving rates in economics data \
nwith 0.01 bandwidth,"
x = "Personal Saving Rate," y = "Density")+

 theme_classic()+

theme(plot.title = element_text(hjust = 0.5))
```

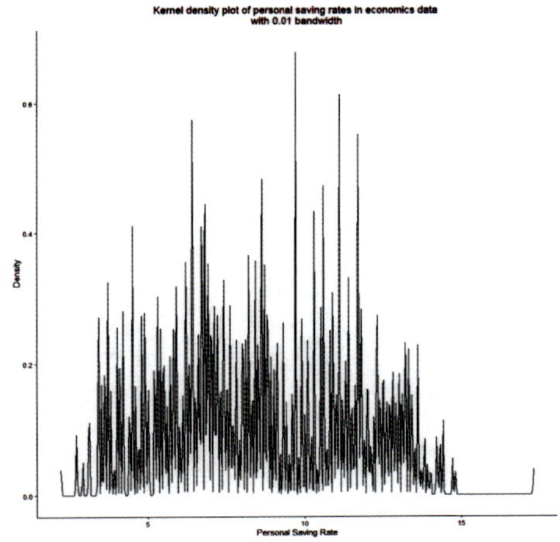

The resulting plot is less smooth than the plot with a default band width of 0.75.

Example using bw = 5.

```
ggplot(data= economics, aes(x = psavert))+ geom_density(bw = 5)+
 labs(title = "Kernel density plot of personal saving rates in economics data \
nwith 5 bandwidth,"
x = "Personal Saning Rate," y = "Density")+
 theme_classic()+
 theme(plot.title = element_text(hjust = 0.5))
```

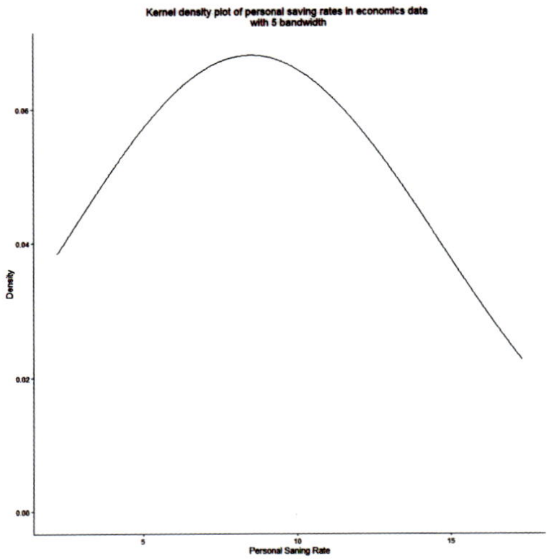

The resulting plot is more smooth than the density plot with a default band width of 0.75.

1.4.5. Violin Plots

A violin plot is a blend of a box plot and a density plot which is a mirrored density plot.

1.4.5.1. Violin Plot for a Symmetric Distribution

The geom_violin function plots a violin plot and requires two aesthetics (x for locating the symmetry line of the violin plot and y for the continuous variable you want to visualize on the y-axis). To draw a violin plot of the psavert column from the economics data, we will use the following functions:

1. The ggplot function with arguments:
   i. data = economics which is the data frame containing the psavert column.
   ii. aes(y = psavert,x = 1), to plot the personal saving rates on the y-axis and symmetry line at 1 value on the x-axis.

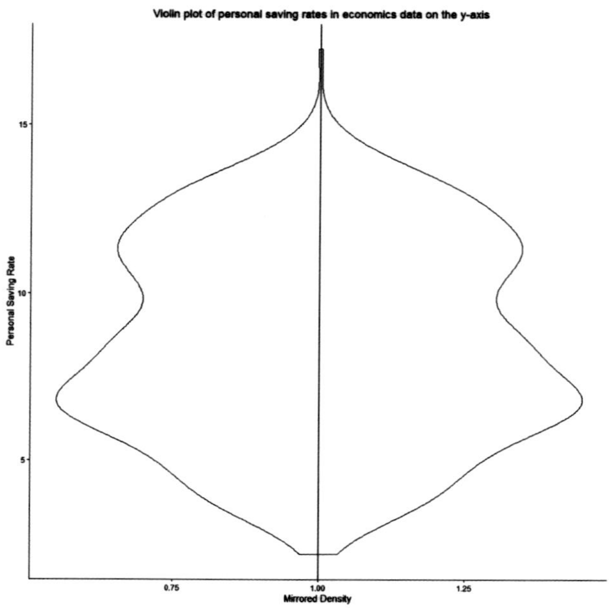

2. The geom_violin function to create the violin plot.

3. The geom_vline function with the argument, xintercept = 1, plots the vertical line at x-axis value = 1.
4. The labs, theme_classic, and theme functions as described above.

```
ggplot(data= economics, aes(x = 1,y = psavert))+ geom_violin()+
  geom_vline(xintercept = 1)+
 labs(title = "Violin plot of personal saving rates in economics data on the y-axis,"
 y = "Personal Saving Rate," x = "Mirrored Density")+
 theme_classic()+
 theme(plot.title = element_text(hjust = 0.5))
```

As noted previously, the highest density (peak) of personal saving rates was at values between 5 and 10.

Alternatively, we can plot the personal saving rates on the x-axis and the symmetry line on the y-axis by reversing the aesthetics to be y = 1 and x = psavert. In addition, we use the geom_hline function with the argument, yintercept = 1 to plot a horizontal line at 1 value.

```
ggplot(data= economics, aes(y = 1,x = psavert))+ geom_violin()+
  geom_hline(yintercept = 1)+
 labs(title = "Violin plot of personal saving rates in economics data on the x-axis,"
 x = "Personal Saving Rate," y = "Mirrored Density")+
 theme_classic()+
 theme(plot.title = element_text(hjust = 0.5))
```

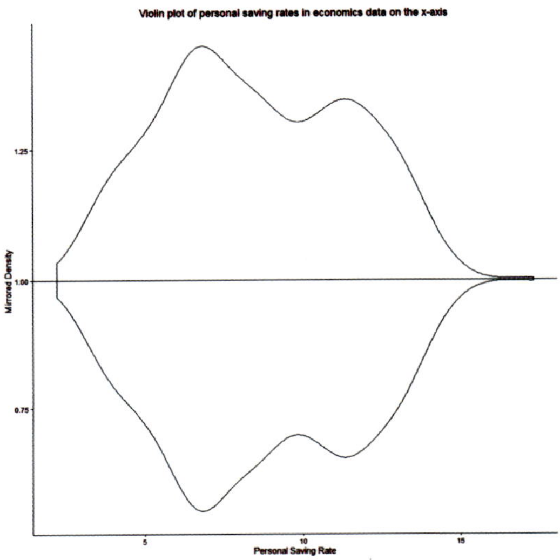

1.4.5.2. Violin Plot for Right-Skewed Distribution

Using the same functions, we can plot a violin plot for the pce column.

```
ggplot(data= economics, aes(x = pce, y = 1))+ geom_violin()+
 geom_hline(yintercept = 1)+
 labs(title = "Violin plot of personal consumption expenditures from the economics
data,"
 x = "Personal Consumption Expenditures (billions of dollars),"
 y = "Mirrored Density")+
 theme_classic()+
 theme(plot.title = element_text(hjust = 0.5))
```

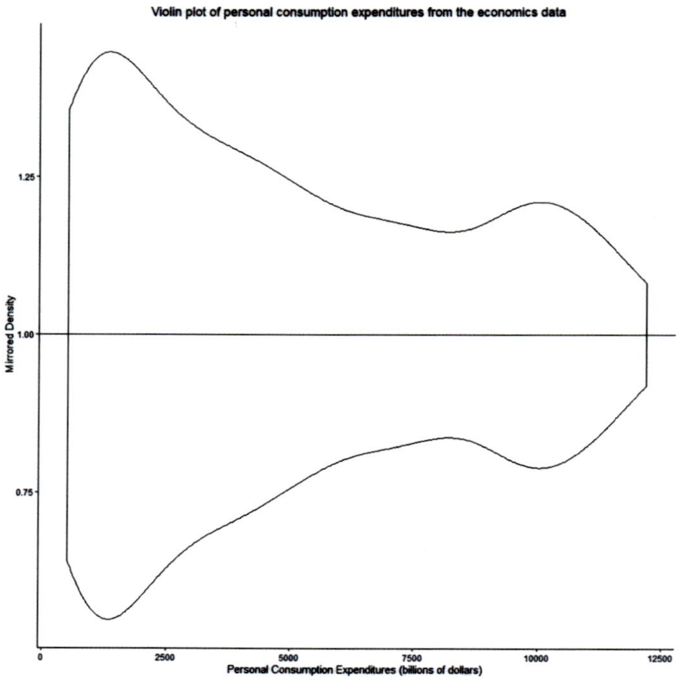

We see that the personal consumption expenditures have a right-skewed distribution with a low density of large values. Using the same functions, we can plot a violin plot for the poptotal column values from the midwest data on the x-axis.

```
ggplot(data= midwest, aes(x = poptotal, y = 1))+ geom_violin()+
 geom_hline(yintercept = 1)+
 labs(title = "Violin plot of total population from the midwest data,"
 x = "Total Population," y = "Mirrored Density")+
```

```
theme_classic()+
theme(plot.title = element_text(hjust = 0.5))
```

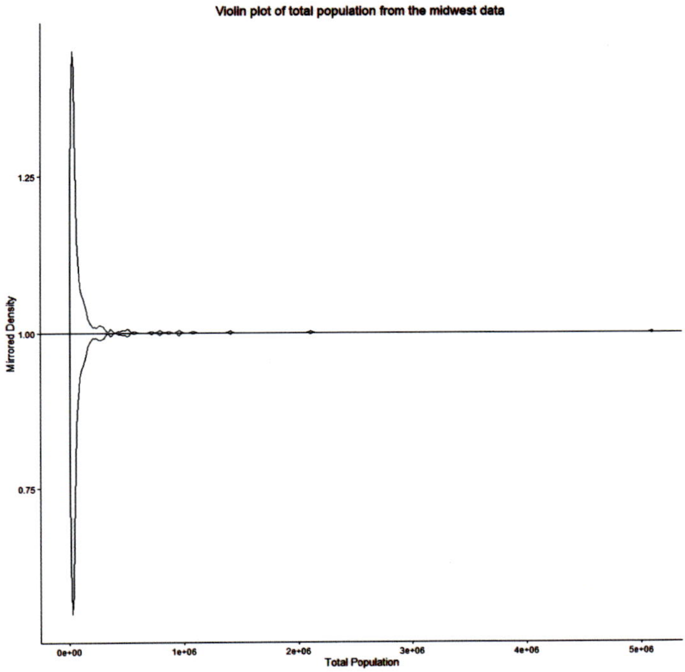

We see that the highest density was at low values (< 1000000) and larger values have a much lower density, so the total population has a right-skewed distribution.

1.4.5.3. Violin Plot for Left-Skewed Distribution

Using the same functions, we can plot a violin plot of the percent white column values on the x-axis from the midwest data.

```
ggplot(data= midwest, aes(x = percwhite, y = 1))+ geom_violin()+
 geom_hline(yintercept = 1)+
 labs(title = "Violin plot of White percentage from midwest data,"
 x = "White Percentage," y = "Mirrored Density")+
 theme_classic()+
 theme(plot.title = element_text(hjust = 0.5))
```

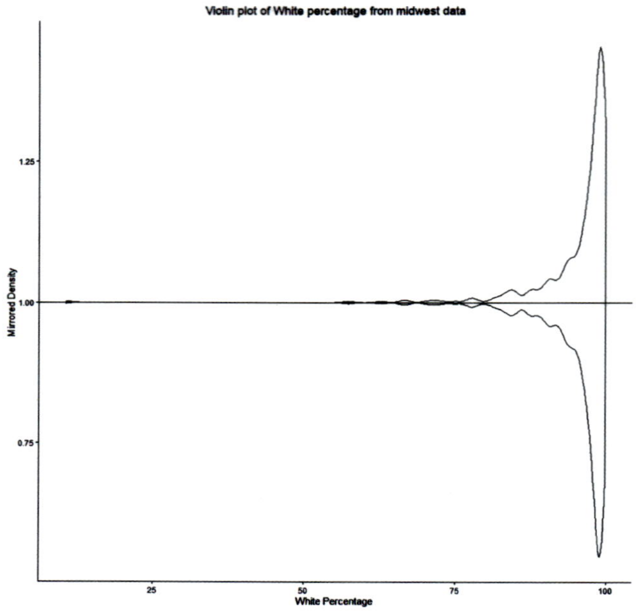

We see that the highest density was at high values (at about 100%) and smaller values have a much lower density, so the percentage white has a left-skewed distribution.

1.4.5.4. Bandwidth

The degree of density plot smoothness in the violin plot is controlled by the bandwidth parameter bw. The default value of the personal saving rate of economics data is 0.75 as noted before.

Larger values will result in more smoothing, while smaller values will produce less smoothing.

Example using bw = 0.1 within the geom_violin function.

```
ggplot(data= economics, aes(x = psavert, y = 1))+
 geom_violin(bw = 0.1)+ geom_hline(yintercept = 1)+
 labs(title = "Violin plot of personal saving rates in economics data \nwith 0.1 bandwidth,"
    x = "Personal Saving Rate," y = "Mirrored Density")+
 theme_classic()+
 theme(plot.title = element_text(hjust = 0.5))
```

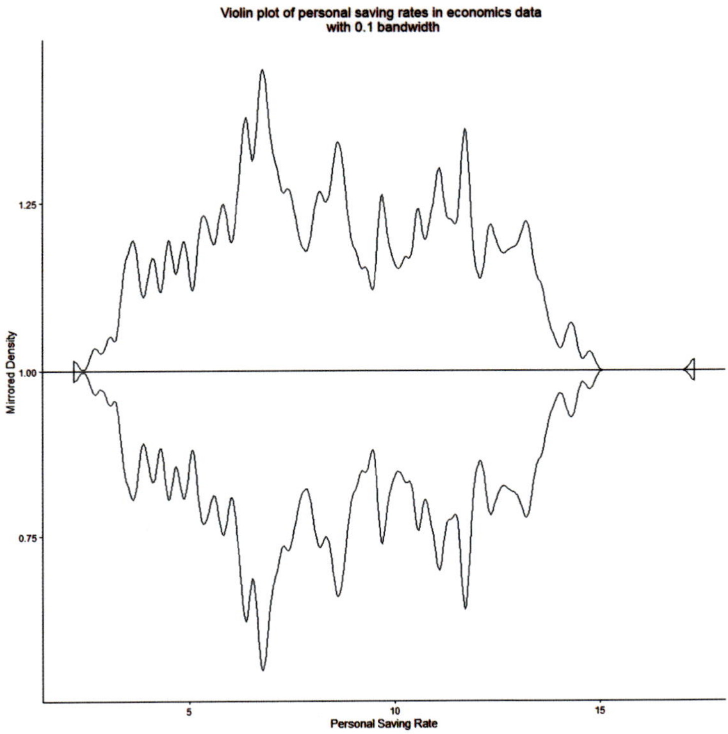

The resulting plot is less smooth than the plot with a default band width of 0.75.

Example using bw = 3.

```
ggplot(data= economics, aes(x = psavert, y = 1))+
 geom_violin(bw = 3)+ geom_hline(yintercept = 1)+
 labs(title = "Violin plot of personal saving rates in economics data \nwith 3 bandwidth,"
 x = "Personal Saning Rate," y = "Mirrored Density")+
 theme_classic()+
 theme(plot.title = element_text(hjust = 0.5))
```

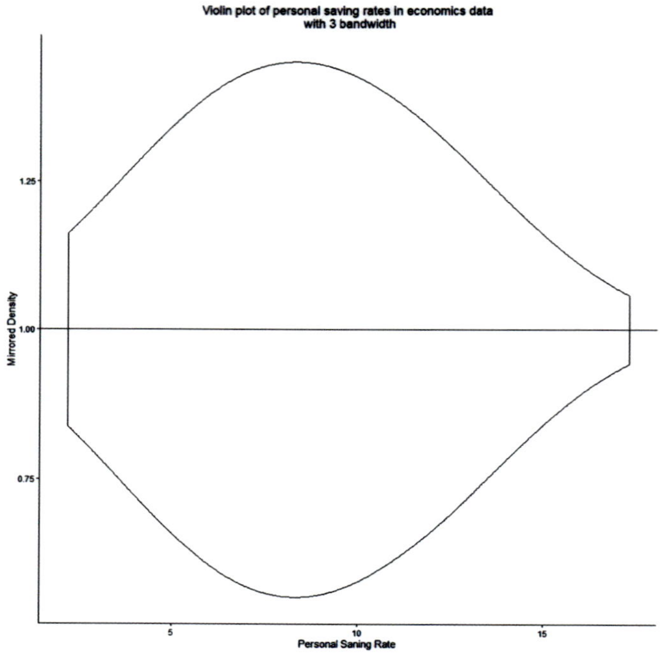

The resulting plot is more smooth than the density plot with a default band width of 0.75.

1.4.5.5. Quantiles

The draw_quantiles argument within the geom_violin function can draw lines at specified quantiles of the data.

Example drawing quantiles at 0.25, 0.5, and 0.75 that correspond to Q1, Q2, Q3.

```
ggplot(data= economics, aes(x = psavert, y = 1))+
 geom_violin(draw_quantiles = c(0.25,0.5,0.75))+ geom_hline(yintercept = 1)+
 labs(title = "Violin plot of personal saving rates in economics data \nwith
0.25,0.5, and 0.75 quantiles,"
 x = "Personal Saving Rate," y = "Mirrored Density")+
 theme_classic()+
 theme(plot.title = element_text(hjust = 0.5))
```

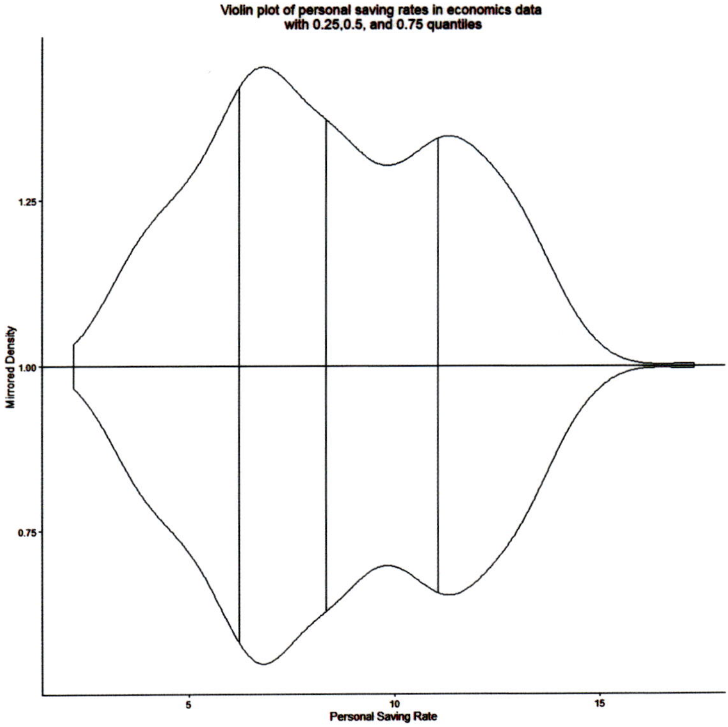

Example drawing quantiles at 0.1, 0.5, and 0.9 that correspond to 10%, 50% (median), and 90%.

```
ggplot(data= economics, aes(x = psavert, y = 1))+
 geom_violin(draw_quantiles = c(0.1,0.5,0.9))+ geom_hline(yintercept = 1)+
 labs(title = "Violin plot of personal saving rates in economics data \nwith 10%,50%, and 90%,"
 x = "Personal Saving Rate," y = "Mirrored Density")+
 theme_classic()+
 theme(plot.title = element_text(hjust = 0.5))
```

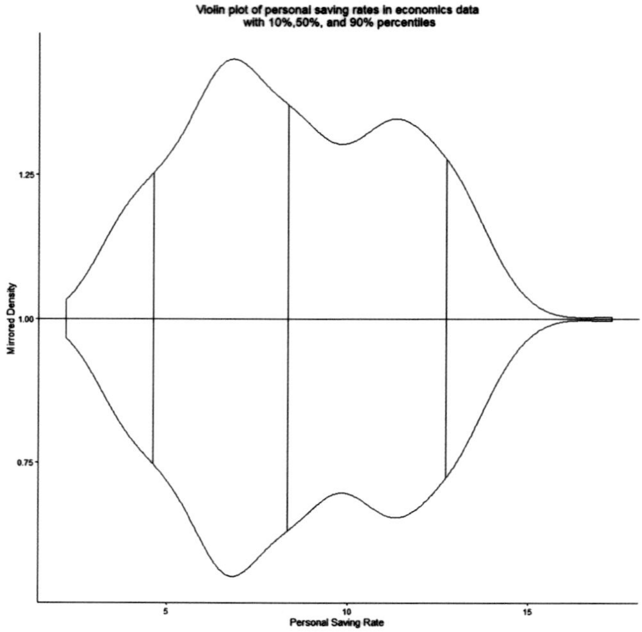

1.4.6. QQ Plot

The QQ plot (Quantile-Quantile Plot) is a plot used to assess the normal distribution of any numerical data.

If the data follow a normal distribution then a plot of the theoretical percentiles of the normal distribution on the x-axis versus the observed sample percentiles on the y-axis should be approximately linear. A reference line is plotted and if all data points fall along this reference line, we can assume normality.

1.4.6.1. QQ Plot of Symmetric Distribution

The ggqqplot from the ggpubr package can plot the QQ plot of any numerical column. To plot the QQ plot of personal saving rates from the economics data, we first load the ggpubr package into the R session using the library function. Then we use the ggqqplot function with the following arguments:

1. data = economics which is the data frame containing the psavert column
2. x = "psavert" which is the column to be plotted.

3. title, xlab, and ylab arguments to add title, x-axis, and y-axis titles.

We also use the theme function to plot the title in the top middle of the graph.

```
library(ggpubr)
ggqqplot(data = economics, x = "psavert,"
title = "QQ plot of personal saving rates from economics data,"
 xlab = "Theoretical percentiles," ylab = "Sample percentiles")+
 theme(plot.title = element_text(hjust = 0.5))
```

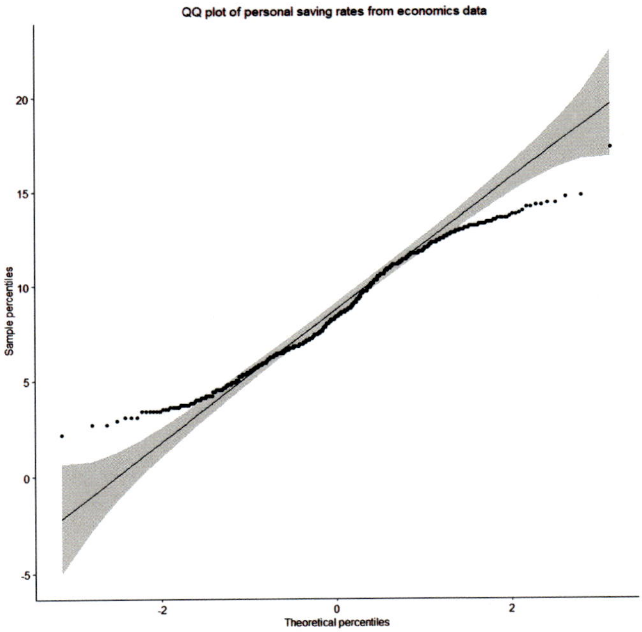

The reference line is plotted with its 95% confidence interval. Because not all data points fall along this reference line or within the confidence band, we cannot assume the normality of personal saving rates.

Using the same functions, we can plot a QQ plot of the area column in the midwest data.

```
ggqqplot(data = midwest, x = "area,"
title = "QQ plot of area values from midwest data,"
xlab = "Theoretical percentiles," ylab = "Sample percentiles")+
 theme(plot.title = element_text(hjust = 0.5))
```

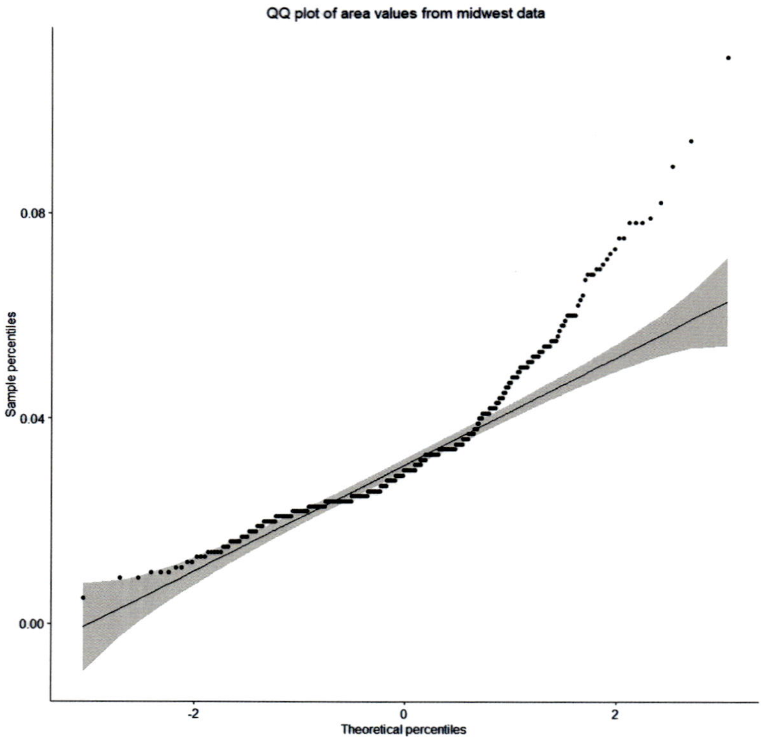

Some large data points do not fall along the reference line or within the 95% confidence band, so we can not assume the normality of area rates.

1.4.6.2. QQ Plot of Right-Skewed Distribution

Using the same functions, we can plot a QQ plot of the pce column from the economics data.

```
ggqqplot(data = economics, x = "pce,"
title = "QQ plot of personal consumption expenditures from economics data,"
xlab = "Theoretical percentiles," ylab = "Sample percentiles")+
 theme(plot.title = element_text(hjust = 0.5))
```

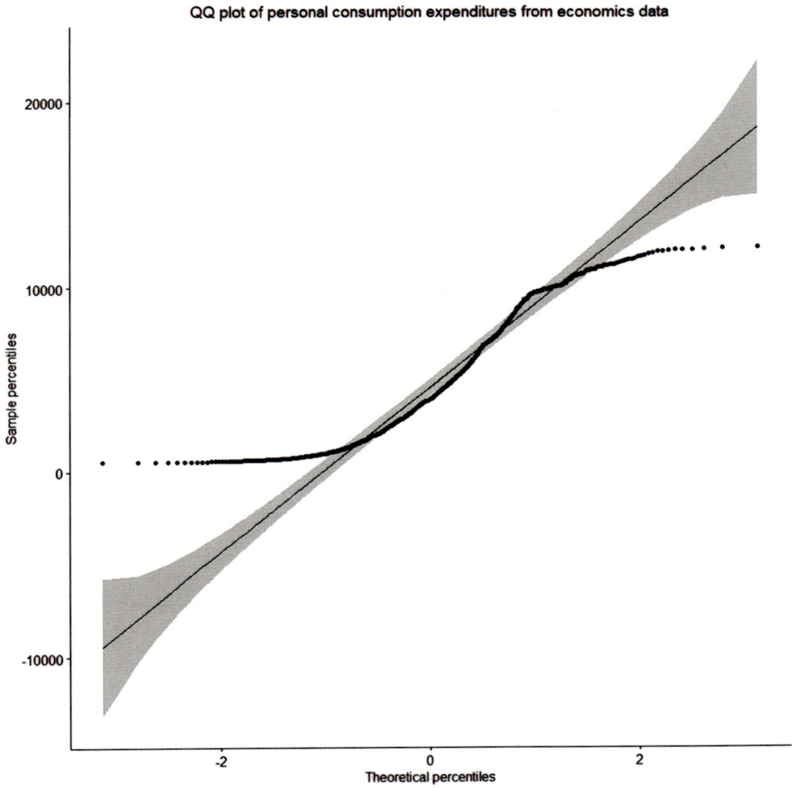

The personal consumption expenditures have a right-skewed distribution with large values outside the confidence band of the reference line. To plot a QQ plot of the poptotal column from the midwest data.

```
ggqqplot(data = midwest, x = "poptotal,"
title = "QQ plot of total population from midwest data,"
xlab = "Theoretical percentiles," ylab = "Sample percentiles")+
 theme(plot.title = element_text(hjust = 0.5))
```

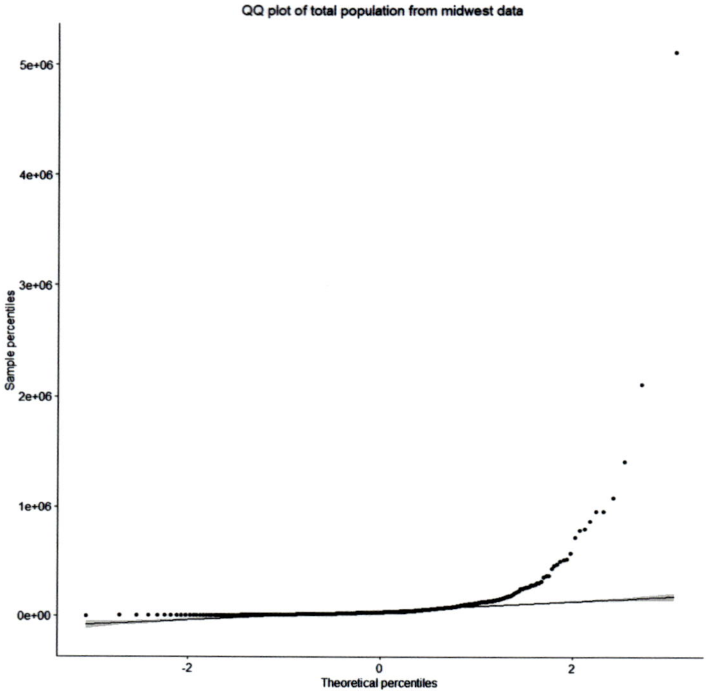

Similarly, the total population has a right-skewed distribution with large values outside the confidence band of the reference line.

1.4.6.3. QQ Plot of Left-Skewed Distribution

Using the same functions, we can plot a QQ plot of the percent white column from the midwest data.

```
ggqqplot(data = midwest, x = "percwhite,"

    title = "QQ plot of percent white from midwest data,"

    xlab = "Theoretical percentiles," ylab = "Sample percentiles")+

 theme(plot.title = element_text(hjust = 0.5))
```

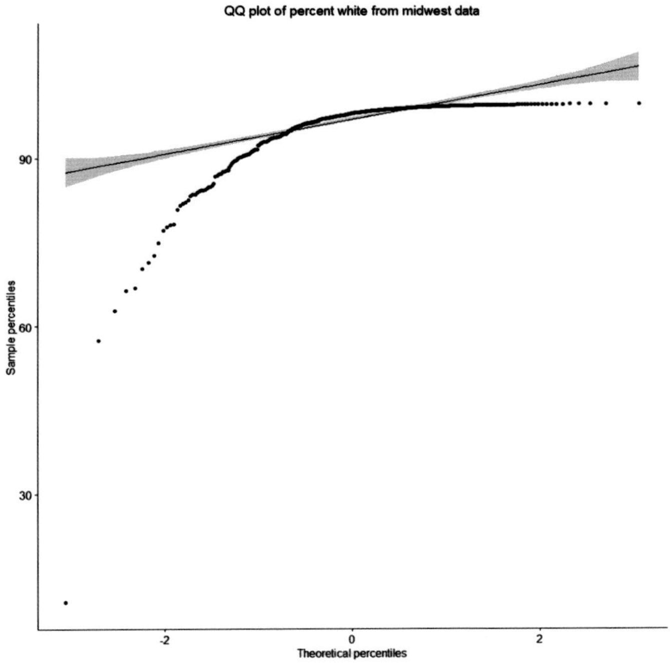

The percent white has left skewed distribution with small values greatly outside the confidence band of the reference line.

1.5. STATISTICAL TESTS FOR CONTINUOUS UNIVARIATE ANALYSIS

After estimating the sample mean (sample estimate), we may wish to infer the underlying population mean (population parameter) from this sample mean using some statistical tests because this estimate (sample mean) is subjected to sampling error.

1.5.1. t-Test for One Sample Mean

1.5.1.1. Hypothesis Testing

In hypothesis testing, we start with two exclusive possibilities for the unknown truth (population parameters). Then, we use the sample data to choose between these two possibilities for the truth.

The two possibilities are the null hypothesis, Ho, and the alternative hypothesis, Ha.

The null hypothesis, Ho, states that our sample parameter equals a reference value.

The alternative hypothesis, Ha, is the hypothesis that contradicts the null hypothesis. The alternative hypothesis states that our population parameter is less than $<$, greater than $>$, or not equal to $\neq$. a reference value.

1.5.1.2. Types of Hypothesis Testing

1. **One-tailed Hypothesis Testing** is a test in which the alternative hypothesis states that the sample parameter is less than $<$ or greater than $>$ a reference value.
2. **Two-Tailed Hypothesis Testing** is a test in which the alternativeypothesis states that the sample parameter is not equal to $\neq$ a reference value. Not equal means that the sample parameter can be greater than or less than a reference value.

1.5.1.3. Examples of Hypothesis Testing

1. Examples of One-Tailed Hypothesis Testing:
   i. The mean percent of adults below the poverty line across all US counties is 15%, while the mean percent of adults below the poverty line in midwest counties is 10.9%. We want to test the hypothesis that midwest counties have a mean percent of adults below the poverty line lower than the US average of 15%.

Two hypotheses are considered:

a. The average percent of adults below the poverty line in midwest counties = 15%. This is the null hypothesis.
b. The average percent of adults below the poverty line in midwest counties is < 15%. This is the alternative hypothesis.

ii. Suppose we know from nationwide surveys based on millions of deliveries that the mean birth weight in the United States is 3400 grams. We want to test the hypothesis that mothers with low socioeconomic status deliver babies whose birth weights are lower than this normal average.

Two hypotheses are considered:

a. The average birth weight of babies delivered by these mothers = 3400 grams. This is the null hypothesis.

b. The average birth weight of babies delivered by these mothers is < 3400 grams. This is the alternative hypothesis.

2. Examples of Two-tailed Hypothesis Testing:

   i. We assume cholesterol levels in women in the United States have a mean of 190 mg/dL. It is unknown whether cholesterol levels among recent Asian women immigrants are higher or lower than those in the general U.S. population.

Two hypotheses are considered:

   a. The average cholesterol level of recent Asian women immigrants = 190 mg/dL. This is the null hypothesis.

   b. The average cholesterol level of recent Asian women immigrants ≠ 190 mg/dL. This is the alternative hypothesis.

ii. The standard mean tablet weight for a certain drug is 125 mg.

A new tableting machine is installed and we want to test that this machine is working properly. It is unknown whether the mean tablet weight from this machine is higher or lower than the standard weight of 125 mg.

Two hypotheses are considered:

i. The average tablet weight from this machine = 125 mg. This is the null hypothesis.

ii. The average tablet weight from this machine is ≠ 125 mg. This is the alternative hypothesis.

1.5.1.4. Error Rate in Hypothesis Testing

If Ho is true and Ho is accepted, or if Ha is true and Ho is rejected, then the correct decision has been made.

If Ho is true and Ho is rejected, then an error has been made and it is called type I error. The probability of a type I error is the probability of rejecting the null hypothesis, Ho when Ho is true.

The probability of a type I error is denoted by α and is commonly called the significance level of a test or the rejection level. The default value is 0.05 or 5%.

The p-value is the probability of the test statistic (z or t) or more extreme values, that correspond to our sample results, under the Null hypothesis. If the p-value < significance level, it is a statistically significant result at this significance level, and we reject the Null hypothesis. Our sample data are unlikely under the Ho, they have a probability less than the significance level or 5%.

If the p-value >= significance level, it is a statistically insignificant result at the significance level, and we fail to reject the Null hypothesis. We say fail to reject the Null hypothesis because if we have a p-value of 0.25. This means that our sample data have a probability of 25% under the Null hypothesis which is considered a large percentage. In your opinion, you may consider it small and accept Ha.

All statistical tests, explored in the following sections, give us the sample statistic (t or z value that corresponds to our sample results) and the p-value required for a decision.

1.5.1.5. t-Test for Personal Saving Rate

We note from the above summary statistics that the mean personal saving rate in the economics data is 8.567. We may wish to test the hypothesis that this mean is different from a reference value of 9, so the alternative hypothesis is the mean personal saving rate is higher or lower than the reference value or a two-tailed hypothesis testing.

To conduct a t-test of the personal saving rate in economics data, we use the t_test function with the following arguments:

1. data = economics which is our data frame containing the psavert (personal saving rate column).
2. psavert ~1 which is the formula for one sample testing of psavert column. This means that all personal saving rate values correspond to 1 group.
3. mu= 9 which is our reference value.
4. alternative = "two.sided" which is the alternative hypothesis.

Then, we use the flextable, theme_box, and set_caption functions to convert the result to a table as before.

```
t_test(data = economics, psavert ~1, mu= 9, alternative = "two.sided") %>%
 flextable() %>% theme_box() %>%
 set_caption(caption = "Two-tailed t-test results of personal saving rates in economics data")
```

Table 1.26. *Two-Tailed t-Test Results of Personal Saving Rates in Economics Data*

.y.	Group1	Group2	n	Statistic	df	p
psavert	1	null model	574	-3.497769	573	0.000506

The table 1.26 contains the t statistic = -3.498 which corresponds to our sample results and the p-value = 0.0005 or 0.05%.

The p_value is the probability of our sample results (personal saving rate) under the null hypothesis (where the mean personal saving rate = 9). Since this is a very low probability, we reject the null hypothesis and conclude that the mean personal saving rate in the US is significantly different from 9.

We can continue and do a one-tailed t-test for the personal saving rate with the alternative hypothesis that the mean personal saving rate is less than 9 because our observed mean from the sample is 8.567. We will use the same functions above except that we use the argument, alternative = "less" for the different alternative hypothesis.

```
t_test(data = economics, psavert ~1, mu= 9, alternative = "less") %>%
 flextable() %>% theme_box() %>%
 set_caption(caption = "One-tailed t-test results of personal saving rates in economics data")
```

Table 1.27. One-Tailed t-Test Results of Personal Saving Rates in Economics Data

.y.	Group1	Group2	n	Statistic	df	p
psavert	1	null model	574	-3.497769	573	0.000253

The table 1.27 contains the same t statistic = -3.498 that corresponds to our sample results and the p-value = 0.00025 or 0.025%.

The p_value is the probability of our sample results (personal saving rate) under the null hypothesis (where the mean personal saving rate = 9). Since this is a very low probability, we reject the null hypothesis and conclude that the mean personal saving rate in the US is significantly lower than 9.

1.5.1.6. t-Test for Percent of Adults Below the Poverty Line

The mean percent of adults below the poverty line across all US counties is 15%, while the mean percent of adults below the poverty line in midwest counties is 10.9%. We can do a one-tailed t-test for the mean percent of adults below the poverty line with the alternative hypothesis is that the mean percent of adults below the poverty line in the midwest counties is less than 15 because our observed mean from the sample is 10.9.

```
t_test(data = midwest, percadultpoverty ~1, mu= 15, alternative = "less") %>%
 flextable() %>% theme_box() %>%
 set_caption(caption = "One-tailed t-test results of percent of adults below poverty line in midwest data")
```

Table 1.28. One-Tailed t-Test Results of Percent of Adults Below the Poverty Line in Midwest Data

.y.	group1	group2	n	statistic	df	p
per-cadult-poverty	1	null model	437	-16.69855	436	0.00000000000000000000000000000000000000000000000472

The Table 1.28 contains the same t statistic = -16.699 that corresponds to our sample results and the p-value is very low and nearly equals zero.

The p_value is the probability of our sample results (percent adults below the poverty line) under the null hypothesis (where the mean percent adults below the poverty line = 15). Since this is a very low probability, we reject the null hypothesis and conclude that the mean percent of adults below the poverty line in the midwest counties is significantly lower than 15 which is the mean value of all US counties.

1.5.2. Normality Test for One Sample

The t-test assumes that the data follows a normal distribution or a Gaussian distribution. The t-test is called a parametric test because its validity depends on the data distribution.

With large enough sample sizes (> 30 as in midwest data with 437 rows or economics data with 574 rows), we can ignore the distribution of the data and use the parametric t-test directly. This is because the central limit theorem tells us that no matter what distribution things have, the sampling distribution tends to be normal if the sample is large enough (n > 30).

However, to inspect normality for some numerical data, we can use visual plots (histogram, density plot, or QQ plot as described above) or statistical tests such as Shapiro-Wilk normality Test.

1.5.2.1. Shapiro-Wilk Normality Test

Shapiro-Wilk normality test is a test comparing the sample distribution to a normal distribution to ascertain whether data show or not a serious deviation from normality.

The null hypothesis of this test is that the sample distribution is normal. If the test is significant, the distribution is not normal. However, the Shapiro-

Wilk normality test is sensitive to sample size. Small samples most often pass normality tests. Therefore, it's important to combine visual inspection and significance tests to make the right decision.

1.5.2.2. Shapiro-Wilk Test for Personal Saving Rate

To conduct the Shapiro-Wilk test for personal saving rate, we use the shapiro_ test function with the following arguments:

1. data = economics which is our data frame containing the required column (personal saving rate).
2. psavert which is our interested column to be tested. Then, we convert the results to a table as before.

```
shapiro_test(data = economics, psavert) %>% flextable() %>% theme_box() %>%
 set_caption(caption = "Shapiro-Wilk test results for personal saving rate in economics data")
```

Table 1.29. *Shapiro-Wilk Test Results for Personal Saving Rate in Economics Data*

Variable	Statistic	p
psavert	0.9754891	0.00000003262322

The Table 1.29 contains the sample statistic = 0.975 which corresponds to our sample results and the p-value which is very low and nearly equals zero.

The p_value is significant (< 0.05), so we reject the null hypothesis and conclude that the personal saving rate values in the economics data are not normally distributed. However, due to the large sample size of 574 observations, we can ignore the normality test results and use the t-test.

1.5.2.3. Shapiro-Wilk Test for Percent Adults Below the Poverty Line

To conduct the Shapiro-Wilk test for the percent of adults below the poverty line in the midwest data, we use the same functions above and modify them accordingly.

```
shapiro_test(data = midwest, percadultpoverty) %>% flextable() %>%
 theme_box() %>%
  set_caption(caption = "Shapiro-Wilk test results for percent adults below poverty line in midwest data")
```

Table 1.30. Shapiro-Wilk Test Results for the Percent Adults Below the Poverty Line in Midwest Data

Variable	Statistic	p
percadultpoverty	0.9020281	0.00000000000000377401

The Table 1.30 contains the sample statistic = 0.90 which corresponds to our sample results and the p-value which is very low and nearly equals zero.

The p_value is significant (< 0.05), so we reject the null hypothesis and conclude that the percent of adults below the poverty line values in the midwest data is not normally distributed. However, due to the large sample size of 437 observations, we can ignore the normality test results and use the t-test.

1.5.3. Test for Outliers

The t-test assumes that the data contains no outliers. Outliers can be detected using the box plot method.

Values above Q3 + 1.5 X IQR or below Q1 – 1.5 X IQR are considered outliers and plotted individually using the box plot described above. In addition, values above Q3 + 3 X IQR or below Q1 – 3 X IQR are considered extreme outliers. They are also plotted individually using the box plot method.

Extreme outliers can be due to data entry errors, measurement errors, or unusual values.

1.5.3.1. Outlier Test for Personal Saving Rate

To conduct the outlier test for personal saving rate, we use the identify_outliers function with the following arguments:

1. data = economics which is our data frame containing the required column (personal saving rate).
2. psavert which is our interested column to be tested. Then, we convert the results to a table as before.

```
identify_outliers(data = economics, psavert) %>% flextable() %>%
 theme_box() %>%
 set_caption(caption = "Outlier test results for personal saving rate in economics
data")
```

Table 1.31. Outlier Test Results for Personal Saving Rate in Economics Data

date	pce	pop	psavert	uempmed	unemploy	is.outlier	is.extreme

We see that the Table 1.31 has no rows meaning that personal saving rate values have no outliers in the economics data.

1.5.3.2. Outlier Test for Percent Adults Below the Poverty Line

To conduct the outlier test for the percent adults below the poverty line in the midwest data, we use the identify_outliers function with the following arguments:

1. data = midwest which is our data frame containing the required column to be tested.
2. percadultpoverty which is our interested column to be tested. Then, we use the select function to select the important columns to be viewed (county, percadultpoverty, is.outlier, is.extreme) instead of viewing all 28 columns of the midwest data. Finally, we convert the results to a table as before.

```
identify_outliers(data = midwest, percadultpoverty) %>%
 select(county, percadultpoverty,is.outlier, is.extreme) %>%
 flextable() %>%
 theme_box() %>%
 set_caption(caption = "Outlier test results for percent adults below poverty
line in midwest data")
```

Table 1.32. Outlier Test Results for Percent Adults Below the Poverty Line in Midwest Data

County	**Percadult-poverty**	**is.outlier**	**is.extreme**
ALEXANDER	27.38565	TRUE	FALSE
HARDIN	25.17428	TRUE	FALSE
JACKSON	32.45848	TRUE	TRUE
MCDONOUGH	22.40338	TRUE	FALSE
POPE	24.41487	TRUE	FALSE
PULASKI	23.86774	TRUE	FALSE
MONROE	22.99900	TRUE	FALSE
CLARE	22.17195	TRUE	FALSE
HOUGHTON	23.69715	TRUE	FALSE
ISABELLA	28.47915	TRUE	FALSE
LAKE	25.07071	TRUE	FALSE
MECOSTA	28.22996	TRUE	FALSE

County	**Percadult-poverty**	**is.outlier**	**is.extreme**
ADAMS	25.75226	TRUE	FALSE
ATHENS	31.74428	TRUE	TRUE
MEIGS	23.66729	TRUE	FALSE
PIKE	22.22396	TRUE	FALSE
SCIOTO	23.52317	TRUE	FALSE
VINTON	22.22598	TRUE	FALSE
MENOMINEE	43.31246	TRUE	TRUE

We have a Table 1.32 of 4 columns and 19 rows meaning that there are 19 outliers in the percent adult below the poverty line.

The 2 logical columns is. outlier and is.extreme identify if the value is an outlier or an extreme outlier. For example, the county ALEXANDER has a value of 27.39 which is an outlier but not an extreme outlier. On the other hand, the county JACKSON has a value of 32.46 which is an outlier and also an extreme outlier.

1.5.4. Wilcoxon Test for One Sample

The Wilcoxon signed rank test is used to determine if the median of the sample is equal to a value. This is a non-parametric equivalent of one-sample t-test and can be used when the required assumptions of the t-test are not met (normality and no outliers).

For example, we see that the percent adults below the poverty line in the midwest data contain some outliers so the t-test cannot be used in that case. However, the minimum sample size for the Wilcoxon test should be 6, or the test cannot become significant.

1.5.4.1. Wilcoxon Test for Percent of Adults Below the Poverty Line

To conduct a Wilcoxon test for the percent of adults below the poverty line in the midwest data, we use the wilcox_test function with the following arguments:

1. data = midwest which is our data frame containing the desired column (percent adults below the poverty line).
2. percadultpoverty ~1 which is the formula for one sample testing. This means that all percent of adults below the poverty line values correspond to 1 group.

3. mu= 15 which is our reference value.
4. alternative = “less” which is the alternative hypothesis. The alternative hypothesis is that the median percent of adults below the poverty line in the midwest counties is less than 15 reference value.

```
wilcox_test(data = midwest, percadultpoverty ~1, mu= 15,
 alternative = "less") %>%
 flextable() %>% theme_box() %>%
 set_caption(caption = "One-tailed Wilcoxon test results of percent of adults
below poverty line in midwest data")
```

Table 1.33. One-Tailed Wilcoxon Test Results of Percent of Adults Below the Poverty Line in Midwest Data

.y.	group1	group2	n	statistic	p
per-cadult-poverty	1	null model	437	11,566	0.000000000000000000000000000000000000000000000000031

The Table 1.33 contains the sample statistic = 11566 which corresponds to our sample results and the p-value is very low and nearly equals zero.

The p_value is the probability of our sample results (percent adults below the poverty line) under the null hypothesis (where the median percent adults below the poverty line = 15). Since this is a very low probability, we reject the null hypothesis and conclude that the median percent of adults below the poverty line in the midwest counties is significantly lower than 15.

CHAPTER 2

UNIVARIATE ANALYSIS OF CATEGORICAL DATA

Contents

2.1. DATA USED IN THIS CHAPTER

2.1.1. The Diamonds Data

The diamonds data is part of the ggplot2 package under the name "diamonds" and contains the prices and other attributes of about 54,000 diamonds. To load this data into our R session, we will load the tidyverse package (which contains the ggplot2 package) using the library function. Then, we will load the diamonds data using the data function.

```
library(tidyverse)

data("diamonds")
```

Then, to see the data structure, we will use the glimpse function.

```
glimpse(diamonds)
## Rows: 53,940
## Columns: 10
## $ carat   <dbl> 0.23, 0.21, 0.23, 0.29, 0.31, 0.24, 0.24, 0.26, 0.22, 0.23, 0.…
## $ cut     <ord> Ideal, Premium, Good, Premium, Good, Very Good, Very Good, Ver…
## $ color   <ord> E, E, E, I, J, J, I, H, E, H, J, J, F, J, E, E, I, J, J, J, I,…
## $ clarity <ord> SI2, SI1, VS1, VS2, SI2, VVS2, VVS1, SI1, VS2, VS1, SI1, VS1, …
## $ depth   <dbl> 61.5, 59.8, 56.9, 62.4, 63.3, 62.8, 62.3, 61.9, 65.1, 59.4, 64…
## $ table   <dbl> 55, 61, 65, 58, 58, 57, 57, 55, 61, 61, 55, 56, 61, 54, 62, 58…
## $ price   <int> 326, 326, 327, 334, 335, 336, 336, 337, 337, 338, 339, 340, 34…
## $ x       <dbl> 3.95, 3.89, 4.05, 4.20, 4.34, 3.94, 3.95, 4.07, 3.87, 4.00, 4.…
## $ y       <dbl> 3.98, 3.84, 4.07, 4.23, 4.35, 3.96, 3.98, 4.11, 3.78, 4.05, 4.…
## $ z       <dbl> 2.43, 2.31, 2.31, 2.63, 2.75, 2.48, 2.47, 2.53, 2.49, 2.39, 2.…
```

The diamonds data contains 53940 rows (diamonds) and 10 columns:

1. carat: the weight of the diamond. It is a double or numeric column with decimals.
2. cut: the quality of the cut. It is an ordered factor with Fair as the lowest cut and Ideal as the best cut.
3. color: the diamond color. It is an ordered factor with D as the best color to J as the worst color.
4. clarity: the clarity of the diamond. It is an ordered factor with I1 as the worst clarity to IF as the best clarity.
5. depth: the total depth percentage. It is a double or numeric column with decimals.
6. table: the width of the top of the diamond relative to the widest point. It is a double or numeric column with decimals.

7. price: the price in US dollars. It is a double or numeric column with decimals.
8. x: the length in mm. It is a double or numeric column with decimals.
9. y: the width in mm. It is a double or numeric column with decimals.
10. z: the depth in mm. It is a double or numeric column with decimals.

2.1.2. The General Social Survey Data

The general social survey data frame is part of the forcats package (which is part of the tidyverse package) under the name "gss_cat." The gss_cat data contains a sample of categorical variables from the General Social Survey of about 21,000 participants. As before, we load the"gss_cat" data frame using the data function. Finally, we explore the data using the glimpse function.

```
data("gss_cat")
glimpse(gss_cat)
## Rows: 21,483
## Columns: 9
## $ year    <int> 2000, 2000, 2000, 2000, 2000, 2000, 2000, 2000, 2000, 2000, 20…
## $ marital <fct> Never married, Divorced, Widowed, Never married, Divorced, Mar…
## $ age     <int> 26, 48, 67, 39, 25, 25, 36, 44, 44, 47, 53, 52, 52, 51, 52, 40…
## $ race    <fct> White, White, White, White, White, White, White, White, White,…
## $ rincome <fct> $8000 to 9999, $8000 to 9999, Not applicable, Not applicable, …
## $ partyid <fct> "Ind,near rep," "Not str republican," "Independent," "Ind,near…
## $ relig   <fct> Protestant, Protestant, Protestant, Orthodox-christian, None, …
## $ denom   <fct> "Southern baptist," "Baptist-dk which," "No denomination," "No…
## $ tvhours <int> 12, NA, 2, 4, 1, NA, 3, NA, 0, 3, 2, NA, 1, NA, 1, 7, NA, 3, 3…
```

The data contains 21,483 rows and 9 columns:

1. year: the year of the survey and its class is integer.
2. marital: the marital status and its class is a factor.
3. age: the participant's age and its class is an integer.
4. race: the participant's race and its class is a factor.
5. rincome: the reported income and its class is a factor.
6. partyid: the party affiliation and its class is a factor.
7. relig: the participant's religion and its class is a factor.
8. denom: the participant's denomination and its class is a factor.
9. tvhours: the hours per day watching TV and its class is an integer.

2.2. TYPES OF CATEGORICAL DATA

There are 2 types of categorical data:

1. **Nominal Categorical Data:** Where the categories have no inherent ordering. Examples are all categorical columns or factors of gss_cat data (marital, race, rincome, partyid, relig, denom).
2. **Ordinal Categorical Data:** Where the categories are ordered. Examples are all categorical columns or ordered factors of diamonds data (cut, color, clarity). The cut column describes the quality of the cut and has the Fair category as the lowest cut and the Ideal category as the best cut.

2.3. SUMMARY STATISTICS

The category proportion (along with the category sample size) is the only measure that is used to describe categorical data.

2.3.1. Proportion and Sample Size of Cut Categories in Diamonds Data

To get the sample size and proportion of the cut column categories in diamonds data, we use the following functions:

1. The count function with the cut argument is applied to the diamonds data frame to give the sample size (number of rows) of cut column categories.
2. The mutate function with the argument, proportion = n/sum(n), to create a new column called "proportion" by dividing n by the sum of n.
3. The flextable, theme_box, and set_caption functions, from the flextable package, convert the result to a table as described in Chapter 1.

All these functions are applied in sequence using the "%>%" operator. Because we are using functions from the flextable package, we should load first the flextable package into our R session using the library function.

```
library(flextable)

diamonds %>% count(cut) %>% mutate(proportion = n/sum(n)) %>%

 flextable() %>% theme_box() %>%

 set_caption(caption = "Sample size and proportion of cut column categories in
diamonds data")
```

Table 2.1. Sample Size and Proportion of Cut Column Categories in Diamonds Data

Cut	n	Proportion
Fair	1,610	0.02984798
Good	4,906	0.09095291
Very Good	12,082	0.22398962
Premium	13,791	0.25567297
Ideal	21,551	0.39953652

We see that:

1. The sample size (or the number of rows) is n. Fair cut has the lowest sample size (1610) and the Ideal cut has the highest sample size (21551).
2. The proportion column contains the proportion of every category. Fair cut has the lowest proportion (0.03 or 3%) and the Ideal cut has the highest proportion (0.4 or 40%).
3. Because the cut is an ordered factor, the categories are arranged by their cut quality which also corresponds to their sample size or proportion.

2.3.2. Proportion and Sample Size of Color Categories in Diamonds Data

We can use the same functions to get the sample size and proportion of color categories in diamonds data.

```
diamonds %>% count(color) %>% mutate(proportion = n/sum(n)) %>%
 flextable() %>% theme_box() %>%
 set_caption(caption = "Sample size and proportion of color column categories
in diamonds data")
```

Table 2.2 *Sample Size and Proportion of Color Column Categories in Diamonds Data*

Color	n	Proportion
D	6,775	0.12560252
E	9,797	0.18162773
F	9,542	0.17690026
G	11,292	0.20934372

H	8,304	0.15394883
I	5,422	0.10051910
J	2,808	0.05205784

Because the color is an ordered factor, the categories are arranged by their color quality from the best color (D) to the worst color (J). However, this arrangement does not correspond to the color sample size or frequency.

To get a Table 2.2 of color column categories arranged by their sample size, we use the additional function arrange with the argument n to arrange the categories in ascending order according to their sample size.

```
diamonds %>% count(color) %>% mutate(proportion = n/sum(n)) %>%
 arrange(n) %>%
 flextable() %>% theme_box() %>%
 set_caption(caption = "Sample size and proportion of color column categories in
diamonds data arranged by their frequency")
```

Table 2.3. *Sample Size and Proportion of Color Column Categories in Diamonds Data Arranged by Their Frequency*

Color	**n**	**Proportion**
J	2,808	0.05205784
I	5,422	0.10051910
D	6,775	0.12560252
H	8,304	0.15394883
F	9,542	0.17690026
E	9,797	0.18162773
G	11,292	0.20934372

We see that:

1. The J color has the lowest sample size (2808) and the G color has the highest sample size (11292).
2. Accordingly, the J color has the lowest proportion (0.052 or 5.2%) and the G color has the highest proportion (0.209 or 20.9%).

2.3.3. Proportion and sample Size of Marital Categories in General Social Survey Data

We can use the same functions to get the sample size and proportion of marital categories in gss_cat data.

```
gss_cat %>% count(marital) %>% mutate(proportion = n/sum(n)) %>%
 flextable() %>% theme_box() %>%
 set_caption(caption = "Sample size and proportion of marital column categories in gss_cat data")
```

Table 2.4 *Sample Size and Proportion of Marital Column Categories in gss_cat Data*

Marital	n	Proportion
No answer	17	0.0007913234
Never married	5,416	0.2521063166
Separated	743	0.0345854862
Divorced	3,383	0.1574733510
Widowed	1,807	0.0841130196
Married	10,117	0.4709305032

We have 6 different marital categories. However, they are not arranged by their sample size. We can use the arrange function to arrange the categories by their sample size.

```
gss_cat %>% count(marital) %>% mutate(proportion = n/sum(n)) %>%
 arrange(n) %>%
 flextable() %>% theme_box() %>%
 set_caption(caption = "Sample size and proportion of marital column categories in gss_cat data arranged by their frequency")
```

Table 2.5. *Sample Size and Proportion of Marital Column Categories in gss_cat Data Arranged by Their Frequency*

Marital	n	Proportion
No answer	17	0.0007913234
Separated	743	0.0345854862
Widowed	1,807	0.0841130196
Divorced	3,383	0.1574733510
Never married	5,416	0.2521063166
Married	10,117	0.4709305032

We see that:

1. The "No answer" category has the lowest sample size (17) and the "Married" status has the highest sample size (10,117).

2. Accordingly, the "No answer" category has the lowest proportion (0.0008 or 0.08%) and the "Married" status has the highest proportion (0.47 or 47%).

2.3.4. Proportion and Sample Size of Religion Categories in General Social Survey Data

We can use the same functions to get the sample size and proportion of religion categories in gss_cat data.

```
gss_cat %>% count(relig) %>% mutate(proportion = n/sum(n)) %>%
 flextable() %>% theme_box() %>%
 set_caption(caption = "Sample size and proportion of religion categories in gss_cat data")
```

Table 2.6. *Sample Size and Proportion of Religion Categories in gss_cat Data*

Relig.	n	Proportion
No answer	93	0.0043290043
Don't know	15	0.0006982265
Inter-nondenominational	109	0.0050737793
Native american	23	0.0010706140
Christian	689	0.0320718708
Orthodox-christian	95	0.0044221012
Moslem/islam	104	0.0048410371
Other eastern	32	0.0014895499
Hinduism	71	0.0033049388
Buddhism	147	0.0068426197
Other	224	0.0104268491
None	3,523	0.1639901317
Jewish	388	0.0180607923
Catholic	5,124	0.2385141740
Protestant	10,846	0.5048643113

We have 15 different religions. However, they are not arranged by their sample size. We can use the arrange function to arrange the categories by their sample size.

```
gss_cat %>% count(relig) %>% mutate(proportion = n/sum(n)) %>%
 arrange(n) %>%
 flextable() %>% theme_box() %>%
 set_caption(caption = "Sample size and proportion of religions in gss_cat data
arranged by their frequency")
```

Table 2.7. *Sample Size and Proportion of Religions in gss_cat Data Arranged by Their Frequency*

Relig	**n**	**Proportion**
Don't know	15	0.0006982265
Native american	23	0.0010706140
Other eastern	32	0.0014895499
Hinduism	71	0.0033049388
No answer	93	0.0043290043
Orthodox-christian	95	0.0044221012
Moslem/islam	104	0.0048410371
Inter-nondenomina-tional	109	0.0050737793
Buddhism	147	0.0068426197
Other	224	0.0104268491
Jewish	388	0.0180607923
Christian	689	0.0320718708
None	3,523	0.1639901317
Catholic	5,124	0.2385141740
Protestant	10,846	0.5048643113

We see that:

1. The "Don't know" category has the lowest sample size (15) and the "Protestant" has the highest sample size (10,846).
2. Accordingly, the "Don't know" category has the lowest proportion (0.0007 or 0.07%), and the "Protestant" has the highest proportion (0.505 or 50.5%).

2.4. SUMMARY PLOTS

2.4.1. Bar Plot

The geom_bar function is used to plot a bar graph where each bar has a height equal to the number of rows or observations at each level of the categorical variable.

The geom_bar function requires only one aesthetic (x or y) which is the categorical variable you want to plot.

2.4.1.1. Bar Plot of Cut Column in Diamonds Data

To plot a bar plot of the cut column from the diamonds data, we will use the following functions:

1. The ggplot function, applied to diamonds data, with argument aes(x = cut) to plot cut categories on the x-axis.
2. The geom_bar function to create the bar plot.
3. The labs function with the title x, and y arguments to add a title, x-axis title, and y-axis title.

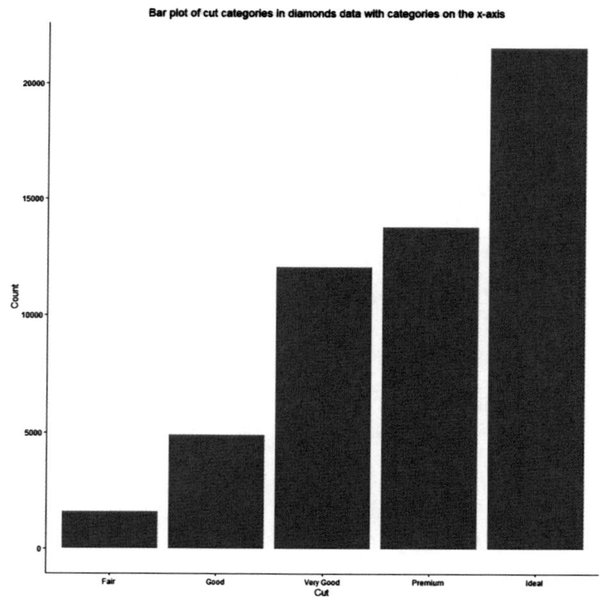

We see that the ideal cut has the highest count or frequency (highest bar) and the fair cut has the lowest count or frequency (shortest bar).

4. The theme_classic function removes the default gray background with white lines.
5. The theme function with the argument plot.title = element_text(hjust = 0.5), where hjust is for horizontal justification, to put the plot title in the top center of the graph.

```
diamonds %>% ggplot(aes(x = cut))+ geom_bar()+
 labs(title = “Bar plot of cut categories in diamonds data with categories on the x-axis,”
x = “Cut,” y = “Count”)+
 theme_classic()+
 theme(plot.title = element_text(hjust = 0.5))
```

2.4.1.2. Bar Plot of the color Column in Diamonds Data

We can use the same Functions to plot the color categories on the x-axis.

```
diamonds %>% ggplot(aes(x = color))+ geom_bar()+
 labs(title = “Bar plot of color categories in diamonds data with categories on the x-axis,”
 x = “Color,” y = “Count”)+
 theme_classic()+
 theme(plot.title = element_text(hjust = 0.5))
```

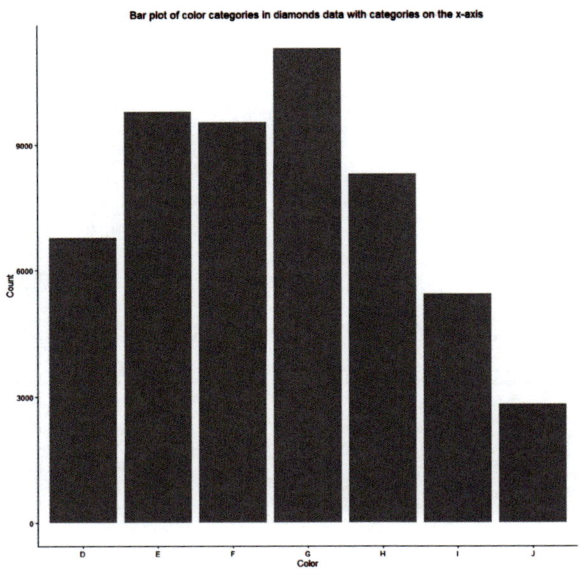

We see that the G color has the highest count or frequency (highest bar) and the J color has the lowest count or frequency (shortest bar).

2.4.1.3. Bar Plot of the Religion Column in General Social Survey Data

We can use the same functions to plot the religion categories on the x-axis from the general social survey data.

```
gss_cat %>% ggplot(aes(x = relig))+ geom_bar()+
 labs(title = "Bar plot of religions in general social survey data with religions on the x-axis,"
x = "Religion," y = "Count")+
 theme_classic()+
 theme(plot.title = element_text(hjust = 0.5))
```

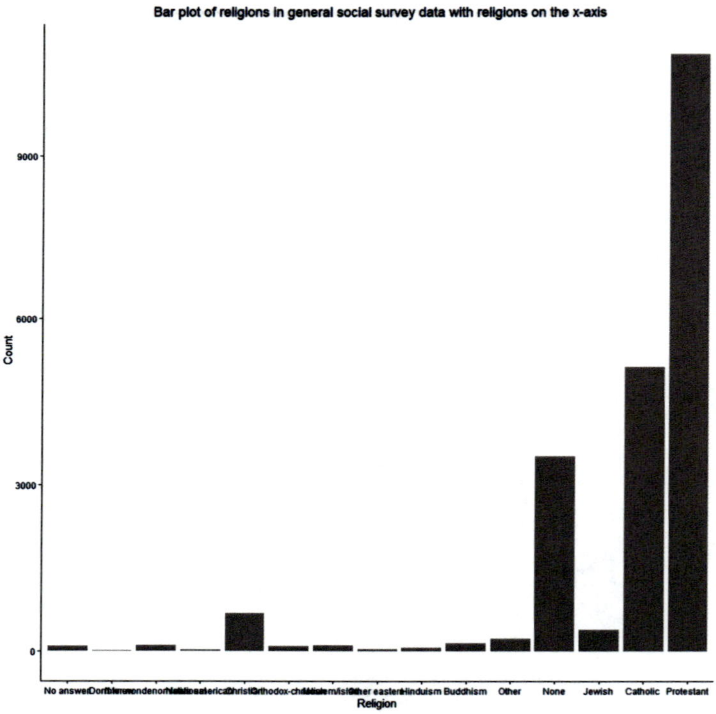

We see that the 15 religions are crowded and not appearing correctly. We can use the argument, axis.text.x = element_text(angle = 60, hjust = 1), inside the theme function to put the x-axis text at an angle = 60 with 1 horizontal justification. We also use the "\n" to break the long title into 2 lines.

```
gss_cat %>% ggplot(aes(x = relig))+ geom_bar()+
 labs(title = "Bar plot of religions in general social survey data \nwith religions on the x-axis at an angle of 60,"
```

```
x = "Religion," y = "Count")+
 theme_classic()+
 theme(plot.title = element_text(hjust = 0.5),
axis.text.x = element_text(angle = 60, hjust = 1))
```

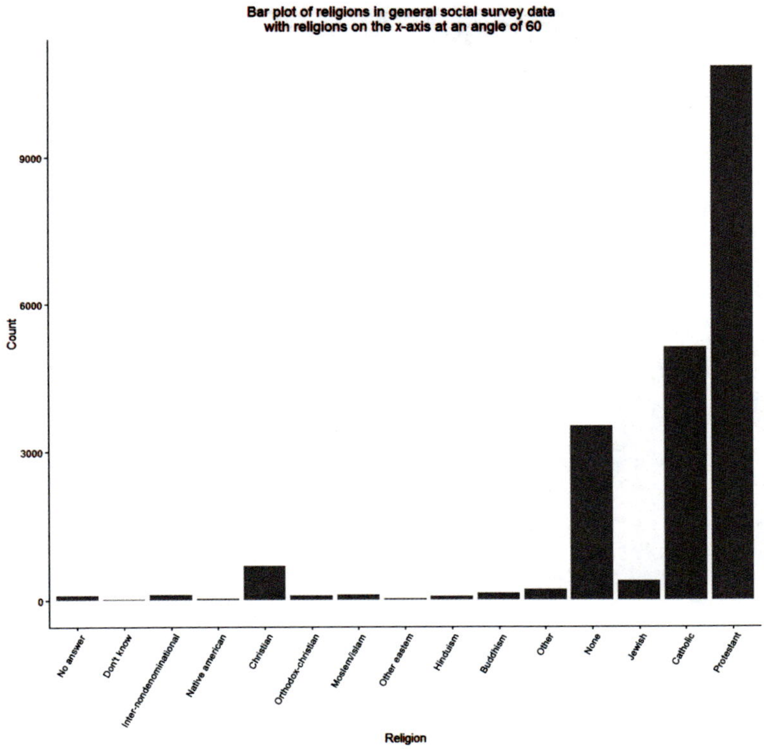

Alternatively, we can plot the religions on the y-axis.

2.4.1.4. Bar Plot with Categories on the Y-Axis

When we have many categories as for the 15 religions in the general social survey data, we can put the categories on the y-axis to avoid crowding on the x-axis. We will use the same functions above except that we use the argument aes(y = relig) to plot the religions on the y-axis. We will modify the labs and theme functions accordingly.

```
gss_cat %>% ggplot(aes(y = relig))+ geom_bar()+
  labs(title = "Bar plot of religions in general social survey data \nwith
religions on the y-axis,"
y = "Religion," x = "Count")+
```

```
theme_classic()+
theme(plot.title = element_text(hjust = 0.5))
```

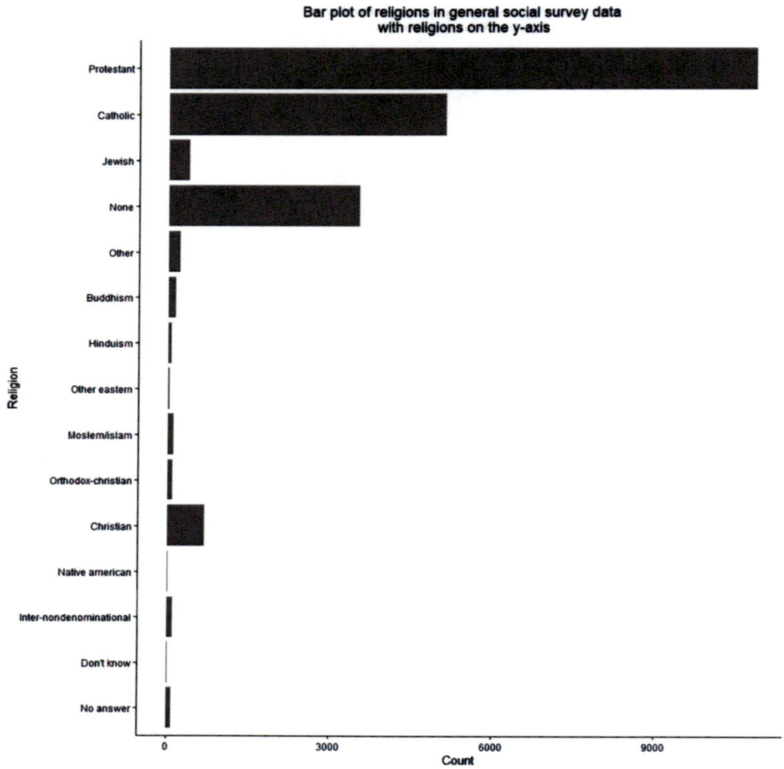

We see that all religion names appear clearly. The Protestant religion has the highest frequency. However, the less frequent religion is not clear.

2.4.1.5. Bar Plot with Ordered Categories by Frequency

We can use the mutate and fct_infreq functions to convert the religion column to a factor with religions arranged by their frequency. Then, we use the same above functions.

```
gss_cat %>% mutate(relig = fct_infreq(relig)) %>%
 ggplot(aes(y = relig))+ geom_bar()+
  labs(title = "Bar plot of religions in general social survey data \n with religions on the y-axis arranged by their frequency,"
y = "Religion," x = "Count")+
 theme_classic()+
 theme(plot.title = element_text(hjust = 0.5))
```

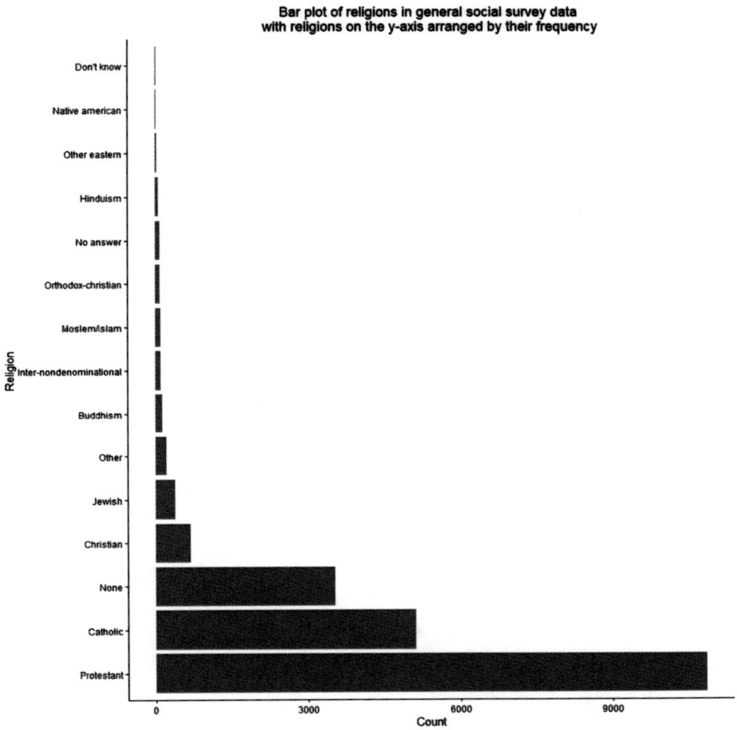

Here we see that Protestant is the most frequent religion while the "Don't know" category is the least frequent.

2.4.1.6. Bar Plot with Labeled Bars by Counts

For a more informative plot, we can plot a bar plot with bars labeled by their counts. To plot this plot for the religion column, we use the following functions:

1. The count function with the argument relig gives a data frame with 15 rows (for 15 religions) with a count column (n) for each religion.
2. The mutate and fct_reorder functions to convert the religion to a factor with religions arranged by their n or frequency value.
3. The ggplot function with argument aes(x = n, y = relig) plots counts on the x-axis and religions on the y-axis.
4. The geom_bar function with the argument stat = "identity" to create the bar plot. The default stat of the geom_bar function is "count" which will not be used here because every religion is represented by only 1 row.

5. The geom_label function with the argument aes(label = n) to plot a label of count (n) on the top of each bar.
6. The labs, theme_classic, and theme functions as before.

```
gss_cat %>% count(relig) %>% mutate(relig = fct_reorder(relig,n)) %>%
 ggplot(aes(y = relig, x = n))+ geom_bar(stat = "identity")+
 geom_label(aes(label = n))+
 labs(title = "Bar plot of religions in general social survey data \
nwith religions arranged by their frequency and labeled bars,"
y = "Religion," x = "Count")+
 theme_classic()+
 theme(plot.title = element_text(hjust = 0.5))
```

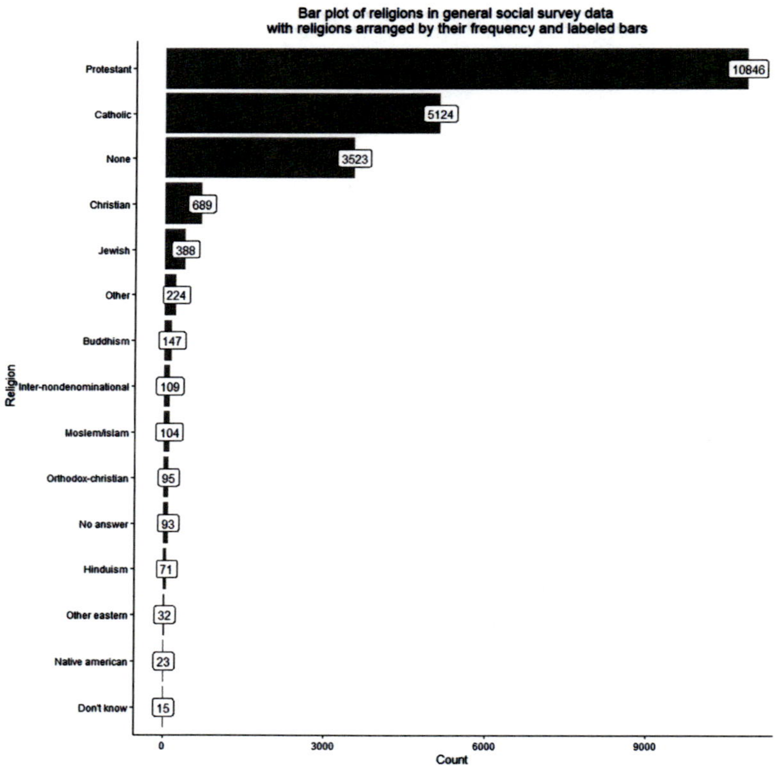

We see that Protestant is the most frequent religion with a frequency of 10846, while the "Don't know" category is the less frequent with a frequency of only 15.

As another example, we can plot the clarity categories from the diamonds data on the x-axis with labeled and arranged bars.

```
diamonds %>% count(clarity) %>%
 mutate(clarity = fct_reorder(clarity,n)) %>%
 ggplot(aes(x = clarity, y = n))+ geom_bar(stat = "identity")+
 geom_label(aes(label = n))+
 labs(title = "Bar plot of clarity categories in diamonds data \nwith clarities arranged by their frequency and labeled bars,"
 x = "Clarity," y = "Count")+
 theme_classic()+
 theme(plot.title = element_text(hjust = 0.5))
```

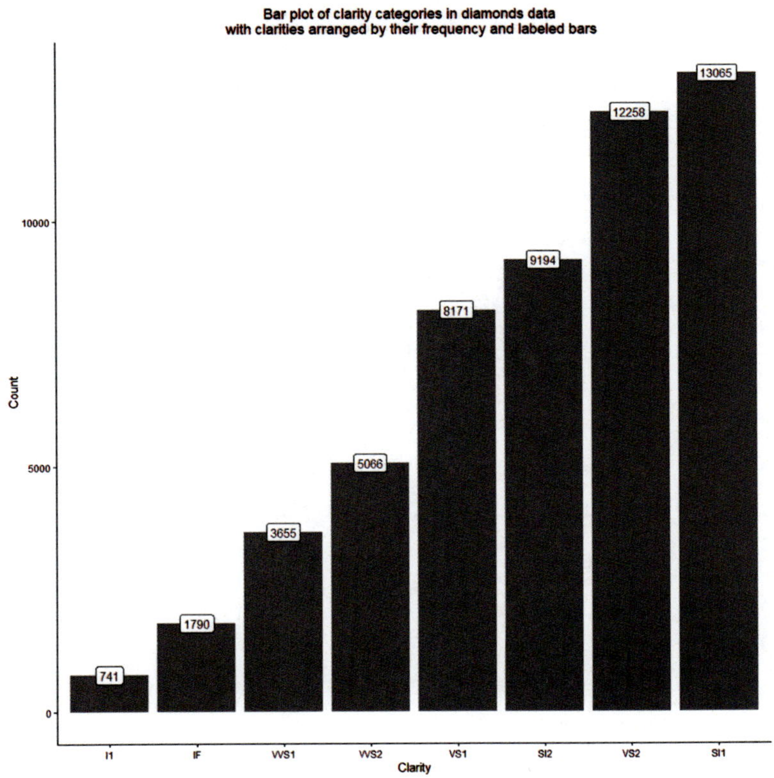

We see that "SI1" is the most frequent clarity with a frequency of 13065, while the "I1" category is the least frequent with a frequency of 741.

2.4.2. Lollipop Plot

The lollipop plot is the same as the bar plot and consists of 2 parts, the point and a line. The point represents the count and the line connects the point to its corresponding category.

The geom_point and geom_segment functions can be used to plot the 2 parts of the lollipop plot. However, both functions require 2 or more aesthetics and not only 1 aesthetic as the geom_bar function. This will be explained below.

2.4.2.1. Lollipop Plot of Cut Column in Diamonds Data

To plot a lollipop plot of the cut column from the diamonds data, we will use the following functions:

1. The count function with the argument cut, applied to the diamonds data, gives a data frame with 5 rows (for 5 cut categories) with a count column (n) for each category.
2. The ggplot function with argument aes(x = cut, y = n) plots cut categories on the x-axis and their counts on the y-axis.
3. The geom_point function to draw the point for each cut category. We increase the point size to size 3 so the resulting plot resembles a lollipop.
4. The geom_segment function with the argument, aes(y = 0, yend = n, x = cut, xend = cut), to draw a line for each cut category that:
   - Starts at y = 0 and ends at n or counts at the y-axis.
   - Starts and ends at the same cut category on the x-axis.
5. The labs, theme_classic, and theme functions as described above.

```
diamonds %>% count(cut) %>%
 ggplot(aes(x = cut, y = n))+ geom_point(size = 3)+
 geom_segment(aes(y = 0, yend = n, x = cut, xend = cut))+
  labs(title = "Lollipop plot of cut categories in diamonds data \nwith cut categories on the x-axis,"
x = "Cut," y = "Count")+
 theme_classic()+
 theme(plot.title = element_text(hjust = 0.5))
```

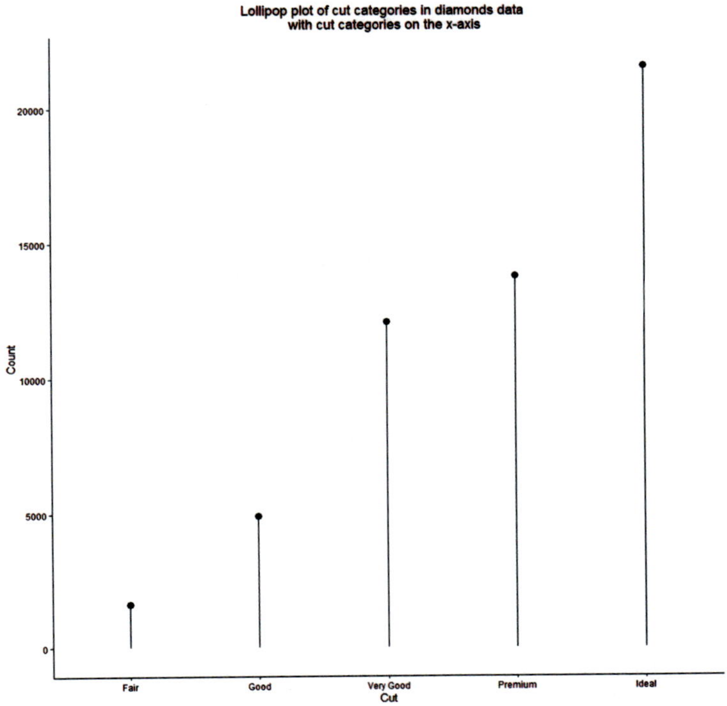

We see that the ideal cut has the highest count or frequency (longest lollipop) and the fair cut has the lowest count or frequency (shortest lollipop).

2.4.2.2. Lollipop Plot with Categories on the Y-axis

When we have many categories as for the 15 religions in the general social survey data, we can put the categories on the y-axis to avoid crowding on the x-axis. We will use the same functions above except that:

1. We use the argument aes(y = relig, x = n) inside the ggplot function to plot the religions on the y-axis and their counts on the x-axis.
2. We use the argument aes(x = 0, xend = n, y = relig, yend = relig) inside the geom_segment function to draw a line for each religion that starts at x = 0 and ends at n or counts at the x-axis and starts and ends at the same religion on the y-axis.

We will modify the labs and theme functions accordingly.

```
gss_cat %>% count(relig) %>%
 ggplot(aes(y = relig, x = n))+ geom_point(size = 3)+
```

```
  geom_segment(aes(x = 0, xend = n, y = relig, yend = relig))+
 labs(title = "Lollipop plot of religions in general social survey data \nwith
religions on the y-axis,"
y = "Religion," x = "Count")+
 theme_classic()+
 theme(plot.title = element_text(hjust = 0.5))
```

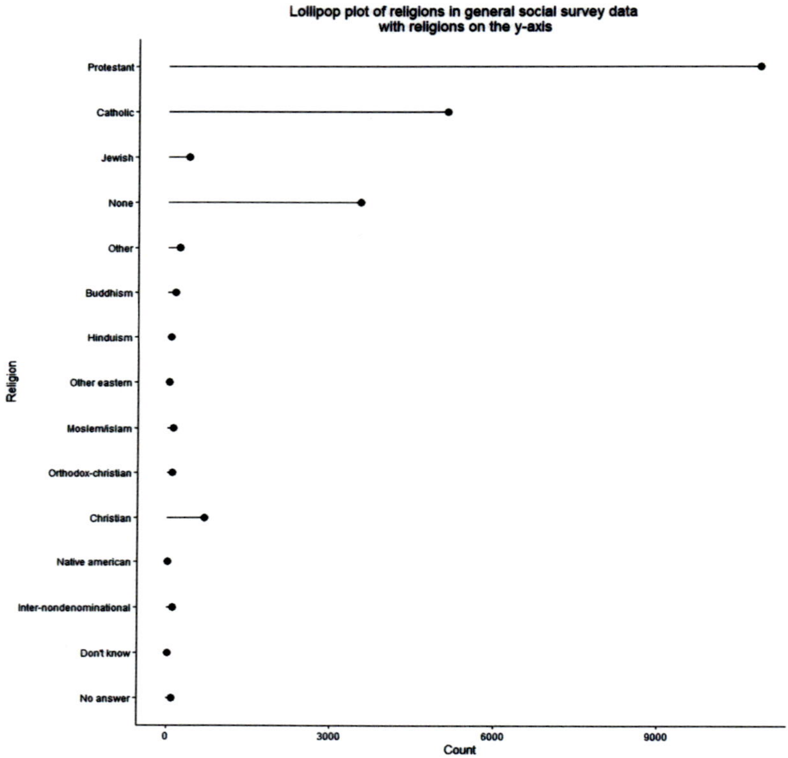

We see that all religion names appear clearly. The protestant religion has the highest frequency. However, the less frequent religion is not clear.

2.4.2.3. Lollipop Plot with Ordered Categories by Frequency

We can use the mutate and fct_reorder functions to convert the religion to a factor with religions arranged by their n or frequency. Then, we use the same above functions.

```
gss_cat %>% count(relig) %>% mutate(relig = fct_reorder(relig,n)) %>%
 ggplot(aes(y = relig, x = n))+ geom_point(size = 3)+
```

```
  geom_segment(aes(x = 0, xend = n, y = relig, yend = relig))+
 labs(title = "Lollipop plot of religions in general social survey data \nwith
religions on the y-axis arranged by their frequency,"
y = "Religion," x = "Count")+
theme_classic()+
 theme(plot.title = element_text(hjust = 0.5))
```

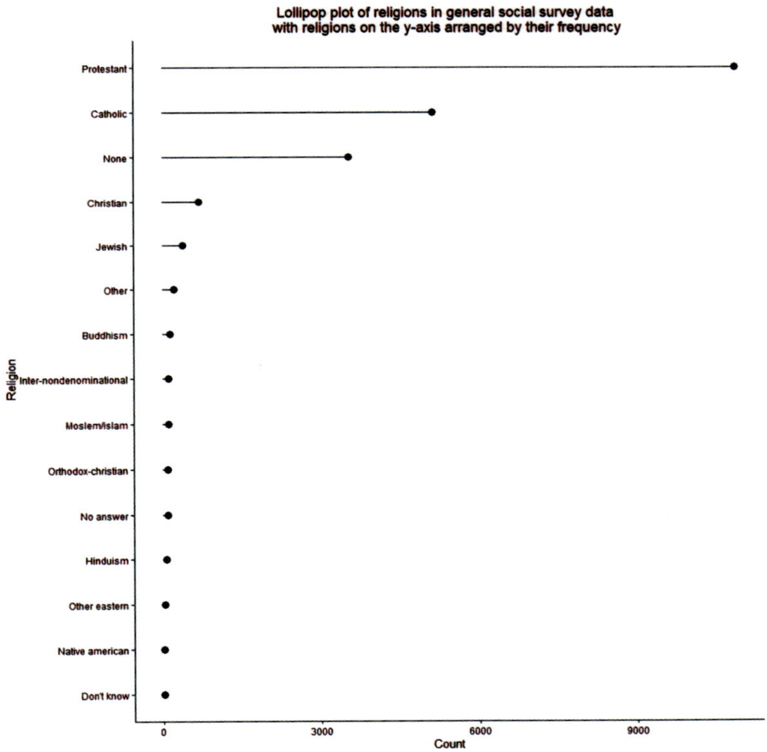

Here we see that Protestant is the most frequent religion while the "Don't know" category is the least frequent.

2.4.2.4. Lollipop Plot Labeled with Counts

We will use the same functions in 2.4.2.3. with the addition of the geom_label function with the arguments:

- aes(label = n) so the label for each lollipop will be its count or n.
- nudge_x = 500 to offset the labels from the points of lollipops by 500 points on the x-axis, or the labels will hide the points of lollipops.

- size = 3 to decrease the label size to avoid crowding

```
gss_cat %>% count(relig) %>% mutate(relig = fct_reorder(relig,n)) %>%
 ggplot(aes(y = relig, x = n))+ geom_point(size = 3)+
  geom_segment(aes(x = 0, xend = n, y = relig, yend = relig))+
 geom_label(aes(label = n), nudge_x = 500, size = 3)+
 labs(title = "Lollipop plot of religions in general social survey data \nwith religions arranged and labeled by their frequency,"
y = "Religion," x = "Count")+
 theme_classic()+
 theme(plot.title = element_text(hjust = 0.5))
```

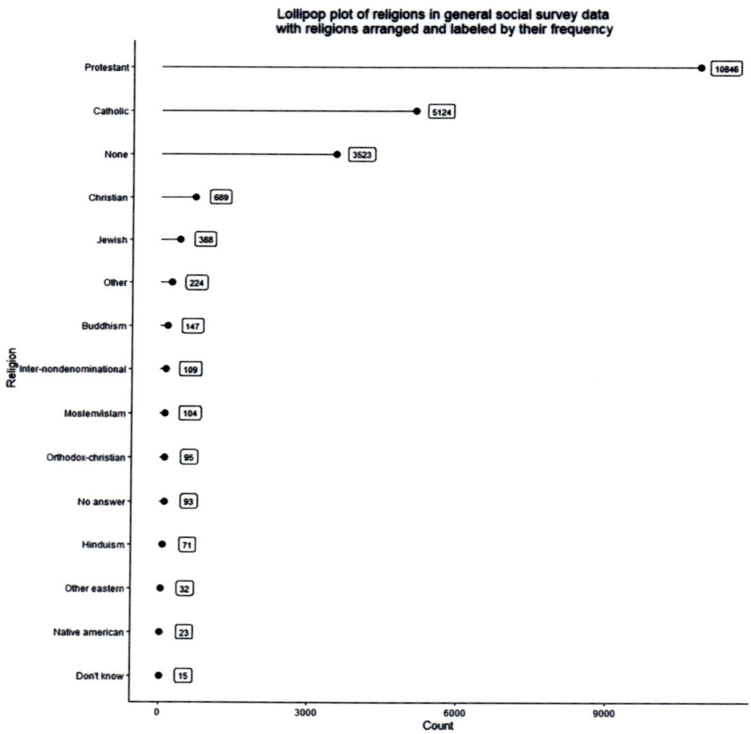

We see that Protestant is the most frequent religion with a frequency of 10846, while the "Don't know" category is the less frequent with a frequency of only 15.

As another example, we can plot the denomination categories from the general social survey data on the y-axis with labeled and arranged lollipops.

```
gss_cat %>% count(denom) %>% mutate(denom = fct_reorder(denom,n)) %>%
 ggplot(aes(y = denom, x = n))+ geom_point(size = 3)+
  geom_segment(aes(x = 0, xend = n, y = denom, yend = denom))+
 geom_label(aes(label = n), nudge_x = 500, size = 3)+
 labs(title = "Lollipop plot of denomination categories in general social survey
data \nwith categories arranged and labeled by their frequency,"
y = "Denomination," x = "Count")+
 theme_classic()+
 theme(plot.title = element_text(hjust = 0.5))
```

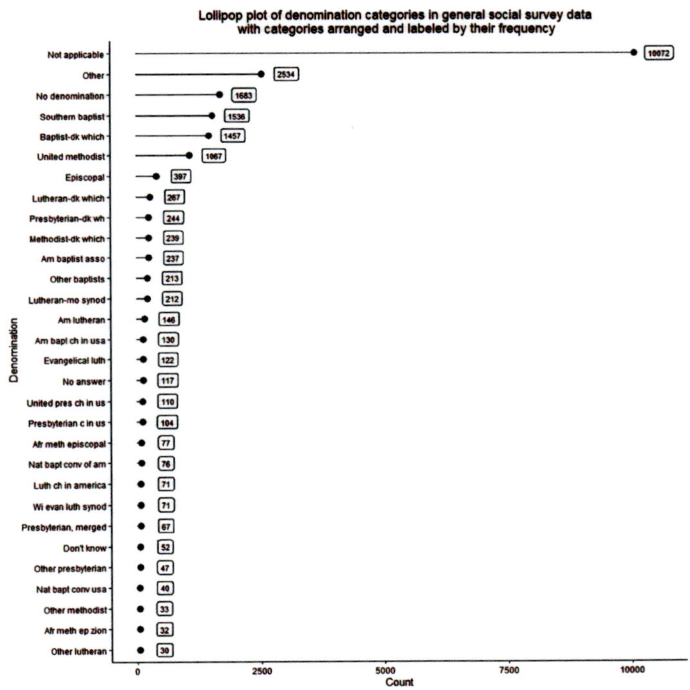

We see that the "Not applicable" category is the most frequent category with a frequency of 10072, while the "Other lutheran" category is the less frequent with a frequency of 30.

To give a different color for each category, we can use the color= denom argument inside the ggplot function. We also use the color= "Denomination" inside the labs function to modify the legend title.

```
gss_cat %>% count(denom) %>% mutate(denom = fct_reorder(denom,n)) %>%
 ggplot(aes(y = denom, x = n, color = denom))+ geom_point(size = 3)+
  geom_segment(aes(x = 0, xend = n, y = denom, yend = denom))+
```

```
geom_label(aes(label = n), nudge_x = 500, size = 3)+
labs(title = "Lollipop plot of denomination categories in general social survey
data \nwith colored categories arranged and labeled by their frequency,"
y = "Denomination," x = "Count," color = "Denomination")+
theme_classic()+
theme(plot.title = element_text(hjust = 0.5))
```

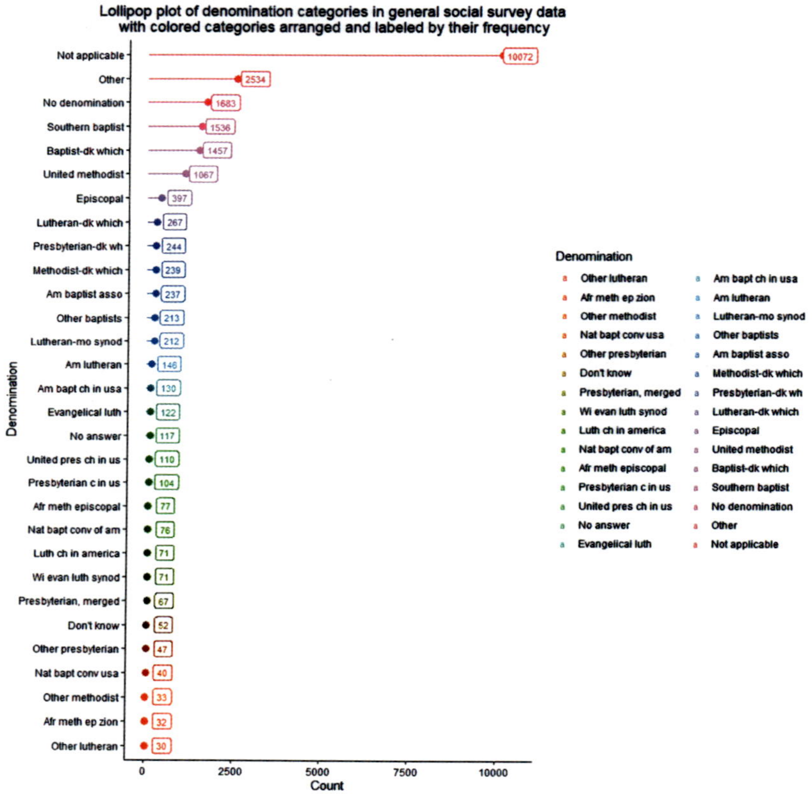

We see that each lollipop and label has a different color for each category.

2.4.3. Pie Chart

The pie chart is used if the goal is to compare each category with the whole. The pie chart is most useful when the number of categories is small. However, if the goal is to compare the frequency of categories, it is better to use bar or lollipop charts because humans are better at judging the length of bars or lollipops than the volume of pie slices.

To plot a pie chart, we must have a table of categories and their percentages that sum up to 100%.

2.4.3.1. Pie chart for Cut Categories in Diamonds Data

We generate a data frame with the count and percentage of each cut category using the formula percentage = nX100/sum(n) as done before in section 2.3.1. Instead of proportions, we will create percentages by multiplying the formula of proportion by 100. We convert the result to a table as before.

```
diamonds %>% count(cut) %>% mutate(percentage = n*100/sum(n)) %>%
 flextable() %>% theme_box() %>%
 set_caption(caption = "Sample size and percentage of cut column categories in
diamonds data")
```

Table 2.8. *Sample Size and Percentage of cut Column Categories in Diamonds Data*

Cut	n	Percentage
Fair	1,610	2.984798
Good	4,906	9.095291
Very Good	12,082	22.398962
Premium	13,791	25.567297
Ideal	21,551	39.953652

To create a pie plot from this data, we use the following functions:

1. the ggplot function with the arguments, aes(y = percentage, fill = cut, x = ""), to plot the percentage on the y-axis and a different fill color for each cut category. This will produce 1 bar with 5 parts for 5 cut categories.
2. The geom_bar function with the arguments, stat = "identity" and color = "black," to draw a black border around each category.
3. The coord_polar function produces a pie chart circle from the bar plot. We use the argument, theta = "y" to map the y values (percentage) to angles.
4. The labs function with the arguments title and fill to add a title and a legend title respectively. We also use the y = "" and x="" arguments to delete the y-axis and x-axis titles respectively since they have no meaning.
5. The theme_void function removes x- and y-axes and keeps only the pie chart circle.

6. The theme function with plot.title argument to place the title at the top center of the plot.

```
diamonds %>% count(cut) %>% mutate(percentage = n*100/sum(n)) %>%
 ggplot(aes(y = percentage, fill = cut, x = "")) +
  geom_bar(stat = "identity," color = "black")+
 coord_polar(theta = "y")+
 labs(title = "Pie chart for percentage of different cut categories in diamonds data,"
y = "," x = "," fill = "Cut")+
 theme_void()+
 theme(plot.title = element_text(hjust = 0.5))
```

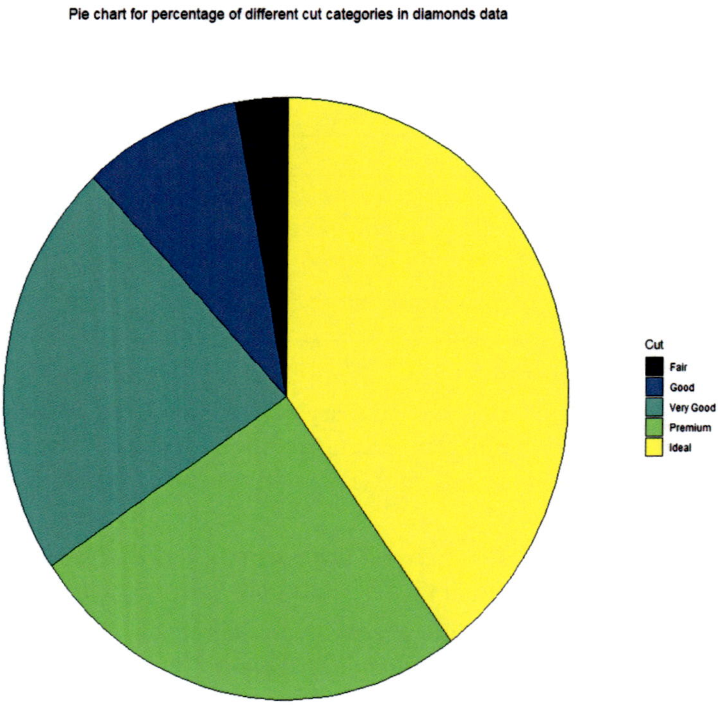

We see that the largest slice (most frequent category) was for the ideal cut and the smallest slice (lowest frequent category) was for the fair cut.

2.4.3.2. Pie Chart for Marital Status Categories in General Social Survey Data

Using the same functions, we can draw a pie chart for the marital status categories in the general social survey data.

```
gss_cat %>% count(marital) %>% mutate(percentage = n*100/sum(n)) %>%
 ggplot(aes(y = percentage, fill = marital, x = "")) +
  geom_bar(stat = "identity," color = "black")+
 coord_polar(theta = "y")+
 labs(title = "Pie chart for percentage of different marital categories in general social survey data,"
 y = ",," x = ",," fill = "Marital status")+
 theme_void()+
 theme(plot.title = element_text(hjust = 0.5))
```

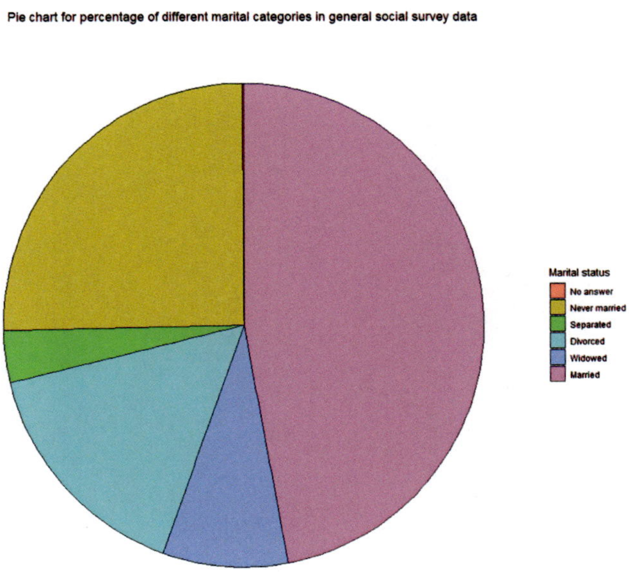

We see that the largest slice (most frequent category) was for the married status and the smallest slice (lowest frequent category) was for the "No answer" category.

2.4.3.3. Pie Chart for Religions in General Social Survey Data

Using the same functions, we can draw a pie chart for the religion categories in the general social survey data

```
gss_cat %>% count(relig) %>% mutate(percentage = n*100/sum(n)) %>%
 ggplot(aes(y = percentage, fill = relig, x = "")) +
  geom_bar(stat = "identity," color = "black")+
 coord_polar(theta = "y")+
 labs(title = "Pie chart for percentage of different religions in general social survey data,"
y = "," x = "," fill = "Religion")+
 theme_void()+
 theme(plot.title = element_text(hjust = 0.5))
```

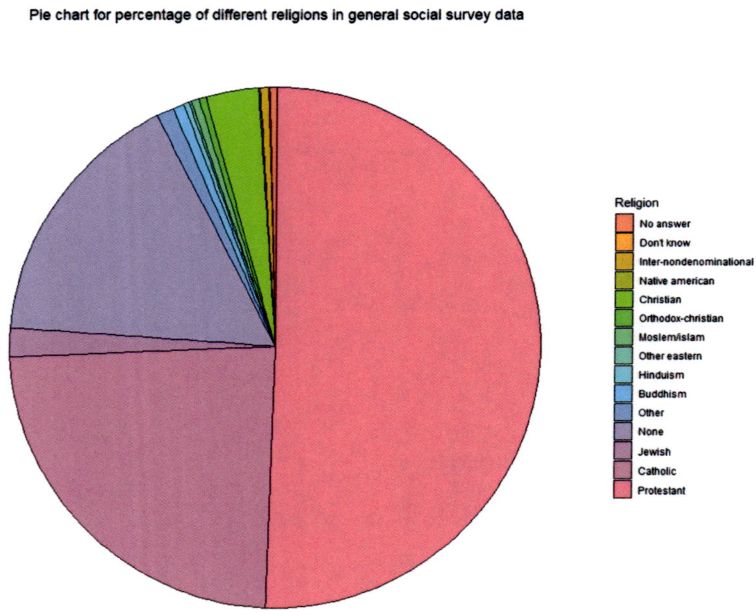

We see that the largest slice (most frequent religion) was the protestant but the smallest slice (lowest frequent religion) is difficult to discern.

2.4.4. Tree Map

In a tree map, each tile represents a single category, with the area of the tile proportional to the categorical counts.

A tree map is similar to a pie chart in that it displays proportions by varying the area of a shape. A tree map has two advantages over a pie chart:

1. We can display many more categories. In a pie chart, there is an upper limit to the number of categories that can be added to the circle. On the other hand, in a tree map, we can display hundreds, or thousands, of categories.
2. A tree map allows us to arrange the data categories hierarchically. In other words, we can group the proportions by using other categorical variables in the data.

We will use the treemapify package for plotting tree maps of different categorical columns so we load it first into our R session using the library function.

2.4.4.1. Treemap for the Cut Categories in Diamonds Data

To draw this plot, we will use the following functions:

1. The count function with the cut argument is applied to the diamonds data to produce a count for each one of the 5 cut categories.
2. The ggplot function with the argument, aes(fill = cut, area = n), so a tile will be drawn for each cut category, with a different fill color, and the tile area is proportional to the count of each cut category.
3. The geom_treemap function to draw the 5 tiles corresponding to 5 cut categories.
4. The labs function with title and fill arguments to add a title and legend title respectively.
5. The theme function with plot.title argument to place the title at the top center of the plot.

```
library(treemapify)
diamonds %>% count(cut) %>%
 ggplot(aes(fill = cut, area = n)) +
 geom_treemap() +
 labs(title = "Tree map of cut categories in Diamonds data,"
 fill = "Cut")+
 theme(plot.title = element_text(hjust = 0.5))
```

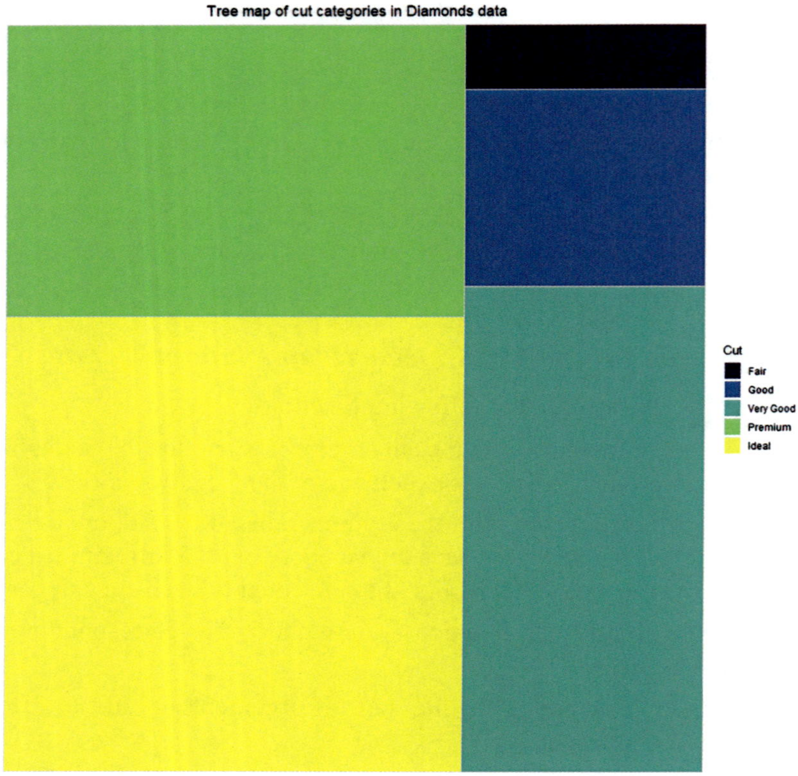

We see that the ideal cut has the largest tile (most frequent), and the fair cut has the smallest tile (least frequent).

2.4.4.2. Treemap for the Color Categories in Diamonds Data

Using the same functions above.

```
diamonds %>% count(color) %>%
 ggplot(aes(fill = color, area = n)) +
 geom_treemap() +
 labs(title = "Tree map of color categories in Diamonds data,"
 fill = "Color")+
 theme(plot.title = element_text(hjust = 0.5))
```

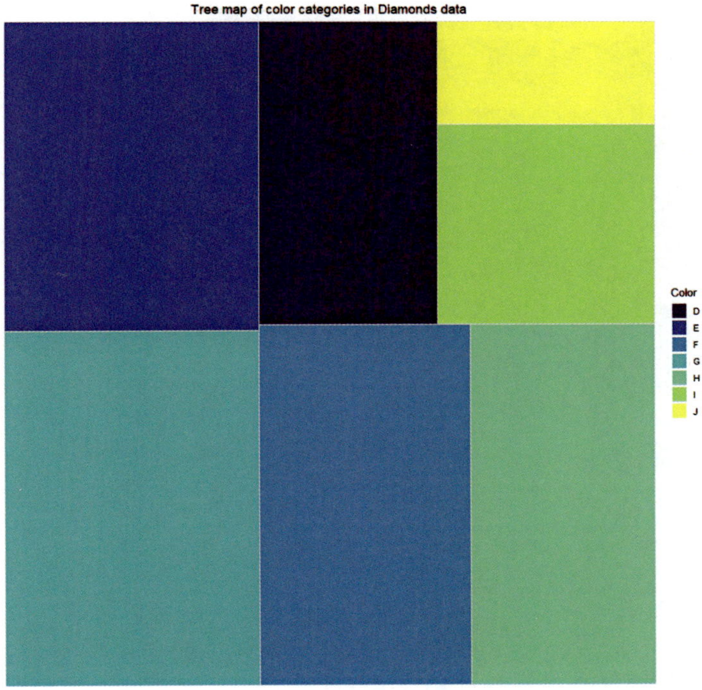

It is difficult to discern which color category is the most frequent. It is better if we add the color name to each tile.

2.4.4.3. Treemap with Labeled Tiles

we can add the text for each tile using the geom_treemap_text function with the argument, aes(label = color), to place the corresponding color name in each tile.

```
diamonds %>% count(color) %>%
 ggplot(aes(fill = color, area = n)) +
 geom_treemap() +
 geom_treemap_text(aes(label = color))+
 labs(title = "Tree map of color categories in Diamonds data with labeled tiles,"
 fill = "Color")+
 theme(plot.title = element_text(hjust = 0.5))
```

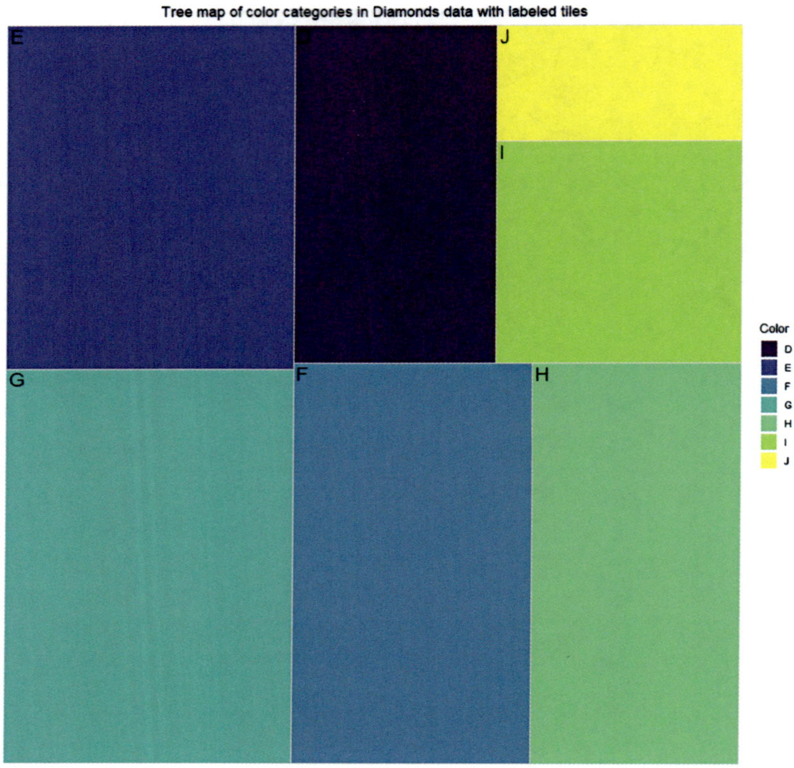

The default black color is difficult to discern in dark color so it is better to use white color using the color="white" argument within the geom_treemap_text function.

```
diamonds %>% count(color) %>%
 ggplot(aes(fill = color, area = n)) +
 geom_treemap() +
 geom_treemap_text(aes(label = color), color = "white")+
 labs(title = "Tree map of color categories in Diamonds data with white labeled
tiles,"
 fill = "Color")+
 theme(plot.title = element_text(hjust = 0.5))
```

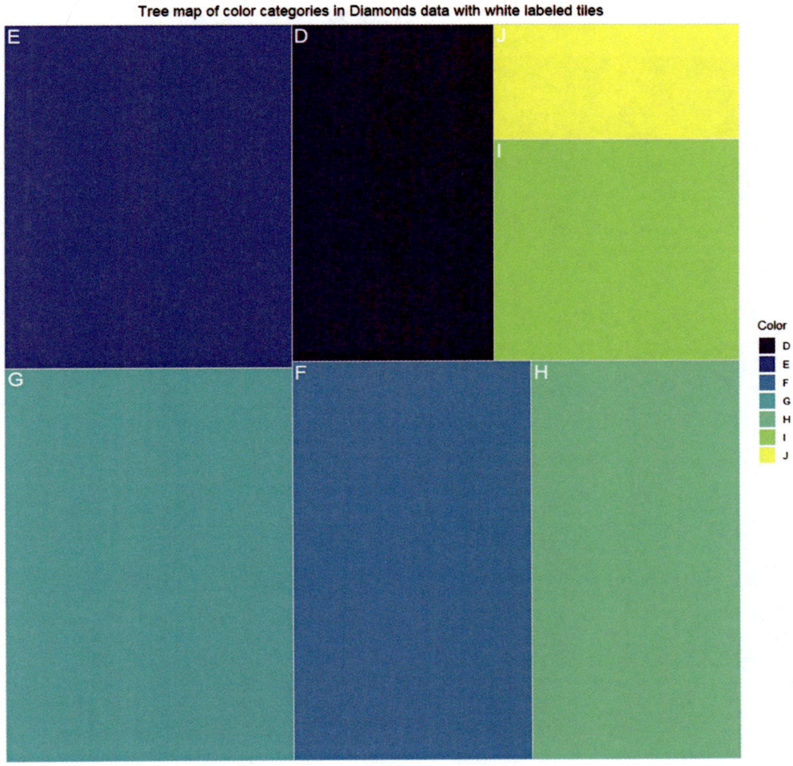

We can also place the labels in the center of each tile using the place = "center" argument within the geom_treemap_text function.

```
diamonds %>% count(color) %>%
 ggplot(aes(fill = color, area = n)) +
 geom_treemap() +
 geom_treemap_text(aes(label = color), color = "white,"
place = "center")+
 labs(title = "Tree map of color categories in Diamonds data \nwith centered white labeled tiles,"

   fill = "Color")+

 theme(plot.title = element_text(hjust = 0.5))
```

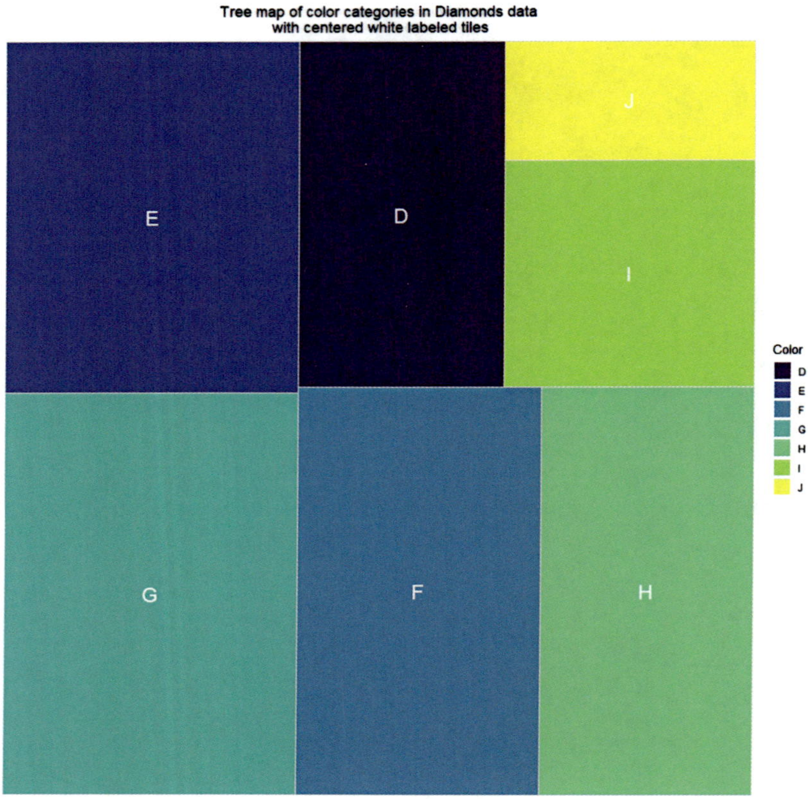

We can also label the tiles by their frequency along with their names. Inside the geom_treemap_text function, we will use the argument, aes(label = paste(color,n, sep = "\n"), to paste the color name to its frequency with a "\n" separator (sep argument) so the result will be in 2 lines.

```
diamonds %>% count(color) %>%
 ggplot(aes(fill = color, area = n)) +
 geom_treemap() +
 geom_treemap_text(aes(label = paste(color,n, sep = "\n")), color = "white,"
place = "center")+
 labs(title = "Tree map of color categories in Diamonds data \nwith tiles
labeleled by names and frequency,"
 fill = "Color")+
 theme(plot.title = element_text(hjust = 0.5))
```

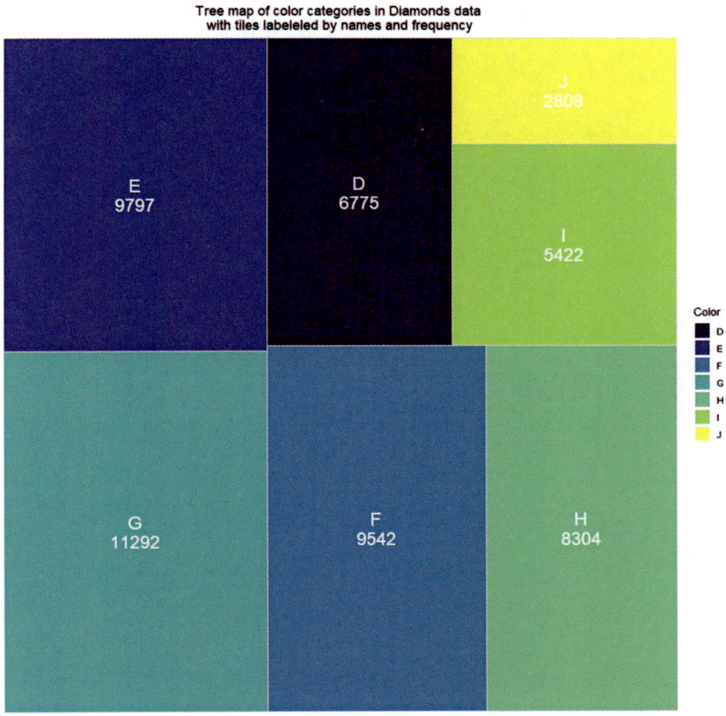

We see that the G color is the most frequent with a frequency of 11292 and the J color is the least frequent with a frequency of 2808.

2.4.4.4. Treemap for Religions in the General Social Survey Data

We can use the same functions to plot a treemap of the religions in the general social survey data.

```
gss_cat %>% count(relig) %>%
 ggplot(aes(fill = relig, area = n)) +
 geom_treemap() +
 geom_treemap_text(aes(label = paste(relig,n, sep = "\n")), color = "white,"
place = "center")+
 labs(title = "Tree map of religions in general social survey data \nwith most
tiles labeleled by names and frequency,"
 fill = "Religion")+
 theme(plot.title = element_text(hjust = 0.5))
```

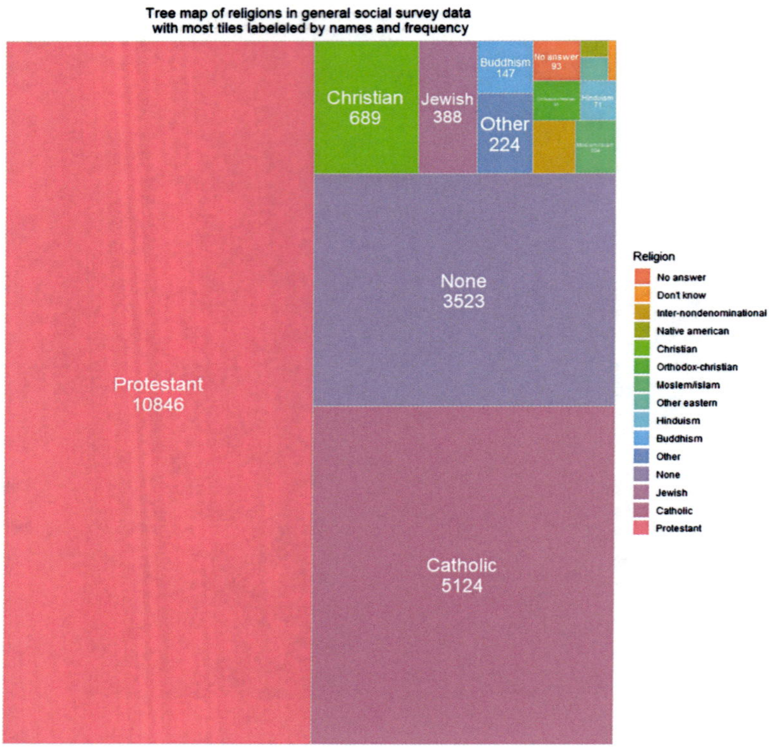

We see that the least frequent tiles are not labeled. This can be corrected using the min.size = 0 argument within the geom_treemap_text function.

```
gss_cat %>% count(relig) %>%
 ggplot(aes(fill = relig, area = n)) +
 geom_treemap() +
 geom_treemap_text(aes(label = paste(relig,n, sep = "\n")), color = "white,"
place = "center," min.size = 0)+
 labs(title = "Tree map of religions in general social survey data \nwith all
tiles labeleled by names and frequency,"
 fill = "Religion")+

 theme(plot.title = element_text(hjust = 0.5))
```

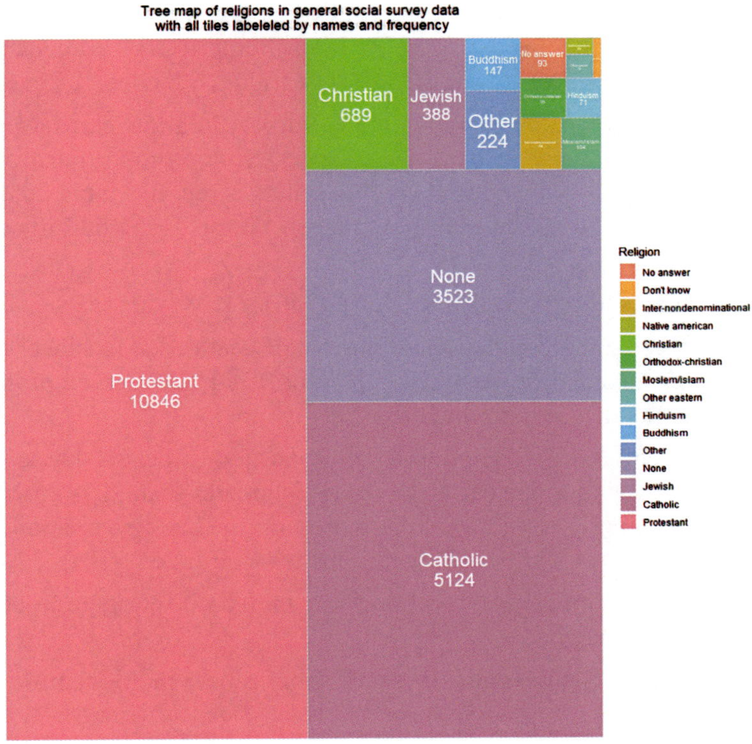

2.5. STATISTICAL TESTS

2.5.1. Binomial and Multinomial Tests

The binomial and multinomial tests are used to test if a categorical variable has a homogeneity between its categories or to compare the categories' proportions to expected proportions. The binomial test is used when the categorical variable has 2 categories only (binary) and the multinomial test is used with a categorical variable with more than 2 categories.

The binomial and multinomial tests are alternatives to proportion and Chi-square tests when the sample size is small. The sample size is small when is less than 5 where:

- n = sample size.
- is the probability or proportion of success or the null hypothesis.
- is the probability or proportion of failure and equals 1-.

2.5.1.1. Binomial Test for Small Sample Data

This example is modified from Rosner, Bernard (Bernard A.). Fundamentals of Biostatistics. Boston :Brooks/Cole, Cengage Learning, 8th edition, 2016.

If 13 deaths have occurred among male workers in a nuclear power plant and in 5 of them the cause of death was cancer. So the proportion from this sample is 5/13 = 0.38 or 38%. Based on vital statistics reports, about 20% of all deaths can be attributed to some form of cancer. So this is the null hypothesis proportion.

This is a small sample because 0.2 X 0.8 X 13 = 2.08 which is < 5.

Null hypothesis: The population proportion of deaths due to cancer among male workers in a nuclear power plant = 20% or 0.2. The observed proportion of 0.38 or 38% was due to sampling error.

Alternative hypothesis: The population proportion of deaths due to cancer among male workers in a nuclear power plant is greater than 20% or 0.2. The observed proportion of 0.38 or 38% truly represents the background population of male workers in a nuclear power plant. This is a one-tailed test.

We will use the binom_test function from the rstatix package to conduct this test with the arguments:

- x = 5 which is the count of deaths from cancer in this sample.
- n = 13 which is the sample size.
- p = 0.2 which is the null hypothesis proportion
- alternative = "greater" which is the alternative hypothesis. Then we convert the results to a table as before.

Because we are using the rstatix package, we must load it into our R session using the library function.

```
library(rstatix)
binom_test(x = 5, n = 13, p = 0.2, alternative = "greater") %>%
 flextable() %>% theme_box() %>%
  set_caption(caption = "One-tailed binomial test results of cancer deaths proportion among male workers in a nuclear power plant")
```

Table 2.9. One-Tailed Binomial Test Results of Cancer Deaths Proportion Among Male Workers in a Nuclear Power Plant

n	estimate	conf.low	conf. high	p	p.signif
13	0.3846154	0.1656594	1	0.09913061	ns

The Table 2.8 contains the estimated sample proportion= 0.38 or 38% and the p-value = 0.099.

The p_value is the probability of our sample results (cancer deaths proportion among male workers in a nuclear power plant) under the null hypothesis (where the actual proportion = 0.2 or 20%). Since this probability is greater than 0.05, we fail to reject the null hypothesis and conclude that the proportion of deaths from cancer is not significantly different for nuclear-power-plant workers than for men in the general population.

This is also evident from the reported 95% confidence interval from 0.166 or 16.6% to 1 or 100%. Since this interval contains the null hypothesis proportion, we accept the null hypothesis that the proportion of cancer deaths among male workers in a nuclear power plant equals 0.2 or 20%.

2.5.1.2. Binomial Test for Race Column in the General Social Survey Data

If we apply the count function with the argument race on the gss_cat data, we will get the 3 races that are presented in this data.

```
gss_cat %>% count(race) %>% flextable() %>% theme_box() %>%
 set_caption(caption = "Count of different races in the general social survey
data")
```

Table 2.10. *Count of Different Races in the General Social Survey Data*

Race	n
Other	1,959
Black	3,129
White	16,395

We see that White is the most frequent race with a count of 16395, followed by Black with a count of 3129, and other (races) with a count of 1959.

To convert this column to a binary column, we will use the fct_lump function inside the mutate function with the arguments:

- race which is the column to be mutated or changed.
- n=1 to keep only the most frequent race and all other races are lumped in the "Other" race.

```
gss_cat %>% mutate(race = fct_lump(race, n = 1)) %>%
 count(race) %>% flextable() %>% theme_box() %>%
 set_caption(caption = "Count of two races after race lumping \n in the general
social survey data")
```

Table 2.11. *Count of Two Races After Race Lumping in the General Social Survey Data*

Race	n
White	16,395
Other	5,088

We see that White has the same count of 16395, while the other (races) has a count of 5088 which is the sum of the counts of 2 previous races, black and other, 3129+1959 = 5088. The proportion of White in this data = 16395/21483 = 0.763 or 76.3%.

We know from the United States census that 71% of the population in the United States are White. So we may wish to test the hypothesis that the proportion of whites in the general social survey data is different from the general US census.

Null hypothesis: The population (actual) proportion of White in the general social survey data = 71% or 0.71. The observed proportion of 0.763 or 76.3% was due to sampling error.

Alternative hypothesis: The population (actual) proportion of White in the general social survey data is different from 71% or 0.71. This is a two-tailed test because the actual proportion may be less or greater than 71%.

Again, we will use the binom_test function to conduct this test with the arguments:

- x = 16395 which is the count of White in this sample.
- n = 21483 which is the sample size or the number of rows in this data.
- p = 0.71 which is the null hypothesis proportion
- alternative = "two.sided" which is the alternative hypothesis. Then we convert the results to a table as before.

```
binom_test(x = 16395, n = 21483, p = 0.71, alternative = "two.sided") %>%

 flextable() %>% theme_box() %>%

 set_caption(caption = "Two-tailed binomial test results of White proportion
in the general social survey data")
```

Table 2.12. *Two-Tailed Binomial Test Results of White Proportion in the General Social Survey Data*

n	Estimate	conf.low	conf.high	p	p.signif
21,483	0.7631616	0.7574178	0.768834	0.0000 000000 000000 000000 000000 000000 000000 000000 000000 000000 000000 000119 439	****

The Table 2.11 contains the estimated sample proportion of 0.763 or 76.3% and the p-value which is very low and nearly equals zero.

The p_value is the probability of our sample results (White proportion in the general social survey data) under the null hypothesis (where the actual proportion = 0.71 or 71%). Since this probability is very low, we reject the null hypothesis and conclude that the proportion of whites in the general social survey data is significantly different from the white proportion in the US census. This means that the general social survey data is not representative of the general population in the US.

This is also evident from the reported 95% confidence interval from 0.757 or 75.7% to 0.769 or 76.9%. Since this interval does not contain the null hypothesis proportion, we accept the alternative hypothesis that the proportion of whites in the general social survey data is different from that in the general population of the US.

2.5.1.3. Multinomial Test for Race Column in the General Social Survey Data

We see that we have 3 races in the general social survey data. We may test the proportions of these races using 2 approaches:

1. Are the 3 races equally common? This is a test of homogeneity.
2. Are the races' proportions equivalent to certain proportions? This is called the goodness-of-fit test where we compare multiple observed proportions to expected probabilities.

2.5.1.3.1. Test for Homogeneity

We will test the homogeneity of races within those participants with a reported income of less than 1000 USD. We use the following functions:

1. The filter function with the argument rincome=="Lt $1000" filters for participants with a reported income less than 1000 USD.
2. The count function with race argument to count the different races within those participants.

```
gss_cat %>% filter(rincome=="Lt $1000") %>% count(race) %>%
 flextable() %>% theme_box() %>%
 set_caption(caption = "Count of different races in participants with a reported income less than 1000 USD ")
```

Table 2.13. *Count of Different Races in Participants with a Reported Income Less Than 1000 USD*

Race	n
Other	36
Black	51
White	199

We see that White is the most frequent race with a count of 199, followed by Black with a count of 51, and other (races) with a count of 36. To test the homogeneity of races within this subset, we do these steps:

1. We create a vector called "races" that contains the counts for each race.
2. We use the multinom_test function with the arguments:
   i. x = races which is the sample counts.
   ii. p = c(1/3,1/3,1/3) which are the probabilities or proportions under the null hypothesis. If the 3 races are homogeneous in those participants with income less than 1000 USD, the expected proportion = 1/3 = 0.33 or 33%. Then we convert the results to a table as before.

```
races<-c(white =199, black=51, other=36)
races
## white black other
##   199    51    36
multinom_test(x = races,


        p = c(1/3,1/3,1/3)) %>%
 flextable() %>% theme_box() %>%
```

```
set_caption(caption = "Multinomial test of homogeneity for races within
participants with income less than 1000 USD")
```

Table 2.14. *Multinomial Test of Homogeneity for Races Within Participants with Income Less Than 1000 USD*

p		p.signif
0.000000000000000000000 0000000000003624663		****

The table 2.13 contains the p-value which is very low and nearly equals zero.

The p_value is the probability of our sample results (race proportion in participants with less than 1000 USD income) under the null hypothesis (where all 3 proportions = 0.33 or 33%). Since this probability is very low, we reject the null hypothesis and conclude that the proportion of some races is different from other races in those participants with income less than 1000 USD.

A subsequent test is to perform pairwise comparisons between groups to find out which race pair is different in its components. In other words, which race proportion is significantly different from 0.5 relative to any other race.

We use the pairwise_binom_test function to perform a pairwise comparison (binomial test) with the arguments:

- x = races which is the named vector with counts.
- p.adjust.method = "fdr" which is the method for adjusting the p-value in multiple comparisons. The "fdr" is for the false discovery rate.
- alternative = "two.sided" which is the alternative hypothesis.

```
pairwise_binom_test(x = races, p.adjust.method = "fdr,"
alternative = "two.sided") %>%
 flextable() %>% theme_box() %>%
 set_caption(caption = "Pairwise comparisons for races within participants with
income less than 1000 USD")
```

Table 2.15. *Pairwise Comparisons for Races Within Participants with Income Less Than 1000 USD*

Group1	Group2	n	Estimate	conf.low	conf.high	p	p.adj	p.adj. signif
white	black	250	0.7960000	0.7406598	0.8441733	0.00000000 000000000 000078206 72314546	0.0000000 00000000 000001170 000000	****
white	other	235	0.8468085	0.7942799	0.8903422	0.00000000 000000000 000000000 01601867	0.0000000 00000000 00000000 0000481	****
black	other	87	0.5862069	0.4755393	0.6908337	0.13290188 519546225 487388824 14909313	0.1330000 00000000 00710542 7357601	ns

We have 3 pairwise comparisons:

1. Comparing white with a count of 199 to black with a count of 51. So the total sample size = 199+51 = 250. The estimated proportion of white in this sample = 199/250 = 0.796 or 79.6% and 95% confidence interval = 0.74–0.84. The 95% confidence interval does not contain the null hypothesis proportion of 0.5 and the adjusted p-value is very low. So, we reject the null hypothesis and conclude that white proportion is significantly different from (larger than) the black proportion in this sample.
2. Comparing white with a count of 199 to other with a count of 36. So the total sample size = 199+36 = 235. The estimated proportion of white in this sample = 199/235 = 0.847 or 84.7% and 95% confidence interval = 0.79–0.89. The 95% confidence interval does not contain the null hypothesis proportion of 0.5 and the adjusted p-value is very low. So, we reject the null hypothesis and conclude that white proportion is significantly different from (larger than) the other proportion in this sample.
3. Comparing black with a count of 51 to other with a count of 36. So the total sample size = 51+36 = 87. The estimated proportion of black in this sample = 51/87 = 0.586 or 58.6% and 95% confidence interval = 0.476–0.69. The 95% confidence interval contains the null hypothesis proportion of 0.5 and the adjusted p-value larger than 0.05. So, we fail to reject the null hypothesis and conclude that the black proportion is statistically equivalent to the other proportion in this sample.

2.5.1.3.2. Goodness-of-Fit Test

For the goodness-of-fit test, we must have another vector of probabilities or proportions that sum to 1. So, we do these steps:

1. We create another vector called "races_prob" that contains the probability for each race. We assume that the expected probability of white is 0.8 or 80%, the expected probability of black is 0.1 or 10%, and the expected probability of other is 0.1 or 10%. Note that 0.8+0.1+0.1 = 1.
2. We use the multinom_test function with the arguments:
   i. x = races which is the sample counts.
   ii. p = races_prob which are the probabilities or proportions under the null hypothesis that we want to test. Then we convert the results to a table as before.

```
races_prob<-c(white =0.8, black=0.1, other=0.1)
races_prob
## white black other
##   0.8   0.1   0.1
multinom_test(x = races,
p = races_prob) %>%
 flextable() %>% theme_box() %>%
  set_caption(caption = "Multinomial goodness-of-fit test for races within
participants with income less than 1000 USD")
```

Table 2.16. *Multinomial Goodness-of-Fit Test for Races Within Participants with Income Less Than 1000 USD*

p	p.signif
0.0000324622	****

The Table 2.15 contains the p-value which is very low and nearly equals zero.

The p_value is the probability of our sample results (race proportion in participants with less than 1000 USD income) under the null hypothesis (where the proportions are stored in the races_prob vector). Since this probability is very low, we reject the null hypothesis and conclude that the proportion of some races is different from the expected probabilities in the races_prob vector.

A subsequent test is to perform pairwise comparisons between each race and its expected probability to find out which race is different from its expected probability. We use the pairwise_binom_test_against_p function to perform a pairwise comparison (binomial test) with the arguments:

- x = races which is the named vector with counts.
- p = races_prob which is the vector holding the expected probabilities.
- p.adjust.method = "fdr" which is the method for adjusting the p-value in multiple comparisons. The "fdr" is for the false discovery rate.
- alternative = "two.sided" which is the alternative hypothesis.

```
pairwise_binom_test_against_p(x = races, p = races_prob,
p.adjust.method = "fdr,"
alternative = "two.sided") %>%
 flextable() %>% theme_box() %>%
  set_caption(caption = "Pairwise comparisons for races against expected probabilities")
```

Table 2.17. *Pairwise Comparisons for Races Against Expected Probabilities*

Group	Observed	Expected	n	Estimate	conf.low	conf.high	p	p.adj	p.adj. signif
white	199	228.8	286	0.6958042	0.63890187	0.7485954	0.00003054810	0.0000686	****
black	51	28.6	286	0.1783217	0.13574917	0.2277023	0.00004571957	0.0000686	****
other	36	28.6	286	0.1258741	0.08974017	0.1699832	0.13993011724	0.1400000	ns

We have 3 pairwise comparisons:

1. Comparing white with a count of 199 and a proportion of 199/286= 0.696 to its expected probability of 0.8. The 95% confidence interval = 0.64–0.75. The 95% confidence interval does not contain the null hypothesis proportion of 0.8 and the adjusted p-value is very low. So, we reject the null hypothesis and conclude that white proportion is significantly different from (smaller than) the expected probability of 0.8.
2. Comparing black with a count of 51 and a proportion of 51/286= 0.178 to its expected probability of 0.1. The 95% confidence interval = 0.136–0.228. The 95% confidence interval does not contain the null hypothesis proportion of 0.1 and the adjusted p-value is very low. So, we reject the null hypothesis and conclude that black proportion is significantly different from (larger than) the expected probability of 0.1 in this sample.
3. Comparing other with a count of 36 and a proportion of 36/286= 0.126 to its expected probability of 0.1. The 95% confidence interval = 0.09–0.17. The 95% confidence interval contains the null hypothesis proportion of 0.1 and the adjusted p-value is greater

than 0.05. So, we accept the null hypothesis and conclude that other proportion is not significantly different from (equivalent to) the expected probability of 0.1.

2.5.2. Proportion Test

The proportion test is used for binary categorical variables to either evaluate the homogeneity of proportions or to test that the proportions are equal to certain given values when the sample size is large.

2.5.2.1. Test for Homogeneity in the Race Column of the General Social Survey Data

We see above after the race factor lumping that White has a count of 16395 and the other (races) has a count of 5088. We can test if these two races are homogeneous or in other words, they have a proportion of 0.5.

- **Null Hypothesis:** The population (actual) proportion of whites or other in the general social survey data = 0.5.
- **Alternative Hypothesis:** The population (actual) proportion of White or other in the general social survey data is different from 0.5. This is a two-tailed test because the actual proportion may be less or greater than 50%.

We will use the prop_test function to conduct this test with the arguments:

- x = 16395 which is the count of White in this sample.
- n = 21483 which is the sample size or the number of rows in this data.
- p = 0.5 which is the null hypothesis proportion.
- alternative = "two.sided" which is the alternative hypothesis. Then we convert the results to a table as before.

```
prop_test(x = 16395, n = 21483, p = 0.5, alternative = "two.sided") %>%
 flextable() %>% theme_box() %>%
 set_caption(caption = "Two-tailed proportion test for homogeneity of white and other proportion in the general social survey data")
```

Table 2.18. *Two-Tailed Proportion test for Homogeneity of White and Other Proportions in the General Social Survey Data*

n	Statistic	df	p	p.signif
21,483	5,950.083	1	0	****

The Table 2.17 contains the estimated sample statistic= = 5950.083 and the p-value which equals zero.

The p_value is the probability of our sample results (White proportion in the general social survey data) under the null hypothesis (where the white proportion = 0.5 or 50%). Since this probability is zero, we reject the null hypothesis and conclude that the proportion of whites in the general social survey data is significantly different from (larger than) 0.5. This means that the two races are not equally distributed in the population from which this sample was taken.

2.5.2.2. Test for Equality of the Race Column to a Certain Proportion

We know from the United States census that 71% of the population in the United States are White. So we may wish to test the hypothesis that the proportion of whites in the general social survey data is different from the general US census.

- **Null Hypothesis:** The population (actual) proportion of White in the general social survey data = 71% or 0.71. The observed proportion of 0.763 or 76.3% was due to sampling error. This means also that the proportion of other race = 1–0.71 = 0.29.
- **Alternative Hypothesis:** The population (actual) proportion of White in the general social survey data is different from 71% or 0.71. This is a two-tailed test.

We use the prop_test function with the same arguments as above except that p = 0.71 which is the new null hypothesis proportion.

```
prop_test(x = 16395, n = 21483, p = 0.71, alternative = "two.sided") %>%
 flextable() %>% theme_box() %>%
 set_caption(caption = "Two-tailed proportion test for equality of white and
other proportion to certain proportions")
```

Table 2.19. *Two-Tailed Proportion Test for Equality of White and other Proportions to Certain Proportions*

n	Statistic	df	p	p.signif
21,483	294.6143	1	0.0000000000000000000000 0000000000000000000000000 000000000000000000000491	****

The Table 2.18 contains the estimated sample statistic= 294.6143 and the p-value which is very low and nearly equals zero.

The p_value is the probability of our sample results (White proportion in the general social survey data) under the null hypothesis (where the white proportion = 0.71 or 71%). Since this probability is very low, we reject the null hypothesis and conclude that the proportion of White in the population, from which this sample was taken, is significantly different from (larger than) 0.71. This means also that the proportion of other race is significantly lower than 0.29 or 29%.

2.5.3. Chi-Square Test

The Chi-square test is used for categorical variables (with many categories) to either evaluate the homogeneity of proportions or to test that the proportions are equal to certain given values when the sample size is large.

2.5.3.1. Test for Homogeneity in the Race Column of the General Social Survey Data

We have seen above that the race column has 3 categories. White is the most frequent race with a count of 16395, followed by Black with a count of 3129, and other (races) with a count of 1959.

To test the homogeneity of races within this column, we do these steps:

1. We create a vector called "races2" that contains the counts for each race.
2. We use the chisq_test function with the arguments:
    1. x = races which is the sample counts.
    2. p = c(1/3,1/3,1/3) which are the probabilities or proportions under the null hypothesis. If the 3 races are homogeneous in the general social survey data, the expected proportion = 1/3 = 0.33 or 33%. Then we convert the results to a table as before.

```
races2<-c(white = 16395, black = 3129, other = 1959)
races2
## white black other
## 16395 3129 1959
chisq_test(x= races2, p = c(1/3,1/3,1/3)) %>% flextable() %>%
 theme_box() %>%
 set_caption(caption = "Chi-square test for homogeneity of races in the
general social survey data")
```

Table 2.20. Chi-Square Test for Homogeneity of Races in the General Social Survey Data

n	**Statistic**	**p**	**df**	**Method**	**p.signif**
3	17,956.23	0	2	Chi-square test	****

The Table 2.19 contains the p-value which equals zero, the sample statistic = 17956.23, and n = 3 because we have 3 categories.

The p_value is the probability of our sample results (race proportions in the general social survey data) under the null hypothesis (where all 3 proportions = 0.33 or 33%). Since this probability equals zero, we reject the null hypothesis and conclude that the proportion of some races is different from other races in the general social survey data.

A subsequent test is to perform pairwise comparisons between races to find out which race pair is different in its components. In other words, which race proportion is significantly different from 0.5 relative to any other race.

We use the pairwise_chisq_gof_test function to perform a pairwise comparison with the arguments:

- x = races2 which is the named vector with counts.
- p.adjust.method = "fdr" which is the method for adjusting the p-value in multiple comparisons. The "fdr" is for the false discovery rate.

```
pairwise_chisq_gof_test(x = races2,
p.adjust.method = "fdr") %>%
 flextable() %>% theme_box() %>%
 set_caption(caption = "Pairwise comparisons for races in the general social survey data")
```

Table 2.21. *Pairwise Comparisons for Races in the General Social Survey Data*

n	Group1	Group2	Statistic	p	df	p.adj	p.adj.signif
2	white	black	9,013.8679	0.000000000000000000000000000000000000000000000000000000000000000	1	0.00000000000000000000000000000000000000000000000000000000000000	****

n	Group1	Group2	Statistic	p	df	p.adj	p.adj.signif
2	white	other	11,354.3694	0.000000000000000 0000000000000000 0000000000000000 000000000000000	1	0.00000000000000 000000000000000 000000000000000 000000000000000 0000	****
2	black	other	269.0448	0.000000000000000 0000000000000000 0000000000000000 000000000000183	1	0.00000000000000 000000000000000 000000000000000 000000000000000 0183	****

We have 3 pairwise comparisons:

1. Comparing white with a count of 16395 to black with a count of 3129. The adjusted p-value is very low, so we reject the null hypothesis and conclude that white proportion is significantly different from (larger than) the black proportion in this sample.
2. Comparing whites with a count of 16395 to other with a count of 1959. The adjusted p-value is very low, so we reject the null hypothesis and conclude that white proportion is significantly different from (larger than) the other race proportion in this sample.
3. Comparing black with a count of 3129 to other with a count of 1959. The adjusted p-value is very low, so we reject the null hypothesis and conclude that the black proportion is significantly different from (larger than) other race proportion in this sample.

2.5.3.2. Test for Homogeneity in the Cut Column of Diamonds Data

We have seen above that the cut column has 5 categories. Ideal is the most frequent cut with a count of 21551, and fair is the least frequent cut with a count of 1610. To test the homogeneity of different cuts within this column, we do these steps:

1. We create a vector called "cuts" that contains the counts for each cut.
2. We use the chisq_test function with the arguments:

i. x = cuts which is the sample counts.

ii. p = c(1/5,1/5,1/5,1/5,1/5) which are the probabilities or proportions under the null hypothesis. If the 5 cuts are homogeneous in the data, the expected proportion = 1/5 = 0.2 or 20%. Then we convert the results to a table as before.

```
cuts<-c(ideal = 21551, premium = 13791, very_good = 12082,
    good = 4906, fair = 1610)
cuts
##    ideal  premium very_good    good   fair
##    21551    13791     12082    4906   1610
chisq_test(x= cuts, p = c(1/5,1/5,1/5,1/5,1/5)) %>% flextable() %>%
 theme_box() %>%
 set_caption(caption = "Chi-square test for homogeneity of cuts in the diamonds
data")
```

Table 2.22. *Chi-Square Test for Homogeneity of Cuts in the Diamonds Data*

n	Statistic	p	df	Method	p.signif
5	22,744.55	0	4	Chi-square test	****

The Table 2.21 contains the p-value which equals zero, the sample statistic = 22744.55, and n = 5 because we have 5 categories.

The p_value is the probability of our sample results (cut proportions in the diamonds data) under the null hypothesis (where all 5 proportions = 0.2 or 20%). Since this probability equals zero, we reject the null hypothesis and conclude that the proportion of some cuts is different from other cuts in the diamonds data.

A subsequent test is to perform pairwise comparisons between cuts to find out which cut pair is different in its components. In other words, which cut proportion is significantly different from 0.5 relative to any other cut.

We use the pairwise_chisq_gof_test function to perform a pairwise comparison with the arguments:

- x = cuts which is the named vector with counts.
- p.adjust.method = "fdr" which is the method for adjusting the p-value in multiple comparisons. The "fdr" is for the false discovery rate.

```
pairwise_chisq_gof_test(x = cuts,
p.adjust.method = "fdr") %>%
 flextable() %>% theme_box() %>%
 set_caption(caption = "Pairwise comparisons for cuts in the diamonds data")
```

Table 2.23. *Pairwise Comparisons for Cuts in the Diamonds Data*

n	group1	group2	statistic	p	df	p.adj	p.adj. signif
2	ideal	premium	1,703.8538	0.000000000000000 0000000000000	1	0.00000000000000 00000000000000	****
2	ideal	very_good	2,665.8925	0.00000000000000 00000000000000	1	0.0000000000000000 000000000000	****
2	ideal	good	10,471.9365	0.000000000000000 0000000000000	1	0.000000000000000 0000000000000	****
2	ideal	fair	17,168.6663	0.0000000000000000 000000000000	1	0.000000000000000 0000000000000	****
2	premium	very_good	112.8853	0.0000000000000000 000000000229	1	0.0000000000000000 000000000229	****
2	premium	good	4,222.2402	0.0000000000000000 000000000000	1	0.0000000000000000 000000000000	****
2	premium	fair	9,634.2290	0.00000000000000000 00000000000	1	0.0000000000000000 000000000000	****
2	very_ good	good	3,031.2559	0.00000000000000000 00000000000	1	0.00000000000000000 00000000000	****
2	very_ good	fair	8,009.2597	0.000000000000000 0000000000000	1	0.00000000000000000 00000000000	****
2	good	fair	1,667.2216	0.0000000000000000 00000000000	1	0.00000000000000000 00000000000	****

We have 10 pairwise comparisons:

1. Comparing ideal with a count of 21551 to premium with a count of 13791. The adjusted p-value is very low, so we reject the null hypothesis and conclude that the ideal proportion is significantly different from (larger than) the premium proportion in the population from which this sample was taken.
2. Comparing ideal with a count of 21551 to very good with a count of 12082. The adjusted p-value is very low, so we reject the null hypothesis and conclude that the ideal proportion is significantly different from (larger than) the very good proportion in the population from which this sample was taken.
3. Comparing ideal with a count of 21551 to good with a count of 4906. The adjusted p-value is very low, so we reject the null hypothesis and conclude that the ideal proportion is significantly different from (larger than) the good proportion in the population from which this sample was taken.

4. The ideal proportion is significantly larger than the fair proportion.
5. The premium proportion is significantly larger than very good, good, and fair proportions.
6. The very good proportion is significantly larger than good and fair proportions.
7. The good proportion is significantly larger than the fair proportion.

2.5.3.3. Goodness-of-Fit Test

For the goodness-of-fit test, we must have another vector of probabilities or proportions that sum to 1. So, we do these steps:

1. We create another vector called "cuts_prob" that contains the probability for each cut. We assume that the expected probability of ideal cut is 0.3 or 30%, the expected probability of premium is 0.2 or 20%, the expected probability of very good is 0.2 or 20%, the expected probability of good is 0.15 or 15%, and the expected probability of fair is 0.15 or 15%. Note that 0.3+0.2+0.2+0.15+0.15 = 1.
2. We use the chisq_test function with the arguments:

i. x = cuts which is the sample counts.

ii. p = cuts_prob which are the probabilities or proportions under the null hypothesis that we want to test. Then we convert the results to a table as before.

```
cuts_prob<-c(ideal= 0.3, premium = 0.2, very_good = 0.2,
        good = 0.15, fair = 0.15)
cuts_prob
##    ideal  premium very_good   good   fair
##    0.30    0.20    0.20    0.15    0.15
chisq_test(x = cuts,
p = cuts_prob) %>%
 flextable() %>% theme_box() %>%
 set_caption(caption = "Chi-square goodness-of-fit test for cuts in the diamonds data")
```

Table 2.24. *Chi-Square Goodness-of-Fit Test for Cuts in the Diamonds Data*

n	Statistic	p	df	Method	p.signif
5	9,217.649	0	4	Chi-square test	****

The Table 2.23 contains the p-value which equals zero.

The p_value is the probability of our sample results (cut proportions in diamonds data) under the null hypothesis (where the proportions are stored in the cuts_prob vector). Since this probability equals zero, we reject the null hypothesis and conclude that the proportion of some cuts is different from the expected probabilities in the cuts_prob vector.

A subsequent test is to perform pairwise comparisons between each cut and its expected probability to find out which cut is different from its expected probability.

We use the pairwise_chisq_test_against_p function to perform a pairwise comparison with the arguments:

- x = cuts which is the named vector with counts.
- p = cuts_prob which is the vector holding the expected probabilities.
- p.adjust.method = "fdr" which is the method for adjusting the p-value in multiple comparisons. The "fdr" is for the false discovery rate.

```
pairwise_chisq_test_against_p(x = cuts, p = cuts_prob,
p.adjust.method = "fdr") %>%
 flextable() %>% theme_box() %>%
  set_caption(caption = "Pairwise comparisons for cuts against expected
probabilities")
```

Table 2.25. *Pairwise Comparisons for Cuts Against Expected Probabilities*

Group	Observed	Expected	n	Statistic	p	df	p.adj	**p.adj. signif**
ideal	21,551	16,182	2	2,544.817	0.000000e+00	1	0.00000e+00	****
premium	13,791	10,788	2	1,044.912	3.110000e-229	1	3.89000e-229	****
very_good	12,082	10,788	2	194.016	4.220000e-44	1	4.22000e-44	****
good	4,906	8,091	2	1,475.019	1.037538e-322	1	1.72923e-322	****
fair	1,610	8,091	2	6,107.492	0.000000e+00	1	0.00000e+00	****

We have 5 pairwise comparisons:

1. Comparing the ideal with a count of 21551 and a proportion of 21551/53940= 0.4 to its expected probability of 0.3, where 53940 is the number of rows or diamonds in our data. The expected count will be 0.3 X 53940 = 16182 and the adjusted p-value equals zero,

so we reject the null hypothesis and conclude that ideal proportion is significantly different from (larger than) the expected probability of 0.3.

2. Comparing the premium with a count of 13791 and a proportion of 13791/53940= 0.256 to its expected probability of 0.2. The expected count will be 0.2 X 53940 = 10788 and the adjusted p-value is very low, so we reject the null hypothesis and conclude that the premium proportion is significantly different from (larger than) the expected probability of 0.2.
3. Comparing very good with a count of 12082 and a proportion of 12082/53940= 0.224 to its expected probability of 0.2. The expected count will be 0.2 X 53940 = 10788 and the adjusted p-value is very low, so we reject the null hypothesis and conclude that the very good proportion is significantly different from (larger than) the expected probability of 0.2.
4. Comparing good with a count of 4906 and a proportion of 4906/53940= 0.091 to its expected probability of 0.15. The expected count will be 0.15 X 53940 = 8091 and the adjusted p-value is very low, so we reject the null hypothesis and conclude that the good proportion is significantly different from (smaller than) the expected probability of 0.15.
5. Comparing fair with a count of 1610 and a proportion of 1610/53940= 0.0298 to its expected probability of 0.15. The expected count will be 0.15 X 53940 = 8091 and the adjusted p-value is very low, so we reject the null hypothesis and conclude that the fair proportion is significantly different from (smaller than) the expected probability of 0.15.

CHAPTER 3

BIVARIATE ANALYSIS FOR CONTINUOUS-CONTINUOUS DATA

Contents

3.1. DATA USED IN THIS CHAPTER

3.1.1. Body Measurements of Physically Active Individuals Data

The Body measurements of physically active individuals data is stored under the name "bdims." The data is part of the openintro package and its source is Heinz G, Peterson LJ, Johnson RW, and Kerk CJ. 2003. Exploring Relationships in Body Dimensions. Journal of Statistics Education 11(2). To load this data into our R session, we will load the openintro package using the library function. Then, we will load the bdims data using the data function. We will also load the tidyverse package because it contains many packages for data analysis like dplyr, tidyr, ggplot2, etc.

```
library(openintro)
library(tidyverse)
data("bdims")
```

Then, to see the data structure, we will use the glimpse function from the dplyr package.

```
glimpse(bdims)
## Rows: 507
## Columns: 25
## $ bia_di <dbl> 42.9, 43.7, 40.1, 44.3, 42.5, 43.3, 43.5, 44.4, 43.5, 42.0, 40.…
## $ bii_di <dbl> 26.0, 28.5, 28.2, 29.9, 29.9, 27.0, 30.0, 29.8, 26.5, 28.0, 29.…
## $ bit_di <dbl> 31.5, 33.5, 33.3, 34.0, 34.0, 31.5, 34.0, 33.2, 32.1, 34.0, 33.…
## $ che_de <dbl> 17.7, 16.9, 20.9, 18.4, 21.5, 19.6, 21.9, 21.8, 15.5, 22.5, 20.…
## $ che_di <dbl> 28.0, 30.8, 31.7, 28.2, 29.4, 31.3, 31.7, 28.8, 27.5, 28.0, 30.…
## $ elb_di <dbl> 13.1, 14.0, 13.9, 13.9, 15.2, 14.0, 16.1, 15.1, 14.1, 15.6, 13.…
## $ wri_di <dbl> 10.4, 11.8, 10.9, 11.2, 11.6, 11.5, 12.5, 11.9, 11.2, 12.0, 10.…
## $ kne_di <dbl> 18.8, 20.6, 19.7, 20.9, 20.7, 18.8, 20.8, 21.0, 18.9, 21.1, 19.…
## $ ank_di <dbl> 14.1, 15.1, 14.1, 15.0, 14.9, 13.9, 15.6, 14.6, 13.2, 15.0, 14.…
## $ sho_gi <dbl> 106.2, 110.5, 115.1, 104.5, 107.5, 119.8, 123.5, 120.4, 111.0, …
## $ che_gi <dbl> 89.5, 97.0, 97.5, 97.0, 97.5, 99.9, 106.9, 102.5, 91.0, 93.5, 9…
## $ wai_gi <dbl> 71.5, 79.0, 83.2, 77.8, 80.0, 82.5, 82.0, 76.8, 68.5, 77.5, 81.…
## $ nav_gi <dbl> 74.5, 86.5, 82.9, 78.8, 82.5, 80.1, 84.0, 80.5, 69.0, 81.5, 81.…
## $ hip_gi <dbl> 93.5, 94.8, 95.0, 94.0, 98.5, 95.3, 101.0, 98.0, 89.5, 99.8, 98…
## $ thi_gi <dbl> 51.5, 51.5, 57.3, 53.0, 55.4, 57.5, 60.9, 56.0, 50.0, 59.8, 60.…
## $ bic_gi <dbl> 32.5, 34.4, 33.4, 31.0, 32.0, 33.0, 42.4, 34.1, 33.0, 36.5, 34.…
## $ for_gi <dbl> 26.0, 28.0, 28.8, 26.2, 28.4, 28.0, 32.3, 28.0, 26.0, 29.2, 27.…
## $ kne_gi <dbl> 34.5, 36.5, 37.0, 37.0, 37.7, 36.6, 40.1, 39.2, 35.5, 38.3, 38.…
## $ cal_gi <dbl> 36.5, 37.5, 37.3, 34.8, 38.6, 36.1, 40.3, 36.7, 35.0, 38.6, 40.…
## $ ank_gi <dbl> 23.5, 24.5, 21.9, 23.0, 24.4, 23.5, 23.6, 22.5, 22.0, 22.2, 23.…
## $ wri_gi <dbl> 16.5, 17.0, 16.9, 16.6, 18.0, 16.9, 18.8, 18.0, 16.5, 16.9, 16.…
```

```
## $ age  <int> 21, 23, 28, 23, 22, 21, 26, 27, 23, 21, 23, 22, 20, 26, 23, 22,…
## $ wgt  <dbl> 65.6, 71.8, 80.7, 72.6, 78.8, 74.8, 86.4, 78.4, 62.0, 81.6, 76.…
## $ hgt  <dbl> 174.0, 175.3, 193.5, 186.5, 187.2, 181.5, 184.0, 184.5, 175.0, …
## $ sex  <int> 1, 1, 1, 1, 1, 1, 1, 1, 1, 1, 1, 1, 1, 1, 1, 1, 1, 1, 1, 1, 1, …
```

We see that the bdims data contains 507 rows and 25 columns:

1. bia_di: respondent's biacromial diameter in centimeters. It is a double or numeric column with decimals.
2. bii_di: respondent's biliac diameter (pelvic breadth) in centimeters. It is a double or numeric column with decimals.
3. bit_di: respondent's bitrochanteric diameter in centimeters. It is a double or numeric column with decimals.
4. che_de: respondent's chest depth in centimeters, measured between spine and sternum at nipple level, mid-expiration. It is a numeric column with decimals.
5. che_di: respondent's chest diameter in centimeters, measured at nipple level, mid-expiration. It is a numeric column.
6. elb_di: respondent's elbow diameter in centimeters, measured as the sum of two elbows. It is a numeric column.
7. wri_di: respondent's wrist diameter in centimeters, measured as the sum of two wrists. It is a numeric column.
8. kne_di: respondent's knee diameter in centimeters, measured as the sum of two knees. It is a numeric column.
9. ank_di: respondent's ankle diameter in centimeters, measured as the sum of two ankles. It is a numeric column.
10. sho_gi: respondent's shoulder girth in centimeters, measured over deltoid muscles. It is a numeric column.
11. che_gi: respondent's chest girth in centimeters, measured at nipple line in males and just above breast tissue in females, mid-expiration. It is a numeric column.
12. wai_gi: respondent's waist girth in centimeters, measured at the narrowest part of the torso below the rib cage as the average of contracted and relaxed position. It is a numeric column.
13. nav_gi: respondent's navel (abdominal) girth in centimeters, measured at the umbilicus and iliac crest using the iliac crest as a landmark. It is a numeric column.
14. hip_gi: respondent's hip girth in centimeters, measured at a level of bitrochanteric diameter. It is a numeric column.

15. thi_gi: respondent's thigh girth in centimeters, measured below the gluteal fold as the average of right and left girths. It is a numeric column.
16. bic_gi: respondent's bicep girth in centimeters, measured when flexed as the average of right and left girths. It is a numeric column.
17. for_gi: respondent's forearm girth in centimeters, measured when extended, palm up as the average of right and left girths. It is a numeric column.
18. kne_gi: respondent's knee diameter in centimeters, measured as the sum of two knees. It is a numeric column.
19. cal_gi: respondent's calf maximum girth in centimeters, measured as the average of right and left girths. It is a numeric column.
20. ank_gi: respondent's ankle minimum girth in centimeters, measured as the average of right and left girths. It is a numeric column.
21. wri_gi: respondent's wrist minimum girth in centimeters, measured as the average of right and left girths. It is a numeric column.
22. age: respondent's age in years. It is an integer column.
23. wgt: respondent's weight in kilograms. It is a numeric column.
24. hgt: respondent's height in centimeters. It is a numeric column.
25. sex: It is an integer column with 1 if the respondent is male, and 0 if female.

3.1.2. Nutrition in Fast Food

The nutrition amounts in different fast food items are stored in the "fastfood" data frame which is part of the openintro package. To load this data into our R session, we will use the data function followed by the glimpse function to see the data structure.

```
data("fastfood")
glimpse(fastfood)
## Rows: 515
## Columns: 17
## $ restaurant <chr> "Mcdonalds," "Mcdonalds," "Mcdonalds," "Mcdonalds," "Mcdon…
## $ item    <chr> "Artisan Grilled Chicken Sandwich," "Single Bacon Smokehou…
## $ calories  <dbl> 380, 840, 1130, 750, 920, 540, 300, 510, 430, 770, 380, 62…
## $ cal_fat   <dbl> 60, 410, 600, 280, 410, 250, 100, 210, 190, 400, 170, 300,…
## $ total_fat  <dbl> 7, 45, 67, 31, 45, 28, 12, 24, 21, 45, 18, 34, 20, 34, 8, …
## $ sat_fat   <dbl> 2.0, 17.0, 27.0, 10.0, 12.0, 10.0, 5.0, 4.0, 11.0, 21.0, 4…
## $ trans_fat  <dbl> 0.0, 1.5, 3.0, 0.5, 0.5, 1.0, 0.5, 0.0, 1.0, 2.5, 0.0, 1.5…
## $ cholesterol <dbl> 95, 130, 220, 155, 120, 80, 40, 65, 85, 175, 40, 95, 125, …
```

```
## $ sodium     <dbl> 1110, 1580, 1920, 1940, 1980, 950, 680, 1040, 1040, 1290, …
## $ total_carb <dbl> 44, 62, 63, 62, 81, 46, 33, 49, 35, 42, 38, 48, 48, 67, 31…
## $ fiber      <dbl> 3, 2, 3, 2, 4, 3, 2, 3, 2, 3, 2, 3, 3, 5, 2, 2, 3, 3, 5, 2…
## $ sugar      <dbl> 11, 18, 18, 18, 18, 9, 7, 6, 7, 10, 5, 11, 11, 11, 6, 3, 1…
## $ protein     <dbl> 37, 46, 70, 55, 46, 25, 15, 25, 25, 51, 15, 32, 42, 33, 13…
## $ vit_a      <dbl> 4, 6, 10, 6, 6, 10, 10, 0, 20, 20, 2, 10, 10, 10, 2, 4, 6,…
## $ vit_c      <dbl> 20, 20, 20, 25, 20, 2, 2, 4, 4, 6, 0, 10, 20, 15, 2, 6, 15…
## $ calcium     <dbl> 20, 20, 50, 20, 20, 15, 10, 2, 15, 20, 15, 35, 35, 35, 4, …
## $ salad      <chr> "Other," "Other," "Other," "Other," "Other," "Other," "Oth…
```

The data contains 515 rows and 17 columns:

1. restaurant: Name of restaurant. It is a character column.
2. item: Name of the item or fast food. It is a character column.
3. calories: Number of calories. It is a numeric column.
4. cal_fat: Calories from fat. It is a numeric column.
5. total_fat: the total fat. It is a numeric column.
6. sat_fat: the saturated fat. It is a numeric column.
7. trans_fat: the trans fat. It is a numeric column.
8. cholesterol: the cholesterol. It is a numeric column.
9. sodium: the sodium present. It is a numeric column.
10. total_carb: the total carbohydrates. It is a numeric column.
11. fiber: the fiber present. It is a numeric column.
12. sugar: the sugar present. It is a numeric column.
13. protein: the protein present. It is a numeric column.
14. vit_a: the Vitamin A present. It is a numeric column.
15. vit_c: the Vitamin C present. It is a numeric column.
16. calcium: the Calcium present. It is a numeric column.
17. salad: with salad or not. It is a character column.

3.2. SUMMARY STATISTICS

3.2.1. The Correlation Coefficient

The correlation coefficient determines the relationship between 2 continuous variables. The correlation coefficient is a dimensionless quantity and ranges between -1 and 1. Generally, we have one of 3 conditions for the value of the correlation coefficient:

1. If the correlation is greater than 0, then the 2 variables are positively

correlated and if one of them increases, the other variable tends to increase, and vice versa.

2. If the correlation is less than 0, then the 2 variables are negatively correlated and if one of them increases, the other variable tends to decrease, and vice versa.
3. If the correlation is nearly 0, then the 2 variables are uncorrelated, and if one of them increases or decreases, the other variable remains the same, and vice versa.

Generally, if the absolute value of the correlation coefficient is greater than 0.5, then this correlation is a relatively strong one. If the absolute value of the correlation coefficient is smaller than 0.5, then this correlation is a relatively weak one.

3.2.2. Types of Correlation Coefficients

There are 3 types of correlation coefficients:

1. Pearson correlation coefficient: which is a parametric correlation coefficient that measures the association between the two variables. The Pearson correlation requires:
   i. The relation between the 2 variables is linear. This can be checked using a scatter plot showing this linear relation.
   ii. The 2 variables follow a normal distribution. This can be checked using the QQ plot and Shapiro-Wilk test as described in Chapter 1.
2. Spearman correlation coefficient: is a non-parametric correlation coefficient and can be used for non-normally distributed variables. In addition, Spearman correlation can be used for non-linear relations. The Spearman correlation computes the correlation between the ranks of one variable to the ranks of the other variable.
3. Kendall correlation coefficient: is a non-parametric correlation coefficient and can be used for non-normally distributed variables. Also, the Kendall correlation can be used for non-linear relations. The Kendall correlation method measures the correspondence between the ranking of the 2 variables.

3.2.3. Correlation Between Ankle Diameter (ank_di) and Bitrochanteric Diameter (bit_di) in Bdims Data

3.2.3.1. Plot a Scatter Plot

Using the following functions:

1. The ggplot function applied on the bdims data with the arguments, aes(x = ank_di, y = bit_di), to plot the ankle diameter on the x-axis and bitrochanteric diameter on the y-axis.
2. The geom_point function to draw a scatter plot.
3. The geom_smooth function with the argument, method = "lm," to add the linear fit line to the scatter plot.
4. The labs, theme_classic, and theme functions as described in previous chapters.

```
bdims %>% ggplot(aes(x = ank_di, y = bit_di))+ geom_point()+
 geom_smooth(method = "lm")+
 labs(title = "Scatter plot of bitrochanteric diameter vs. ankle diameter in bdims data \n with linear fit line," x = "Ankle diameter,"
 y = "Bitrochanteric diameter")+
 theme_classic()+
 theme(plot.title = element_text(hjust = 0.5))
```

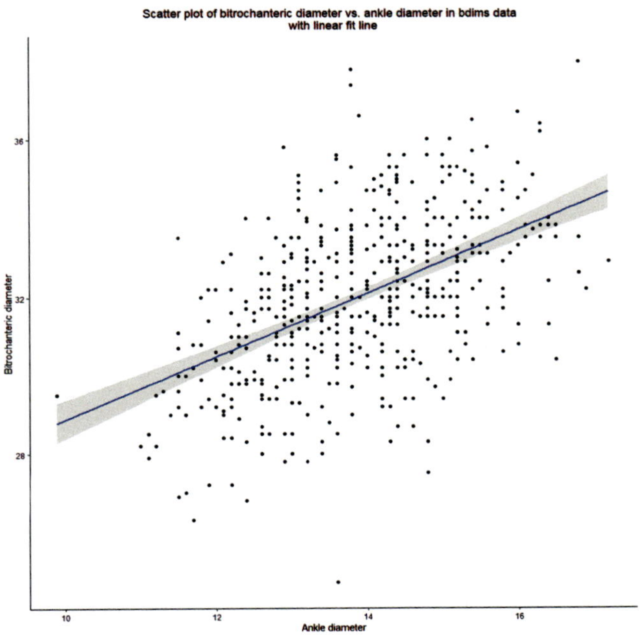

We see that all points are scattered around the linear fit line so the relation is linear.

3.2.3.2. Plot a QQ Plot

We plot a QQ plot for the ankle diameter and the bitrochanteric diameter, as described in Chapter 1, using the ggqqplot function from the ggpubr package.

```
library(ggpubr)
ggqqplot(data = bdims, x = "ank_di,"
title = "QQ plot of ankle diameter from bdims data,"
xlab = "Theoretical percentiles," ylab = "Sample percentiles")+
 theme(plot.title = element_text(hjust = 0.5))
```

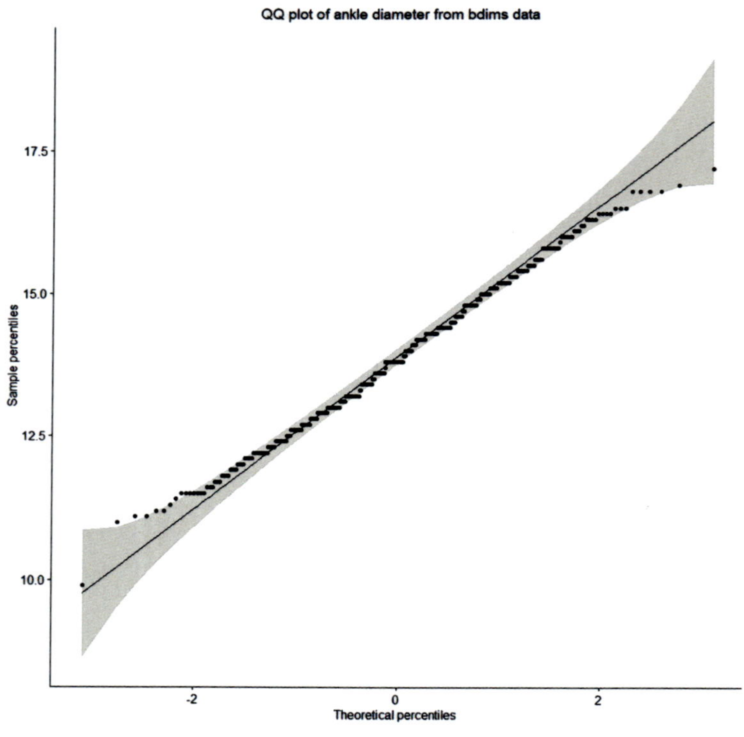

We see that nearly all data points fall along this reference line or within the confidence band, so we can assume the normality of ankle diameters.

```
ggqqplot(data = bdims, x = "bit_di,"
title = "QQ plot of bitrochanteric diameter from bdims data,"
xlab = "Theoretical percentiles," ylab = "Sample percentiles")+
 theme(plot.title = element_text(hjust = 0.5))
```

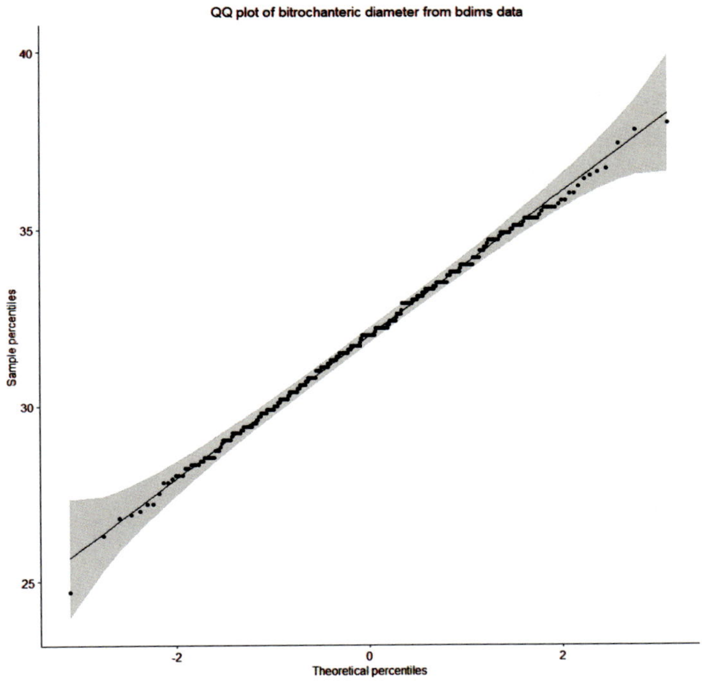

Similarly, We see that all data points fall along this reference line or within the confidence band, so we can assume the normality of bitrochanteric diameters.

3.2.3.3. Shapiro-Wilk Test

We do a Shapiro-Wilk test for the ankle diameter and the bitrochanteric diameter, as described in Chapter 1, using the shapiro_test function from the rstatix package. We convert the results to a table using the flextable package functions.

```
library(rstatix)
library(flextable)
shapiro_test(data = bdims, ank_di) %>% flextable() %>% theme_
box() %>%
  set_caption(caption = "Shapiro-Wilk test results for ankle
diameter in the body measurements data")
```

Table 3.1. *Shapiro-Wilk Test Results for Ankle Diameter in the Body Measurements Data*

Variable	Statistic	p
ank_di	0.9949495	0.09594954

The Table 3.1 contains the sample statistic = 0.995 which corresponds to our sample results and the p-value which is larger than the cut-off point of 0.05.

The p_value is insignificant, so we fail to reject the null hypothesis and conclude that the ankle diameter in the body measurements data is normally distributed.

```
shapiro_test(data = bdims, bit_di) %>% flextable() %>% theme_
box() %>%
   set_caption(caption = "Shapiro-Wilk test results for
bitrochanteric diameter in the body measurements data")
```

Table 3.2. *Shapiro-Wilk Test Results for Bitrochanteric Diameter in the Body Measurements Data*

Variable	Statistic	p
bit_di	0.9979092	0.7928441

The Table 3.2 contains the sample statistic = 0.998 which corresponds to our sample results and the p-value which is larger than the cut-off point of 0.05.

The p_value is insignificant, so we fail to reject the null hypothesis and conclude that the bitrochanteric diameter in the body measurements data is normally distributed.

Because the ankle and bitrochanteric diameters show a linear relation and both are normally distributed, we can use the Pearson correlation method to examine the relation between the ankle and bitrochanteric diameter.

3.2.3.4. Pearson Correlation

We get the Pearson correlation coefficient between the ankle diameter and the bitrochanteric diameter, we use the cor_test function with the following arguments:

- ank_di, bit_di which are the 2 columns we want to get the correlation between them.
- method = "pearson" which is the correlation method.
- alternative = "two.sided" which is the alternative hypothesis for testing the significance of the correlation. The null hypothesis is that

the correlation equals zero or no correlation. The "greater" alternative hypothesis corresponds to positive correlation (correlation > 0) and the "less" alternative hypothesis corresponds to negative correlation (correlation < 0). We convert the result to a table as before.

```
bdims %>% cor_test(ank_di, bit_di, method = "pearson,"
         alternative = "two.sided") %>% flextable() %>%
 theme_box() %>%
 set_caption(caption = "Pearson correlation test results for the
correlation between ankle and bitrochanteric diameter in the
body measurements data")
```

Table 3.3. *Pearson Correlation Test Results for the Correlation Between Ankle and Bitrochanteric Diameter in the Body Measurements Data*

var1	var2	cor	statistic	p	conf.low	conf.high	method
ank_di	bit_di	0.5	12.8161	0.000000 00000000 00000000 00000000 00938	0.4267328	0.5583983	Pearson

We see that:

1. The pearson correlation = 0.5.
2. The sample statistic = 12.8161 which corresponds to our sample results and the p-value which is very low and nearly equals zero. The p_value is significant, so we reject the null hypothesis and conclude that the correlation between the ankle and bitrochanteric diameter in the body measurements data is different from zero. In other words, they are positively associated so as the ankle diameter increases, the bitrochanteric diameter increases on average.
3. The 95% confidence interval = 0.43–0.56. This means that we are 95% confident that the underlying population from which this sample was taken can have a correlation as low as 0.43 and as high as 0.56.

3.2.4. Correlation Between Weight and Height in Bdims Data

3.2.4.1. Plot a Scatter Plot

Using the same previous functions.

```
bdims %>% ggplot(aes(x = wgt, y = hgt))+ geom_point()+
 geom_smooth(method = "lm")+
 labs(title = "Scatter plot of height vs. weight in bdims data with linear fit
line,"
```

```
    x = "Weight,"
    y = "Height")+
  theme_classic()+
  theme(plot.title = element_text(hjust = 0.5))
```

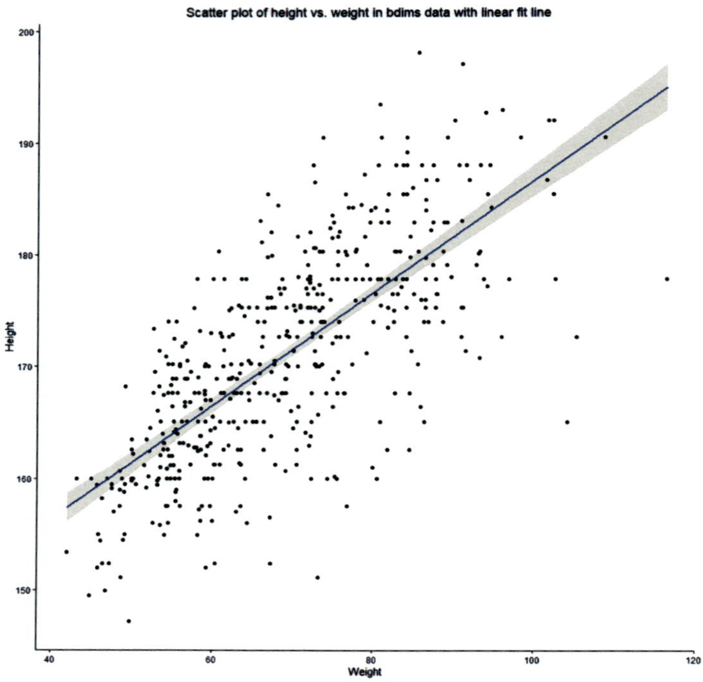

We see that all points are scattered around the linear fit line so the relation is linear.

3.2.4.2. Plot a QQ Plot

We plot a QQ plot for the weight and the height columns as described previously.

```
ggqqplot(data = bdims, x = "wgt,"
     title = "QQ plot of weight values from bdims data,"
     xlab = "Theoretical percentiles," ylab = "Sample percentiles")+
theme(plot.title = element_text(hjust = 0.5))
```

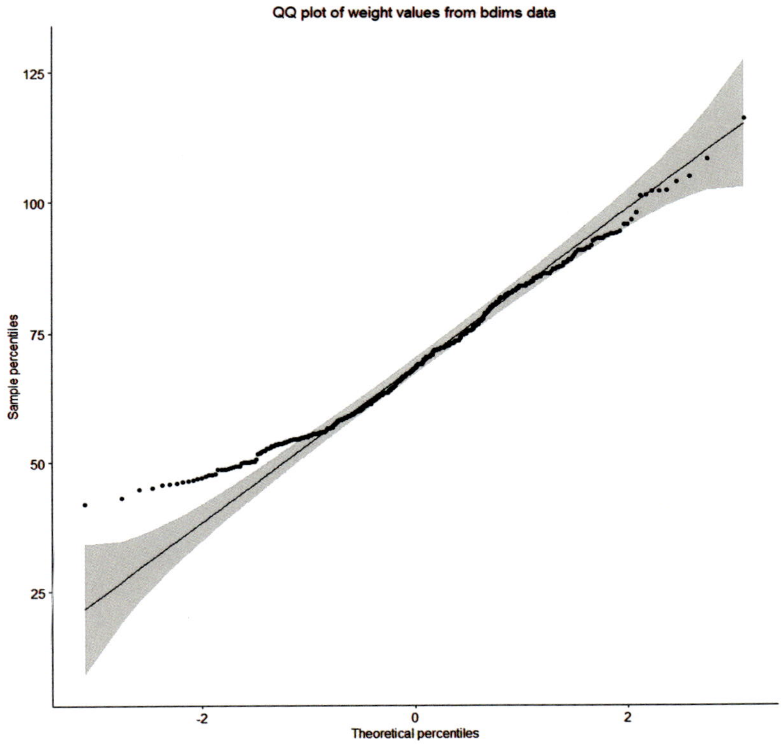

We see that many data points are outside the confidence band, so we can not assume the normality of the weight values.

```
ggqqplot(data = bdims, x = "hgt,"

    title = "QQ plot of height values from bdims data,"

    xlab = "Theoretical percentiles," ylab = "Sample percentiles")+

 theme(plot.title = element_text(hjust = 0.5))
```

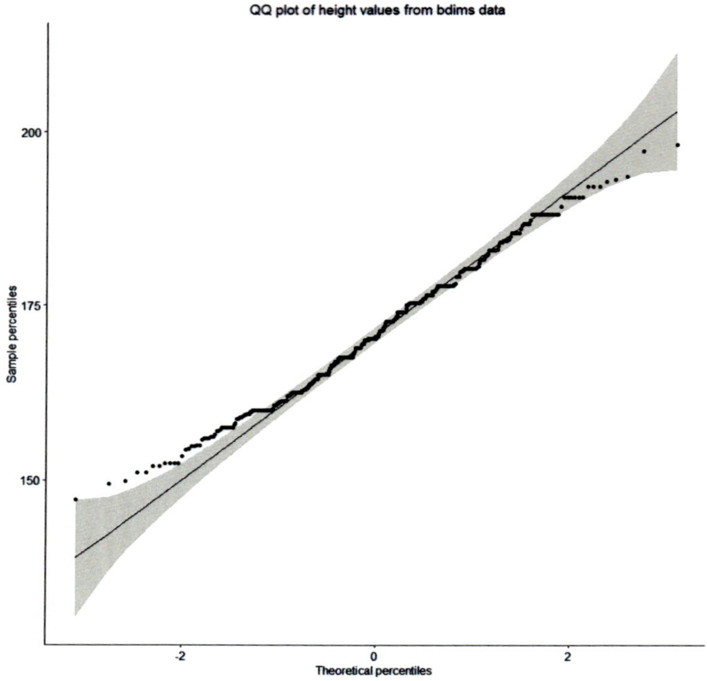

Similarly, we see that many data points are outside the confidence band, so we can not assume the normality of the height values.

3.2.4.3. Shapiro-Wilk Test

We do a Shapiro-Wilk test for the weight and the height values.

```
shapiro_test(data = bdims, wgt) %>% flextable() %>% theme_box() %>%
 set_caption(caption = "Shapiro-Wilk test results for the weight in the body measurements data")
```

Table 3.4. Shapiro-Wilk Test Results for the Weight in the Body Measurements Data

Variable	Statistic	p
wgt	0.9791889	0.00000123279

The Table 3.4 contains the sample statistic = 0.979 which corresponds to our sample results and the p-value which is smaller than the cut-off point of 0.05.

The p_value is significant, so we reject the null hypothesis and conclude that the weight values in the body measurements data are not normally distributed.

```
shapiro_test(data = bdims, hgt) %>% flextable() %>% theme_box() %>%
  set_caption(caption = "Shapiro-Wilk test results for height in the body measurements data")
```

Table 3.5. *Shapiro-Wilk Test Results for Height in the Body Measurements Data*

Variable	Statistic	p
hgt	0.9923302	0.01044543

The Table 3.5 contains the sample statistic = 0.992 which corresponds to our sample results and the p-value which is smaller than the cut-off point of 0.05.

The p_value is significant, so we reject the null hypothesis and conclude that the height in the body measurements data is not normally distributed.

Because the weight and height values are not normally distributed, we can use the Spearman or Kendall correlation method to examine the relation between these 2 columns.

3.2.4.4. Spearman Correlation

To get the Spearman correlation coefficient between the weight and the height, we use the cor_test function with the following arguments:

- wgt, hgt which are the 2 columns we want to get the correlation between them.
- method = "spearman" which is the correlation method.
- alternative = "two.sided" which is the alternative hypothesis for testing the significance of the correlation. The null hypothesis is that the correlation equals zero or no correlation.

```
bdims %>% cor_test(wgt, hgt, method = "spearman,"
        alternative = "two.sided") %>% flextable() %>%

 theme_box() %>%

 set_caption(caption = "Spearman correlation test results for the correlation between weight and height in the body measurements data")
```

Table 3.6. Spearman Correlation Test Results for the Correlation Between Weight and Height in the Body Measurements Data

var1	var2	cor	Statistic	p	Method
wgt	hgt	0.73	5,824,225	0.000000000000000000000000000000000000000000000000000000000000000000000000000000000000000000000000373	Spearman

We see that:

1. The Spearman correlation = 0.73.
2. The sample statistic = 5824225 which corresponds to our sample results and the p-value which is very low and nearly equals zero. The p_value is significant, so we reject the null hypothesis and conclude that the correlation between the weight and height in the body measurements data is different from zero. In other words, they are positively associated so as the weight increases, the height increases on average.

3.2.4.5. Kendall Correlation

To get the Kendall correlation coefficient between the weight and the height, we use the cor_test function with the following arguments:

- wgt, hgt which are the 2 columns we want to get the correlation between them.
- method = "kendall" which is the correlation method.
- alternative = "two.sided" which is the alternative hypothesis for testing the significance of the correlation. The null hypothesis is that the correlation equals zero or no correlation.

```
bdims %>% cor_test(wgt, hgt, method = "kendall,"
         alternative = "two.sided") %>% flextable() %>%

 theme_box() %>%

 set_caption(caption = "Kendall correlation test results for the correlation
between weight and height in the body measurements data")
```

Table 3.7. *Kendall Correlation Test Results for the Correlation Between Weight and Height in the Body Measurements Data*

var1	var2	cor	Statistic	p	Method
wgt	hgt	0.54	18.10245	0.0000 000000 000000 000000 000000 000000 000000 000000 000000 000000 000000 000000 00305	Kendall

We see that:

1. The Kendall correlation = 0.54.
2. The sample statistic = 18.10245 which corresponds to our sample results and the p-value is very low and nearly equals zero. The p_ value is significant, so we reject the null hypothesis and conclude that the Kendall correlation between the weight and height in the body measurements data is different from zero. In other words, they are positively associated so as the weight increases, the height increases on average.

3.2.5. Correlation Between Cholesterol and Calories in the Fast Food Data

3.2.5.1. Plot a Scatter Plot

Using the same previous functions.

```
fastfood %>% ggplot(aes(x = cholesterol, y = calories))+ geom_point()+
 geom_smooth(method = "lm")+
 labs(title = "Scatter plot of calories vs. cholesterol in fast food data with linear fit line,"

    x = "Cholesterol,"

    y = "Calories")+
```

```
theme_classic()+
theme(plot.title = element_text(hjust = 0.5))
```

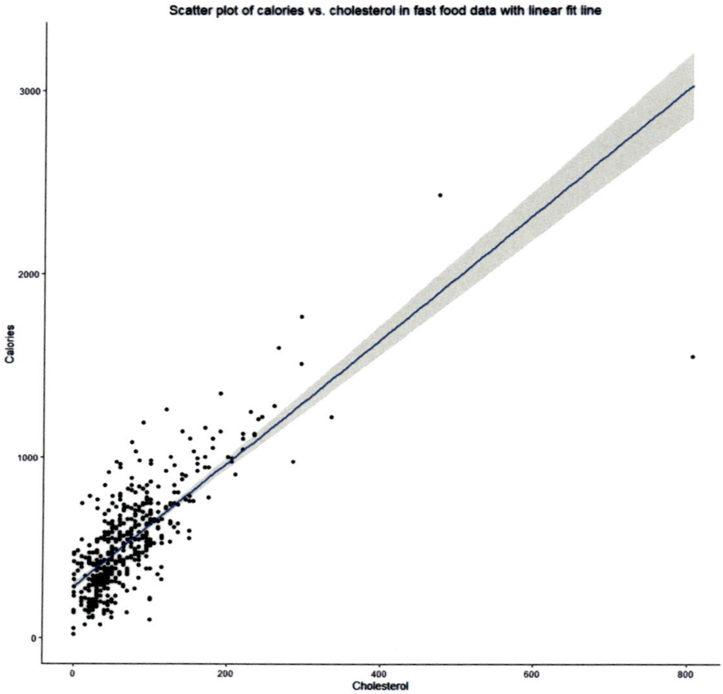

We see that all points are scattered around the linear fit line so the relation is linear.

3.2.5.2. Plot a QQ Plot

We plot a QQ plot for the cholesterol and for the calories columns as described previously.

```
ggqqplot(data = fastfood, x = "cholesterol,"

    title = "QQ plot of cholesterol values from fast food data,"

    xlab = "Theoretical percentiles," ylab = "Sample percentiles")+

theme(plot.title = element_text(hjust = 0.5))
```

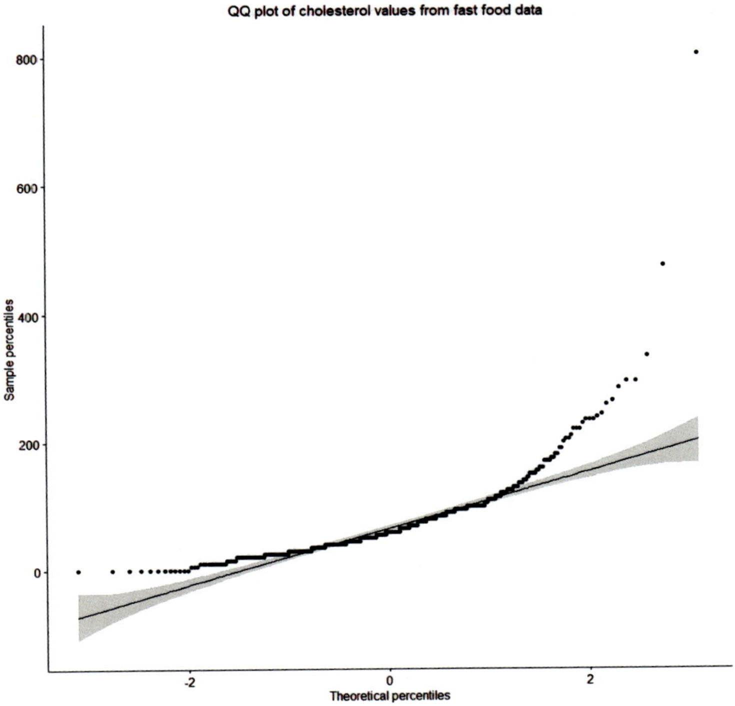

We see that many data points are outside the confidence band, so we can not assume the normality of the cholesterol values.

```
ggqqplot(data = fastfood, x = "calories,"

    title = "QQ plot of calories values from fast food data,"

    xlab = "Theoretical percentiles," ylab = "Sample percentiles")+

 theme(plot.title = element_text(hjust = 0.5))
```

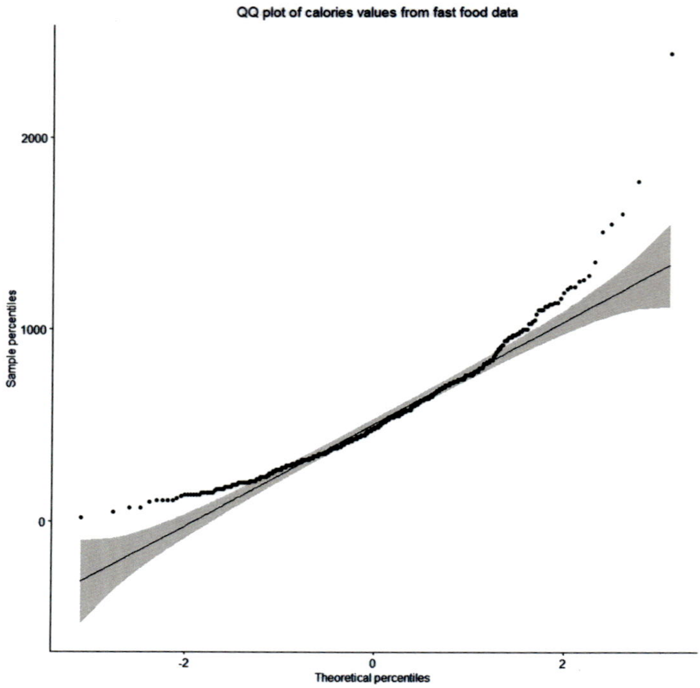

Similarly, we see that many data points are outside the confidence band, so we can not assume the normality of the calories values.

3.2.5.3. Shapiro-Wilk Test

We do a Shapiro-Wilk test for the cholesterol and the calories values.

```
shapiro_test(data = fastfood, cholesterol) %>% flextable() %>%

 theme_box() %>%

 set_caption(caption = "Shapiro-Wilk test results for the cholesterol in the fast food data")
```

Table 3.8. *Shapiro-Wilk Test Results for the Cholesterol in the Fast Food Data*

Variable	Statistic	p
cholesterol	0.7064736	0.000000000000000000000000005103688

The table contains the sample statistic = 0.706 which corresponds to our sample results and the p-value which is smaller than the cut-off point of 0.05.

The p_value is significant, so we reject the null hypothesis and conclude that the cholesterol values in the fast food data are not normally distributed.

```
shapiro_test(data = fastfood, calories) %>% flextable() %>% theme_box() %>%

 set_caption(caption = "Shapiro-Wilk test results for calories in the fast food
data")
```

Table 3.9. *Shapiro-Wilk Test Results for Calories in the Fast Food Data*

Variable	Statistic	p
calories	0.9214142	0.00000000000000009594792

The table contains the sample statistic = 0.921 which corresponds to our sample results and the p-value which is smaller than the cut-off point of 0.05.

The p_value is significant, so we reject the null hypothesis and conclude that the calories in the fast food data are not normally distributed.

Because the cholesterol and calories values are not normally distributed, we can use the Spearman or Kendall correlation method to examine the relation between these 2 columns.

3.2.5.4. Spearman Correlation

To get the Spearman correlation coefficient between the cholesterol and calories values, we use the same functions described above and convert the result to a table as before.

```
fastfood %>% cor_test(cholesterol,calories, method = "spearman,"
          alternative = "two.sided") %>% flextable() %>%

 theme_box() %>%

 set_caption(caption = "Spearman correlation test results for the correlation
between cholesterol and calories in the fast food data")
```

Table 3.10. Spearman Correlation Test Results for the Correlation Between Cholesterol and Calories in the Fast Food Data

var1	var2	cor	Statistic	p	Method
cholesterol	calories	0.73	6,142,437	0.00000000000000 000000000000000 000000000000000 000000000000000 000000000000000 000000000000665	Spearman

We see that:

1. The Spearman correlation = 0.73.
2. The sample statistic = 6142437 which corresponds to our sample results and the p-value which is very low and nearly equals zero. The p_value is significant, so we reject the null hypothesis and conclude that the correlation between the cholesterol and calories in the fast food data is different from zero. In other words, they are positively associated so as the cholesterol increases, the calories increase on average.

3.2.6. Correlation Between Cholesterol and Vitamin A

3.2.6.1. Plot a Scatter Plot

Using the same previous functions.

```
fastfood %>% ggplot(aes(x = cholesterol, y = vit_a))+ geom_point()+
 geom_smooth(method = "lm")+

 labs(title = "Scatter plot of vitamin A vs. cholesterol in fast food data with
linear fit line,"

    x = "Cholesterol,"

    y = "vitamin A")+

 theme_classic()+

 theme(plot.title = element_text(hjust = 0.5))
```

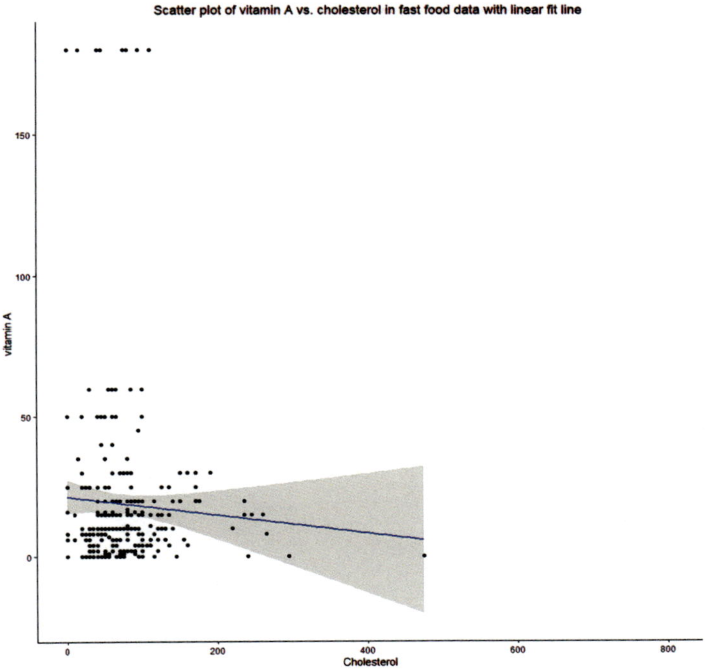

We see that nearly all points are scattered around the linear fit line so the relation is nearly linear. However, some large outliers in vitamin A are far from the linear fit line.

3.2.6.2. Plot a QQ Plot

We plot a QQ plot for the vitamin A column as described previously. The QQ plot of cholesterol is drawn in the previous example.

```
ggqqplot(data = fastfood, x = "vit_a,"

    title = "QQ plot of vitamin A values from fast food data,"

    xlab = "Theoretical percentiles," ylab = "Sample percentiles")+

 theme(plot.title = element_text(hjust = 0.5))
```

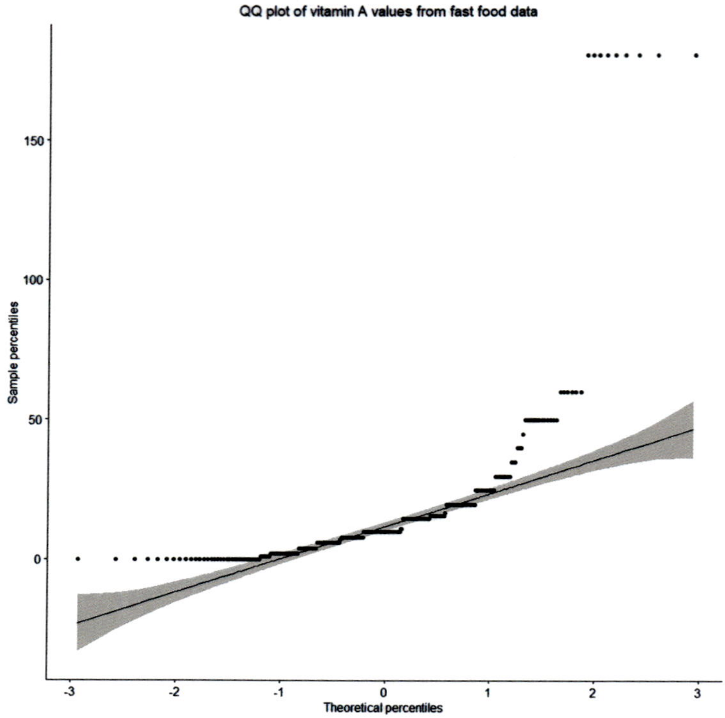

We see that many data points are outside the confidence band, so we can not assume the normality of the vitamin A values.

3.2.6.3. Shapiro-Wilk Test

We do a Shapiro-Wilk test for the vitamin A values.

```
shapiro_test(data = fastfood, vit_a) %>% flextable() %>%

 theme_box() %>%

 set_caption(caption = "Shapiro-Wilk test results for vitamin A in the fast food data")
```

Table 3.11. *Shapiro-Wilk Test Results for Vitamin A in the Fast Food Data*

Variable	**Statistic**	**p**
vit_a	0.4983948	0.000000000000 00000000000000 02535053

The Table 3.11 contains the sample statistic = 0.498 which corresponds to our sample results and the p-value which is smaller than the cut-off point of 0.05.

The p_value is significant, so we reject the null hypothesis and conclude that vitamin A values in the fast food data are not normally distributed.

Because the cholesterol and vitamin A values are not normally distributed, we can use the Spearman or Kendall correlation method to examine the relation between these 2 columns.

3.2.6.4. Spearman Correlation

We use the same functions described above and convert the result to a table as before.

```
fastfood %>% cor_test(cholesterol,vit_a, method = "spearman,"
         alternative = "two.sided") %>% flextable() %>%

theme_box() %>%

set_caption(caption = "Spearman correlation test results for the correlation between cholesterol and vitamin A in the fast food data")
```

Table 3.12. Spearman Correlation Test Results for the Correlation Between Cholesterol and Vitamin A in the Fast Food Data

var1	**var2**	**cor**	**Statistic**	**p**	**Method**
cholesterol	vit_a	0.069	4,232,745	0.235	Spearman

We see that:

1. The Spearman correlation = 0.069 which is a very low value.
2. The sample statistic = 4232745 corresponds to our sample results and the p-value which is larger than the cut-off value of 0.05. The p_value is insignificant, so we fail to reject the null hypothesis and conclude that there is no correlation between cholesterol and vitamin A in the fast food data. In other words, when one of the variables increases or decreases, the other variable remains nearly the same.

3.2.7. Correlation Between All Numeric Variables in Body Measurements Data

3.2.7.1. The Correlation Matrix

We can get all pairwise correlations between all numeric columns in the body measurements data using the cor_mat function (to produce a correlation matrix) with the argument method = “spearman” because not all variables are normally distributed as we see above.

```
bdims %>% cor_mat(method = "spearman")
## # A tibble: 25 × 26
##  rowname bia_di bii_di bit_di che_de che_di elb_di wri_di kne_di ank_di sho_gi
## * <chr>   <dbl> <dbl> <dbl> <dbl> <dbl> <dbl> <dbl> <dbl> <dbl> <dbl>
## 1 bia_di  1    0.3  0.48  0.61  0.78  0.78  0.74  0.66  0.68  0.81
## 2 bii_di  0.3  1    0.68  0.36  0.32  0.31  0.28  0.42  0.36  0.26
## 3 bit_di  0.48  0.68  1   0.47  0.51  0.52  0.47  0.6  0.5  0.47
## 4 che_de  0.61  0.36  0.47  1   0.68  0.7  0.65  0.6  0.63  0.76
## 5 che_di  0.78  0.32  0.51  0.68  1   0.78  0.75  0.67  0.69  0.87
## 6 elb_di  0.78  0.31  0.52  0.7  0.78  1   0.85  0.75  0.83  0.83
## 7 wri_di  0.74  0.28  0.47  0.65  0.75  0.85  1   0.73  0.78  0.8
## 8 kne_di  0.66  0.42  0.6  0.6  0.67  0.75  0.73  1   0.75  0.69
## 9 ank_di  0.68  0.36  0.5  0.63  0.69  0.83  0.78  0.75  1   0.72
## 10 sho_gi  0.81  0.26  0.47  0.76  0.87  0.83  0.8  0.69  0.72  1
## # i 15 more rows
## # i 15 more variables: che_gi <dbl>, wai_gi <dbl>, nav_gi <dbl>, hip_gi <dbl>,
## #  thi_gi <dbl>, bic_gi <dbl>, for_gi <dbl>, kne_gi <dbl>, cal_gi <dbl>,
## #  ank_gi <dbl>, wri_gi <dbl>, age <dbl>, wgt <dbl>, hgt <dbl>, sex <dbl>
```

The result is a correlation matrix or a data frame with 25 rows (for 25 columns in the body measurements data) and 26 columns (for 25 columns of the data plus a “rowname” column for the column names). The upper triangle of the matrix is the same as the lower triangle with a diagonal of ones because it is the correlation of the variable with itself.

3.2.7.2. Long Correlation Matrix

Because the correlation matrix is so wide and symmetric along its diagonal, we can gather these columns and extract the lower triangle using the following functions after the cor_mat function:

- The pull_lower_triangle function extracts the lower triangle of the correlation matrix.

- The cor_gather function to gather all columns. Then, we convert the result to a table as before.
- The mutate and round function to round the p-values to 5 decimal places.

```
bdims %>% cor_mat(method = "spearman") %>% pull_lower_triangle() %>%

 cor_gather() %>% mutate(p = round(p,5)) %>%

  flextable() %>% theme_box() %>%

 set_caption(caption = "Spearman correlation matrix of numeric columns of body
measurements data in long format with p-values")
```

Table 3.13. *Spearman Correlation Matrix of Numeric Columns of Body Measurements Data in Long Format with p-Values*

var1	var2	cor	p
bii_di	bia_di	0.30000	0.00000
bit_di	bia_di	0.48000	0.00000
che_de	bia_di	0.61000	0.00000
che_di	bia_di	0.78000	0.00000
elb_di	bia_di	0.78000	0.00000
wri_di	bia_di	0.74000	0.00000
kne_di	bia_di	0.66000	0.00000
ank_di	bia_di	0.68000	0.00000
sho_gi	bia_di	0.81000	0.00000
che_gi	bia_di	0.74000	0.00000
wai_gi	bia_di	0.68000	0.00000
nav_gi	bia_di	0.33000	0.00000
hip_gi	bia_di	0.34000	0.00000
thi_gi	bia_di	0.13000	0.00257
bic_gi	bia_di	0.71000	0.00000
for_gi	bia_di	0.76000	0.00000
kne_gi	bia_di	0.53000	0.00000
cal_gi	bia_di	0.52000	0.00000
ank_gi	bia_di	0.61000	0.00000
wri_gi	bia_di	0.79000	0.00000

age	bia_di	0.11000	0.01030
wgt	bia_di	0.75000	0.00000
hgt	bia_di	0.76000	0.00000
sex	bia_di	0.79000	0.00000
bit_di	bii_di	0.68000	0.00000
che_de	bii_di	0.36000	0.00000
che_di	bii_di	0.32000	0.00000
elb_di	bii_di	0.31000	0.00000
wri_di	bii_di	0.28000	0.00000
kne_di	bii_di	0.42000	0.00000
ank_di	bii_di	0.36000	0.00000
sho_gi	bii_di	0.26000	0.00000
che_gi	bii_di	0.32000	0.00000
wai_gi	bii_di	0.41000	0.00000
nav_gi	bii_di	0.56000	0.00000
hip_gi	bii_di	0.55000	0.00000
thi_gi	bii_di	0.42000	0.00000
bic_gi	bii_di	0.29000	0.00000
for_gi	bii_di	0.28000	0.00000
kne_gi	bii_di	0.46000	0.00000
cal_gi	bii_di	0.40000	0.00000
ank_gi	bii_di	0.33000	0.00000
wri_gi	bii_di	0.27000	0.00000
age	bii_di	0.26000	0.00000
wgt	bii_di	0.48000	0.00000
hgt	bii_di	0.36000	0.00000
sex	bii_di	0.10000	0.02390
che_de	bit_di	0.47000	0.00000
che_di	bit_di	0.51000	0.00000
elb_di	bit_di	0.52000	0.00000
wri_di	bit_di	0.47000	0.00000
kne_di	bit_di	0.60000	0.00000
ank_di	bit_di	0.50000	0.00000

sho_gi	bit_di	0.47000	0.00000
che_gi	bit_di	0.49000	0.00000
wai_gi	bit_di	0.57000	0.00000
nav_gi	bit_di	0.61000	0.00000
hip_gi	bit_di	0.75000	0.00000
thi_gi	bit_di	0.53000	0.00000
bic_gi	bit_di	0.49000	0.00000
for_gi	bit_di	0.49000	0.00000
kne_gi	bit_di	0.62000	0.00000
cal_gi	bit_di	0.58000	0.00000
ank_gi	bit_di	0.54000	0.00000
wri_gi	bit_di	0.49000	0.00000
age	bit_di	0.26000	0.00000
wgt	bit_di	0.66000	0.00000
hgt	bit_di	0.48000	0.00000
sex	bit_di	0.27000	0.00000
che_di	che_de	0.68000	0.00000
elb_di	che_de	0.70000	0.00000
wri_di	che_de	0.65000	0.00000
kne_di	che_de	0.60000	0.00000
ank_di	che_de	0.63000	0.00000
sho_gi	che_de	0.76000	0.00000
che_gi	che_de	0.82000	0.00000
wai_gi	che_de	0.81000	0.00000
nav_gi	che_de	0.62000	0.00000
hip_gi	che_de	0.56000	0.00000
thi_gi	che_de	0.36000	0.00000
bic_gi	che_de	0.77000	0.00000
for_gi	che_de	0.74000	0.00000
kne_gi	che_de	0.58000	0.00000
cal_gi	che_de	0.57000	0.00000
ank_gi	che_de	0.60000	0.00000
wri_gi	che_de	0.71000	0.00000

age	che_de	0.31000	0.00000
wgt	che_de	0.81000	0.00000
hgt	che_de	0.58000	0.00000
sex	che_de	0.65000	0.00000
elb_di	che_di	0.78000	0.00000
wri_di	che_di	0.75000	0.00000
kne_di	che_di	0.67000	0.00000
ank_di	che_di	0.69000	0.00000
sho_gi	che_di	0.87000	0.00000
che_gi	che_di	0.87000	0.00000
wai_gi	che_di	0.79000	0.00000
nav_gi	che_di	0.50000	0.00000
hip_gi	che_di	0.50000	0.00000
thi_gi	che_di	0.30000	0.00000
bic_gi	che_di	0.80000	0.00000
for_gi	che_di	0.81000	0.00000
kne_gi	che_di	0.58000	0.00000
cal_gi	che_di	0.59000	0.00000
ank_gi	che_di	0.64000	0.00000
wri_gi	che_di	0.78000	0.00000
age	che_di	0.22000	0.00000
wgt	che_di	0.82000	0.00000
hgt	che_di	0.64000	0.00000
sex	che_di	0.72000	0.00000
wri_di	elb_di	0.85000	0.00000
kne_di	elb_di	0.75000	0.00000
ank_di	elb_di	0.83000	0.00000
sho_gi	elb_di	0.83000	0.00000
che_gi	elb_di	0.82000	0.00000
wai_gi	elb_di	0.74000	0.00000
nav_gi	elb_di	0.46000	0.00000
hip_gi	elb_di	0.45000	0.00000
thi_gi	elb_di	0.21000	0.00000

bic_gi	elb_di	0.82000	0.00000
for_gi	elb_di	0.87000	0.00000
kne_gi	elb_di	0.59000	0.00000
cal_gi	elb_di	0.58000	0.00000
ank_gi	elb_di	0.69000	0.00000
wri_gi	elb_di	0.86000	0.00000
age	elb_di	0.20000	0.00000
wgt	elb_di	0.82000	0.00000
hgt	elb_di	0.75000	0.00000
sex	elb_di	0.79000	0.00000
kne_di	wri_di	0.73000	0.00000
ank_di	wri_di	0.78000	0.00000
sho_gi	wri_di	0.80000	0.00000
che_gi	wri_di	0.79000	0.00000
wai_gi	wri_di	0.71000	0.00000
nav_gi	wri_di	0.41000	0.00000
hip_gi	wri_di	0.43000	0.00000
thi_gi	wri_di	0.20000	0.00001
bic_gi	wri_di	0.78000	0.00000
for_gi	wri_di	0.83000	0.00000
kne_gi	wri_di	0.60000	0.00000
cal_gi	wri_di	0.58000	0.00000
ank_gi	wri_di	0.68000	0.00000
wri_gi	wri_di	0.88000	0.00000
age	wri_di	0.22000	0.00000
wgt	wri_di	0.79000	0.00000
hgt	wri_di	0.70000	0.00000
sex	wri_di	0.75000	0.00000
ank_di	kne_di	0.75000	0.00000
sho_gi	kne_di	0.69000	0.00000
che_gi	kne_di	0.67000	0.00000
wai_gi	kne_di	0.66000	0.00000
nav_gi	kne_di	0.47000	0.00000

hip_gi	kne_di	0.56000	0.00000
thi_gi	kne_di	0.39000	0.00000
bic_gi	kne_di	0.70000	0.00000
for_gi	kne_di	0.74000	0.00000
kne_gi	kne_di	0.72000	0.00000
cal_gi	kne_di	0.68000	0.00000
ank_gi	kne_di	0.68000	0.00000
wri_gi	kne_di	0.75000	0.00000
age	kne_di	0.20000	0.00001
wgt	kne_di	0.78000	0.00000
hgt	kne_di	0.62000	0.00000
sex	kne_di	0.59000	0.00000
sho_gi	ank_di	0.72000	0.00000
che_gi	ank_di	0.73000	0.00000
wai_gi	ank_di	0.68000	0.00000
nav_gi	ank_di	0.46000	0.00000
hip_gi	ank_di	0.43000	0.00000
thi_gi	ank_di	0.21000	0.00000
bic_gi	ank_di	0.71000	0.00000
for_gi	ank_di	0.75000	0.00000
kne_gi	ank_di	0.57000	0.00000
cal_gi	ank_di	0.56000	0.00000
ank_gi	ank_di	0.70000	0.00000
wri_gi	ank_di	0.77000	0.00000
age	ank_di	0.26000	0.00000
wgt	ank_di	0.76000	0.00000
hgt	ank_di	0.70000	0.00000
sex	ank_di	0.71000	0.00000
che_gi	sho_gi	0.93000	0.00000
wai_gi	sho_gi	0.85000	0.00000
nav_gi	sho_gi	0.52000	0.00000
hip_gi	sho_gi	0.52000	0.00000
thi_gi	sho_gi	0.32000	0.00000

bic_gi	sho_gi	0.90000	0.00000
for_gi	sho_gi	0.90000	0.00000
kne_gi	sho_gi	0.62000	0.00000
cal_gi	sho_gi	0.62000	0.00000
ank_gi	sho_gi	0.69000	0.00000
wri_gi	sho_gi	0.85000	0.00000
age	sho_gi	0.20000	0.00000
wgt	sho_gi	0.88000	0.00000
hgt	sho_gi	0.68000	0.00000
sex	sho_gi	0.79000	0.00000
wai_gi	che_gi	0.90000	0.00000
nav_gi	che_gi	0.63000	0.00000
hip_gi	che_gi	0.59000	0.00000
thi_gi	che_gi	0.37000	0.00000
bic_gi	che_gi	0.92000	0.00000
for_gi	che_gi	0.90000	0.00000
kne_gi	che_gi	0.62000	0.00000
cal_gi	che_gi	0.62000	0.00000
ank_gi	che_gi	0.69000	0.00000
wri_gi	che_gi	0.84000	0.00000
age	che_gi	0.26000	0.00000
wgt	che_gi	0.91000	0.00000
hgt	che_gi	0.63000	0.00000
sex	che_gi	0.76000	0.00000
nav_gi	wai_gi	0.74000	0.00000
hip_gi	wai_gi	0.68000	0.00000
thi_gi	wai_gi	0.42000	0.00000
bic_gi	wai_gi	0.85000	0.00000
for_gi	wai_gi	0.82000	0.00000
kne_gi	wai_gi	0.66000	0.00000
cal_gi	wai_gi	0.64000	0.00000
ank_gi	wai_gi	0.68000	0.00000
wri_gi	wai_gi	0.77000	0.00000

age	wai_gi	0.36000	0.00000
wgt	wai_gi	0.91000	0.00000
hgt	wai_gi	0.59000	0.00000
sex	wai_gi	0.70000	0.00000
hip_gi	nav_gi	0.80000	0.00000
thi_gi	nav_gi	0.59000	0.00000
bic_gi	nav_gi	0.58000	0.00000
for_gi	nav_gi	0.50000	0.00000
kne_gi	nav_gi	0.58000	0.00000
cal_gi	nav_gi	0.51000	0.00000
ank_gi	nav_gi	0.53000	0.00000
wri_gi	nav_gi	0.45000	0.00000
age	nav_gi	0.44000	0.00000
wgt	nav_gi	0.70000	0.00000
hgt	nav_gi	0.33000	0.00000
sex	nav_gi	0.23000	0.00000
thi_gi	hip_gi	0.81000	0.00000
bic_gi	hip_gi	0.57000	0.00000
for_gi	hip_gi	0.53000	0.00000
kne_gi	hip_gi	0.71000	0.00000
cal_gi	hip_gi	0.66000	0.00000
ank_gi	hip_gi	0.59000	0.00000
wri_gi	hip_gi	0.47000	0.00000
age	hip_gi	0.24000	0.00000
wgt	hip_gi	0.75000	0.00000
hgt	hip_gi	0.35000	0.00000
sex	hip_gi	0.17000	0.00011
bic_gi	thi_gi	0.42000	0.00000
for_gi	thi_gi	0.36000	0.00000
kne_gi	thi_gi	0.62000	0.00000
cal_gi	thi_gi	0.62000	0.00000
ank_gi	thi_gi	0.42000	0.00000
wri_gi	thi_gi	0.26000	0.00000

age	thi_gi	0.00097	0.98300
wgt	thi_gi	0.54000	0.00000
hgt	thi_gi	0.14000	0.00130
sex	thi_gi	-0.05900	0.18200
for_gi	bic_gi	0.94000	0.00000
kne_gi	bic_gi	0.64000	0.00000
cal_gi	bic_gi	0.65000	0.00000
ank_gi	bic_gi	0.70000	0.00000
wri_gi	bic_gi	0.86000	0.00000
age	bic_gi	0.22000	0.00000
wgt	bic_gi	0.89000	0.00000
hgt	bic_gi	0.61000	0.00000
sex	bic_gi	0.76000	0.00000
kne_gi	for_gi	0.66000	0.00000
cal_gi	for_gi	0.68000	0.00000
ank_gi	for_gi	0.74000	0.00000
wri_gi	for_gi	0.91000	0.00000
age	for_gi	0.17000	0.00012
wgt	for_gi	0.89000	0.00000
hgt	for_gi	0.67000	0.00000
sex	for_gi	0.80000	0.00000
cal_gi	kne_gi	0.79000	0.00000
ank_gi	kne_gi	0.75000	0.00000
wri_gi	kne_gi	0.66000	0.00000
age	kne_gi	0.12000	0.00835
wgt	kne_gi	0.79000	0.00000
hgt	kne_gi	0.56000	0.00000
sex	kne_gi	0.40000	0.00000
ank_gi	cal_gi	0.74000	0.00000
wri_gi	cal_gi	0.64000	0.00000
age	cal_gi	0.12000	0.00645
wgt	cal_gi	0.77000	0.00000
hgt	cal_gi	0.48000	0.00000
sex	cal_gi	0.40000	0.00000

wri_gi	ank_gi	0.77000	0.00000
age	ank_gi	0.16000	0.00022
wgt	ank_gi	0.78000	0.00000
hgt	ank_gi	0.59000	0.00000
sex	ank_gi	0.55000	0.00000
age	wri_gi	0.19000	0.00001
wgt	wri_gi	0.84000	0.00000
hgt	wri_gi	0.71000	0.00000
sex	wri_gi	0.79000	0.00000
wgt	age	0.24000	0.00000
hgt	age	0.11000	0.01520
sex	age	0.16000	0.00039
hgt	wgt	0.73000	0.00000
sex	wgt	0.68000	0.00000
sex	hgt	0.71000	0.00000

The result is a data frame with 300 rows and 4 columns:

- var1 which is one continuous variable.
- var2 which is another continuous variable.
- cor which is the Spearman correlation coefficient between var1 and var2.
- p which is the p-value for the test of significance of this correlation coefficient.

To make this table more informative, we use the following functions after the cor_gather function:

- The arrange function with the argument cor to arrange the correlation coefficients in ascending order.
- The add_significance function with the arguments, p.col = "p," output.col = "significance," to add p-value significance symbols according to the "p" in the "significance" column.
- The mutate function with the argument p = scientific(p) to convert the large decimals of p-values to scientific notations (1e05, 1.5e-02) using the scientific function from the scales package.

```
library(scales)
bdims %>% cor_mat(method = "spearman") %>% pull_lower_triangle() %>%
```

```
cor_gather() %>%

arrange(cor) %>%

add_significance(p.col = "p," output.col = "significance") %>%

mutate(p = scientific(p)) %>%


 flextable() %>% theme_box() %>%

set_caption(caption = "Spearman correlation matrix of numeric columns of body measurements data in ascending order and significance symbols")
```

Table 3.14. *Spearman Correlation Matrix of Numeric Columns of Body Measurements Data in Ascending Order and Significance Symbols*

var1	var2	cor	p	Significance
sex	thi_gi	-0.05900	1.82e-01	ns
age	thi_gi	0.00097	9.83e-01	ns
sex	bii_di	0.10000	2.39e-02	*
age	bia_di	0.11000	1.03e-02	*
hgt	age	0.11000	1.52e-02	*
age	kne_gi	0.12000	8.35e-03	**
age	cal_gi	0.12000	6.45e-03	**
thi_gi	bia_di	0.13000	2.57e-03	**
hgt	thi_gi	0.14000	1.30e-03	**
age	ank_gi	0.16000	2.24e-04	***
sex	age	0.16000	3.94e-04	***
sex	hip_gi	0.17000	1.13e-04	***
age	for_gi	0.17000	1.16e-04	***
age	wri_gi	0.19000	1.38e-05	****
age	elb_di	0.20000	3.33e-06	****
thi_gi	wri_di	0.20000	6.75e-06	****
age	kne_di	0.20000	5.55e-06	****
age	sho_gi	0.20000	3.29e-06	****
thi_gi	elb_di	0.21000	1.49e-06	****

thi_gi	ank_di	0.21000	3.18e-06	****
age	che_di	0.22000	3.45e-07	****
age	wri_di	0.22000	8.23e-07	****
age	bic_gi	0.22000	8.97e-07	****
sex	nav_gi	0.23000	1.01e-07	****
age	hip_gi	0.24000	7.73e-08	****
wgt	age	0.24000	5.19e-08	****
sho_gi	bii_di	0.26000	4.61e-09	****
age	bii_di	0.26000	2.92e-09	****
age	bit_di	0.26000	2.93e-09	****
age	ank_di	0.26000	4.71e-09	****
age	che_gi	0.26000	1.69e-09	****
wri_gi	thi_gi	0.26000	5.08e-09	****
wri_gi	bii_di	0.27000	9.49e-10	****
sex	bit_di	0.27000	1.17e-09	****
wri_di	bii_di	0.28000	1.04e-10	****
for_gi	bii_di	0.28000	1.94e-10	****
bic_gi	bii_di	0.29000	4.29e-11	****
bii_di	bia_di	0.30000	1.13e-11	****
thi_gi	che_di	0.30000	1.11e-11	****
elb_di	bii_di	0.31000	4.10e-13	****
age	che_de	0.31000	8.31e-13	****
che_di	bii_di	0.32000	2.47e-13	****
che_gi	bii_di	0.32000	1.36e-13	****
thi_gi	sho_gi	0.32000	3.79e-13	****
nav_gi	bia_di	0.33000	1.94e-14	****
ank_gi	bii_di	0.33000	4.94e-14	****
hgt	nav_gi	0.33000	1.18e-14	****
hip_gi	bia_di	0.34000	1.53e-15	****
hgt	hip_gi	0.35000	1.68e-16	****
che_de	bii_di	0.36000	1.38e-16	****
ank_di	bii_di	0.36000	1.04e-16	****

hgt	bii_di	0.36000	2.39e-17	****
thi_gi	che_de	0.36000	6.16e-17	****
age	wai_gi	0.36000	1.48e-16	****
for_gi	thi_gi	0.36000	1.06e-16	****
thi_gi	che_gi	0.37000	4.36e-18	****
thi_gi	kne_di	0.39000	9.95e-20	****
cal_gi	bii_di	0.40000	4.47e-21	****
sex	kne_gi	0.40000	6.67e-21	****
sex	cal_gi	0.40000	4.03e-21	****
wai_gi	bii_di	0.41000	2.70e-22	****
nav_gi	wri_di	0.41000	1.65e-22	****
kne_di	bii_di	0.42000	5.59e-23	****
thi_gi	bii_di	0.42000	4.67e-23	****
thi_gi	wai_gi	0.42000	1.53e-23	****
bic_gi	thi_gi	0.42000	7.06e-23	****
ank_gi	thi_gi	0.42000	1.01e-22	****
hip_gi	wri_di	0.43000	3.40e-24	****
hip_gi	ank_di	0.43000	8.80e-24	****
age	nav_gi	0.44000	3.50e-25	****
hip_gi	elb_di	0.45000	4.56e-26	****
wri_gi	nav_gi	0.45000	2.08e-26	****
kne_gi	bii_di	0.46000	1.78e-28	****
nav_gi	elb_di	0.46000	2.76e-27	****
nav_gi	ank_di	0.46000	2.94e-28	****
che_de	bit_di	0.47000	2.52e-29	****
wri_di	bit_di	0.47000	8.91e-29	****
sho_gi	bit_di	0.47000	4.59e-29	****
nav_gi	kne_di	0.47000	3.07e-29	****
wri_gi	hip_gi	0.47000	6.98e-30	****
bit_di	bia_di	0.48000	4.77e-30	****
wgt	bii_di	0.48000	3.24e-30	****
hgt	bit_di	0.48000	3.81e-31	****
hgt	cal_gi	0.48000	3.28e-31	****

che_gi	bit_di	0.49000	4.09e-32	****
bic_gi	bit_di	0.49000	2.42e-32	****
for_gi	bit_di	0.49000	1.49e-31	****
wri_gi	bit_di	0.49000	1.71e-31	****
ank_di	bit_di	0.50000	9.88e-33	****
nav_gi	che_di	0.50000	2.44e-33	****
hip_gi	che_di	0.50000	1.01e-33	****
for_gi	nav_gi	0.50000	9.10e-34	****
che_di	bit_di	0.51000	2.18e-35	****
cal_gi	nav_gi	0.51000	1.81e-35	****
cal_gi	bia_di	0.52000	1.56e-36	****
elb_di	bit_di	0.52000	3.79e-36	****
nav_gi	sho_gi	0.52000	2.51e-36	****
hip_gi	sho_gi	0.52000	3.64e-36	****
kne_gi	bia_di	0.53000	7.88e-38	****
thi_gi	bit_di	0.53000	2.76e-38	****
ank_gi	nav_gi	0.53000	2.02e-37	****
for_gi	hip_gi	0.53000	2.07e-37	****
ank_gi	bit_di	0.54000	2.06e-40	****
wgt	thi_gi	0.54000	1.50e-40	****
hip_gi	bii_di	0.55000	1.12e-40	****
sex	ank_gi	0.55000	8.10e-41	****
nav_gi	bii_di	0.56000	2.48e-43	****
hip_gi	che_de	0.56000	2.02e-42	****
hip_gi	kne_di	0.56000	3.98e-43	****
cal_gi	ank_di	0.56000	9.92e-44	****
hgt	kne_gi	0.56000	1.13e-43	****
wai_gi	bit_di	0.57000	3.36e-44	****
cal_gi	che_de	0.57000	1.97e-45	****
kne_gi	ank_di	0.57000	1.32e-44	****
bic_gi	hip_gi	0.57000	2.12e-45	****
cal_gi	bit_di	0.58000	4.11e-47	****
kne_gi	che_de	0.58000	3.05e-46	****

hgt	che_de	0.58000	2.95e-46	****
kne_gi	che_di	0.58000	8.01e-48	****
cal_gi	elb_di	0.58000	1.80e-46	****
cal_gi	wri_di	0.58000	1.79e-46	****
bic_gi	nav_gi	0.58000	3.83e-47	****
kne_gi	nav_gi	0.58000	9.56e-47	****
cal_gi	che_di	0.59000	6.57e-49	****
kne_gi	elb_di	0.59000	8.48e-50	****
sex	kne_di	0.59000	3.94e-48	****
hip_gi	che_gi	0.59000	2.44e-48	****
hgt	wai_gi	0.59000	5.40e-48	****
thi_gi	nav_gi	0.59000	1.92e-48	****
ank_gi	hip_gi	0.59000	2.19e-48	****
hgt	ank_gi	0.59000	7.16e-49	****
kne_di	bit_di	0.60000	1.31e-51	****
kne_di	che_de	0.60000	2.33e-51	****
ank_gi	che_de	0.60000	1.23e-51	****
kne_gi	wri_di	0.60000	1.38e-50	****
che_de	bia_di	0.61000	1.04e-53	****
ank_gi	bia_di	0.61000	5.53e-54	****
nav_gi	bit_di	0.61000	1.28e-53	****
hgt	bic_gi	0.61000	5.72e-52	****
kne_gi	bit_di	0.62000	2.21e-55	****
nav_gi	che_de	0.62000	1.30e-55	****
hgt	kne_di	0.62000	7.17e-56	****
kne_gi	sho_gi	0.62000	1.29e-55	****
cal_gi	sho_gi	0.62000	4.16e-55	****
kne_gi	che_gi	0.62000	3.31e-55	****
cal_gi	che_gi	0.62000	1.18e-54	****
kne_gi	thi_gi	0.62000	1.81e-55	****
cal_gi	thi_gi	0.62000	2.17e-54	****
ank_di	che_de	0.63000	1.57e-57	****
nav_gi	che_gi	0.63000	2.52e-58	****

hgt	che_gi	0.63000	4.15e-58	****
ank_gi	che_di	0.64000	3.43e-60	****
hgt	che_di	0.64000	3.02e-60	****
cal_gi	wai_gi	0.64000	1.53e-60	****
kne_gi	bic_gi	0.64000	8.06e-59	****
wri_gi	cal_gi	0.64000	8.12e-61	****
wri_di	che_de	0.65000	4.03e-61	****
sex	che_de	0.65000	2.20e-61	****
cal_gi	bic_gi	0.65000	1.99e-61	****
kne_di	bia_di	0.66000	1.18e-64	****
wgt	bit_di	0.66000	2.99e-65	****
wai_gi	kne_di	0.66000	7.98e-66	****
kne_gi	wai_gi	0.66000	3.68e-65	****
cal_gi	hip_gi	0.66000	1.06e-65	****
kne_gi	for_gi	0.66000	6.17e-66	****
wri_gi	kne_gi	0.66000	1.06e-64	****
kne_di	che_di	0.67000	9.66e-67	****
che_gi	kne_di	0.67000	2.24e-68	****
hgt	for_gi	0.67000	4.29e-66	****
ank_di	bia_di	0.68000	1.81e-71	****
wai_gi	bia_di	0.68000	9.41e-71	****
bit_di	bii_di	0.68000	4.62e-69	****
che_di	che_de	0.68000	8.65e-71	****
ank_gi	wri_di	0.68000	2.69e-71	****
cal_gi	kne_di	0.68000	2.17e-70	****
ank_gi	kne_di	0.68000	7.52e-70	****
wai_gi	ank_di	0.68000	2.97e-69	****
hgt	sho_gi	0.68000	1.39e-69	****
hip_gi	wai_gi	0.68000	2.18e-70	****
ank_gi	wai_gi	0.68000	2.51e-70	****
cal_gi	for_gi	0.68000	4.33e-69	****
sex	wgt	0.68000	2.20e-71	****
ank_di	che_di	0.69000	2.37e-73	****

ank_gi	elb_di	0.69000	1.43e-71	****
sho_gi	kne_di	0.69000	1.17e-73	****
ank_gi	sho_gi	0.69000	2.28e-74	****
ank_gi	che_gi	0.69000	2.04e-73	****
elb_di	che_de	0.70000	5.38e-75	****
hgt	wri_di	0.70000	1.05e-74	****
bic_gi	kne_di	0.70000	3.15e-77	****
ank_gi	ank_di	0.70000	8.49e-76	****
hgt	ank_di	0.70000	1.26e-76	****
sex	wai_gi	0.70000	2.36e-77	****
wgt	nav_gi	0.70000	3.99e-76	****
ank_gi	bic_gi	0.70000	5.98e-75	****
bic_gi	bia_di	0.71000	2.04e-79	****
wri_gi	che_de	0.71000	4.43e-78	****
wai_gi	wri_di	0.71000	1.48e-79	****
bic_gi	ank_di	0.71000	1.43e-79	****
sex	ank_di	0.71000	1.30e-79	****
kne_gi	hip_gi	0.71000	3.11e-80	****
hgt	wri_gi	0.71000	1.78e-77	****
sex	hgt	0.71000	1.71e-77	****
sex	che_di	0.72000	2.75e-81	****
kne_gi	kne_di	0.72000	4.49e-81	****
sho_gi	ank_di	0.72000	1.68e-81	****
kne_di	wri_di	0.73000	2.99e-85	****
che_gi	ank_di	0.73000	3.82e-86	****
hgt	wgt	0.73000	3.73e-86	****
wri_di	bia_di	0.74000	3.41e-89	****
che_gi	bia_di	0.74000	6.00e-88	****
for_gi	che_de	0.74000	1.61e-90	****
wai_gi	elb_di	0.74000	2.34e-87	****
for_gi	kne_di	0.74000	8.97e-89	****
nav_gi	wai_gi	0.74000	1.23e-89	****
ank_gi	for_gi	0.74000	1.51e-87	****

ank_gi	cal_gi	0.74000	1.69e-89	****
wgt	bia_di	0.75000	5.19e-91	****
hip_gi	bit_di	0.75000	2.32e-92	****
wri_di	che_di	0.75000	9.52e-92	****
kne_di	elb_di	0.75000	2.44e-91	****
hgt	elb_di	0.75000	1.48e-91	****
sex	wri_di	0.75000	1.84e-93	****
ank_di	kne_di	0.75000	6.83e-92	****
wri_gi	kne_di	0.75000	3.04e-92	****
for_gi	ank_di	0.75000	1.53e-93	****
wgt	hip_gi	0.75000	4.61e-92	****
ank_gi	kne_gi	0.75000	2.73e-91	****
for_gi	bia_di	0.76000	1.01e-96	****
hgt	bia_di	0.76000	9.50e-96	****
sho_gi	che_de	0.76000	8.39e-97	****
wgt	ank_di	0.76000	7.42e-95	****
sex	che_gi	0.76000	1.55e-95	****
sex	bic_gi	0.76000	3.46e-95	****
bic_gi	che_de	0.77000	1.62e-99	****
wri_gi	ank_di	0.77000	2.12e-101	****
wri_gi	wai_gi	0.77000	6.04e-99	****
wgt	cal_gi	0.77000	2.39e-102	****
wri_gi	ank_gi	0.77000	3.68e-101	****
che_di	bia_di	0.78000	1.42e-106	****
elb_di	bia_di	0.78000	3.30e-104	****
elb_di	che_di	0.78000	1.53e-103	****
wri_gi	che_di	0.78000	1.54e-104	****
ank_di	wri_di	0.78000	4.58e-107	****
bic_gi	wri_di	0.78000	1.06e-104	****
wgt	kne_di	0.78000	1.55e-106	****
wgt	ank_gi	0.78000	1.11e-103	****
wri_gi	bia_di	0.79000	1.92e-108	****
sex	bia_di	0.79000	2.48e-108	****

wai_gi	che_di	0.79000	9.19e-111	****
sex	elb_di	0.79000	5.95e-111	****
che_gi	wri_di	0.79000	1.51e-107	****
wgt	wri_di	0.79000	9.67e-109	****
sex	sho_gi	0.79000	2.66e-111	****
cal_gi	kne_gi	0.79000	2.45e-111	****
wgt	kne_gi	0.79000	1.78e-111	****
sex	wri_gi	0.79000	4.58e-110	****
bic_gi	che_di	0.80000	9.64e-114	****
sho_gi	wri_di	0.80000	4.46e-112	****
hip_gi	nav_gi	0.80000	1.65e-115	****
sex	for_gi	0.80000	2.67e-112	****
sho_gi	bia_di	0.81000	1.57e-117	****
wai_gi	che_de	0.81000	1.62e-120	****
wgt	che_de	0.81000	1.61e-120	****
for_gi	che_di	0.81000	7.29e-119	****
thi_gi	hip_gi	0.81000	6.58e-120	****
che_gi	che_de	0.82000	6.76e-126	****
wgt	che_di	0.82000	2.57e-126	****
che_gi	elb_di	0.82000	2.18e-124	****
bic_gi	elb_di	0.82000	5.25e-123	****
wgt	elb_di	0.82000	4.03e-123	****
for_gi	wai_gi	0.82000	1.03e-124	****
ank_di	elb_di	0.83000	1.14e-132	****
sho_gi	elb_di	0.83000	3.58e-131	****
for_gi	wri_di	0.83000	4.75e-131	****
wri_gi	che_gi	0.84000	2.96e-135	****
wgt	wri_gi	0.84000	7.26e-136	****
wri_di	elb_di	0.85000	1.16e-144	****
wai_gi	sho_gi	0.85000	1.67e-139	****
wri_gi	sho_gi	0.85000	6.03e-143	****
bic_gi	wai_gi	0.85000	2.68e-141	****
wri_gi	elb_di	0.86000	5.71e-147	****

wri_gi	bic_gi	0.86000	6.99e-148	****
sho_gi	che_di	0.87000	2.96e-158	****
che_gi	che_di	0.87000	4.67e-156	****
for_gi	elb_di	0.87000	1.64e-153	****
wri_gi	wri_di	0.88000	5.39e-162	****
wgt	sho_gi	0.88000	4.21e-164	****
wgt	bic_gi	0.89000	3.21e-172	****
wgt	for_gi	0.89000	3.69e-172	****
bic_gi	sho_gi	0.90000	4.24e-182	****
for_gi	sho_gi	0.90000	2.10e-181	****
wai_gi	che_gi	0.90000	1.06e-187	****
for_gi	che_gi	0.90000	1.72e-181	****
wgt	che_gi	0.91000	1.51e-191	****
wgt	wai_gi	0.91000	3.41e-200	****
wri_gi	for_gi	0.91000	2.37e-197	****
bic_gi	che_gi	0.92000	2.93e-205	****
che_gi	sho_gi	0.93000	2.13e-217	****
for_gi	bic_gi	0.94000	9.81e-247	****

We see that:

- The lowest correlation coefficient was between sex and thigh girth (thi_gi) and equals -0.059. However, this correlation was insignificant or ns.
- There are no more negative correlations and all other correlation coefficients are positive.
- The highest correlation was between forearm girth (for_gi) and bicep girth (bic_gi) and equals 0.94. It was significantly greater than 0 with a very low p-value. This means that as the forearm girth increases, the bicep girth increases on average and vice versa.

3.2.8. Correlation Between all Numeric Variables in fast Food Data

We can use the same functions to get the long correlation matrix between all numeric variables in fast food data. However, because not all columns in the fast food data are numeric, we select the numeric ones using the select function with the argument where(is.numeric) to select numeric columns only.

```
fastfood %>% select(where(is.numeric)) %>% cor_mat(method = "spearman") %>%
pull_lower_triangle() %>%

 cor_gather() %>%

 arrange(cor) %>%

 add_significance(p.col = "p," output.col = "significance") %>%

 mutate(p = scientific(p)) %>%


  flextable() %>% theme_box() %>%

 set_caption(caption = "Spearman correlation matrix of numeric columns of fast
food data in ascending order and significance symbols")
```

Table 3.15. *Spearman Correlation Matrix of Numeric Columns of Fast Food Data in Ascending Order and Significance Symbols*

var1	var2	cor	p	Significance
vit_c	trans_fat	-0.2100	2.43e-04	***
vit_c	cal_fat	-0.1800	1.92e-03	**
vit_c	total_fat	-0.1700	2.26e-03	**
fiber	trans_fat	-0.1300	4.91e-03	**
vit_c	sat_fat	-0.1200	3.06e-02	*
fiber	cholesterol	-0.0370	4.04e-01	ns
vit_a	cal_fat	-0.0098	8.65e-01	ns
vit_a	total_fat	-0.0092	8.74e-01	ns
vit_a	trans_fat	0.0059	9.19e-01	ns
vit_a	total_carb	0.0140	8.05e-01	ns
vit_c	calories	0.0230	6.87e-01	ns
fiber	sat_fat	0.0440	3.26e-01	ns
vit_a	calories	0.0560	3.33e-01	ns
vit_a	sodium	0.0560	3.34e-01	ns
vit_a	cholesterol	0.0690	2.35e-01	ns
fiber	cal_fat	0.0700	1.17e-01	ns

fiber	total_fat	0.0730	1.00e-01	ns
vit_c	cholesterol	0.0850	1.40e-01	ns
vit_c	sodium	0.1100	5.59e-02	ns
vit_a	protein	0.1300	2.31e-02	*
vit_a	sat_fat	0.1400	1.20e-02	*
calcium	trans_fat	0.1500	9.01e-03	**
vit_c	total_carb	0.1500	9.79e-03	**
protein	fiber	0.1700	1.23e-04	***
total_carb	trans_fat	0.1900	1.44e-05	****
vit_c	protein	0.2400	2.52e-05	****
calcium	cal_fat	0.2500	1.29e-05	****
calcium	total_fat	0.2500	9.49e-06	****
sugar	trans_fat	0.2500	1.00e-08	****
calcium	cholesterol	0.2500	1.43e-05	****
sugar	fiber	0.2900	3.09e-11	****
fiber	calories	0.3000	3.51e-12	****
fiber	sodium	0.3100	1.63e-12	****
sodium	trans_fat	0.3200	9.55e-14	****
total_carb	cholesterol	0.3300	1.09e-14	****
vit_a	sugar	0.3300	4.54e-09	****
sugar	cal_fat	0.3400	9.13e-16	****
sugar	total_fat	0.3500	3.00e-16	****
protein	trans_fat	0.3600	1.97e-17	****
sugar	sat_fat	0.3700	5.27e-18	****
calcium	sat_fat	0.4000	2.04e-13	****
calcium	vit_c	0.4100	4.00e-14	****
total_carb	sat_fat	0.4200	2.51e-23	****
calcium	sodium	0.4200	1.16e-14	****
vit_a	fiber	0.4300	4.88e-15	****
sugar	cholesterol	0.4500	1.75e-26	****
calcium	protein	0.4500	1.18e-16	****
calcium	vit_a	0.4500	1.20e-16	****
trans_fat	calories	0.4700	3.32e-30	****

vit_c	sugar	0.4700	4.84e-18	****
sugar	sodium	0.4800	3.49e-31	****
cholesterol	trans_fat	0.4900	2.12e-32	****
total_carb	cal_fat	0.5000	1.34e-34	****
calcium	calories	0.5100	5.67e-22	****
total_carb	total_fat	0.5100	4.33e-35	****
protein	sugar	0.5200	3.11e-37	****
protein	total_carb	0.5300	7.59e-39	****
sugar	calories	0.5500	1.91e-41	****
fiber	total_carb	0.5600	1.03e-43	****
trans_fat	cal_fat	0.5700	1.50e-45	****
trans_fat	total_fat	0.5700	4.64e-46	****
protein	sat_fat	0.5800	5.07e-47	****
calcium	sugar	0.5800	3.53e-29	****
sugar	total_carb	0.5900	7.95e-49	****
vit_c	fiber	0.5900	2.04e-29	****
sodium	sat_fat	0.6200	1.22e-55	****
calcium	total_carb	0.6200	1.15e-33	****
calcium	fiber	0.6200	3.76e-33	****
protein	cal_fat	0.6300	1.73e-58	****
protein	total_fat	0.6300	5.75e-59	****
vit_c	vit_a	0.6300	2.05e-34	****
sodium	cholesterol	0.6700	1.71e-68	****
sodium	cal_fat	0.7000	1.93e-77	****
sodium	total_fat	0.7000	1.66e-77	****
trans_fat	sat_fat	0.7000	2.37e-77	****
cholesterol	sat_fat	0.7100	3.13e-81	****
total_carb	sodium	0.7100	2.07e-80	****
cholesterol	cal_fat	0.7200	2.70e-84	****
cholesterol	total_fat	0.7200	5.59e-85	****
cholesterol	calories	0.7300	6.65e-87	****
sat_fat	calories	0.7500	4.62e-96	****
total_carb	calories	0.7800	2.93e-106	****

protein	sodium	0.7800	1.62e-105	****
protein	calories	0.8000	2.57e-113	****
sodium	calories	0.8400	2.72e-137	****
sat_fat	cal_fat	0.8500	2.79e-146	****
sat_fat	total_fat	0.8500	1.92e-146	****
cal_fat	calories	0.8700	1.87e-163	****
total_fat	calories	0.8800	1.22e-164	****
protein	cholesterol	0.8800	6.37e-167	****
total_fat	cal_fat	1.0000	0.00e+00	****

We see that:

1. The lowest correlation was -0.21 and was between vitamin C and trans fat. There was a significant correlation with p-value < 0.05. This means that as the concentration of vitamin C increases the concentration of trans fat decreases and vice versa.
2. The highest correlation was 1.00 and was between total fat and calories from fat (cal_fat). It was a significant correlation with a zero p-value. This means that as the concentration of total fat increases, the calories from fat increase too, and vice versa.

3.3. SUMMARY PLOTS

3.3.1. Scatter Plot

The scatter plot is explained above to see the linear dependence between 2 variables. Here, we will plot another scatter plot for a significant small negative correlation, a significant small positive correlation, and a significant large positive correlation.

3.3.1.1. Scatter Plot for Significant Small Negative Correlation

We noticed that the Spearman correlation between vitamin C and trans fat is significant, small, and negative (-0.21). We can plot a scatter plot of trans fat on the y-axis vs. vitamin C on the x-axis with a linear fit line as described previously.

```
fastfood %>% ggplot(aes(x = vit_c, y = trans_fat))+ geom_point()+
 geom_smooth(method = "lm")+


 labs(title = "Scatter plot of trans fat vs. vitamin C in fast food data \n with linear fit line," x = "vitamin C,"
```

```
    y = "Trans fat")+
  theme_classic()+
  theme(plot.title = element_text(hjust = 0.5))
```

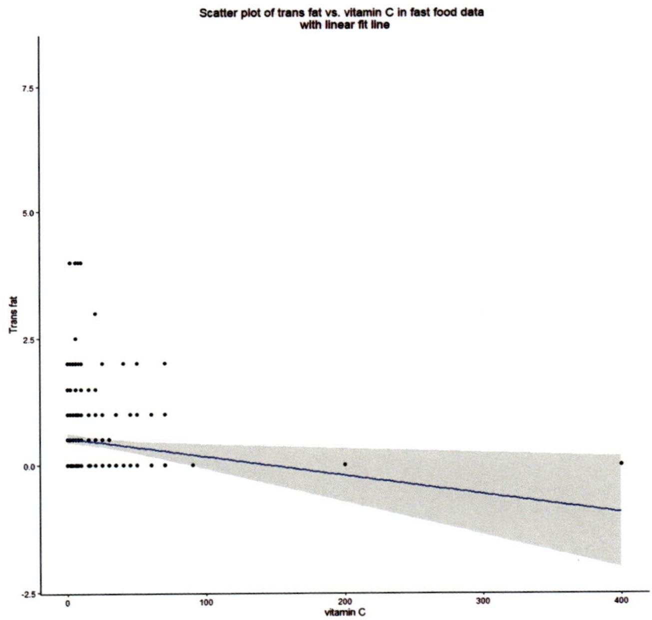

We see that the linear fit line has a negative slope and many points are scattered around this linear fit line. That is why the correlation was negative and small.

3.3.1.2. Scatter Plot for a Significant Small Positive Correlation

We noticed that the Spearman correlation between vitamin C and protein is significant, small, and positive (0.24). We can plot a scatter plot of protein on the y-axis vs. vitamin C on the x-axis with a linear fit line as described previously.

```
fastfood %>% ggplot(aes(x = vit_c, y = protein))+ geom_point()+
  geom_smooth(method = "lm")+
  labs(title = "Scatter plot of protein vs. vitamin C in fast food data \n with
```

```
linear fit line," x = "vitamin C,"

    y = "Protein")+

  theme_classic()+

  theme(plot.title = element_text(hjust = 0.5))
```

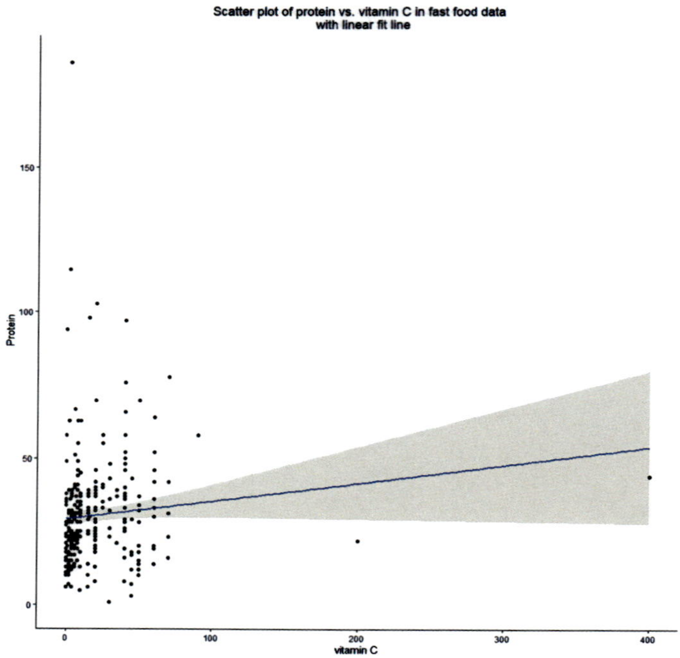

We see that the linear fit line has a positive slope and many points are scattered around this linear fit line. That is why the correlation was positive and small.

3.3.1.3. Scatter Plot for a Significant Large Positive Correlation

We noticed that the Spearman correlation between total fat and calories from fat is significant, large, and perfectly positive (1.00). We can plot a scatter plot of calories from fat on the y-axis vs. total fat on the x-axis with a linear fit line as described previously.

```
fastfood %>% ggplot(aes(x = total_fat, y = cal_fat))+ geom_point()+
```

```
geom_smooth(method = "lm")+

labs(title = "Scatter plot of calories from fat vs. total fat in fast food data
\n with linear fit line," x = "Total fat,"

   y = "Calories from fat")+

theme_classic()+

theme(plot.title = element_text(hjust = 0.5))
```

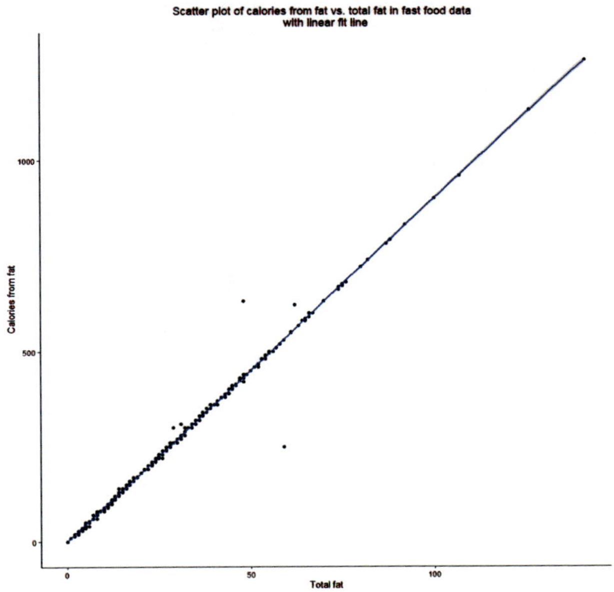

We see that the linear fit line has a positive slope and many points are aligned along this linear fit line. That is why the correlation was perfectly positive and large.

3.3.2. Visualize the Correlation Matrix

The cor_plot function can be applied to the result of the cor_mat function. The produced plot is created using the base R functions (and not the ggplot function), so to add a title, we use the title function after the cor_plot function.

3.3.2.1. Visualize the Correlation Matrix of Body Measurements Data

```
bdims %>% cor_mat(method = "spearman") %>% cor_plot()
title("Spearman correlation matrix of numeric columns in body measurements data\n using cor_plot function")
```

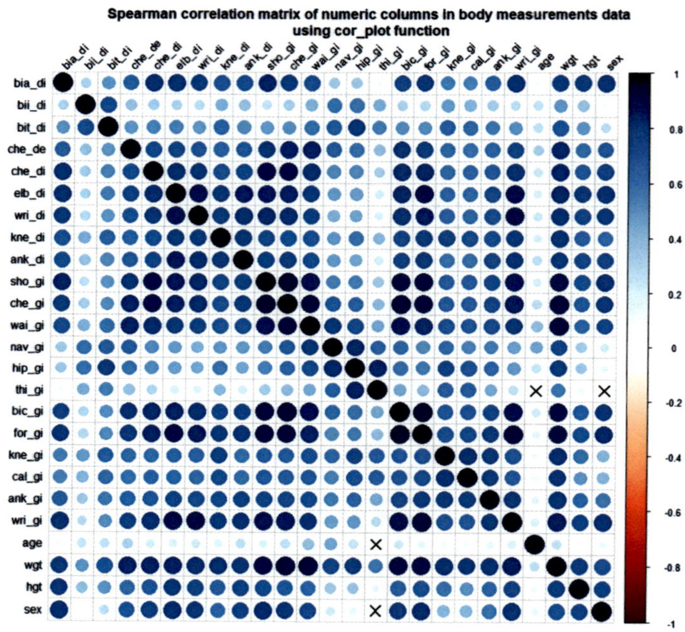

We see that:

1. The positive correlations are plotted as blue circles, while the negative correlations are plotted as red circles (none in this data).
2. The areas and color shades of circles correspond to the absolute value of the correlation coefficient. So, a larger positive correlation coefficient will be shown as larger darker blue circles than a smaller positive correlation coefficient.
3. The insignificant correlations are marked by crosses (X). For example, between age and thigh girth (thi_gi).

We see that the lower triangle is a mirror image of the upper triangle so we can extract the lower or upper triangle using the type argument within the cor_plot function. This also will reduce the crowding of visualizing the whole correlation matrix.

```
bdims %>% cor_mat(method = “spearman”) %>% cor_plot(type = “lower”)
title(“Lower triangle of spearman correlation matrix of numeric columns in body measurements data\n using cor_plot function”)
```

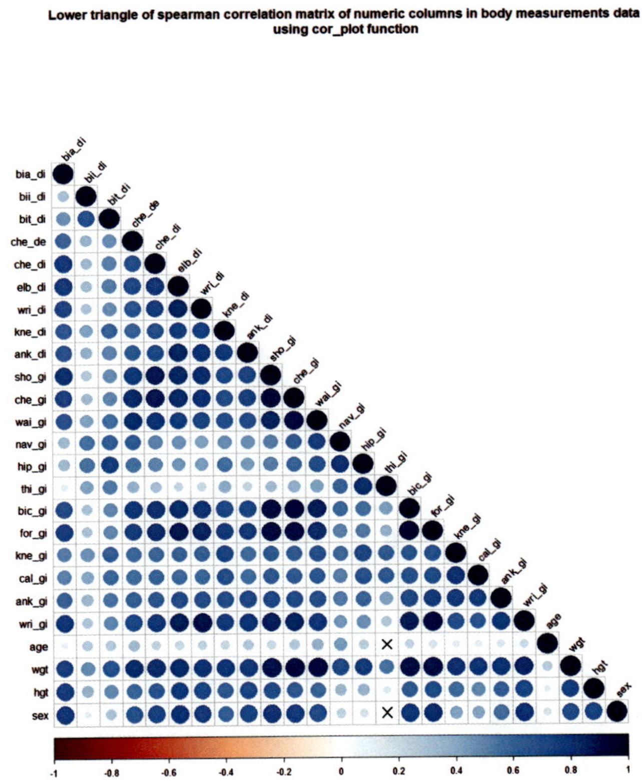

3.3.2.2. *Visualize the Correlation Matrix of Fast Food Data*

We can also plot the lower triangle of the Spearman correlation matrix of the fast food data.

```
fastfood %>% select(where(is.numeric)) %>% cor_mat(method = “spearman”) %>%
cor_plot(type = “lower”)

title(“Lower triangle of spearman correlation matrix of numeric columns in fast food data\n using cor_plot function”)
```

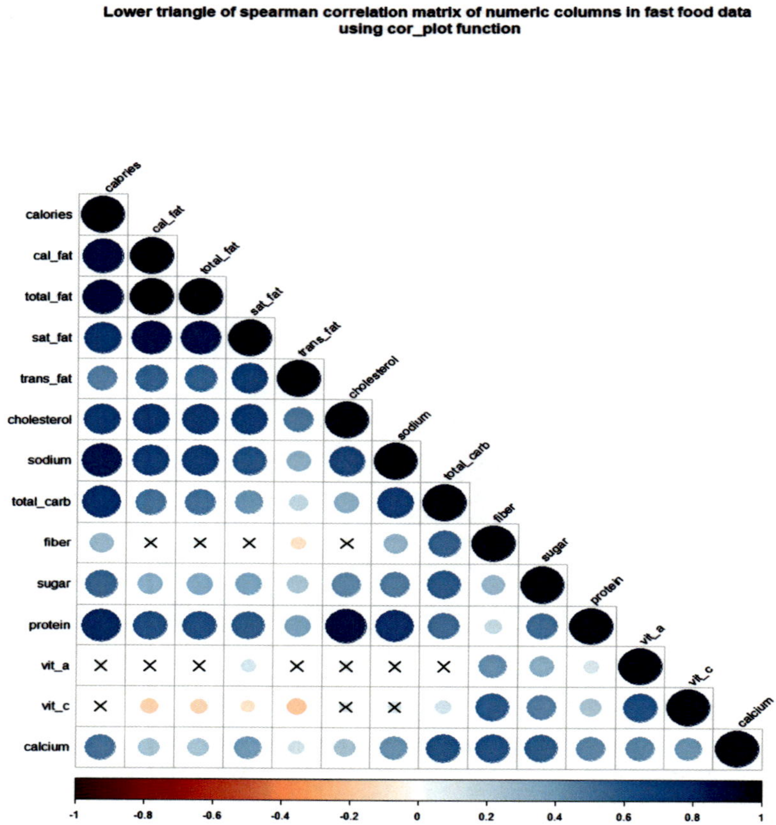

A more informative plot is to label the circles with their corresponding correlation coefficient using label = TRUE argument within the cor_plot function.

```
fastfood %>% select(where(is.numeric)) %>% cor_mat(method = "spearman") %>%
cor_plot(type = "lower," label = TRUE)

title("Lower triangle of spearman correlation matrix with labels of numeric
columns in fast food data\n using cor_plot function")
```

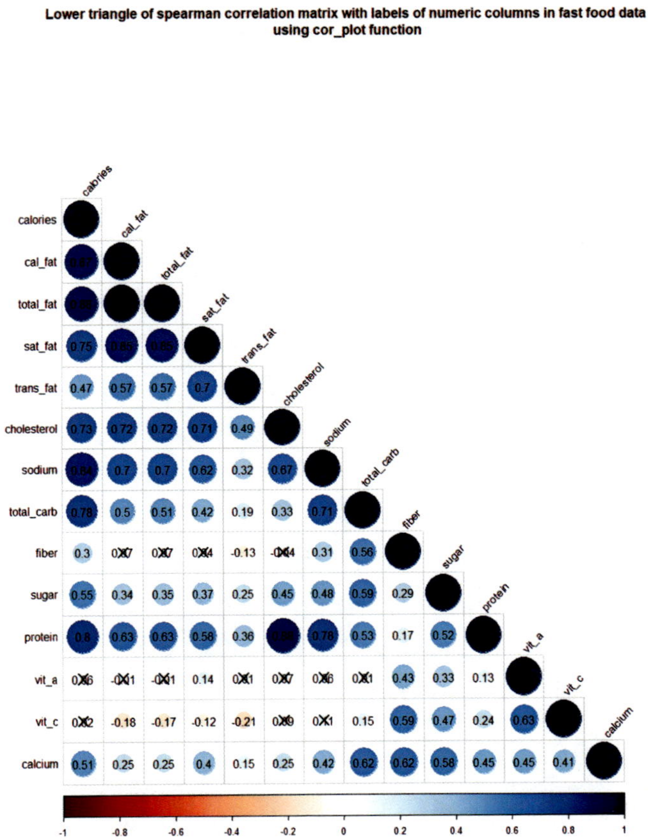

To see the correlation coefficients more clearly, we can color the text white using the font.label argument within the cor_plot function.

```
fastfood %>% select(where(is.numeric)) %>% cor_mat(method = "spearman") %>%

 cor_plot(type = "lower," label = TRUE, font.label = list(color = "white"))

title("Lower triangle of spearman correlation matrix with white labels of numeric columns in fast food data\n using cor_plot function")
```

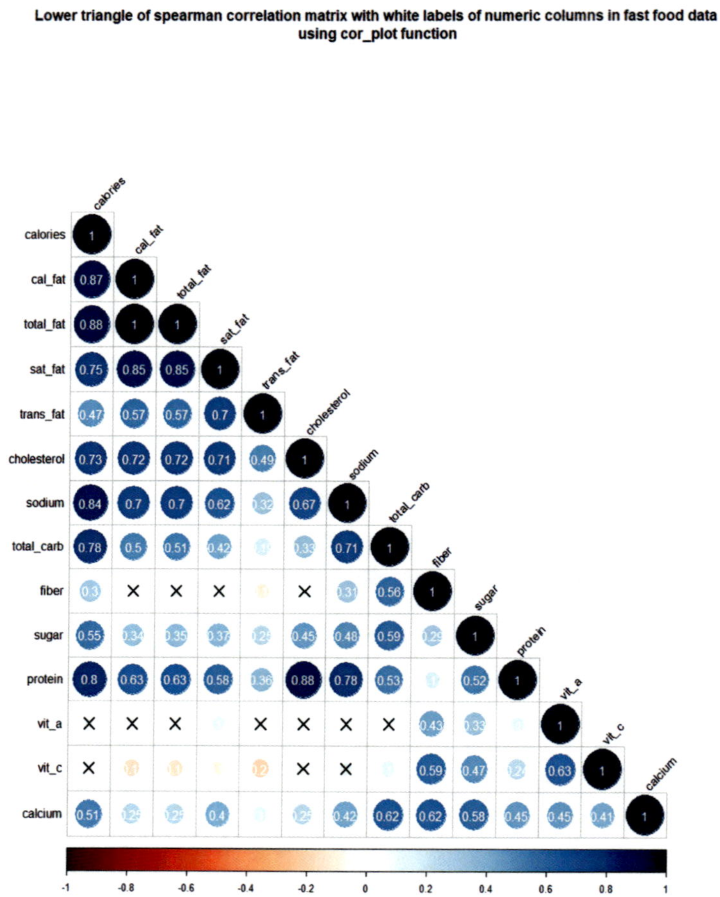

3.4. STATISTICAL TESTS

We can test the correlation for significance as described above.

CHAPTER 4

BIVARIATE ANALYSIS FOR CONTINUOUS-CATEGORICAL DATA

Contents

4.1. DATA USED IN THIS CHAPTER

4.1.1. US Births Data

A random sample of 1000 births from the US births data released in 2014 is stored under the name "births14." The data is part of the openintro package and its source is: United States Department of Health and Human Services. Centers for Disease Control and Prevention. National Center for Health Statistics. Natality Detail File, 2014 United States. Inter-university Consortium for Political and Social Research, 2016–10–07. doi:10.3886/ICPSR36461.v1.

To load this data into our R session, we will load the openintro package using the library function. Then, we will load the "births14" data using the data function. We will also load the tidyverse package because it contains many packages for data analysis like dplyr, tidyr, ggplot2, etc.

```
library(openintro)
data("births14")
library(tidyverse)
```

To see the data structure, we will use the glimpse function from the dplyr package.

```
glimpse(births14)
## Rows: 1,000
## Columns: 13
## $ fage        <int> 34, 36, 37, NA, 32, 32, 37, 29, 30, 29, 30, 34, 28, 28,…
## $ mage        <dbl> 34, 31, 36, 16, 31, 26, 36, 24, 32, 26, 34, 27, 22, 31,…
## $ mature       <chr> "younger mom," "younger mom," "mature mom," "younger mo…
## $ weeks       <dbl> 37, 41, 37, 38, 36, 39, 36, 40, 39, 39, 42, 40, 40, 39,…
## $ premie       <chr> "full term," "full term," "full term," "full term," "pr…
## $ visits       <dbl> 14, 12, 10, NA, 12, 14, 10, 13, 15, 11, 14, 16, 20, 15,…
## $ gained       <dbl> 28, 41, 28, 29, 48, 45, 20, 65, 25, 22, 40, 30, 31, NA,…
## $ weight       <dbl> 6.96, 8.86, 7.51, 6.19, 6.75, 6.69, 6.13, 6.74, 8.94, 9…
## $ lowbirthweight <chr> "not low," "not low," "not low," "not low," "not low," …
## $ sex      <chr> "male," "female," "female," "male," "female," "female,"…
## $ habit      <chr> "nonsmoker," "nonsmoker," "nonsmoker," "nonsmoker," "no…
## $ marital     <chr> "married," "married," "married," "not married," "marrie…
## $ whitemom     <chr> "white," "white," "not white," "white," "white," "white…
```

We see that the "births14" data contains 1000 rows and 13 columns:

1. fage: Father's age in years. It is an integer column.
2. mage: Mother's age in years. It is a double or numeric column.
3. mature: Maturity status of the mother. It is a character column.

4. weeks: Length of pregnancy in weeks. It is a double or numeric column.
5. premie: Whether the birth was classified as premature (premie) or full-term. It is a character column.
6. visits: Number of hospital visits during pregnancy. It is a double or numeric column.
7. gained: Weight gained by mother during pregnancy in pounds. It is a double or numeric column.
8. weight: Weight of the baby at birth in pounds. It is a double or numeric column.
9. lowbirthweight: Whether the baby was classified as low birthweight (low) or not (not low). It is a character column.
10. sex: Sex of the baby, female or male. It is a character column.
11. habit: Status of the mother as a nonsmoker or a smoker. It is a character column.
12. marital: Whether the mother is married or not married at birth. It is a character column.
13. whitemom: Whether mom is white or not white. It is a character column.

4.1.2. Cherry Blossom Run Data in 2009

The Details for all 14,974 runners in the 2009 Cherry Blossom Run, which is an annual road race that takes place in Washington DC, are stored in the "run09" data frame that is part of the cherryblossom package. The cherryblossom package is loaded automatically when we load the openintro package. So, to load this data into our R session, we will use the data function as before followed by the glimpse function to get the data structure.

```
data("run09")
glimpse(run09)
## Rows: 14,974
## Columns: 14
## $ place    <int> 1, 2, 3, 4, 5, 6, 7, 8, 9, 10, 11, 12, 13, 14, 15, 16, 17, 1…
## $ time     <dbl> 53.533, 53.917, 53.967, 54.433, 54.450, 54.533, 54.633, 54.6…
## $ net_time <dbl> 53.533, 53.917, 53.967, 54.433, 54.450, 54.533, 54.633, 54.6…
## $ pace     <dbl> 5.367, 5.400, 5.400, 5.450, 5.450, 5.467, 5.467, 5.467, 5.48…
## $ age      <int> 21, 21, 22, 19, 36, 28, 25, 31, 23, 26, 23, 35, 28, 28, 26, …
## $ gender   <fct> F, F, F, F, F, F, F, F, F, F, F, F, F, F, F, F, F, F, F, F, …
## $ first    <fct> Lineth, Belianesh Zemed, Teyba, Abebu, Catherine, Olga, Sall…
```

```
## $ last      <fct> Chepkurui, Gebre, Naser, Gelan, Ndereba, Romanova, Meyerhoff…
## $ city      <fct> Kenya, Ethiopia, Ethiopia, Ethiopia, Kenya, Russia, United S…
## $ state     <fct> NR, NR, NR, NR, NR, NR, NR, NR, NR, NR, NR, NR, NR, CO, NR, …
## $ country   <fct> KEN, ETH, ETH, ETH, KEN, RUS, USA, KEN, ETH, RUS, ETH, ROM, …
## $ div       <int> 2, 2, 2, 1, 5, 3, 3, 4, 2, 3, 2, 5, 3, 3, 3, 3, 3, 5, 4, 2, …
## $ div_place <int> 1, 2, 3, 1, 1, 1, 2, 1, 4, 3, 4, 2, 4, 5, 6, 7, 8, 3, 2, 5, …
## $ div_tot   <int> 953, 953, 953, 71, 1130, 2706, 2706, 1678, 953, 2706, 953, 1…
```

The data is composed of 14974 rows (runners) and 14 columns:

1. place: Finishing position. Separate positions are provided for each gender. It is an integer column.
2. time: The total run time. It is a double or numeric column.
3. net_time: The run time from the start line to the finish line. It is a double or numeric column.
4. pace: Average time per mile, in minutes. It is a double or numeric column.
5. age: runner's age. It is a double or numeric column.
6. gender: runner's gender. It is a factor column with 2 levels "F" for females and "M" for males.
7. first: runner's first name. It is a factor column with many levels.
8. last: runner's last name. It is a factor column with many levels.
9. city: runner's hometown city. It is a factor column with many levels.
10. state: runner's hometown state. It is a factor column with many levels.
11. country: runner's hometown country. It is a factor column with many levels.
12. div: Running division (age group). It is an integer column.
13. div_place: Division place broken up by gender. It is an integer column.
14. div_tot: Total number of people in the division split by gender. It is an integer column.

4.2. SUMMARY STATISTICS

4.2.1. Summary Statistics for Location: The Mean

As we see in Chapter 1, there are different measures of the central tendency (central location) of numerical data like the mean, the median, and percentiles.

To examine the relation between a continuous and a categorical variable, we can calculate the mean of the continuous variable under the different levels of the categorical variable to see how the data center changes between the different levels.

4.2.1.1. The Mean Maternal Age in the Birth Types

To get the mean maternal age for the 2 birth types (premature and full-term), we use the following functions:

- The group_by function with the argument premie applied to the births data frame to split the data frame into different data frames each containing one level of premie column. So we will have 2 data frames, one for full-term births and the other for premature births.
- The get_summary_stats function, from the rstatix package, with the arguments, mage, and show = "mean," to calculate the mean maternal age within each data frame.
- The flextable, theme_box, and set_caption functions convert the result to a table as described in previous chapters.

The functions are applied in sequence using the "%>%" operator. Because we are using rstatix and flextable functions, so we must first load them into our R session using the library function.

```
library(rstatix)
library(flextable)
births14 %>% group_by(premie) %>% get_summary_stats(mage, show = "mean") %>%
 flextable() %>% theme_box() %>%
 set_caption(caption = "Mean maternal age in premature and full-term births of the US births data in 2014")
```

Table 4.1. *Mean Maternal Age in Premature and Full-Term Births of the US Births Data in 2014*

Premie	Variable	n	Mean
full term	mage	876	28.33
premie	mage	124	29.29

We see that:

1. There are 876 full-term births in our data compared to 124 premature births. The total is 1000 births which is the number of rows in our data.

2. The mean maternal age in full-term births is 28.33 years which is lower than that in premature births (29.29 years). So higher maternal age may be associated with premature births.

4.2.1.2. The Mean Number of Visits in the Birth Types

Similarly, we can use the same functions to get the mean number of hospital visits during pregnancy for the 2 birth types (premature and full-term).

```
births14 %>% group_by(premie) %>% get_summary_stats(visits, show = "mean") %>%
 flextable() %>% theme_box() %>%
  set_caption(caption = "Mean number of hospital visits during pregnancy in premature and full-term births of the US births data in 2014")
```

Table 4.2. *Mean Number of Hospital Visits During Pregnancy in Premature and Full-Term Births of the US Births Data in 2014*

Premie	Variable	n	Mean
full term	visits	829	11.516
premie	visits	115	10.165

We see that:

1. There are 829 full-term births in our data with an available number of visits compared to 115 premature births. The total is 944 births which is lower than the number of rows in our data. This means that there are some full-term births and some premature births without a recorded number of visits.
2. The mean number of visits in full-term births is 11.516 which is higher than that in premature births (10.165). So lower number of hospital visits during pregnancy may be associated with premature births.

4.2.1.3. The Mean Run Time in the 2 Genders

Similarly, we can use the same functions to get the mean run time for the 2 genders (males and females) in the Cherry Blossom Run data of 2009.

```
run09 %>% group_by(gender) %>% get_summary_stats(time, show = "mean") %>%
 flextable() %>% theme_box() %>%
 set_caption(caption = "Mean run time in males and females of Cherry Blossom Run data in 2009")
```

Table 4.3. Mean Run Time in Males and Females of Cherry Blossom Run Data in 2009

Gender	Variable	n	mean
F	time	8,323	109.240
M	time	6,651	96.226

We see that:

1. There are 8323 females in our data compared to 6651 males. The total is 14974 persons which is the number of rows in our data.
2. The mean run time in females is 109.240 which is higher than that in males (96.226). So males may be associated with lower run times on average.

4.2.1.4. The Mean Run Time in the Different States

Similarly, we can use the same functions to get the mean run time for runners from the different hometown states in the Cherry Blossom Run data of 2009. To make the resulting table more informative, we use the arrange function with the argument mean to arrange the states in ascending order by their mean run time.

```
run09 %>% group_by(state) %>% get_summary_stats(time, show = "mean") %>%
 arrange(mean) %>%
 flextable() %>% theme_box() %>%
 set_caption(caption = "Mean run time in runners from different states of Cherry
Blossom Run data in 2009")
```

Table 4.4. *Mean Run Time in Runners from Different States of Cherry Blossom Run Data in 2009*

State	Variable	n	Mean
NR	time	59	70.138
AE	time	1	74.467
IA	time	6	91.836
OK	time	4	92.604
WA	time	8	93.102
VT	time	6	93.817
DE	time	61	98.278
AK	time	2	98.475
CO	time	23	99.796

WY	time	1	100.383
NH	time	19	100.950
PA	time	461	101.227
MS	time	3	101.417
WV	time	28	101.580
GA	time	37	101.675
KY	time	9	102.074
NY	time	522	102.141
DC	time	3,464	102.150
NM	time	7	102.364
WI	time	14	102.385
SC	time	11	102.424
RI	time	14	102.688
CA	time	75	102.730
CT	time	73	102.740
KS	time	3	103.017
NE	time	3	103.106
LA	time	2	103.250
IL	time	71	103.411
MA	time	136	104.068
VA	time	5,608	104.083
MD	time	3,558	104.450
MN	time	19	104.459
ME	time	10	104.523
NJ	time	207	104.567
MI	time	34	105.225
MO	time	17	105.468
IN	time	18	105.753
FL	time	55	105.913
UT	time	2	106.175
NC	time	158	107.048
ID	time	1	107.733
TX	time	44	107.791
AL	time	6	109.383

OH	time	80	110.043
TN	time	10	110.120
AZ	time	11	110.379
OR	time	5	111.783
PR	time	3	113.028
NV	time	2	113.258
SD	time	1	113.683
AR	time	2	129.967

We see that:

1. There are 51 different states in our data with different sample sizes. Some states have only 1 runner coming from it ("AE" and "WY").
2. The lowest mean run time was in 59 runners coming from the "NR" state, while the highest mean run time was found in 2 runners coming from the "AR" state. So runners from the "NR" state may be associated with lower run times on the average.

4.2.2. Summary Statistics for Location: The Median

As we saw in Chapter 1, The median is a **robust statistic** that gives the data center without being affected by the extreme values or outliers in the data. So, we can calculate the median of the continuous variable under the different levels of the categorical variable to see how the data center changes between the different levels. In addition, we will also calculate the mean to determine if the data is skewed as we saw in Chapter 1.

4.2.2.1. The Median and Mean Maternal Age in the Birth Types

To get the median and mean maternal age for the 2 birth types (premature and full-term), we will use the same above functions except that we add another argument to the get_summary_stats function. So this function will have the arguments, mage, and show = c("mean," "median"), to calculate the mean and median maternal age within each birth type.

```
births14 %>% group_by(premie) %>% get_summary_stats(mage,

                         show = c("mean,""median")) %>%

 flextable() %>% theme_box() %>%

 set_caption(caption = "Mean and median maternal age in premature and full-
term births of the US births data in 2014")
```

Table 4.5. *Mean and Median Maternal Age in Premature and Full-Term Births of the US Births Data in 2014*

Premie	Variable	n	Mean	Median
full term	mage	876	28.33	28
premie	mage	124	29.29	30

We see that:

1. The median maternal age in full-term births is 28 years which is lower than that in premature births (30 years). So higher maternal age may be associated with premature births.
2. The mean and median maternal age are nearly equal in full-term and premature births. So, we conclude that the maternal age is evenly spaced or normally distributed in the 2 birth types. We will see that in the summary plots below.

4.2.2.2. The Median and Mean Number of Visits in the Birth Types

Similarly, we can use the same functions to get the mean and median number of hospital visits during pregnancy for the 2 birth types (premature and full-term).

```
births14 %>% group_by(premie) %>% get_summary_stats(visits,

                    show = c("mean,""median")) %>%

flextable() %>% theme_box() %>%

set_caption(caption = "Mean and median number of hospital visits during pregnancy
in premature and full-term births of the US births data in 2014")
```

Table 4.6. *Mean and Median Number of Hospital visits During Pregnancy in Premature and Full-Term Births of the US Births Data in 2014*

Premie	Variable	n	Mean	Median
full term	visits	829	11.516	12
premie	visits	115	10.165	10

We see that:

1. The mean number of visits in full-term births is 12 which is higher than that in premature births (10). So lower number of hospital visits during pregnancy may be associated with premature births.

2. The mean nearly equals the median in full-term and premature births. So, we conclude that the number of visits is evenly spaced or normally distributed in the 2 birth types.

4.2.2.3. The Median and Mean Run Time in the 2 Genders

Similarly, we can use the same functions to get the median and mean run time for the 2 genders (males and females) in the Cherry Blossom Run data of 2009.

```
run09 %>% group_by(gender) %>% get_summary_stats(time,

                            show = c("mean,""median")) %>%

 flextable() %>% theme_box() %>%

 set_caption(caption = "Mean and median run time in males and females of Cherry
Blossom Run data in 2009")
```

Table 4.7. Mean and Median Run Time in Males and Females of Cherry Blossom Run Data in 2009

Gender	Variable	n	Mean	Median
F	time	8,323	109.240	109.567
M	time	6,651	96.226	95.717

We see that:

1. The median run time in females is 109.567 which is higher than that in males (95.717). So males may be associated with lower run times.
2. The mean nearly equals the median in females and males. So, we conclude that the run time is evenly spaced or normally distributed in the 2 genders.

4.2.2.4. The Median and Mean Run Time in the Different States

Similarly, we can use the same functions to get the mean and median run time for runners from the different hometown states in the Cherry Blossom Run data of 2009. To make the resulting table more informative, we use the arrange function with the argument median to arrange the states in ascending order by their median run time.

```
run09 %>% group_by(state) %>%
 get_summary_stats(time, show = c("mean,""median")) %>%
 arrange(median) %>%
```

```
flextable() %>% theme_box() %>%

set_caption(caption = "Mean and median run time in runners from different states of Cherry Blossom Run data in 2009")
```

Table 4.8. *Mean and Median Run Time in Runners From Different States of Cherry Blossom Run Data in 2009*

State	Variable	n	Mean	Median
NR	time	59	70.138	55.183
AE	time	1	74.467	74.467
VT	time	6	93.817	92.267
OK	time	4	92.604	92.808
WA	time	8	93.102	93.200
MS	time	3	101.417	93.667
IA	time	6	91.836	96.042
RI	time	14	102.688	97.858
NH	time	19	100.950	97.900
AK	time	2	98.475	98.475
NE	time	3	103.106	98.550
KY	time	9	102.074	98.833
MI	time	34	105.225	99.358
DE	time	61	98.278	99.383
OR	time	5	111.783	99.567
WV	time	28	101.580	99.875
WY	time	1	100.383	100.383
PA	time	461	101.227	100.650
SC	time	11	102.424	100.983
MO	time	17	105.468	101.133
DC	time	3,464	102.150	102.575
NY	time	522	102.141	102.650
WI	time	14	102.385	102.750
CT	time	73	102.740	103.000
TN	time	10	110.120	103.108
LA	time	2	103.250	103.250

CA	time	75	102.730	103.383
CO	time	23	99.796	103.617
MN	time	19	104.459	103.950
MA	time	136	104.068	104.225
VA	time	5,608	104.083	104.308
FL	time	55	105.913	104.600
MD	time	3,558	104.450	104.833
GA	time	37	101.675	104.967
NJ	time	207	104.567	104.967
IL	time	71	103.411	105.300
IN	time	18	105.753	105.750
UT	time	2	106.175	106.175
NM	time	7	102.364	107.617
ID	time	1	107.733	107.733
NC	time	158	107.048	108.450
OH	time	80	110.043	109.592
ME	time	10	104.523	110.534
TX	time	44	107.791	111.242
AZ	time	11	110.379	111.300
AL	time	6	109.383	113.092
NV	time	2	113.258	113.258
PR	time	3	113.028	113.417
SD	time	1	113.683	113.683
KS	time	3	103.017	120.050
AR	time	2	129.967	129.967

We see that:

1. The lowest median run time was in 59 runners coming from the "NR" state (55.183), while the highest median run time was found in 2 runners coming from the "AR" state (129.967). So runners from the "NR" state may be associated with lower run times.
2. There is a great difference between the mean and median run time for runners coming from the "NR" state. So, we conclude that the run time in the "NR" state is **right skewed** because the mean is much larger than the median. On the other hand, the median is larger than the mean in the "CO" state so the run time in this state is **left**

skewed. Other states like "DC" and "NY" have nearly equal mean and median so the run in these states is evenly spaced or normally distributed.

4.2.3. Summary Statistics for Location: The Percentiles

As we saw in Chapter 1, the percentiles including the median are not affected by the extreme values or outliers in the data so they are **robust statistics**. We can calculate the different percentiles of the continuous variable under the different levels of the categorical variable to see how the continuous variable distributes under the different levels.

4.2.3.1. The Percentiles of Maternal Age in the Birth Types

To get the percentiles of maternal age for the 2 birth types (premature and full-term), we will use the same above functions except that we use the get_summary_stats function with the arguments, mage, and type = "quantile," to get the 0% (minimum),25% (Q1), 50% (median), 75% (Q3), and 100% (maximum) percentiles of maternal age within each birth type.

```
births14 %>% group_by(premie) %>% get_summary_stats(mage,

                    type = "quantile") %>%

 flextable() %>% theme_box() %>%

 set_caption(caption = "The different percentiles of maternal age in premature
and full-term births of the US births data in 2014")
```

Table 4.9. *The Different Percentiles of Maternal Age in Premature and Full-Term Births of the US Births Data in 2014*

Premie	Variable	n	0%	25%	50%	75%	100%
full term	mage	876	14	24	28	33	44
premie	mage	124	16	24	30	34	47

We see that:

1. All percentiles (except the 25%) are lower in full-term births than in premature births. So higher maternal age may be associated with premature births.

4.2.3.2. The Percentiles of Visits Number in the Birth Types

```
births14 %>% group_by(premie) %>%
 get_summary_stats(visits, type = "quantile") %>%
 flextable() %>% theme_box() %>%
  set_caption(caption = "The different percentiles of the number of hospital visits during pregnancy in premature and full-term births of the US births data in 2014")
```

Table 4.10. *The Different Percentiles of the Number of Hospital Visits During Pregnancy in Premature and Full-Term Births of the US Births Data in 2014*

Premie	Variable	n	0%	25%	50%	75%	100%
full term	visits	829	0	10	12	14	30
premie	visits	115	0	7	10	12	30

We see that:

All percentiles (except the 0% and 100%) are higher in full-term births than in premature births. So lower number of hospital visits may be associated with premature births.

4.2.3.3. The Percentiles of Run Time in the 2 Genders

```
run09 %>% group_by(gender) %>% get_summary_stats(time,
                         type = "quantile") %>%

 flextable() %>% theme_box() %>%

  set_caption(caption = "The different percentiles of run time in males and females of Cherry Blossom Run data in 2009")
```

Table 4.11. *The Different Percentiles of Run Time in Males and Females of Cherry Blossom Run Data in 2009*

Gender	Variable	n	0%	25%	50%	75%	100%
F	time	8,323	53.533	97.433	109.567	121.242	169.617
M	time	6,651	45.933	82.542	95.717	109.225	157.517

We see that:

1. All percentiles are higher in females than in males. So males appear to be faster than females in this data.

4.2.3.4. The Percentiles of Run Time in the Different States

We also use the arrange function with the argument "`50%`" to arrange the states in ascending order by their median run time.

```
run09 %>% group_by(state) %>%
 get_summary_stats(time, type = "quantile") %>%
 arrange(`50%`) %>%
 flextable() %>% theme_box() %>%
 set_caption(caption = "The different percentiles of run time in runners from different states of Cherry Blossom Run data in 2009")
```

Table 4.12. *The Different Percentiles of Run Time in Runners from Different States of Cherry Blossom Run Data in 2009*

State	Variable	n	0%	25%	50%	75%	100%
NR	time	59	45.933	48.159	55.183	92.450	144.767
AE	time	1	74.467	74.467	74.467	74.467	74.467
VT	time	6	82.833	85.100	92.267	103.008	106.233
OK	time	4	75.200	76.500	92.808	108.912	109.600
WA	time	8	61.350	80.008	93.200	103.854	127.083
MS	time	3	85.450	89.559	93.667	109.400	125.133
IA	time	6	68.317	78.412	96.042	101.708	114.483
RI	time	14	84.417	92.975	97.858	110.229	131.400
NH	time	19	58.233	87.942	97.900	122.559	134.800
AK	time	2	91.467	94.971	98.475	101.979	105.483
NE	time	3	92.900	95.725	98.550	108.208	117.867
KY	time	9	83.100	98.800	98.833	109.083	117.867
MI	time	34	63.200	91.692	99.358	121.600	139.850
DE	time	61	66.033	87.450	99.383	107.100	141.183
OR	time	5	86.817	92.700	99.567	125.983	153.850
WV	time	28	66.717	86.696	99.875	111.933	150.683
WY	time	1	100.383	100.383	100.383	100.383	100.383
PA	time	461	50.700	88.850	100.650	114.017	149.733

SC	time	11	79.617	97.858	100.983	105.267	132.983
MO	time	17	67.683	88.433	101.133	112.383	155.883
DC	time	3,464	53.233	88.767	102.575	115.067	158.133
NY	time	522	53.183	88.171	102.650	116.970	158.083
WI	time	14	65.917	87.113	102.750	121.525	146.067
CT	time	73	61.000	91.717	103.000	117.600	150.600
TN	time	10	80.067	96.825	103.108	125.129	156.867
LA	time	2	86.783	95.016	103.250	111.484	119.717
CA	time	75	60.950	88.167	103.383	117.708	149.333
CO	time	23	48.050	85.884	103.617	115.575	130.133
MN	time	19	48.067	94.284	103.950	119.075	139.300
MA	time	136	53.150	90.170	104.225	117.983	152.467
VA	time	5,608	51.117	90.113	104.308	117.737	169.617
FL	time	55	68.733	88.325	104.600	122.575	148.183
MD	time	3,558	51.183	90.800	104.833	117.929	158.233
GA	time	37	55.733	78.017	104.967	120.100	156.783
NJ	time	207	62.333	91.158	104.967	117.775	149.883
IL	time	71	52.400	90.192	105.300	116.017	153.750
IN	time	18	64.167	97.167	105.750	123.383	133.700
UT	time	2	93.367	99.771	106.175	112.579	118.983
NM	time	7	58.333	91.542	107.617	117.350	132.817
ID	time	1	107.733	107.733	107.733	107.733	107.733
NC	time	158	62.567	94.537	108.450	118.850	149.400
OH	time	80	59.667	97.667	109.592	126.238	154.450
ME	time	10	65.300	95.725	110.534	117.304	121.800
TX	time	44	56.783	90.975	111.242	127.312	150.800
AZ	time	11	85.517	98.200	111.300	122.358	134.350
AL	time	6	90.733	97.375	113.092	120.546	124.217
NV	time	2	97.417	105.338	113.258	121.179	129.100
PR	time	3	85.550	99.483	113.417	126.767	140.117
SD	time	1	113.683	113.683	113.683	113.683	113.683
KS	time	3	54.967	87.508	120.050	127.041	134.033
AR	time	2	106.517	118.242	129.967	141.692	153.417

We see that:

1. The lowest median run time was in 59 runners coming from the "NR" state (55.183). However, the maximum run time in the "NR" state is 144.767 which is higher than other maximums from other states like "WA," "NH," "MI," etc.

4.2.4. Summary Statistics for Spread: The Range

The range is the difference between the largest and smallest observations in a sample. As we see in Chapter 1, the disadvantages of the range as a spread measure are:

- The range is very sensitive to extreme values or outliers.
- The range depends on the sample size. The larger the sample size, the larger the range tends to be. This makes it difficult to compare ranges from samples of different sizes.

However, we can calculate the range of the continuous variable under the different levels of the categorical variable to see how the continuous variable spreads under the different levels.

4.2.4.1. The Range of Maternal Age in the Birth Types

To get the range of maternal age in 2 birth types, we will use the functions:

- The group_by function with the argument premie applied to the births data frame to split the data frame into different data frames each containing one level of premie column.
- The get_summary_stats function with the arguments, mage, and show = c("min," "max") to calculate the minimum and maximum maternal age within each data frame.
- The mutate function creates a new column (range) by subtracting the minimum value from the maximum value.
- The flextable, theme_box, and set_caption functions convert the result to a table as described in previous chapters.

```
births14 %>% group_by(premie) %>%
 get_summary_stats(mage, show = c("min,""max")) %>%
 mutate(range = max-min) %>%
 flextable() %>% theme_box() %>%


 set_caption(caption = "The range of maternal age in premature and full-term
births of the US births data in 2014")
```

Table 4.13. *The Range of Maternal Age in Premature and Full-Term Births of the US Births Data in 2014*

Premie	Variable	n	Min	Max	Range
full term	mage	876	14	44	30
premie	mage	124	16	47	31

We see that the premature births had a higher maternal age range than full-term births (31 compared to 30) although they have a lower sample size than the full-term births (124 compared to 876), so we conclude that the maternal age is more spread in premature births than in full-term births.

4.2.4.2. The Range of Visits Number in the Birth Types

```
births14 %>% group_by(premie) %>%
 get_summary_stats(visits, show = c("min,""max")) %>%
 mutate(range = max-min) %>%
 flextable() %>% theme_box() %>%
  set_caption(caption = "The range of the number of hospital visits during pregnancy in premature and full-term births of the US births data in 2014")
```

Table 4.14. *The Range of the Number of Hospital Visits During Pregnancy in Premature and Full-Term Births of the US Births Data in 2014*

Premie	Variable	n	Min	Max	Range
full term	visits	829	0	30	30
premie	visits	115	0	30	30

We see that the premature births had an equal maternal age range to that of full-term births (range = 30 in 2 birth types) although they had a lower sample size than the full-term births (115 compared to 829), so we conclude that the maternal age is equally spread in premature births and full-term births.

4.2.4.3. The Range of Run Time in the 2 Genders

```
run09 %>% group_by(gender) %>% get_summary_stats(time,
                    show = c("min,""max")) %>%
 mutate(range = max-min) %>%
 flextable() %>% theme_box() %>%
```

```
set_caption(caption = "The range of run time in males and females of Cherry
Blossom Run data in 2009")
```

Table 4.15. *The Range of Run Time in Males and Females of Cherry Blossom Run Data in 2009*

Gender	Variable	n	Min	Max	Range
F	time	8,323	53.533	169.617	116.084
M	time	6,651	45.933	157.517	111.584

We see that females had a higher run time range than males (116.084 compared to 111.584). This may be due that females had a higher sample size than males in this data (8323 compared to 6651), so other summary statistics of spread need to be calculated.

4.2.4.4. The Range of Run Time in the Different States

We also use the arrange function to arrange the states by their range in ascending order.

```
run09 %>% group_by(state) %>% get_summary_stats(time,

                          show = c("min,""max")) %>%

 mutate(range = max-min) %>%

 arrange(range) %>%

 flextable() %>% theme_box() %>%

 set_caption(caption = "The range of run time in runners from different states
of Cherry Blossom Run data in 2009")
```

Table 4.16. *The Range of Run Time in Runners From Different States of Cherry Blossom Run Data in 2009*

State	Vari-able	n	Min	Max	Range
AE	time	1	74.467	74.467	0.000
ID	time	1	107.733	107.733	0.000
SD	time	1	113.683	113.683	0.000
WY	time	1	100.383	100.383	0.000

AK	time	2	91.467	105.483	14.016
VT	time	6	82.833	106.233	23.400
NE	time	3	92.900	117.867	24.967
UT	time	2	93.367	118.983	25.616
NV	time	2	97.417	129.100	31.683
LA	time	2	86.783	119.717	32.934
AL	time	6	90.733	124.217	33.484
OK	time	4	75.200	109.600	34.400
KY	time	9	83.100	117.867	34.767
MS	time	3	85.450	125.133	39.683
IA	time	6	68.317	114.483	46.166
AR	time	2	106.517	153.417	46.900
RI	time	14	84.417	131.400	46.983
AZ	time	11	85.517	134.350	48.833
SC	time	11	79.617	132.983	53.366
PR	time	3	85.550	140.117	54.567
ME	time	10	65.300	121.800	56.500
WA	time	8	61.350	127.083	65.733
OR	time	5	86.817	153.850	67.033
IN	time	18	64.167	133.700	69.533
NM	time	7	58.333	132.817	74.484
DE	time	61	66.033	141.183	75.150
NH	time	19	58.233	134.800	76.567
MI	time	34	63.200	139.850	76.650
TN	time	10	80.067	156.867	76.800
KS	time	3	54.967	134.033	79.066
FL	time	55	68.733	148.183	79.450
WI	time	14	65.917	146.067	80.150
CO	time	23	48.050	130.133	82.083
WV	time	28	66.717	150.683	83.966
NC	time	158	62.567	149.400	86.833
NJ	time	207	62.333	149.883	87.550
MO	time	17	67.683	155.883	88.200

CA	time	75	60.950	149.333	88.383
CT	time	73	61.000	150.600	89.600
MN	time	19	48.067	139.300	91.233
TX	time	44	56.783	150.800	94.017
OH	time	80	59.667	154.450	94.783
NR	time	59	45.933	144.767	98.834
PA	time	461	50.700	149.733	99.033
MA	time	136	53.150	152.467	99.317
GA	time	37	55.733	156.783	101.050
IL	time	71	52.400	153.750	101.350
DC	time	3,464	53.233	158.133	104.900
NY	time	522	53.183	158.083	104.900
MD	time	3,558	51.183	158.233	107.050
VA	time	5,608	51.117	169.617	118.500

We see that:

1. When the sample size is 1 for the "AE," "ID," "SD," and "WY" states, the range is 0 because the minimum and maximum are the same numbers.
2. The lowest range was for the "AK" and "VT" states (14.016 and 23.400 respectively). However, this may be due to low sample sizes, 2 and 6 respectively. So, more measures of spread need to be calculated.
3. The highest range was for the "VA" and "MD" states (118.500 and 107.05 respectively). However, this may be due to large sample sizes, 5608 and 3558 respectively. So, more measures of spread need to be calculated.

4.2.5. Summary Statistics for Spread: The Standard Deviation

As we saw in Chapter 1, the standard deviation is the square root of the average squared differences from the sample mean. A large standard deviation indicates that data points are far from the mean and far from each other, while a small standard deviation indicates the opposite. A zero standard deviation indicates that all values within our data are identical.

The standard deviation is affected by outliers. However, we can calculate it for the different levels of categorical variable to see how the continuous variable spreads under these levels.

4.2.5.1. The Standard Deviation of Maternal Age in the Birth Types

To get the standard deviation of maternal age in 2 birth types, we will use the same above functions except that the get_summary_stats function will have the arguments, mage, and show = "sd" to calculate the standard deviation of maternal age within each birth type.

```
births14 %>% group_by(premie) %>%

 get_summary_stats(mage, show = "sd") %>%


 flextable() %>% theme_box() %>%


 set_caption(caption = "The standard deviation of maternal age in premature and full-term births of the US births data in 2014")
```

Table 4.17. *The Standard Deviation of Maternal Age in Premature and Full-Term Births of the US Births Data in 2014*

Premie	Variable	n	sd
full term	mage	876	5.721
premie	mage	124	5.982

We see that the maternal age standard deviation (sd) is higher in premature births than in full-term births (5.982 compared to 5.721), so we conclude that the maternal age is more spread in premature births than in full-term births in this data.

4.2.5.2. The Standard Deviation of Visits Number in the Birth Types

```
births14 %>% group_by(premie) %>%

 get_summary_stats(visits, show = "sd") %>%


 flextable() %>% theme_box() %>%


 set_caption(caption = "The standard deviation of the number of hospital visits during pregnancy in premature and full-term births of the US births data in 2014")
```

Table 4.18. The Standard Deviation of the Number of Hospital Visits During Pregnancy in Premature and Full-Term births of the US Births Data in 2014

Premie	Variable	n	sd
full term	visits	829	3.884
premie	visits	115	5.329

We see that the visits standard deviation is higher in premature births than in full-term births (5.329 compared to 3.884), so we may conclude that the number of visits is more spread in premature births than in full-term births in this data.

4.2.5.3. The Standard Deviation of Run Time in the 2 Genders

```
run09 %>% group_by(gender) %>% get_summary_stats(time,

                                show = "sd") %>%

 flextable() %>% theme_box() %>%

 set_caption(caption = "The standard deviation of run time in males and females of Cherry Blossom Run data in 2009")
```

Table 4.19. The Standard Deviation of Run Time in Males and Females of Cherry Blossom Run Data in 2009

Gender	Variable	n	sd
F	time	8,323	17.453
M	time	6,651	19.095

We see that females had a lower run time standard deviation than males (17.453 compared to 19.095). So, we may conclude that the run time in females is less spread than that in males.

4.2.5.4. The Standard Deviation of Run Time in the Different States

We also use the arrange function to arrange the states by their standard deviation in ascending order.

```
run09 %>% group_by(state) %>% get_summary_stats(time,

                                show = "sd") %>%
```

```
arrange(sd) %>%

flextable() %>% theme_box() %>%

set_caption(caption = "The standard deviation of run time in runners from different states of Cherry Blossom Run data in 2009")
```

Table 4.20. *The Standard Deviation of Run Time in Runners from Different States of Cherry Blossom Run Data in 2009*

State	Variable	n	sd
AK	time	2	9.911
KY	time	9	10.293
VT	time	6	10.386
NE	time	3	13.092
SC	time	11	13.932
AL	time	6	14.478
RI	time	14	15.075
DE	time	61	15.277
AZ	time	11	17.478
IA	time	6	17.696
CT	time	73	17.926
UT	time	2	18.113
DC	time	3,464	18.138
ME	time	10	18.142
PA	time	461	18.676
NJ	time	207	18.813
NC	time	158	18.945
OK	time	4	19.113
VA	time	5,608	19.217
MD	time	3,558	19.492
IL	time	71	19.559
NY	time	522	19.890
MI	time	34	20.176
WA	time	8	20.426
MA	time	136	20.460

MS	time	3	20.946
IN	time	18	21.059
MN	time	19	21.240
OH	time	80	21.389
FL	time	55	21.553
CA	time	75	21.601
NV	time	2	22.403
CO	time	23	22.556
TN	time	10	22.920
TX	time	44	23.227
MO	time	17	23.240
LA	time	2	23.288
NH	time	19	23.610
WI	time	14	24.185
WV	time	28	24.488
NM	time	7	25.337
GA	time	37	25.755
PR	time	3	27.286
OR	time	5	27.875
NR	time	59	28.123
AR	time	2	33.163
KS	time	3	42.195
AE	time	1	
ID	time	1	
SD	time	1	
WY	time	1	

We see that:

1. When the sample size is 1 as for the "AE," "ID," "SD," and "WY" states, the standard deviation is missing because the sample size is 1 with no variation.
2. The lowest standard deviation was for the "AK" and "KY" states (9.911 and 10.293 respectively). So, the run time of runners from these states is less spread than in other states, although they have a low sample size (2 and 9 runners respectively).

3. The highest standard deviation was for the "KS" and "AR" states (42.195 and 33.163 respectively). So, the run time of runners from these states is more spread than in other states, although they have a low sample size (3 and 2 runners respectively).

4.2.6. Summary Statistics for Spread: The Interquartile Range (IQR)

As we saw in Chapter 1, the interquartile range (IQR) is the difference between the first and third quartiles (Q3-Q1) and provides an estimate of the data spread. The IQR contains the middle 50% of our data. The interquartile range is a **robust statistic** since it is less sensitive to outliers or sample size than the standard deviation or the range. We can calculate the IQR for the different levels of categorical variable to see how the continuous variable spreads under these levels.

4.2.6.1. The IQR of Maternal Age in the Birth Types

To get the IQR of maternal age in the 2 birth types, we will use the same above functions except that the get_summary_stats function will have the arguments, mage, and show = "iqr" to calculate the IQR of maternal age within each birth type.

```
births14 %>% group_by(premie) %>%

 get_summary_stats(mage, show = "iqr") %>%


 flextable() %>% theme_box() %>%

 set_caption(caption = "The interquartile range of maternal age in premature and
full-term births of the US births data in 2014")
```

Table 4.21. *The Interquartile Range of Maternal Age in Premature and Full-Term Births of the US Births Data in 2014*

Premie	Variable	n	iqr
full term	mage	876	9
premie	mage	124	10

We see that the maternal age IQR is higher in premature births than in full-term births (10 compared to 9), so we may conclude that the maternal age is more spread in premature births than in full-term births in this data.

4.2.6.2. The IQR of Visits Number in the Birth Types

```
births14 %>% group_by(premie) %>%
 get_summary_stats(visits, show = "iqr") %>%
 flextable() %>% theme_box() %>%
 set_caption(caption = "The IQR of the number of hospital visits during pregnancy
in premature and full-term births of the US births data in 2014")
```

Table 4.22. *The IQR of the Number of Hospital Visits During Pregnancy in Premature and Full-term Births of the US Births Data in 2014*

Premie	Variable	n	iqr
full term	visits	829	4
premie	visits	115	5

We see that the visits IQR is higher in premature births than in full-term births (5 compared to 4), so we may conclude that the number of visits is more spread in premature births than in full-term births in this data.

4.2.6.3. The IQR of Run Time in the 2 Genders

```
run09 %>% group_by(gender) %>% get_summary_stats(time,

                         show = "iqr") %>%

flextable() %>% theme_box() %>%

 set_caption(caption = "The IQR of run time in males and females of Cherry
Blossom Run data in 2009")
```

Table 4.23. *The IQR of Run Time in Males and Females of Cherry Blossom Run Data in 2009*

Gender	Variable	n	iqr
F	time	8,323	23.808
M	time	6,651	26.683

We see that females had lower run time IQR than males (23.808 compared to 26.683). So, we may conclude that the run time in females is less spread than that in males.

4.2.6.4. The IQR of Run Time in the Different States

We also use the arrange function to arrange the states by their IQR value in ascending order.

```
run09 %>% group_by(state) %>% get_summary_stats(time,

                            show = "iqr") %>%

 arrange(iqr) %>%

 flextable() %>% theme_box() %>%

 set_caption(caption = "The IQR of run time in runners from different states of
Cherry Blossom Run data in 2009")
```

Table 4.24. *The IQR of Run Time in Runners from Different States of Cherry Blossom Run Data in 2009*

State	Variable	n	iqr
AE	time	1	0.000
ID	time	1	0.000
SD	time	1	0.000
WY	time	1	0.000
AK	time	2	7.008
SC	time	11	7.408
KY	time	9	10.283
NE	time	3	12.484
UT	time	2	12.808
NV	time	2	15.841
LA	time	2	16.467
RI	time	14	17.254
VT	time	6	17.908
DE	time	61	19.650
MS	time	3	19.841
ME	time	10	21.579
AL	time	6	23.171
IA	time	6	23.296

AR	time	2	23.450
WA	time	8	23.846
MO	time	17	23.950
AZ	time	11	24.158
NC	time	158	24.313
MN	time	19	24.791
PA	time	461	25.167
WV	time	28	25.238
NM	time	7	25.808
IL	time	71	25.824
CT	time	73	25.883
IN	time	18	26.216
DC	time	3,464	26.300
NJ	time	207	26.617
MD	time	3,558	27.129
PR	time	3	27.284
VA	time	5,608	27.624
MA	time	136	27.813
TN	time	10	28.304
OH	time	80	28.570
NY	time	522	28.800
CA	time	75	29.541
CO	time	23	29.691
MI	time	34	29.909
OK	time	4	32.412
OR	time	5	33.283
FL	time	55	34.250
WI	time	14	34.412
NH	time	19	34.617
TX	time	44	36.338
KS	time	3	39.533
GA	time	37	42.083
NR	time	59	44.291

We see that:

1. When the sample size is 1 as for the "AE," "ID," "SD," and "WY" states, the IQR is 0 because the sample size is 1 with no variation.
2. The lowest IQR was for the "AK" and "SC" states (7.008 and 7.408 respectively). So, the run time of runners from these states is less spread than in other states.
3. The highest IQR was for the "NR" and "GA" states (44.291 and 42.083 respectively). So, the run time of runners from these states is more spread than in other states.

4.2.7. Summary Statistics for Spread: The Median Absolute Deviation (MAD)

The MAD is another robust statistic for measuring the variability of numeric data. MAD is the median absolute distance that the data points are from the median. We can calculate the MAD for the different levels of categorical variable to see how the continuous variable spreads under these levels.

4.2.7.1. The MAD of Maternal Age in the Birth Types

To get the MAD of maternal age in the 2 birth types, we will use the same above functions except that the get_summary_stats function will have the arguments, mage, and show = "mad" to calculate the MAD of maternal age within each birth type.

```
births14 %>% group_by(premie) %>%

 get_summary_stats(mage, show = "mad") %>%

 flextable() %>% theme_box() %>%

 set_caption(caption = "The median absolute deviation of maternal age in premature and full-term births of the US births data in 2014")
```

Table 4.25. The Median Absolute Deviation of Maternal Age in Premature and Full-Term Births of the US Births Data in 2014

Premie	Variable	n	mad
full term	mage	876	5.930
premie	mage	124	7.413

We see that the maternal age MAD is higher in premature births than in full-term births (7.413 compared to 5.930), so we may conclude that the maternal age is more spread in premature births than in full-term births in this data.

4.2.7.2. The MAD of Visits Number in the Birth Types

```
births14 %>% group_by(premie) %>%
 get_summary_stats(visits, show = "mad") %>%
 flextable() %>% theme_box() %>%
 set_caption(caption = "The median absolute deviation of the number of hospital visits during pregnancy in premature and full-term births of the US births data in 2014")
```

Table 4.26. The Median Absolute Deviation of the Number of hospital Visits During Pregnancy in Premature and full-Term Births of the US Births Data in 2014

Premie	Variable	n	MAD
full term	visits	829	2.965
premie	visits	115	4.448

We see that the visits MAD is higher in premature births than in full-term births (4.448 compared to 2.965), so we may conclude that the number of visits is more spread in premature births than in full-term births in this data.

4.2.7.3. The MAD of Run Time in the 2 Genders

```
run09 %>% group_by(gender) %>% get_summary_stats(time,
                        show = "mad") %>%

 flextable() %>% theme_box() %>%

 set_caption(caption = "The MAD of run time in males and females of Cherry Blossom Run data in 2009")
```

Table 4.27. *The MAD of Run Time in Males and Females of Cherry Blossom Run Data in 2009*

Gender	Variable	n	MAD
F	time	8,323	17.643
M	time	6,651	19.769

We see that females had lower run time MAD than males (17.643 compared to 19.769). So, we may conclude that the run time in females is less spread than that in males.

4.2.7.4. The MAD of Run Time in the Different States

We also use the arrange function to arrange the states by their MAD value in ascending order.

```
run09 %>% group_by(state) %>% get_summary_stats(time,
                    show = "mad") %>%
 arrange(mad) %>%
 flextable() %>% theme_box() %>%
 set_caption(caption = "The MAD of run time in runners from different states of Cherry Blossom Run data in 2009")
```

Table 4.28. The MAD of Run Time in Runners from Different States of Cherry Blossom Run Data in 2009

State	Variable	n	MAD
AE	time	1	0.000
ID	time	1	0.000
SD	time	1	0.000
WY	time	1	0.000
KY	time	9	1.804
SC	time	11	6.672
NE	time	3	8.377
AK	time	2	10.390
NR	time	59	12.058
MS	time	3	12.183
RI	time	14	12.837
VT	time	6	12.973
DE	time	61	14.034
ME	time	10	14.987
AL	time	6	15.148

IA	time	6	17.902
CT	time	73	18.335
OH	time	80	18.383
IL	time	71	18.755
MO	time	17	18.829
OR	time	5	18.903
PA	time	461	18.903
UT	time	2	18.989
MN	time	19	19.026
DC	time	3,464	19.311
NJ	time	207	19.398
NC	time	158	19.434
WV	time	28	19.694
MD	time	3,558	20.090
VA	time	5,608	20.584
KS	time	3	20.731
MA	time	136	20.831
WA	time	8	20.856
NY	time	522	21.387
NH	time	19	21.646
CO	time	23	21.818
TN	time	10	22.091
AZ	time	11	22.387
CA	time	75	22.438
MI	time	34	23.178
NV	time	2	23.487
OK	time	4	24.216
LA	time	2	24.414
GA	time	37	25.772
FL	time	55	25.994
IN	time	18	26.143
TX	time	44	27.725
WI	time	14	27.762

NM	time	7	28.860
AR	time	2	34.767
PR	time	3	39.585

We see that:

1. When the sample size is 1 as for the "AE," "ID," "SD," and "WY" states, the MAD is 0 because the sample size is 1 with no variation.
2. The lowest MAD was for the "KY" and "SC" states (1.804 and 6.672 respectively). So, the run time of runners from these states is less spread than in other states.
3. The highest MAD was for the "PR" and "AR" states (39.585 and 34.767 respectively). So, the run time of runners from these states is more spread than in other states.

4.3. SUMMARY PLOTS

4.3.1. Histogram

Histograms show the distribution of a continuous variable by dividing the x-axis into bins, counting the number of observations in each bin, and displaying the counts with bars. By producing a histogram for each level of the categorical variable, we can see how the continuous variable distributes under the different levels of the categorical variable.

4.3.1.1. Histograms of Maternal Age in the Birth Types

To produce a histogram with different fill color for each birth type, we use the following functions:

- The ggplot function, applied on the "births14" data frame," with the arguments, aes(x = mage, fill = premie), to plot "mage" or maternal age on the x-axis and the bins will have different fill color for each level of "premie" column. So we will have 2 different fill colors, one for full-term births and the other for premature births.
- The geom_histogram function with the argument, color = "black," to make the histogram bins have a black border so the fill color can be seen easily.
- The labs function with the arguments, title to plot a plot title, x to plot an x-axis title, y to plot a y-axis title, and fill to plot a legend title.

- The theme_classic and theme functions as described in previous chapters.

```
births14 %>% ggplot(aes(x = mage, fill = premie))+

 geom_histogram(color = "black")+
 labs(title = "Histogram of maternal age in premature and full-term births of the US births data in 2014,"
 x = "Maternal age,"
   y = "Count," fill = "Birth type")+
 theme_classic()+
 theme(plot.title = element_text(hjust = 0.5))
```

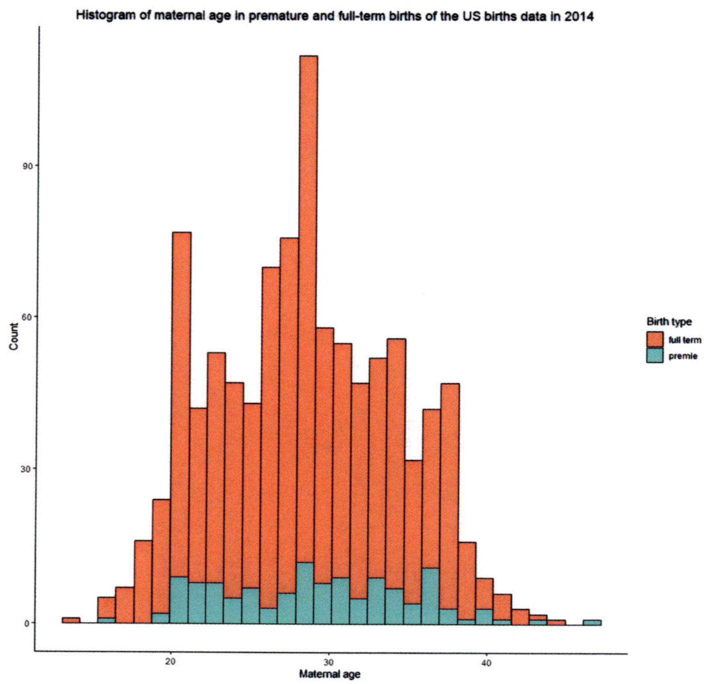

We see that:

- The bins of full-term births are taller than that of premature births indicating that the count of full-term births is higher than that of preterm births and we have seen that above because the sample size of full-term births is 876 compared to only 124 premature births.

- The distribution of maternal age in full-term or premature births is nearly normal with peak count at the center and low counts at the tails (high or small values).

Alternatively, we can plot a separate plot for each birth type by using the function facet_wrap with the arguments, ~premie, nrow = 1, to produce a separate plot for each level of the "premie" column and the 2 plots are in 1 row.

```
births14 %>% ggplot(aes(x = mage, fill = premie))+
 geom_histogram(color = "black")+
  facet_wrap(~premie, nrow = 1)+
 labs(title = "Histogram of maternal age in premature and full-term births of
the US births data in 2014\n using facet_wrap function,"
   x = "Maternal age,"
   y = "Count," fill = "Birth type")+
 theme_classic()+
 theme(plot.title = element_text(hjust = 0.5))
```

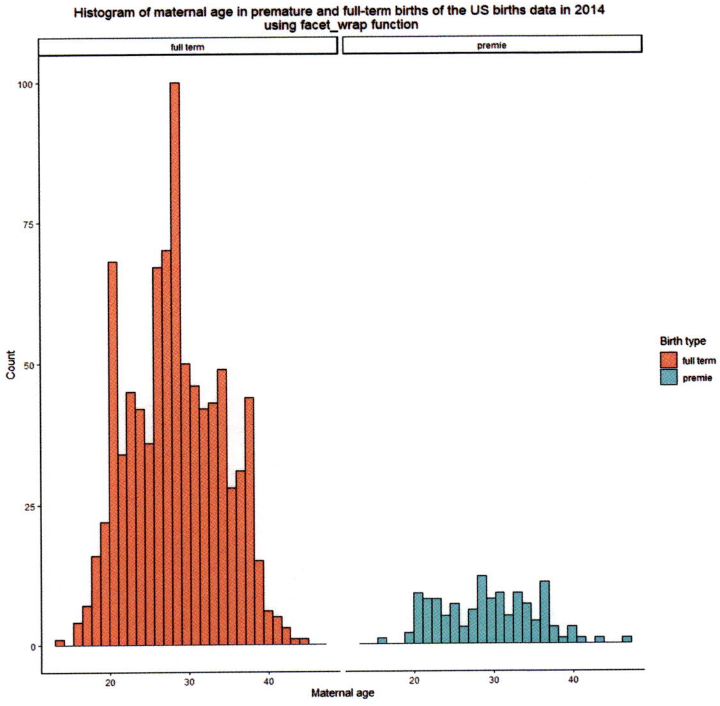

We note the same comments stated above.

4.3.1.2. Histograms of Visits Number in the Birth Types

To produce a histogram of the number of hospital visits with different fill color for each birth type, we use the same above functions except that the ggplot function will have the arguments, aes(x = visits, fill = premie), to plot "visits" or number of visits during pregnancy on the x-axis and the bins will have different fill color for each birth type.

```
births14 %>% ggplot(aes(x = visits, fill = premie))+
 geom_histogram(color = "black")+
 labs(title = "Histogram of number of hospital visits during pregnancy\n in premature and full-term births of the US births data in 2014,"
    x = "Number of visits,"
y = "Count," fill = "Birth type")+
 theme_classic()+
 theme(plot.title = element_text(hjust = 0.5))
```

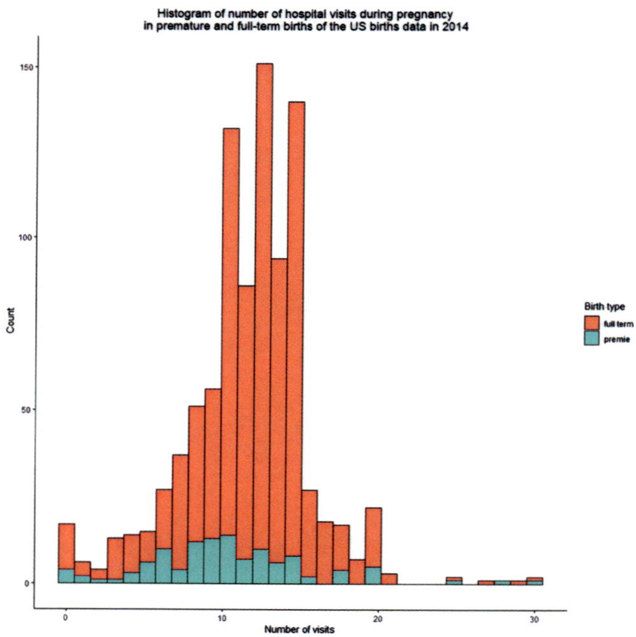

We see that:

- The bins of full-term births are taller than that of premature births indicating that the count of full-term births is higher than that of preterm births.

- The distribution of visits in full-term or premature births is nearly normal with peak count at the center and low counts at the tails (high or small values).
- The distribution of visits in full-term births is more shifted to the right than that of premature births. This means that a higher number of visits may be associated with full-term birth.

Alternatively, we can plot a separate plot for each birth type by using the function facet_wrap with the arguments, ~premie, ncol = 1, to produce a separate plot for each level of the "premie" column and the 2 plots are in 1 column.

```
births14 %>% ggplot(aes(x = visits, fill = premie))+
 geom_histogram(color = "black")+
  facet_wrap(~premie, ncol = 1)+
 labs(title = "Histogram of number of hospital visits during pregnancy\n in premature and full-term births of the US births data in 2014\n using facet_wrap function,"
    x = "Number of visits,"
    y = "Count," fill = "Birth type")+
 theme_classic()+
 theme(plot.title = element_text(hjust = 0.5))
```

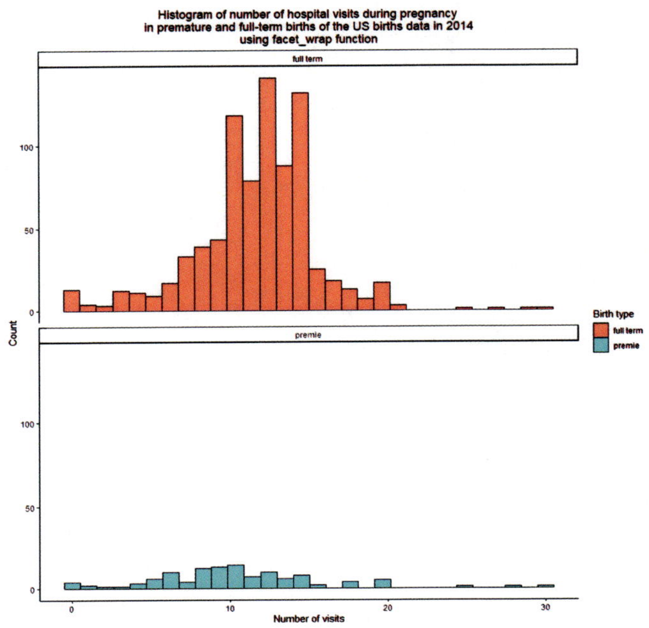

We note the same comments stated above.

4.3.1.3. Histograms of Run Time in the 2 Genders

To produce a histogram of the run time with different fill color for each gender, we use the same above functions except that the ggplot function will be applied on "run09" data and have the arguments, aes(x = time, fill = gender), to plot the run time on the x-axis and the bins will have different fill color for each gender.

```
run09 %>% ggplot(aes(x = time, fill = gender))+
 geom_histogram(color = "black")+
 labs(title = "Histogram of run time in males and females of Cherry Blossom Run data in 2009,"
    x = "Time,"
    y = "Count," fill = "Gender")+
 theme_classic()+
 theme(plot.title = element_text(hjust = 0.5))
```

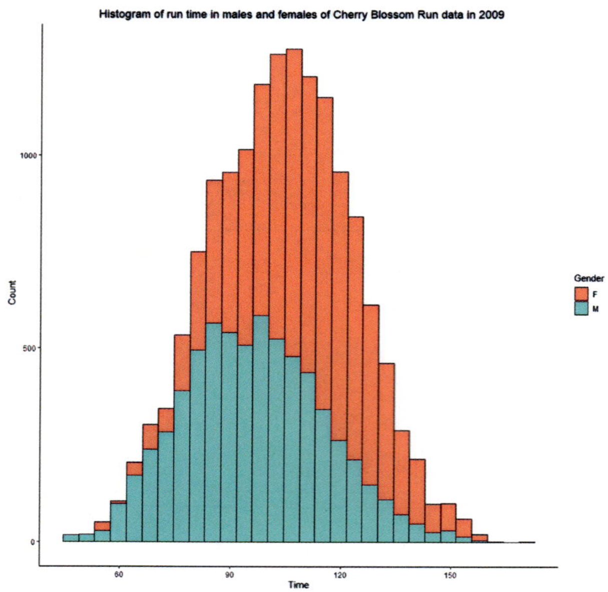

We see that:

- The bins of females are taller than that of males indicating that the count of females is higher than that of males in this data.
- The distribution of run time in females or males is nearly normal with peak count at the center and low counts at the tails (high or small values).

- The distribution of run time in females is more shifted to the right than that of males. This means that females have higher run time (slower) than males.

Alternatively, we can plot a separate plot for each gender by using the function facet_wrap with the arguments, ~gender, ncol = 1, to produce a separate plot for each gender and the 2 plots will be in 1 column.

```
run09 %>% ggplot(aes(x = time, fill = gender))+
 geom_histogram(color = "black")+
  facet_wrap(~gender, ncol = 1)+
 labs(title = "Histogram of run time in males and females of Cherry Blossom Run
data in 2009\n using facet_wrap function,"
 x = "Time,"
    y = "Count," fill = "Gender")+
 theme_classic()+
 theme(plot.title = element_text(hjust = 0.5))
```

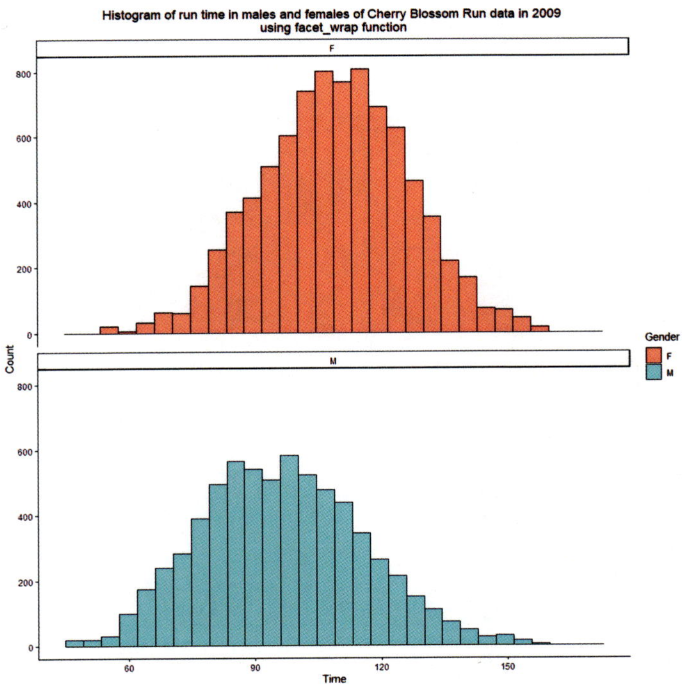

We note the same comments stated above.

4.3.1.4. Histograms of Run Time in Runners from Different States

Because we have 51 different states in our data, we cannot plot the bins from all states in 1 plot as the plot will be very crowded. Alternatively, we can plot a separate plot for each state by using the function facet_wrap with the arguments, ~state, scales = “free,” to produce a separate plot for each state and each plot will have its x-axis and y-axis with separate limits. We also remove the unnecessary legend by using the argument, show.legend = FALSE, inside the geom_histogram function.

```
run09 %>% ggplot(aes(x = time, fill = state))+
 geom_histogram(color = “black,” show.legend = FALSE)+
  facet_wrap(~state, scales = “free”)+
 labs(title = “Histogram of run time in runners from different states of Cherry Blossom Run data in 2009\n using facet_wrap function,”
    x = “Time,”
    y = “Count”)+
theme_classic()+
 theme(plot.title = element_text(hjust = 0.5))
```

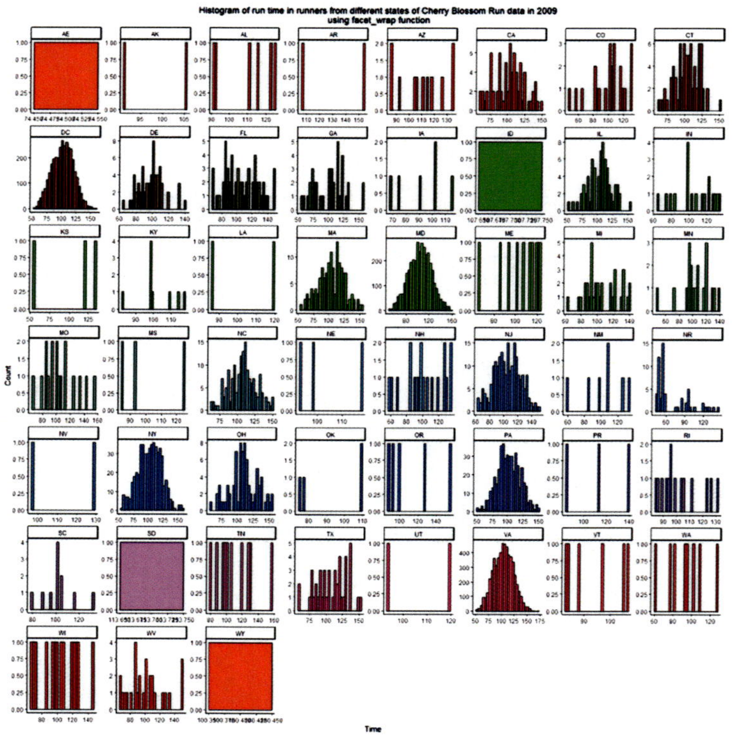

We note that each state has its x-axis and y-axis with a specific limit according to its values. For example, the "AZ" state has x-axis values from 90 to 130, while the "CT" state has x-axis values from 75 to 150.

4.3.2. Box Plot

As we see in Chapter 1, the box plot displays the distribution of a continuous variable by displaying the median, two hinges two whiskers, and all outliers individually. The lower and upper hinges correspond to the first and third quartiles (Q1 and Q3)respectively. The upper whisker extends from Q3 to the largest value no further than 1.5 X IQR from Q3. The lower whisker extends from Q1 to the smallest value at most 1.5 X IQR from Q1. Data beyond the end of the whiskers are called "outlying" points and are plotted individually.

By plotting a box plot for each level of the categorical variable, we can see how the continuous variable distributes under these different levels.

4.3.2.1. Box Plots of Maternal Age in the Birth Types

To produce a box plot with different fill color for each birth type, we use the following functions:

- The ggplot function, applied on the "births14" data frame, with the arguments, aes(x = premie, fill = premie, y = mage), to plot the "premie" or the 2 levels of "premie" column on the x-axis, "mage" or maternal age on the y-axis and the box plots will have different fill color for each level of "premie" column. So we will have 2 different fill colors, one for full-term births and the other for premature births.
- The geom_boxplot function plots a box plot.
- The labs, theme_classic, and theme functions as described previously.

```
births14 %>% ggplot(aes(x = premie, fill = premie, y = mage))+

 geom_boxplot()+

 labs(title = "Box plot of maternal age in premature and full-term births of
the US births data in 2014,"

    x = "Birth type,"

    y = "Maternal age," fill = "Birth type")+

 theme_classic()+

 theme(plot.title = element_text(hjust = 0.5))
```

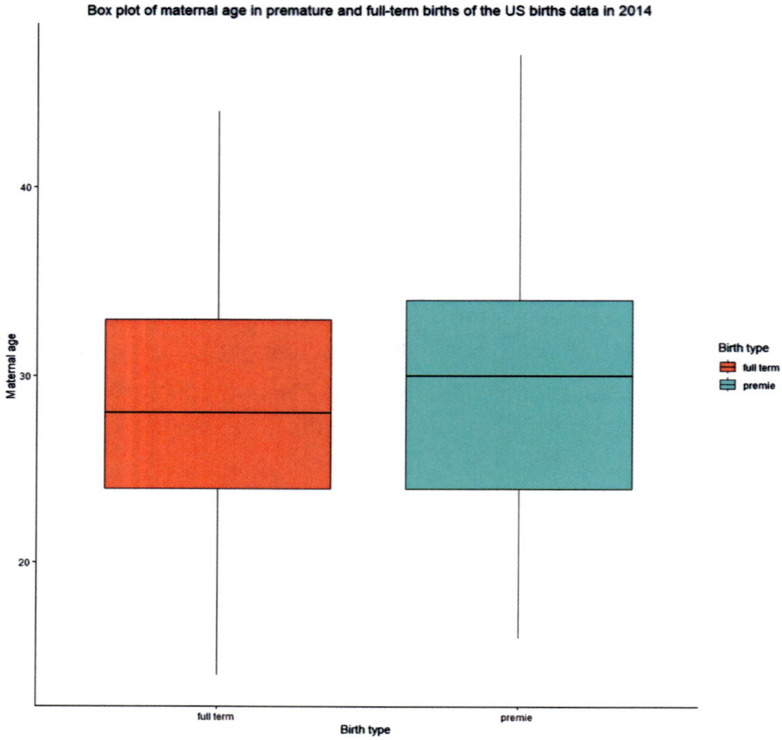

We see that:

- The distribution of maternal age in full-term or premature births is nearly normal with the median line equally spaced from the 1st and 3rd quartiles. There are no outliers in the maternal age for both birth types.
- The box plot of maternal age in premature births is shifted up to that of maternal age in full-term births. This means that high maternal age may be associated with premature births.

4.3.2.2. Box Plots of Number of Visits in the Birth Types

To produce a box plot of the number of visits with different fill color for each birth type, we use the same functions except that the ggplot function will have the arguments, aes(x = premie, fill = premie, y = visits), to plot "premie" or the 2 levels of "premie" column on the x-axis, visits number on the y-axis and the box plots will have different fill color for each level of "premie" column.

```
births14 %>% ggplot(aes(x = premie, fill = premie, y = visits))+
 geom_boxplot()+
  labs(title = "Box plot of number of hospital visits during pregnancy \nin premature and full-term births of the US births data in 2014,"
    x = "Birth type,"
    y = "Number of hospital visits during pregnancy,"
    fill = "Birth type")+
 theme_classic()+
 theme(plot.title = element_text(hjust = 0.5))
```

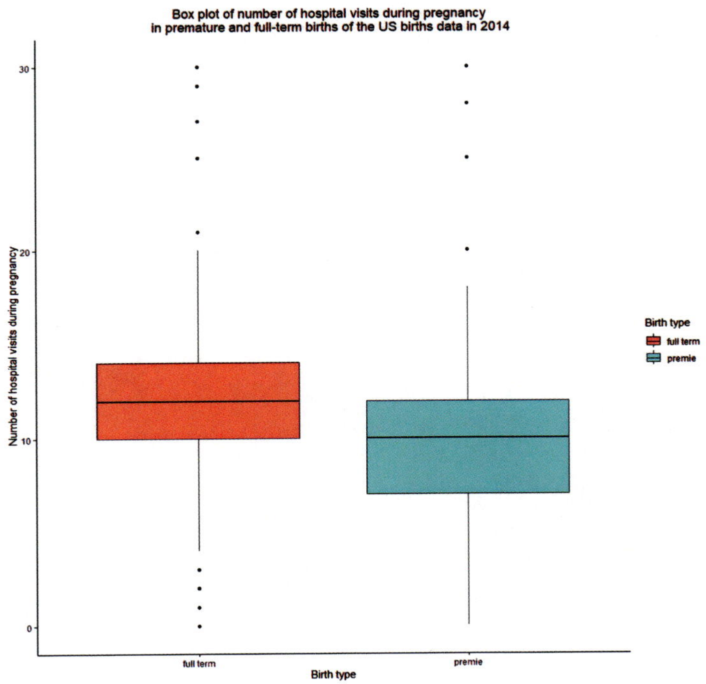

We see that:

- The distribution of the visits number in full-term or premature births is nearly normal with the median line equally spaced from the 1st and 3rd quartiles. However, there are large and small outliers of visits in full-term births and large outliers of visits in premature births.
- The box plot of visits in premature births is shifted down to that of visits in full-term births. This means that the low number of visits may be associated with premature births.

4.3.2.3. Box Plots of Run Time in the 2 Genders

To produce a box plot of the run time with different fill color for each gender, we use the same functions except that the ggplot function will have the arguments, aes(x = gender, fill = gender, y = time), to plot gender on the x-axis, run time on the y-axis and the box plots will have different fill color for each level of the gender column.

```
run09 %>% ggplot(aes(x = gender, fill = gender, y = time))+
 geom_boxplot()+
 labs(title = "Box plot of run time in males and females of Cherry Blossom Run
data in 2009,"
    x = "Gender,"
    y = "Run time,"
    fill = "Gender")+
 theme_classic()+
 theme(plot.title = element_text(hjust = 0.5))
```

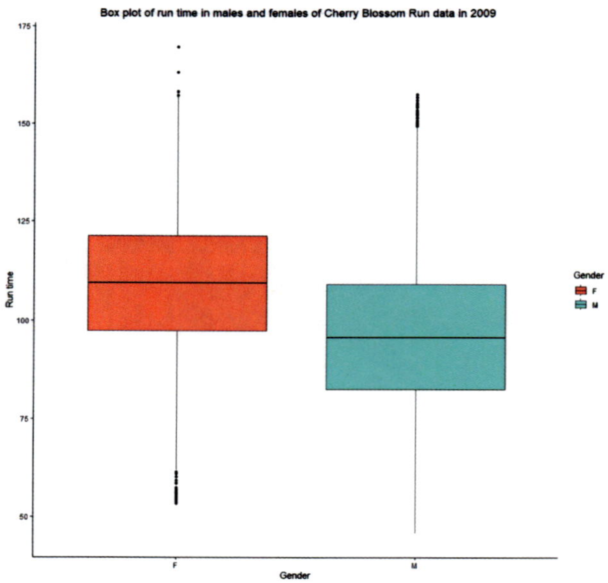

We see that:

- The distribution of the run time in females or males is nearly normal with the median line equally spaced from the 1st and 3rd quartiles. However, there are large and small outliers of run time in females and large outliers of run time in males.

- The box plot of run time in males is shifted down than that of females. This means that males had lower run time (faster) than females.

4.3.2.4. Box Plots of Run Time in Runners from Different States

To produce a box plot of the run time with different fill color for each state, we use the same functions except that the ggplot function will have the arguments, aes(x = state, fill = state, y = time), to plot states on the x-axis, run time on the y-axis and the box plots will have different fill color for each level of the state column.

```
run09 %>% ggplot(aes(x = state, fill = state, y = time))+
 geom_boxplot()+
 labs(title = "Box plot of run time in runners from different states of Cherry Blossom Run data in 2009,"
    x = "State,"
    y = "Run time,"
    fill = "State")+
theme_classic()+
 theme(plot.title = element_text(hjust = 0.5))
```

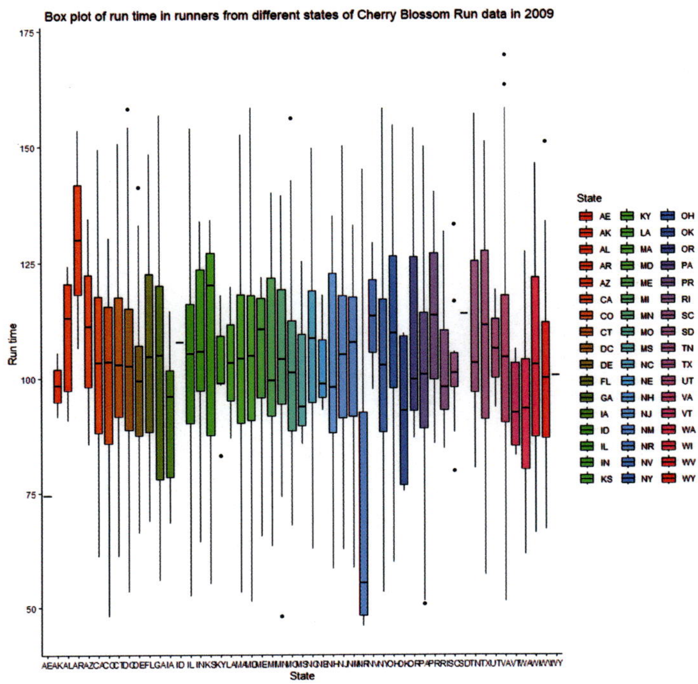

We see that the x-axis is very crowded and some states have only a dash (like "AE" and "WY" states) because their sample size is only 1 (one runner from these states).

We can further customize this plot by:

- Removing the states with a single count ("AE," "ID," "SD," and "WY" states) using the filter function. The filter function will have the "!" operator on the states %in% c("AE," "ID," "SD," "WY") to filter out these states.
- Removing the legend by using the argument show.legend = FALSE within the geom_boxplot function.
- Arranging the states by their median time using the fct_reorder function within the mutate function. The fct_reorder function will have the state, time, .fun = median, to arrange states by their median time in ascending order.

```
run09 %>% filter(!state %in% c("AE," "ID," "SD," "WY")) %>%

 mutate(state = fct_reorder(state,time, .fun = median)) %>%

 ggplot(aes(x = state, fill = state, y = time))+

 geom_boxplot(show.legend = FALSE)+


 labs(title = "Box plot of run time in runners from 47 states of Cherry Blossom
Run data in 2009 \n arranged by median time,"

   x = "State,"

   y = "Run time")+

 theme_classic()+

 theme(plot.title = element_text(hjust = 0.5))
```

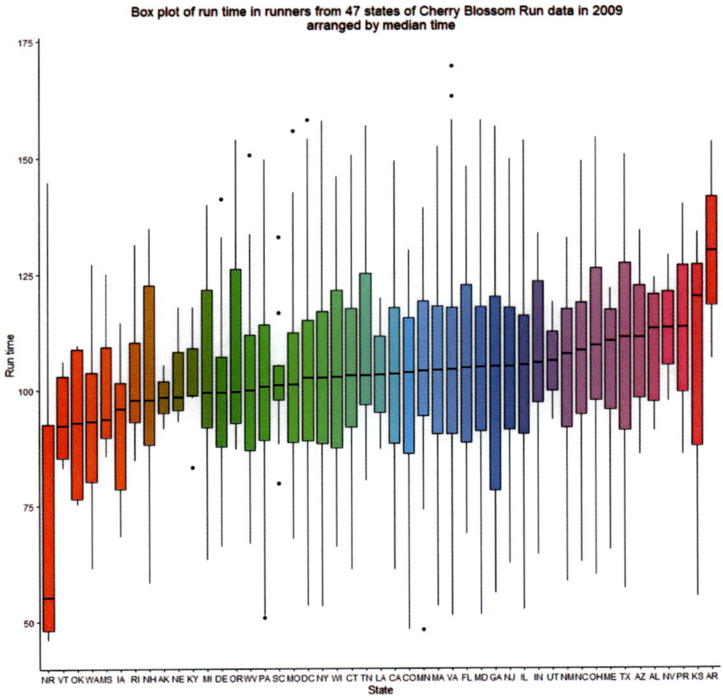

We see that:

- The distribution of the run time in different states may be symmetric with the upper and lower quartiles nearly equally spaced from the median (like "DC" and "NY" states), right skewed with the median line closer to the 1st quartile line than to the 3rd quartile (as "NR" state), or left skewed with the median line closer to the 3rd quartile line than to the 1st quartile line (as "KS" state)
- The lowest median run time was for runners from the "NR" state, while the highest median run time was for runners from the "AR" state. So runners from the "NR" state are faster than other runners from other states.

4.3.3. Strip Plot

A strip chart is a scatter plot used to see the relation between a continuous variable (on the x-axis) and a categorical variable (on the y-axis).

4.3.3.1. Strip Plot of Maternal Age in the Birth Types

To create this plot, we will use the following functions:

- The ggplot function with the arguments, aes(x = mage, y = premie, color = premie), to plot maternal age "mage" on the x-axis and premie column on the y-axis with coloring the points by a different color for each birth type.
- The geom_point function to draw the scatter plot.
- The labs, theme_classic, and theme functions as described before.

```
births14 %>%
ggplot(aes(x = mage, y = premie, color = premie))+
 geom_point()+
 labs(title = "Strip plot of maternal age in premature and full-term births of the US births data in 2014,"
    x = "Maternal age," y = "Birth type,"
    color = "Birth type")+
 theme_classic()+
 theme(plot.title = element_text(hjust = 0.5))
```

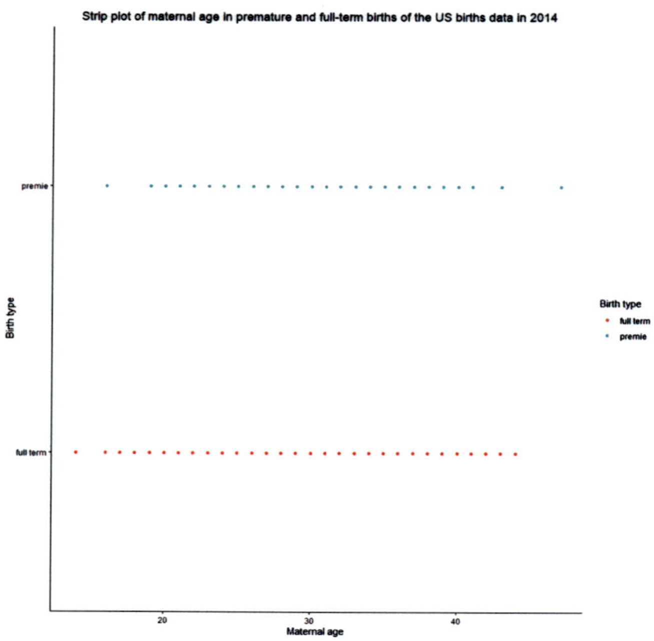

We see that:

- The different data points are superimposed over each other which makes the interpretation difficult.
- The distribution of maternal age in premature births is more shifted to the right (higher) than that of maternal age in full-term births. This means that higher maternal age may be associated with premature births.

lternatively, the continuous categorical relationship can be seen easily if the points are jittered (displaced) using the geom_jitter function. The geom_jitter function adds a small amount of random variation to the location of each data point so the points are less to be superimposed over each other.

As it adds randomness to the location at each point, we must use the set. seed function (with any number of our choice) for a reproducible plot. We simply replace the geom_point function with the geom_jitter function in the above code chunk.

```
set.seed(123)

births14 %>%

ggplot(aes(x = mage, y = premie, color = premie))+

 geom_jitter()+

 labs(title = "Strip plot of maternal age in premature and full-term births of the US births data in 2014\n using geom_jitter function,"

   x = "Maternal age," y = "Birth type,"

   color = "Birth type")+

 theme_classic()+

 theme(plot.title = element_text(hjust = 0.5))
```

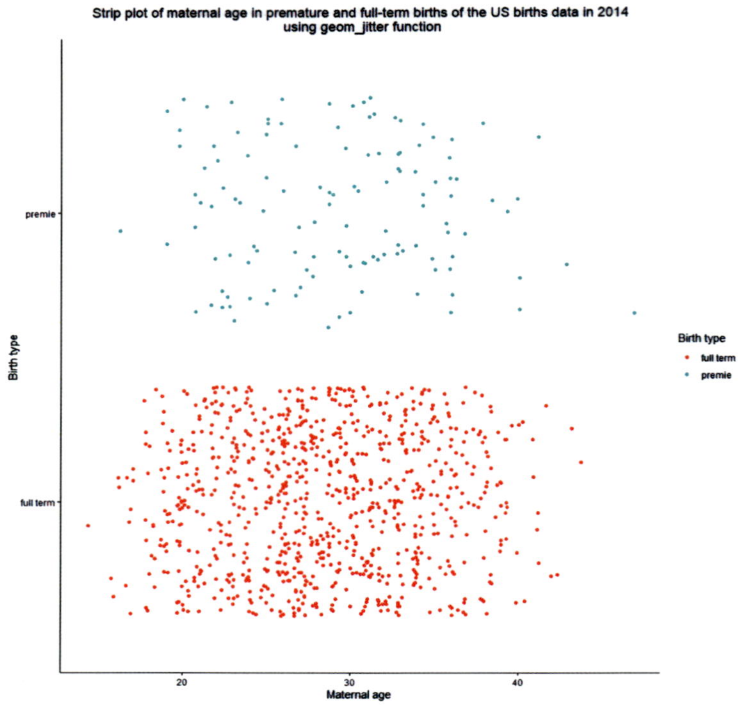

The using of the geom_jitter function has revealed that the sample size of premature births is much lower than that of full-term births.

4.3.3.2. Strip Plot of Visits Number in the Birth Types

To create this plot, we will use the same above functions except that the ggplot function will have the arguments, aes(x = visits, y = premie, color = premie), to plot the visits number on the x-axis and premie column on the y-axis with coloring the points by a different color for each birth type.

```
births14 %>%
ggplot(aes(x = visits, y = premie, color = premie))+
 geom_point()+
 labs(title = "Strip plot of number of hospital visits during pregnancy\n in premature and full-term births of the US births data in 2014,"
    x = "Number of hospital visits during pregnancy," y = "Birth type,"
    color = "Birth type")+
 theme_classic()+
 theme(plot.title = element_text(hjust = 0.5))
```

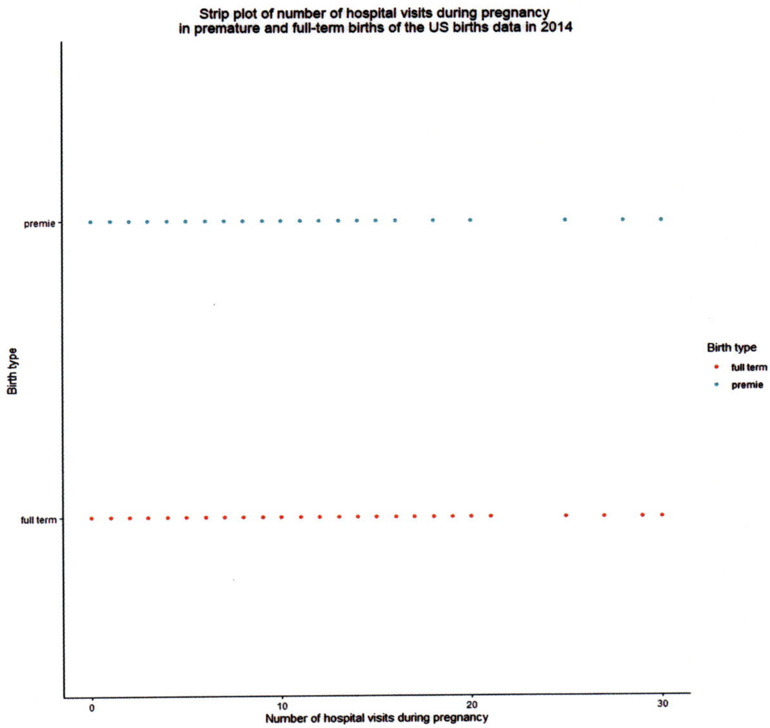

We see that:

- The distribution of visits number in premature births is similar to that of the visits number in full-term births.

Alternatively, the relationship can be seen easily if the points are jittered (displaced) using the geom_jitter function as before.

```
set.seed(123)
births14 %>%
ggplot(aes(x = visits, y = premie, color = premie))+
 geom_jitter()+
  labs(title = "Strip plot of number of hospital visits during pregnancy in premature and full-term births of the US births data in 2014\n using geom_jitter function,"
    x = "Number of hospital visits during pregnancy," y = "Birth type,"
    color = "Birth type")+
theme_classic()+
 theme(plot.title = element_text(hjust = 0.5))
```

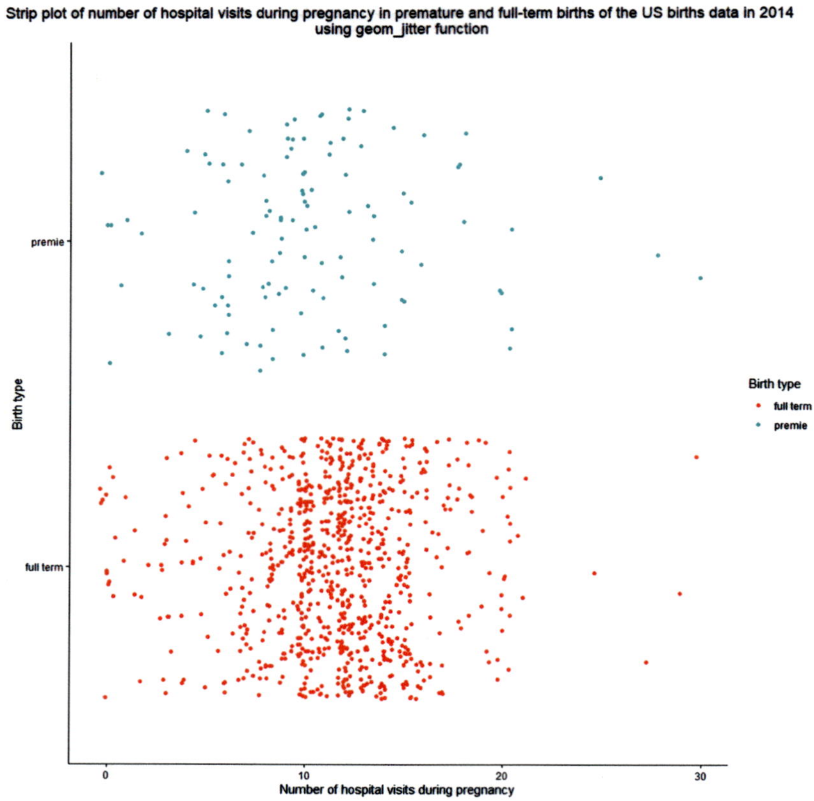

The distribution of visits number in premature and full-term births is still similar. To get a deeper look, we will add a box plot for each jittered point using the geom_boxplot function before the geom_jitter function.

```
set.seed(123)

births14 %>%

ggplot(aes(x = visits, y = premie, color = premie))+

 geom_boxplot()+

 geom_jitter()+
```

```
labs(title = "Strip and box plot of number of hospital visits during pregnancy in premature and full-term births of the US births data in 2014\n using geom_jitter function,"

  x = "Number of hospital visits during pregnancy," y = "Birth type,"

  color = "Birth type")+

theme_classic()+

theme(plot.title = element_text(hjust = 0.5))
```

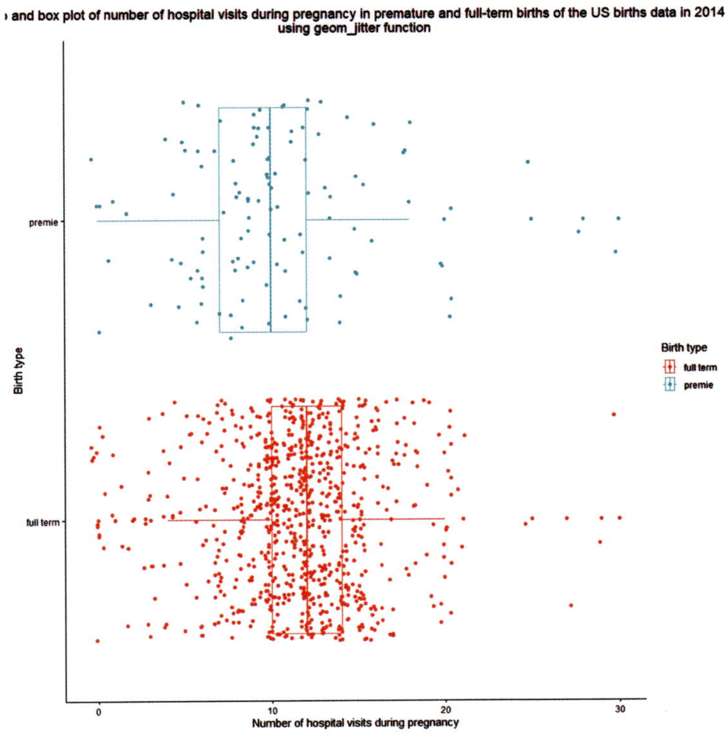

Here, we again see that the box plot of visits number in full-term births is shifted up to that in premature births, so higher visits number may be associated with full-term births.

4.3.3.3. Strip Plot of Run Time in the 2 Genders

To create this plot, we will use the same above functions except that the ggplot function, applied on "run09" data, will have the arguments, aes(x = time, y = gender, color = gender), to plot the run time on the x-axis and the gender column on the y-axis with coloring the points by a different color for each gender.

```
run09 %>%
ggplot(aes(x = time, y = gender, color = gender))+
 geom_point()+
 labs(title = "Strip plot of run time in males and females of Cherry Blossom Run
data in 2009,"
    x = "Run time," y = "Gender,"
    color = "Gender")+
 theme_classic()+
 theme(plot.title = element_text(hjust = 0.5))
```

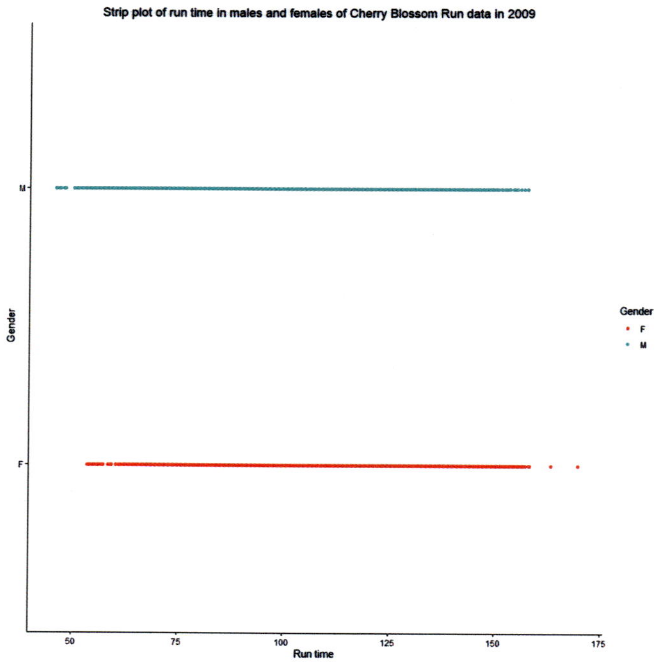

We see that:

- The distribution of run time in females is more shifted to the right (higher) than that in males. This means that females are slower on average than males.

Alternatively, the relationship can be seen more easily if the points are jittered (displaced) using the geom_jitter function as before.

```
set.seed(123)

run09 %>%

ggplot(aes(x = time, y = gender, color = gender))+

 geom_jitter()+

 labs(title = "Strip plot of run time in males and females of Cherry Blossom Run
data in 2009\n using geom_jitter function,"

    x = "Run time," y = "Gender,"
    color = "Gender")+
 theme_classic()+
 theme(plot.title = element_text(hjust = 0.5))
```

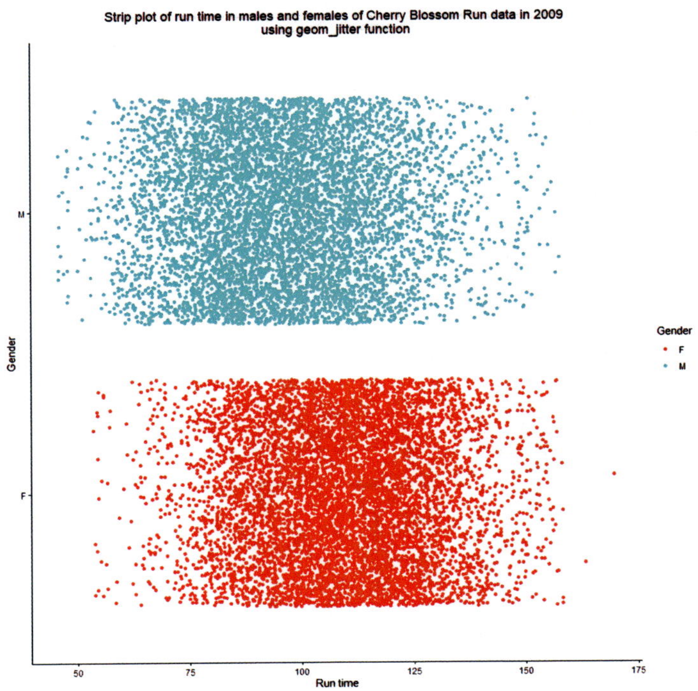

Again, we see that males are faster than females on average.

4.3.3.4. Strip Plot of Run Time in the Different States

To create this plot, we will use the same above functions except that the ggplot function, applied on "run09" data, will have the arguments, aes(x = time, y = state, color = state), to plot the run time on the x-axis and the state column on the y-axis with coloring the points by a different color for each state.

To make this plot more informative, we will use the mutate and fct_reorder functions to order the states by their median run time. We also remove the unnecessary legend as before.

```
run09 %>%
 mutate(state = fct_reorder(state, time, .fun = median)) %>%
ggplot(aes(x = time, y = state, color = state))+
 geom_point(show.legend = FALSE)+
 labs(title = "Strip plot of run time in in runners from different states of Cherry Blossom Run data in 2009\n arranged by median run time,"
   x = "Run time," y = "State")+
 theme_classic()+
 theme(plot.title = element_text(hjust = 0.5))
```

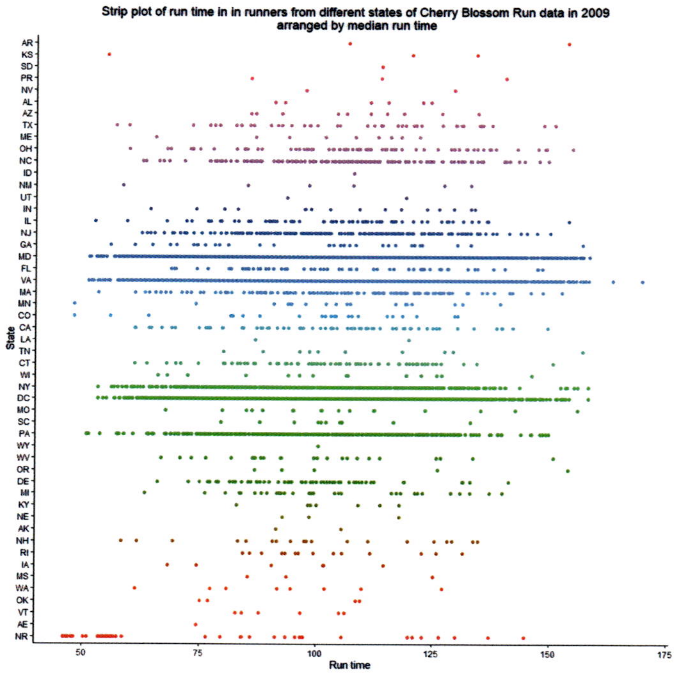

We see that:

- The lowest median run time was found in runners from the "NR" state and the highest median run time was found in runners from the "AR" state. However, there are only 2 runners (2 data points) from the "AR" state.

4.3.4. Cleveland Dot Plot

Cleveland plots are useful when you want to compare a numeric statistic of a continuous variable (like mean, median, minimum, maximum) for different levels of a categorical variable.

4.3.4.1. Cleveland Dot Plot of Mean Maternal Age in the Birth Types

To create this plot, we use the following functions:

- The group_by and get_summary_stats function, as we have done in section 4.2.1.1., to get the mean maternal age in each birth type.
- The ggplot function with the arguments, aes(x = mean,y = premie, color = premie, to plot the mean on the x-axis, the premie column (with 2 levels) on the y-axis, and coloring a different color for each birth type.
- The geom_point function to plot a point for each mean.
- The geom_segment function with the arguments, aes(x = 0, xend = mean, y = premie, yend = premie, to plot a line segment for each birth type. The start of the line segment for each birth type on the x-axis will be from 0 to its mean maternal age, while the start of the line segment for each birth type on the y-axis will be from its birth type to its birth type too.

```
births14 %>% group_by(premie) %>%
get_summary_stats(mage, show = "mean") %>%
 ggplot(aes(x = mean,y = premie, color = premie))+
 geom_point()+
 geom_segment(aes(x = 0, xend = mean,
         y = premie,

         yend = premie))+


 labs(title = "Cleveland plot of mean maternal age in premature and full-term
births\n of the US births data in 2014,"
```

```
    x = "Mean maternal age," y = "Birth type," color = "Birth type")+

  theme_classic()+

  theme(plot.title = element_text(hjust = 0.5))
```

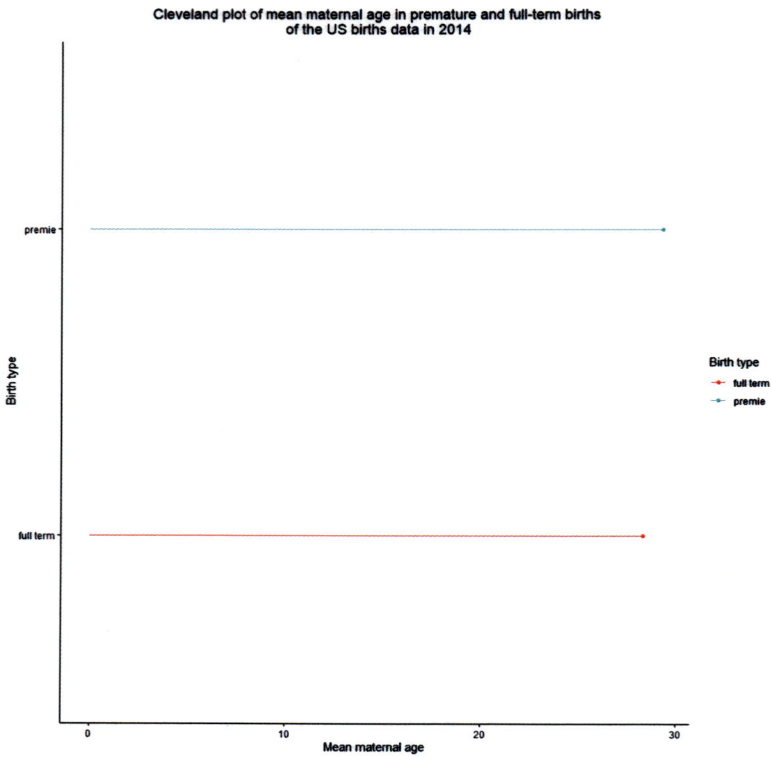

We see that the mean maternal age in premature births is higher than that in full-term births.

We can use the same functions to get the median maternal age in each birth type.

```
births14 %>% group_by(premie) %>%
get_summary_stats(mage, show = "median") %>%

 ggplot(aes(x = median,y = premie, color = premie))+
```

```
geom_point()+

geom_segment(aes(x = 0, xend = median,

         y = premie,

         yend = premie))+
labs(title = "Cleveland plot of median maternal age in premature and full-term births\n of the US births data in 2014,"

   x = "Median maternal age," y = "Birth type," color = "Birth type")+
theme_classic()+
theme(plot.title = element_text(hjust = 0.5))
```

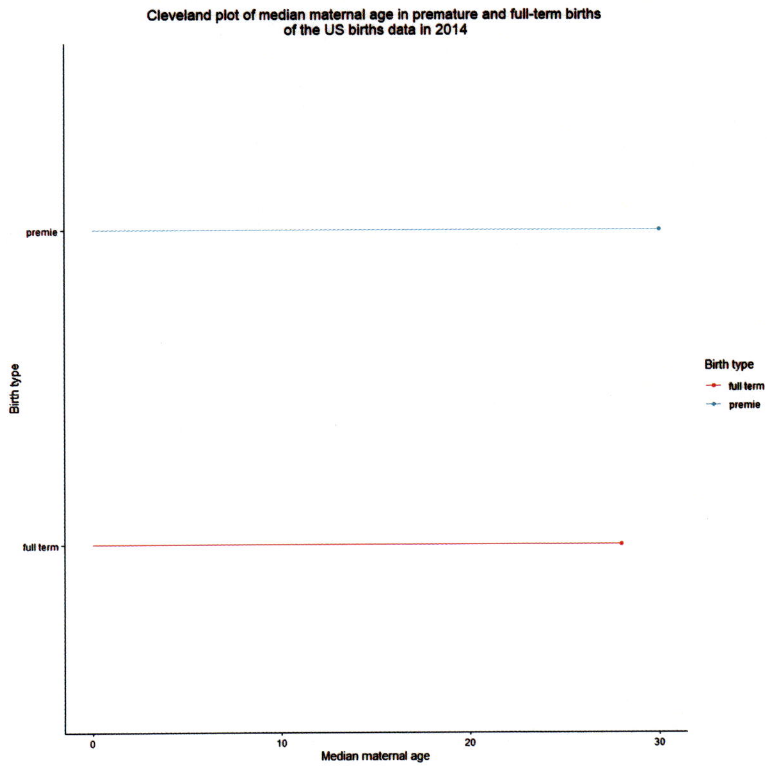

We see that the median maternal age in premature births is higher than that in full-term births.

4.3.4.2. Cleveland Dot Plot of the Mean Number of Hospital Visits in the Birth Types

To create this plot, we use the same above functions and modify them accordingly.

```
births14 %>% group_by(premie) %>%
get_summary_stats(visits, show = "mean") %>%
 ggplot(aes(x = mean,y = premie, color = premie))+
 geom_point()+
 geom_segment(aes(x = 0, xend = mean,
          y = premie,
          yend = premie))+
 labs(title = "Cleveland plot of mean number of hospital visits during pregnancy
\nin premature and full-term births of the US births data in 2014,"
    x = "Mean visits number," y = "Birth type," color = "Birth type")+
 theme_classic()+
 theme(plot.title = element_text(hjust = 0.5))
```

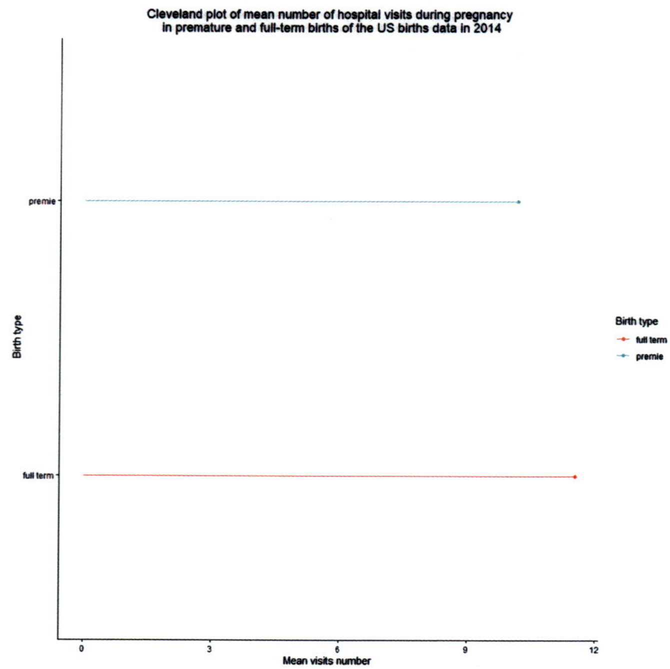

We see that the mean visits number in premature births is lower than that in full-term births.

4.3.4.3. Cleveland Dot Plot of Mean Run Time in the 2 Genders

To create this plot, we use the same above functions and modify them accordingly.

```
run09 %>% group_by(gender) %>%
get_summary_stats(time, show = "mean") %>%
 ggplot(aes(x = mean,y = gender, color = gender))+
 geom_point()+
 geom_segment(aes(x = 0, xend = mean,
          y = gender,
          yend = gender))+
 labs(title = "Cleveland plot of mean run time in males and females of Cherry
Blossom Run data in 2009,"
   x = "Mean run time," y = "Gender," color = "Gender")+
 theme_classic()+
 theme(plot.title = element_text(hjust = 0.5))
```

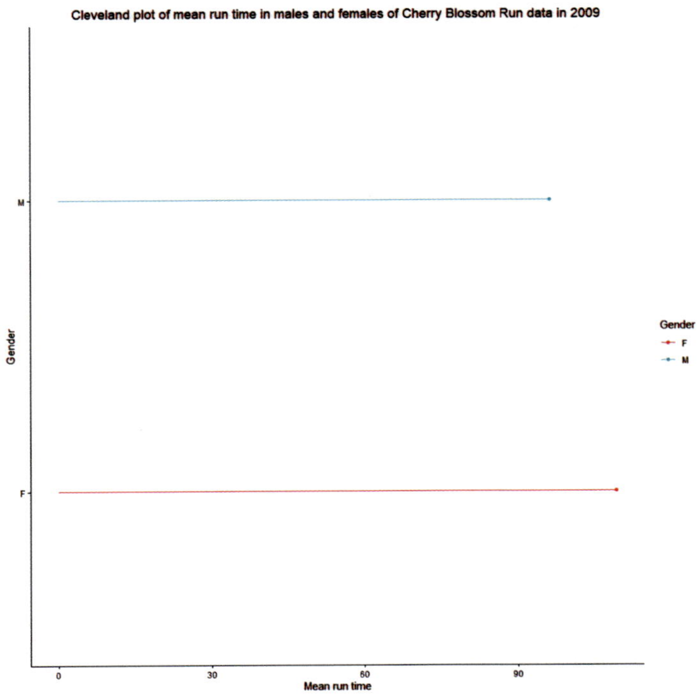

We see that the mean run time in females is higher than that in males, so males are faster than females on average.

4.3.4.4. Cleveland dot plot of mean run time in the different states

To create this plot, we use the same above functions and modify them accordingly. We also use the mutate and fct_reorder functions to order the state by their mean run time in ascending order. Finally, we remove the unnecessary legend by using the argument, show.legend = FALSE, inside the geom_point and geom_segment functions.

```
run09 %>% group_by(state) %>%
get_summary_stats(time, show = "mean") %>%
 mutate(state = fct_reorder(state, mean)) %>%
 ggplot(aes(x = mean,y = state, color = state))+
 geom_point(show.legend = FALSE)+
 geom_segment(aes(x = 0, xend = mean,
y = state,
yend = state), show.legend = FALSE)+
 labs(title = "Cleveland plot of mean run time in runners from different states
\nof Cherry Blossom Run data in 2009,"
 x = "Mean run time," y = "State")+
 theme_classic()+
 theme(plot.title = element_text(hjust = 0.5))
```

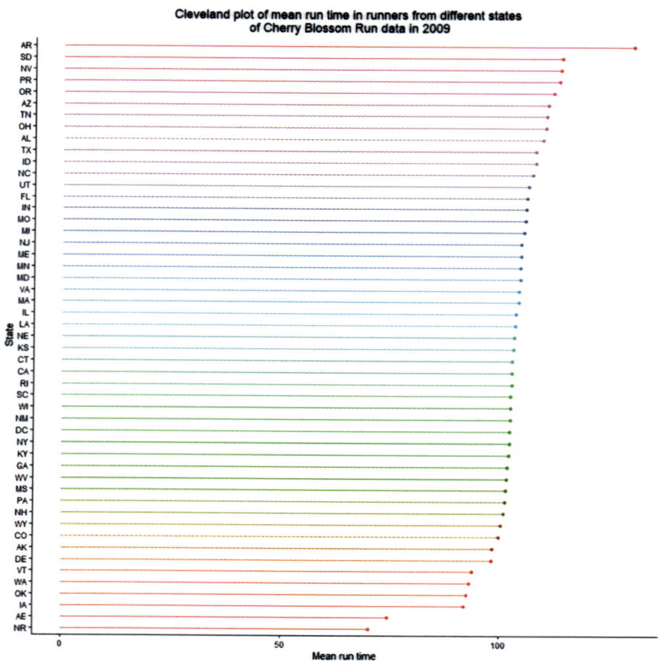

We see that the mean run time in the "NR" state is lower than all other states so runners from this state are faster than runners from other states on average.

4.3.5. Mean Plot with Error Bars

We can compare the continuous variable in different levels of a categorical variable by using the mean plot with error bars. The error bars can represent standard deviations, standard error of the mean, or confidence intervals.

4.3.5.1. Mean Plot with Standard Deviation Error Bars of Maternal Age in the Birth Types

To create this plot, we use the following functions:

- The group_by and get_summary_stats functions as we have done previously. However, the get_summary_stats function will have the arguments, mage, type= "mean_sd," to get the mean and standard deviation of maternal age in each birth type.
- The ggplot function with the arguments, aes(x = premie,y = mean, color = premie, to plot the mean on the y-axis, the premie column (with 2 levels) on the x-axis, and coloring a different color for each birth type.
- The geom_point function to plot a point for each mean.
- The geom_errorbar function with the arguments, aes(ymin = mean – sd, ymax = mean + sd), width = 0.1), so the error bar for each birth type will have a maximum of mean + standard deviation value and a minimum of mean – standard deviation value, and a central point of the mean maternal age for each birth type. The width argument to reduce the width of the error bars to 0.1 of its default width.
- The labs, theme_classic, and theme functions had been described before.

```
births14 %>% group_by(premie) %>%
get_summary_stats(mage, type= "mean_sd") %>%
 ggplot(aes(x = premie, y= mean, color = premie))+ geom_point()+
 geom_errorbar(aes(ymin = mean - sd,
          ymax = mean + sd), width = 0.1)+
 labs(title = "Mean maternal age with 1 standard deviation error bars \nin premature and full-term births of the US births data in 2014,"
    y = "Mean maternal age," x = "Birth type," color = "Birth type")+
 theme_classic()+
 theme(plot.title = element_text(hjust = 0.5))
```

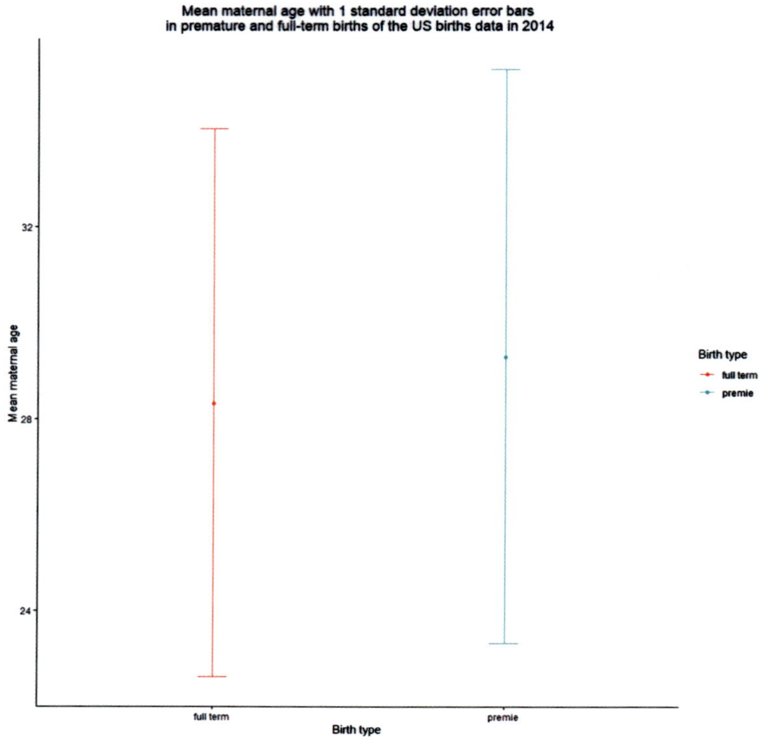

We see that the mean maternal age in premature births is higher than that in full-term births. However, the standard deviation is nearly the same.

4.3.5.2. Mean Plot with Standard Error Bars of Maternal Age in the Birth Types

The standard error of the mean is estimated by where:

- s is the sample standard deviation.
- n is the sample size.

The standard error represents the estimated standard deviation obtained from a set of sample means from repeated samples of size n from the same population.

We can use the same functions to get the mean plot with standard error bars of maternal age in the birth types using the argument type = "mean_se" in the get_summary_stats function.

```
births14 %>% group_by(premie) %>%
get_summary_stats(mage, type= "mean_se") %>%
 ggplot(aes(x = premie, y= mean, color = premie))+ geom_point()+
 geom_errorbar(aes(ymin = mean - se,
          ymax = mean + se), width = 0.1)+
 labs(title = "Mean maternal age with 1 standard error bars \nin premature and
full-term births of the US births data in 2014,"
    y = "Mean maternal age," x = "Birth type," color = "Birth type")+
 theme_classic()+
 theme(plot.title = element_text(hjust = 0.5))
```

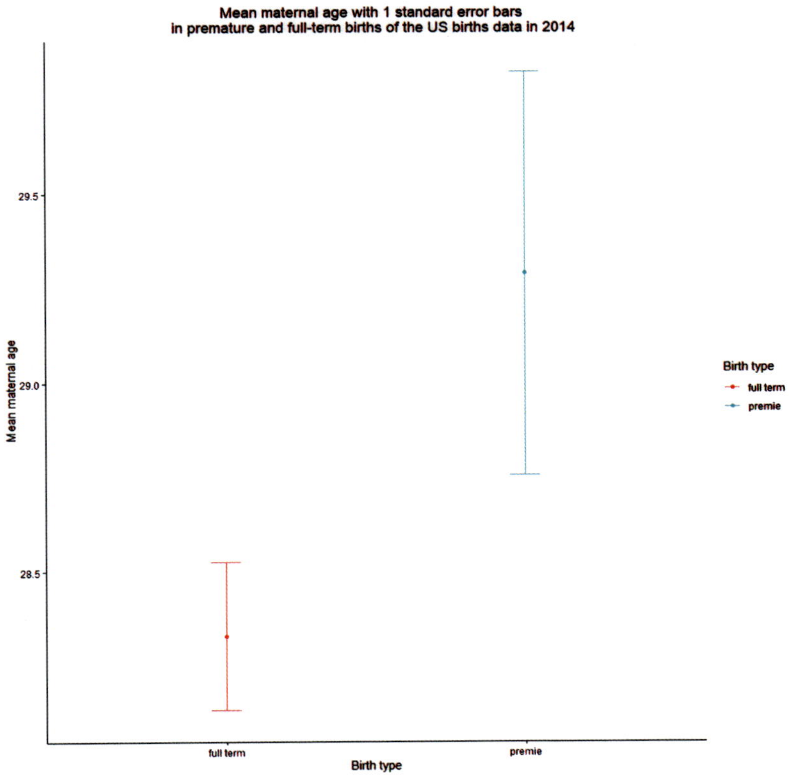

In a normal distribution, about 95% of the data are within 2 standard deviations (error) from the mean, so it is more reasonable if we created the error bars at 2 X se. The 2 X se represents a 95% confidence interval that will capture the true population mean 95% of the time.

```
births14 %>% group_by(premie) %>%
get_summary_stats(mage, type= "mean_se") %>%
 ggplot(aes(x = premie, y= mean, color = premie))+ geom_point()+
 geom_errorbar(aes(ymin = mean - 2*se,
          ymax = mean + 2*se), width = 0.1)+
 labs(title = "Mean maternal age with 2 standard error bars \nin premature and
full-term births of the US births data in 2014,"
    y = "Mean maternal age," x = "Birth type," color = "Birth type")+
 theme_classic()+
 theme(plot.title = element_text(hjust = 0.5))
```

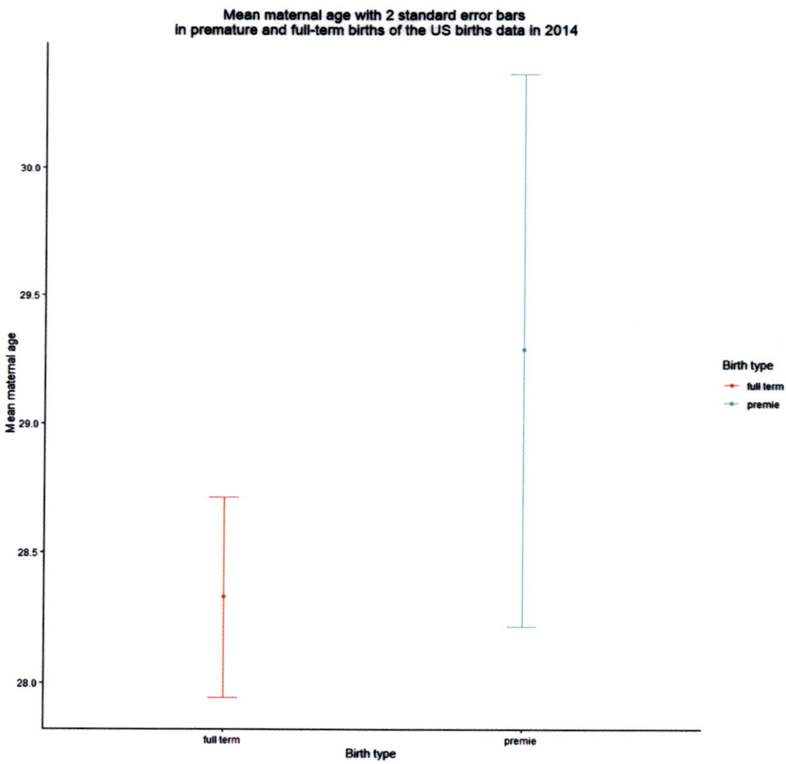

We see that:

- The mean maternal age in premature births is higher than that in full-term births.

- The error bar in premature births is wider than that in full-term births because the sample size is smaller in premature births.
- The 2 error bars overlap indicating that the difference between the mean maternal age in premature and full-term births is not significant or they are statistically equivalent.

4.3.5.3. Mean Plot with 95% Confidence Interval Error Bars of Maternal Age in the Birth Types

The 95% confidence interval of the mean is estimated by or X standard error where:

- s is the standard deviation.
- n is the sample size.
- The value depends on the sample size and can be obtained from the t-distribution table.
- is the level of significance and equals a 100-confidence level. For a 95% confidence interval, = 5% or 0.05, for a 99% confidence interval, = 1% or 0.01, and for a 90% confidence interval, = 10% or 0.1.

Generally, for large sample sizes (> 30), we can be certain by 95% that the true mean is within two standard errors of the estimated mean.

We can use the same functions to get the mean plot with 95% confidence interval error bars of maternal age in the birth types using the argument type = "mean_ci" in the get_summary_stats function.

```
births14 %>% group_by(premie) %>%

get_summary_stats(mage, type= "mean_ci") %>%

 ggplot(aes(x = premie, y= mean, color = premie))+ geom_point()+

 geom_errorbar(aes(ymin = mean - ci,

          ymax = mean + ci), width = 0.1)+

 labs(title = "Mean maternal age with 95% confidence interval error bars \nin premature and full-term births of the US births data in 2014,"

    y = "Mean maternal age," x = "Birth type," color = "Birth type")+

 theme_classic()+


 theme(plot.title = element_text(hjust = 0.5))
```

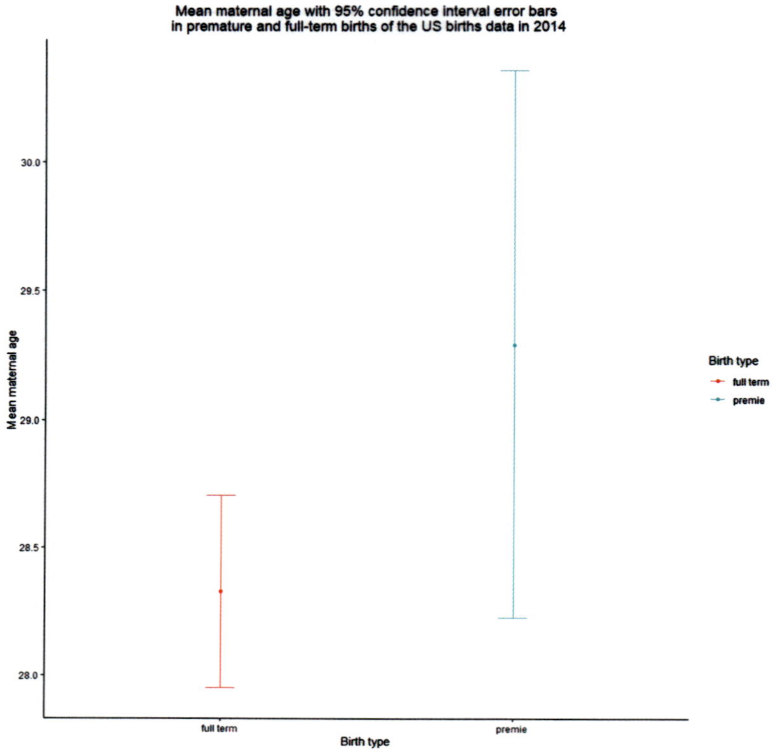

We see that:

- The mean maternal age in premature births is higher than that in full-term births.
- The error bar in premature births is wider than that in full-term births because the sample size is smaller in premature births.
- The 2 error bars overlap indicating that the difference between the mean maternal age in premature and full-term births is not significant or they are statistically equivalent.

4.3.5.4. Mean Plot with 95% Confidence Interval Error Bars of Visits Number in the Birth Types

We can use the same functions to get the mean plot with 95% confidence interval error bars of visits number in the birth types and modify the functions accordingly.

```
births14 %>% group_by(premie) %>%
get_summary_stats(visits, type= "mean_ci") %>%
 ggplot(aes(x = premie, y= mean, color = premie))+ geom_point()+
 geom_errorbar(aes(ymin = mean - ci,
          ymax = mean + ci), width = 0.1)+
 labs(title = "Mean number of hospital visits during pregnancy with 95% confidence interval error bars \nin premature and full-term births of the US births data in 2014,"
    y = "Mean visits number," x = "Birth type," color = "Birth type")+
 theme_classic()+
 theme(plot.title = element_text(hjust = 0.5))
```

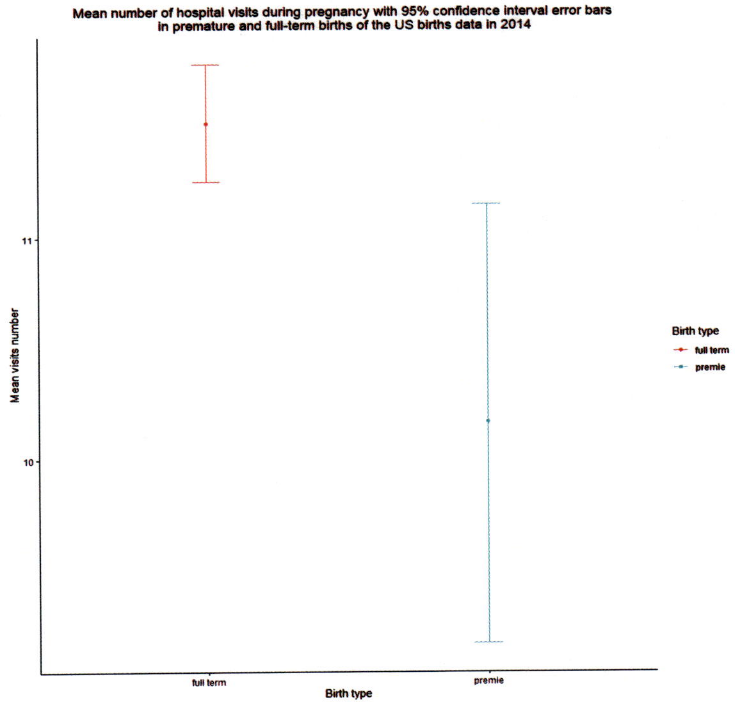

We see that:

- The mean number of visits in premature births is lower than that in full-term births.
- The error bar in premature births is wider than that in full-term births because the sample size is smaller in premature births.

- The 2 error bars do not overlap indicating that the difference between the mean number of hospital visits during pregnancy in premature and full-term births is statistically significant or there is a real difference between the 2 groups in their mean number of visits.

4.3.5.5. Mean Plot with 95% Confidence Interval Error Bars of Run Time in the 2 Genders

We can use the same functions to get the mean plot with 95% confidence interval error bars of run time in the 2 genders of Cherry Blossom Run data in 2009 and modify the functions accordingly.

```
run09 %>% group_by(gender) %>%
get_summary_stats(time, type= "mean_ci") %>%
 ggplot(aes(x = gender, y= mean, color = gender))+ geom_point()+
 geom_errorbar(aes(ymin = mean - ci,
          ymax = mean + ci), width = 0.1)+
 labs(title = "Mean run time with 95% confidence interval error bars\n in males and females of Cherry Blossom Run data in 2009,"
    y = "Mean run time," x = "Gender," color = "Gender")+
 theme_classic()+
 theme(plot.title = element_text(hjust = 0.5))
```

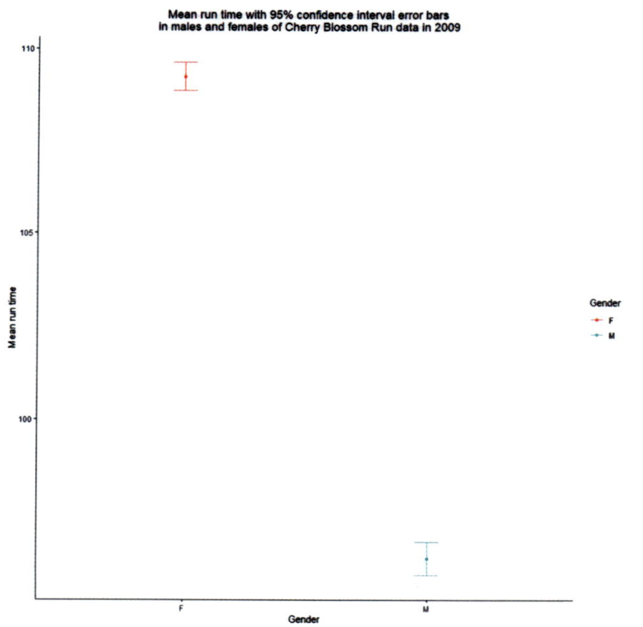

We see that:

- The mean run time in males is lower than that in females.
- The 2 error bars do not overlap indicating that the difference between the mean run time in males and females is statistically significant so we can conclude that males are faster than females on the average in the population from which this sample was taken.

4.3.5.6. Mean Plot with 95% Confidence Interval Error Bars of Run Time in the Runners from Different States

We can use the same functions to get the mean plot with 95% confidence interval error bars of run time in the runner from different states of Cherry Blossom Run data in 2009 and modify the functions accordingly. However, the 95% confidence interval cannot be calculated when the sample size is 1 and produces a "NaN" or not a number value. We remove these rows by using the drop_na function. We can also arrange the states by their mean run time using the mutate and fct_reorder functions. We also remove the unnecessary legend as before.

```
run09 %>% group_by(state) %>%
get_summary_stats(time, type= "mean_ci") %>%
 drop_na() %>% mutate(state = fct_reorder(state,mean)) %>%
 ggplot(aes(x = state, y= mean, color = state))+
 geom_point(show.legend = FALSE)+
 geom_errorbar(aes(ymin = mean - ci,
          ymax = mean + ci), width = 0.1, show.legend = FALSE)+
 labs(title = "Mean run time with 95% confidence interval error bars\n in runners from different states of Cherry Blossom Run data in 2009\n arranged by the mean run time,"
    y = "Mean run time," x = "State")+
 theme_classic()+
 theme(plot.title = element_text(hjust = 0.5))
```

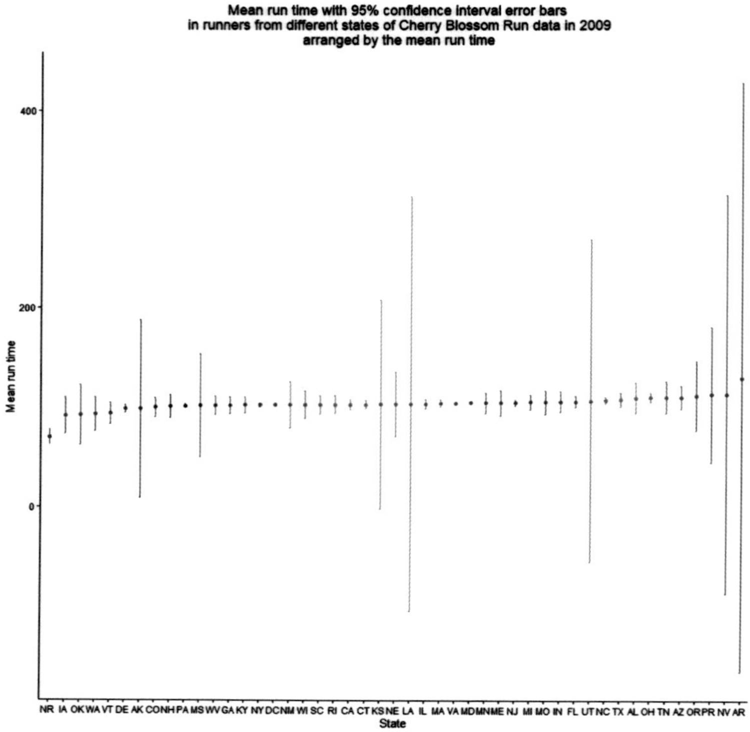

We see that:

- The highest mean run time was in runners from the "AR" state. However, the 95% confidence interval is very large due to the small sample size (2 runners only).
- The lowest mean run time was in runners from the "NR" state and the 95% confidence interval is very tight due to the large sample size (59 runners).
- All the 95% confidence intervals of different states appear to overlap so all runners from all states may have statistically equivalent run time. We will see that in the below statistical tests.

4.4. STATISTICAL TESTS

4.4.1. t-Test for Two Samples

The independent samples t-test (or unpaired samples t-test) is used to compare the mean of two independent groups. For example, compare the mean maternal age in the 2 birth types, full-term, and premature births. Another example is comparing the mean visits number in the 2 birth types, full-term, and premature births. A final example is comparing the mean run time in the 2 genders, males and females. In all these examples, the 2 groups are unrelated or independent.

The independent samples t-test comes in two versions:

- The standard Student's t-test assumes that the variance of the two groups is equal.
- The Welch's t-test does not assume that the variance is the same in the two groups.

4.4.1.1. Assumptions of t-Test

The independent samples t-test assumes the following about the data:

- Independence of the observations. Each subject or observation should belong to one group. There is no relationship between the observations in the 2 groups.
- No significant outliers in the two groups.
- Normality of the data in each group.
- Homogeneity of variances of the data in each group.

4.4.1.2. t-Test for the Mean Maternal Age in the 2 Birth Types

The null hypothesis is that the difference between the mean maternal age in the 2 birth types is 0, while the alternative hypothesis is that the difference between the means is greater than or smaller than 0 or a two-sided test.

To conduct this test, we use the t-test function applied to the "births14" data with the following arguments:

- formula = mage ~ premie which is the formula for two samples t-test. This means that we want to compare the maternal age across the 2 levels of the "premie" column.
- mu = 0 which is the null value that corresponds to the null hypothesis.
- alternative = "two.sided" which is the alternative hypothesis.

Then, we convert the result to a table as before.

```
births14 %>% t_test(formula = mage ~ premie, mu = 0,

           alternative = "two.sided") %>%

  flextable() %>% theme_box() %>%
```

```
set_caption(caption = "Two-sided t-test results of mean maternal age in premature and full-term births of the US births data in 2014")
```

Table 4.29. *Two-Sided t-Test Results of Mean Maternal Age in Premature and Full-Term Births of the US births Data in 2014*

.y.	group1	group2	n1	n2	statistic	df	p
mage	full term	premie	876	124	-1.682214	156.5432	0.0945

We see that:

- The table contains the statistic = -1.68 which corresponds to our sample results and the p-value = 0.0945.
- The p_value is the probability of our sample results (the difference between the 2 group means) under the null hypothesis (where the 2 means are equivalent). Since this probability is larger than the cut-off value of 0.05, we fail to reject the null hypothesis and conclude that the mean maternal age in full-term and premature births is statistically equivalent.

To trust these results, we must test the assumptions of the t-test on our data. The 2 groups are independent with no relation between them. Other tests will be described below.

4.4.1.2.1. Test for Outliers in the Maternal Age in the 2 Birth Types

As described in Chapter 1, we use the identify_outliers function with the argument, mage, after the group_by function with the argument premie to detect any outliers in the maternal age within the 2 birth types. Then, we use the select function to select the important columns to be viewed (premie, mage, is.outlier, is.extreme) instead of viewing all columns of the "births14" data. Finally, we convert the results to a table as before.

```
births14 %>% group_by(premie) %>% identify_outliers(mage) %>%

select(premie,mage, is.outlier, is.extreme) %>%

flextable() %>%

theme_box() %>%
```

```
set_caption(caption = "Outlier test results for maternal age in premature and full-term births of the US births data in 2014")
```

Table 4.30. Outlier Test Results for Maternal Age in Premature and Full-Term Births of the US Births Data in 2014

Premie	mage	is.outlier	is.extreme

We see that the table 4.30 has no rows meaning that maternal age values have no outliers in full-term or premature births.

4.4.1.2.2. Test for Normality of the Maternal Age in the 2 Birth Types

We can use the QQ plot or the Shapiro-Wilk normality test as described in Chapter 1. The ggqqplot function from the ggpubr package can be used to create a QQ plot of the maternal age. To create a separate QQ plot for each birth type, we use the argument facet.by = "premie" to plot a separate QQ plot for full-term and premature births.

```
library(ggpubr)

ggqqplot(data = births14, x = "mage," facet.by = "premie,"

    title = "QQ plot of maternal age in premature and full-term births\n of the US births data in 2014,"

    xlab = "Theoretical percentiles," ylab = "Sample percentiles")+

 theme(plot.title = element_text(hjust = 0.5))
```

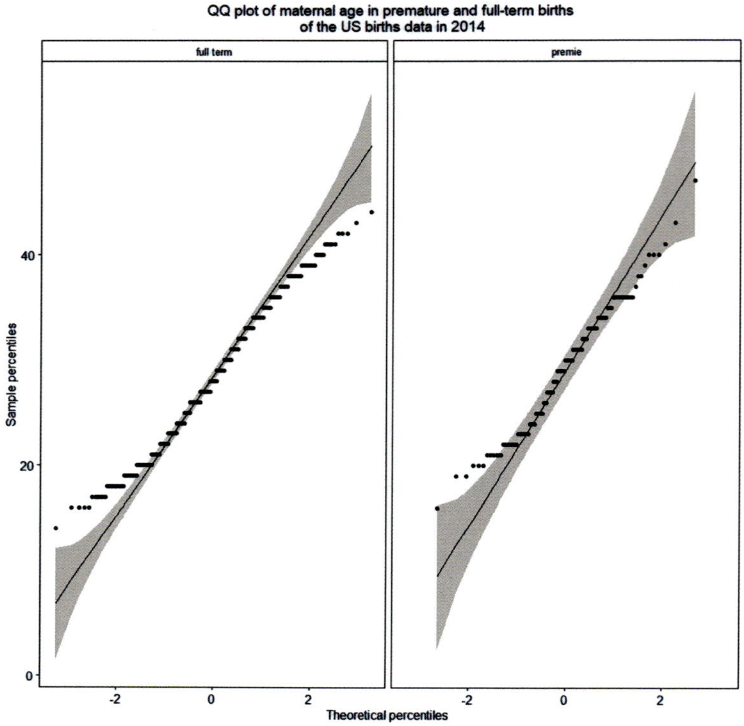

In full-term births, not all data points fall along the reference line or within the confidence band, so we can not assume normality of maternal age in full-term births and we should use the Wilcoxon test which does not need normality of data in the 2 groups.

In premature births, nearly all data points fall along the reference line or within the confidence band, so we can assume the normality of maternal age in full-term births.

For the Shapiro-Wilk normality test, we use the shapiro_test function with the argument "mage" after the group_by function with the argument "premie." This will test the normality of maternal age in full-term and premature births.

```
births14 %>% group_by(premie) %>% shapiro_test(mage) %>% flextable() %>%

 theme_box() %>%

 set_caption(caption = "Shapiro-Wilk test results for maternal age in premature
and full-term births\n of the US births data in 2014")
```

Table 4.31. *Shapiro-Wilk Test Results for Maternal Age in Premature and Full-Term Births of the US Births Data in 2014*

Premie	Variable	Statistic	p
full term	mage	0.9879408	0.000001299452
premie	mage	0.9796766	0.058485020608

In full-term births, the p_value is significant (< 0.05), so we reject the null hypothesis and conclude that the maternal age values in full-term births are not normally distributed. However, due to the large sample size of full-term births (876), we can ignore the normality test results and use the t-test.

In premature births, the p_value is insignificant (> 0.05), so we fail to reject the null hypothesis and conclude that the maternal age values in premature births are normally distributed.

4.4.1.2.3. Test for Homogeneity of Variances of the Maternal Age in the 2 Birth Types

We will use Levene's test for this using the levene_test function. The only argument is the formula "mage ~ premie" to test the equality of variances of the maternal age across the 2 groups of the "premie" column. If the variances of the 2 groups are equal, the p-value should be insignificant or greater than 0.05.

```
births14 %>% levene_test(formula = mage ~ premie) %>% flextable() %>%

  theme_box() %>%

  set_caption(caption = "Levene's test results for maternal age in premature and full-term births\n of the US births data in 2014")
```

Table 4.32. *Levene's Test Results for Maternal Age in Premature and Full-Term Births of the US Births Data in 2014*

df1	df2	Statistic	p
1	998	0.5747473	0.4485576

We see that the p-value is insignificant (> 0.05) so we conclude that the variances of the maternal age in premature and full-term births are equal. The t-test done above was Welch's t-test which does not assume that the variance is equal in the two groups. Because the variance is equal in the 2 groups, we can do the standard Student's t-test by using the argument var.equal = TRUE within the t_test function.

```
births14 %>% t_test(formula = mage ~ premie, mu = 0,

          alternative = "two.sided,"

          var.equal = TRUE) %>%

 flextable() %>% theme_box() %>%

 set_caption(caption = "Two-sided Student's t-test results of mean maternal age in premature and full-term births of the US births data in 2014")
```

Table 4.33. *Two-Sided Student's t-Test Results of Mean Maternal Age in Premature and Full-Term Births of the US Births Data in 2014*

.y.	Group1	Group2	n1	n2	Statistic	df	p
mage	full term	premie	876	124	-1.739637	998	0.0822

The conclusion is the same as that of Welch's t-test with an insignificant p-value, so we fail to reject the null hypothesis and conclude that the mean maternal age in full-term and premature births is statistically equivalent.

4.4.1.3. t-Test for the Mean Number of Hospital Visits During Pregnancy in the 2 Birth Types

The null hypothesis is that the difference between the mean number of visits in the 2 birth types is 0, while the alternative hypothesis is that the difference between the means is greater than or smaller than 0 or a two-sided test.

To conduct this test, we use Welch's t-test using the same functions above.

```
births14 %>% t_test(formula = visits ~ premie, mu = 0,

          alternative = "two.sided") %>%

 flextable() %>% theme_box() %>%

 set_caption(caption = "Two-sided t-test results of mean number of hospital visits during pregnancy in premature and full-term births of the US births data in 2014")
```

Table 4.34. *Two-Sided t-Test Results of the Mean Number of Hospital Visits During Pregnancy in Premature and Full-Term Births of the US Births Data in 2014*

.y.	group1	group2	n1	n2	statistic	df	p
vis-its	full term	premie	829	115	2.62367	131.323	0.00973

We see that:

- The table contains the statistic = 2.62 which corresponds to our sample results and the p-value = 0.00973.
- The p_value is significant, so we reject the null hypothesis and conclude that the mean number of visits in the full-term births is larger than that of the premature births.

To trust these results, we must test the assumptions of the t-test on our data. The 2 groups are independent with no relation between them. Other tests will be described below.

4.4.1.3.1. Test for Outliers in the Number of Visits in the 2 Birth Types

We use the same above functions. Then, we use the select function to select the important columns to be viewed (premie, visits, is.outlier, is.extreme) instead of viewing all columns of the "births14" data. Finally, we convert the results to a table as before.

```
births14 %>% group_by(premie) %>% identify_outliers(visits) %>%

 select(premie,visits, is.outlier, is.extreme) %>%

 flextable() %>%

 theme_box() %>%

 set_caption(caption = "Outlier test results for hospital visits during pregnancy
in premature and full-term births of the US births data in 2014")
```

Table 4.35. *Outlier Test Results for Hospital Visits During Pregnancy in Premature and Full-Term Births of the US Births Data in 2014*

Premie	Visits	is.outlier	is.extreme
full term	2	TRUE	FALSE
full term	29	TRUE	TRUE
full term	0	TRUE	FALSE
full term	3	TRUE	FALSE
full term	2	TRUE	FALSE
full term	25	TRUE	FALSE
full term	0	TRUE	FALSE
full term	3	TRUE	FALSE
full term	21	TRUE	FALSE
full term	2	TRUE	FALSE
full term	0	TRUE	FALSE
full term	0	TRUE	FALSE
full term	3	TRUE	FALSE
full term	0	TRUE	FALSE
full term	0	TRUE	FALSE
full term	0	TRUE	FALSE
full term	1	TRUE	FALSE
full term	30	TRUE	TRUE
full term	0	TRUE	FALSE
full term	3	TRUE	FALSE
full term	21	TRUE	FALSE
full term	0	TRUE	FALSE
full term	0	TRUE	FALSE
full term	3	TRUE	FALSE
full term	0	TRUE	FALSE
full term	27	TRUE	TRUE
full term	3	TRUE	FALSE
full term	1	TRUE	FALSE
full term	3	TRUE	FALSE
full term	21	TRUE	FALSE

full term	1	TRUE	FALSE
full term	0	TRUE	FALSE
full term	1	TRUE	FALSE
full term	3	TRUE	FALSE
full term	3	TRUE	FALSE
full term	3	TRUE	FALSE
full term	3	TRUE	FALSE
full term	3	TRUE	FALSE
full term	0	TRUE	FALSE
premie	20	TRUE	FALSE
premie	28	TRUE	TRUE
premie	20	TRUE	FALSE
premie	20	TRUE	FALSE
premie	20	TRUE	FALSE
premie	20	TRUE	FALSE
premie	30	TRUE	TRUE
premie	25	TRUE	FALSE

We see that the table 4.35 has many rows containing the outlier values of visits number in full-term or premature births, so we should use the Wilcoxon test to compare the visits number between the 2 birth types.

4.4.1.3.2. Test for Normality of the Number of Visits in the 2 Birth Types

We can plot the QQ plot.

```
ggqqplot(data = births14, x = "visits," facet.by = "premie,"

    title = "QQ plot of hospital visits during pregnancy in premature and full-
term births\n of the US births data in 2014,"

    xlab = "Theoretical percentiles," ylab = "Sample percentiles")+

 theme(plot.title = element_text(hjust = 0.5))
```

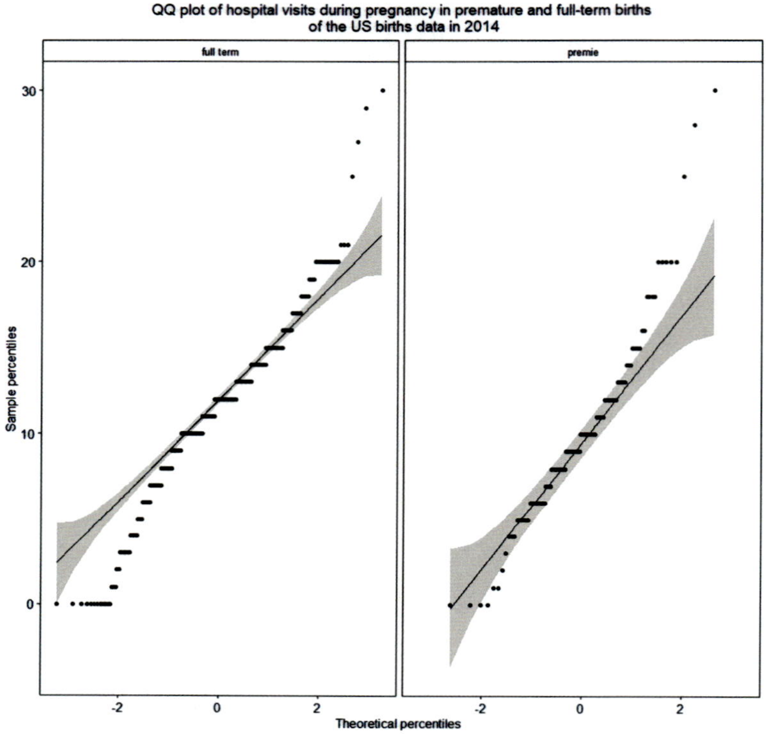

In full-term and premature births, not all data points fall along the reference line or within the confidence band, so we can not assume normality of visits number in the full-term or premature births and we should use the Wilcoxon test which does not need normality of data in the 2 groups. However, due to the large sample size of full-term births or premature births (829 and 115 respectively), we can ignore the normality test results and use the t-test.

We can also use the Shapiro-Wilk normality test as before.

```
births14 %>% group_by(premie) %>% shapiro_test(visits) %>% flextable() %>%

 theme_box() %>%

 set_caption(caption = "Shapiro-Wilk test results for hospital visits during pregnancy in premature and full-term births\n of the US births data in 2014")
```

Table 4.36. *Shapiro-Wilk Test Results for Hospital Visits During Pregnancy in Premature and Full-Term Births of the US Births Data in 2014*

Premie	Variable	Statistic	p
full term	visits	0.9593774	0.00000000000002168143
premie	visits	0.9418316	0.00008177188744695395

In full-term and premature births, the p_value is significant (< 0.05), so we reject the null hypothesis and conclude that the visits number values in the full-term and premature births are not normally distributed. However, due to the large sample size of full-term births or premature births (829 and 115 respectively), we can ignore the normality test results and use the t-test.

4.4.1.3.3. Test for Homogeneity of Variances of the Hospital Visits During Pregnancy in the 2 Birth Types

```
births14 %>% levene_test(formula = visits ~ premie) %>% flextable() %>%

 theme_box() %>%

 set_caption(caption = "Levene's test results for hospital visits during pregnancy in premature and full-term births of the US births data in 2014")
```

Table 4.37. *Levene's Test Results for Hospital Visits During Pregnancy in Premature and Full-Term Births of the US Births Data in 2014*

df1	df2	Statistic	p
1	942	12.91543	0.0003427704

We see that the p-value is significant (< 0.05) so we conclude that the variances of the visits number in premature and full-term births are different and we can only use Welch's t-test conducted above.

4.4.1.4. t-Test for the Mean Run Time in the 2 Genders

The null hypothesis is that the difference between the mean run time in the 2 genders is 0, while the alternative hypothesis is that the difference between the means is greater than or smaller than 0 or a two-sided test.

To conduct this test, we use Welch's t-test using the same functions above.

```
run09 %>% t_test(formula = time ~ gender, mu = 0,

          alternative = "two.sided") %>%
 flextable() %>% theme_box() %>%
```

```
set_caption(caption = "Two-sided t-test results of mean run time in males and females of Cherry Blossom Run data in 2009")
```

Table 4.38. *Two-Sided t-Test Results of Mean Run Time in Males and Females of Cherry Blossom Run Data in 2009*

.y.	Group1	Group2	n1	n2	Statistic	df	p
time	F	M	8,323	6,651	43.04116	13,636.55	0

We see that:

- The table contains the statistic = 43.04 which corresponds to our sample results and the p-value = 0.
- The p_value is significant, so we reject the null hypothesis and conclude that the mean run time in females is larger than that of males. In other words, females are slower than males on average.

To trust these results, we must test the assumptions of the t-test on our data. The 2 groups are independent with no relation between them. Other tests will be described below.

4.4.1.4.1. Test for Outliers in the Run Time in the 2 Genders

We use the same above functions. Then, we use the select function to select the important columns to be viewed (gender, time, is.outlier, is.extreme) instead of viewing all columns of the "run09" data. Finally, we convert the results to a table as before.

```
run09 %>% group_by(gender) %>% identify_outliers(time) %>%

select(gender,time, is.outlier, is.extreme) %>%

flextable() %>%
theme_box() %>%

set_caption(caption = "Outlier test results for run time in males and females of Cherry Blossom Run data in 2009")
```

Table 4.39. *Outlier Test Results for Run Time in Males and Females of Cherry Blossom Run data in 2009*

Gender	Time	is.outlier	is.extreme
F	53.533	TRUE	FALSE
F	53.917	TRUE	FALSE

F	53.967	TRUE	FALSE
F	54.433	TRUE	FALSE
F	54.450	TRUE	FALSE
F	54.533	TRUE	FALSE
F	54.633	TRUE	FALSE
F	54.650	TRUE	FALSE
F	54.717	TRUE	FALSE
F	54.767	TRUE	FALSE
F	55.183	TRUE	FALSE
F	55.200	TRUE	FALSE
F	55.467	TRUE	FALSE
F	55.717	TRUE	FALSE
F	55.850	TRUE	FALSE
F	55.917	TRUE	FALSE
F	56.300	TRUE	FALSE
F	56.733	TRUE	FALSE
F	56.783	TRUE	FALSE
F	57.183	TRUE	FALSE
F	57.417	TRUE	FALSE
F	58.567	TRUE	FALSE
F	58.750	TRUE	FALSE
F	59.367	TRUE	FALSE
F	60.300	TRUE	FALSE
F	61.017	TRUE	FALSE
F	61.100	TRUE	FALSE
F	61.467	TRUE	FALSE
F	157.217	TRUE	FALSE
F	158.133	TRUE	FALSE
F	158.233	TRUE	FALSE
F	158.117	TRUE	FALSE
F	158.083	TRUE	FALSE
F	163.250	TRUE	FALSE
F	169.617	TRUE	FALSE

M	151.417	TRUE	FALSE
M	149.683	TRUE	FALSE
M	151.350	TRUE	FALSE
M	153.250	TRUE	FALSE
M	149.467	TRUE	FALSE
M	150.050	TRUE	FALSE
M	149.650	TRUE	FALSE
M	150.517	TRUE	FALSE
M	152.117	TRUE	FALSE
M	150.683	TRUE	FALSE
M	150.700	TRUE	FALSE
M	153.100	TRUE	FALSE
M	150.517	TRUE	FALSE
M	150.517	TRUE	FALSE
M	152.650	TRUE	FALSE
M	150.417	TRUE	FALSE
M	149.300	TRUE	FALSE
M	152.367	TRUE	FALSE
M	154.083	TRUE	FALSE
M	151.450	TRUE	FALSE
M	155.150	TRUE	FALSE
M	156.733	TRUE	FALSE
M	153.250	TRUE	FALSE
M	156.783	TRUE	FALSE
M	154.450	TRUE	FALSE
M	157.517	TRUE	FALSE
M	155.883	TRUE	FALSE
M	149.783	TRUE	FALSE
M	154.800	TRUE	FALSE
M	151.417	TRUE	FALSE
M	155.017	TRUE	FALSE

We see that the Table 4.39 has many rows containing the outlier values of run time in females and males, so we should use the Wilcoxon test to compare the run time between the 2 genders.

4.4.1.4.2. Test for Normality of the Run Time in the 2 Genders

We can plot the QQ plot.

```
ggqqplot(data = run09, x = "time," facet.by = "gender,"

      title = "QQ plot of run time in males and females of Cherry Blossom Run
data in 2009,"

     xlab = "Theoretical percentiles," ylab = "Sample percentiles")+

 theme(plot.title = element_text(hjust = 0.5))
```

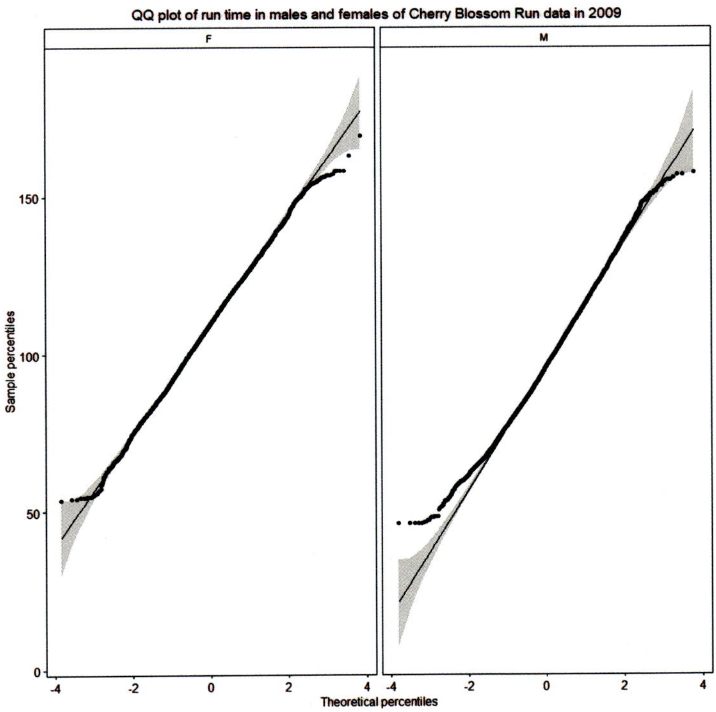

In females and males, not all data points fall along the reference line or within the confidence band, so we can not assume the normality of run time in females or males and we should use the Wilcoxon test which does not need the normality of data in the 2 groups.

4.4.1.4.3. Test for Homogeneity of Variances of the Run Time in the 2 Genders

```
run09 %>% levene_test(formula = time ~ gender) %>% flextable() %>%

  theme_box() %>%

  set_caption(caption = "Levene's test results for run time in males and females of Cherry Blossom Run data in 2009")
```

Table 4.40. *Levene's Test Results for Run Time in Males and Females of Cherry Blossom Run Data in 2009*

df1	df2	Statistic	p
1	14,972	66.96781	0.0000000000000002980299

We see that the p-value is significant (< 0.05) so we conclude that the variances of the run time in females and males are different and we can only use Welch's t-test conducted above.

4.4.2. Wilcoxon Test for Two Samples

The Wilcoxon test is a non-parametric alternative to the two samples t-test for comparing the median of a continuous variable in two independent groups of samples, in case where the data are not normally distributed or contain some outliers. It is also known as the Mann-Whitney or Mann-Whitney U test. However, the sample size should be at least 6 in each group, or the Wilcoxon test cannot become significant.

4.4.2.1. Wilcoxon Test for Maternal Age in Premature and Full-Term Births

The null hypothesis is that the difference between the median maternal age in the 2 birth types is 0, while the alternative hypothesis is that the difference between the medians is greater than or smaller than 0 or a two-sided test.

To conduct this test, we use the wilcox_test function applied to the "births14" data with the following arguments:

- formula = mage ~ premie which is the formula for two samples Wilcoxon test. This means that we want to compare the maternal age across the 2 levels of the "premie" column.
- mu = 0 which is the null value that corresponds to the null hypothesis.
- alternative = "two.sided" which is the alternative hypothesis.

Then, we convert the result to a table as before.

```
births14 %>% wilcox_test(formula = mage ~ premie, mu = 0,

            alternative = "two.sided") %>%

 flextable() %>% theme_box() %>%

 set_caption(caption = "Two-sided Wilcoxon test results of median maternal age
in premature and full-term births of the US births data in 2014")
```

Table 4.41. *Two-Sided Wilcoxon Test Results of Median Maternal Age in Premature and Full-Term Births of the US Births Data in 2014*

.y.	Group1	Group2	n1	n2	Statistic	p
mage	full term	premie	876	124	49,577.5	0.115

We see that:

- The table contains the statistic = 49577.5 which corresponds to our sample results and the p-value = 0.115.
- The p_value is larger than the cut-off value of 0.05, so we fail to reject the null hypothesis and conclude that the median maternal age in full-term and premature births is statistically equivalent.

4.4.2.2. Wilcoxon Test for Hospital Visits During Pregnancy in Premature and Full-Term Births

The null hypothesis is that the difference between the median hospital visits during pregnancy in the 2 birth types is 0, while the alternative hypothesis is that the difference between the medians is greater than or smaller than 0 or a two-sided test.

To conduct this test, we use the same functions above and modify them accordingly.

```
births14 %>% wilcox_test(formula = visits ~ premie, mu = 0,

            alternative = "two.sided") %>%

 flextable() %>% theme_box() %>%

 set_caption(caption = "Two-sided Wilcoxon test results of hospital visits during
pregnancy in premature and full-term births of the US births data in 2014")
```

Table 4.42. *Two-Sided Wilcoxon Test Results of Hospital Visits During Pregnancy in Premature and Full-Term Births of the US Births Data in 2014*

.y.	Group1	Group2	n1	n2	Statistic	p
visits	full term	premie	829	115	59,894.5	0.00000731

We see that:

- The Table 4.42 contains the statistic = 59894.5 which corresponds to our sample results and the p-value which is very low and nearly equals 0.
- The p_value is smaller than the cut-off value of 0.05, so we reject the null hypothesis and conclude that the median hospital visits during pregnancy in full-term births is significantly larger than that of premature births.

4.4.2.3. Wilcoxon Test for Run Time in Females and Males

The null hypothesis is that the difference between the median run time in the 2 genders is 0, while the alternative hypothesis is that the difference between the medians is greater than or smaller than 0 or a two-sided test.

To conduct this test, we use the same functions above and modify them accordingly.

```
run09 %>% wilcox_test(formula = time ~ gender, mu = 0,

            alternative = "two.sided") %>%

 flextable() %>% theme_box() %>%

 set_caption(caption = "Two-sided Wilcoxon test results of run time in males and
females of Cherry Blossom Run data in 2009")
```

Table 4.43. *Two-Sided Wilcoxon Test Results of Run Time in Males and Females of Cherry Blossom Run Data in 2009*

.y.	Group1	Group2	n1	n2	Statistic	p
time	F	M	8,323	6,651	38,522,940	0

We see that:

- The Table 4.43 contains the statistic = 38,522,940 which corresponds to our sample results and the p-value which is 0.

- The p_value is smaller than the cut-off value of 0.05, so we reject the null hypothesis and conclude that the median run time in females is significantly larger than that of males or they are slower than males.

4.4.3. ANOVA Test for More Than Two Samples

The ANOVA (Analysis of Variance) test is used to compare the mean of a continuous variable across multiple groups. The One-way ANOVA test is an extension of the independent two samples t-test for comparing the means across the different levels of 1 group.

If the average variation between group means is large compared to the average variation within groups, then we can conclude that at least one group mean is not equal to the others. That is why the method is called analysis of variance although the main goal is to compare the group means.

The null hypothesis is that all group means are equal, while the alternative hypothesis is that at least one mean is different from another mean.

4.4.3.1. ANOVA Assumptions

The ANOVA test has the same assumptions as that of the independent two samples t-test:

- Independence of the observations. Each subject should belong to only one group. There is no relationship between the observations in each group.
- No significant outliers in the different groups.
- Normality of the data in each group.
- Homogeneity of variances of the data in each group.

If the above assumptions are not met, there is a non-parametric alternative (Kruskal-Wallis test) to the one-way ANOVA.

4.4.3.2. ANOVA Test for the Mean Run Time in Runners from Different States

We saw previously that some states have only 1,2,3, etc runners, so we filter for states with a suitable sample size (> 10 runners) by creating a data frame "df" using the following functions:

- The count function with the argument state is applied to the "run09" data to count the number of runners (rows) for each state.
- The filter function with the argument n > 10 keeps only states with more than 10 runners.

```
df<-run09 %>% count(state) %>% filter(n > 10)
df %>% flextable() %>% theme_box() %>% set_caption(caption = "States with more than 10 runners of Cherry Blossom Run data in 2009")
```

Table 4.44. *States with More than 10 Runners of Cherry Blossom Run Data in 2009*

State	n
AZ	11
CA	75
CO	23
CT	73
DC	3,464
DE	61
FL	55
GA	37
IL	71
IN	18
MA	136
MD	3,558
MI	34
MN	19
MO	17
NC	158
NH	19
NJ	207
NR	59
NY	522
OH	80
PA	461
RI	14
SC	11
TX	44
VA	5,608
WI	14
WV	28

We have 28 different states instead of 51. Then we use this data frame "df" to filter for only these states in the original "run09" data frame using the filter function with the argument state %in% df$state to filter for only these 28 states. We create another data frame "run_filtered" to be used in subsequent analysis.

```
run_filtered<-run09 %>% filter(state %in% df$state)
glimpse(run_filtered)
## Rows: 14,877
## Columns: 14
## $ place    <int> 1, 2, 3, 4, 5, 6, 7, 8, 9, 10, 11, 12, 13, 14, 15, 16, 17, 1…
## $ time     <dbl> 53.533, 53.917, 53.967, 54.433, 54.450, 54.533, 54.633, 54.6…
## $ net_time <dbl> 53.533, 53.917, 53.967, 54.433, 54.450, 54.533, 54.633, 54.6…
## $ pace     <dbl> 5.367, 5.400, 5.400, 5.450, 5.450, 5.467, 5.467, 5.467, 5.48…
## $ age      <int> 21, 21, 22, 19, 36, 28, 25, 31, 23, 26, 23, 35, 28, 28, 26, …
## $ gender   <fct> F, F, F, F, F, F, F, F, F, F, F, F, F, F, F, F, F, F, F, F, …
## $ first    <fct> Lineth, Belianesh Zemed, Teyba, Abebu, Catherine, Olga, Sall…
## $ last     <fct> Chepkurui, Gebre, Naser, Gelan, Ndereba, Romanova, Meyerhoff…
## $ city     <fct> Kenya, Ethiopia, Ethiopia, Ethiopia, Kenya, Russia, United S…
## $ state    <fct> NR, NR, NR, NR, NR, NR, NR, NR, NR, NR, NR, NR, NR, CO, NR, …
## $ country  <fct> KEN, ETH, ETH, ETH, KEN, RUS, USA, KEN, ETH, RUS, ETH, ROM, …
## $ div      <int> 2, 2, 2, 1, 5, 3, 3, 4, 2, 3, 2, 5, 3, 3, 3, 3, 3, 5, 4, 2, …
## $ div_place <int> 1, 2, 3, 1, 1, 1, 2, 1, 4, 3, 4, 2, 4, 5, 6, 7, 8, 3, 2, 5, …
## $ div_tot  <int> 953, 953, 953, 71, 1130, 2706, 2706, 1678, 953, 2706, 953, 1…
```

The run_filtered data frame has the same columns as the original data (14 columns) but a lower number of rows (14877 instead of 14974).

The null hypothesis is that all 28 states' mean run times are equal, while the alternative hypothesis is that at least one state's mean is different from another state's mean.

To conduct this test, we use the anova_test function applied on the "run_filtered" data with the following argument, formula = time ~ state which is the formula for the ANOVA test. This means that we want to compare the mean run time across the different states of the "state" column.

Then, we convert the result to a table as before.

```
run_filtered %>% anova_test(formula = time ~ state) %>% flextable() %>%
 theme_box() %>% set_caption(caption = "ANOVA test results of the mean run time
in runners from 28 states of Cherry Blossom Run data in 2009")
```

Table 4.45. *ANOVA Test Results of the Mean Run Time in Runners from 28 States of Cherry Blossom Run Data in 2009*

Effect	DFn	DFd	F	p	p<.05	ges
state	27	14,849	9.121	0.000 0000 0000 0000 0000 0000 0000 0000 0000 0664	*	0.016

In the table above, we see that:

- The "DFn" is the degrees of freedom in the numerator and "DFd" is the degrees of freedom in the denominator (DFd).
- The obtained F-statistic value that corresponds to our sample results is 9.121.
- The p is the p-value which is the probability of our sample results (the difference between the state means) under the null hypothesis (where all states' means are equivalent). Since this probability is very low, so we reject the null hypothesis and conclude that at least one state run time mean is significantly different from another state mean.
- The "ges" is the generalized eta squared (effect size). This measures the proportion of the variability in the run time that can be explained in terms of the predictor (or the different states). An effect size of 0.016 (1.6%) means that about 1.6% of the variability in run time can be explained by the different states.

4.4.3.3. Post-Hoc Tests

A significant ANOVA test is followed by Tukey honest significant differences using the tukey_hsd function to perform multiple pairwise t-tests between the different states. We will use the same formula of the ANOVA test with the tukey_hsd function and arrange the adjusted p-values (p.adj) by using the arrange function.

```
run_filtered %>% tukey_hsd(time ~ state) %>% arrange(p.adj) %>%
```

```
flextable() %>% theme_box() %>%

set_caption(caption = "Tukey honest significant differences of the mean run time
in runners from 28 states of Cherry Blossom Run data in 2009")
```

Table 4.46. *Tukey Honest Significant Differences in the Mean Run Time in Runners From 28 States of Cherry Blossom Run Data in 2009*

Term	Group 1	Group 2	null. value	Estimate	conf.low	conf.high	p.adj	p.adj. signif
state	CA	NR	0	-32.592467345	-44.9864131	-20.1985216	0.00000000972	****
state	CT	NR	0	-32.602413281	-45.0708889	-20.1339377	0.00000000972	****
state	DC	NR	0	-32.012456556	-41.3633951	-22.6615180	0.00000000972	****
state	DE	NR	0	-28.140571826	-41.1456668	-15.1354768	0.00000000972	****
state	FL	NR	0	-35.775786133	-49.1250988	-22.4264735	0.00000000972	****
state	GA	NR	0	-31.537143381	-46.4727401	-16.6015467	0.00000000972	****
state	IL	NR	0	-33.273229410	-45.8199529	-20.7265060	0.00000000972	****
state	MA	NR	0	-33.930212737	-45.0330935	-22.8273320	0.00000000972	****
state	MD	NR	0	-34.312460071	-43.6613298	-24.9635904	0.00000000972	****
state	MI	NR	0	-35.087499501	-50.4227135	-19.7522855	0.00000000972	****
state	NC	NR	0	-36.909997640	-47.7764842	-26.0435111	0.00000000972	****
state	NJ	NR	0	-34.429368214	-44.9403545	-23.9183819	0.00000000972	****
state	NR	NY	0	32.003582440	22.2212901	41.7858748	0.00000000972	****
state	NR	OH	0	39.904990678	27.6827669	52.1272144	0.00000000972	****
state	NR	PA	0	31.089204235	21.2414085	40.9370000	0.00000000972	****
state	NR	TX	0	37.653736133	23.4670782	51.8403941	0.00000000972	****
state	NR	VA	0	33.945354551	24.6243992	43.2663099	0.00000000972	****
state	NR	WV	0	31.442762107	15.0983827	47.7871415	0.00000001010	****
state	IN	NR	0	-35.615218456	-54.7929367	-16.4375002	0.00000001180	****
state	MN	NR	0	-34.321230152	-53.1082686	-15.5341917	0.00000001420	****
state	MO	NR	0	-35.329970090	-54.9351196	-15.7248205	0.00000001810	****
state	AZ	NR	0	-40.241258860	-63.6318125	-16.8507052	0.00000007330	****
state	CO	NR	0	-29.658875461	-47.1666454	-12.1511055	0.00000013000	****
state	NH	NR	0	-30.812388046	-49.5994265	-12.0253496	0.00000043500	****
state	NR	RI	0	32.550583535	11.3774451	53.7237219	0.00000425000	****
state	NR	WI	0	32.247154964	11.0740166	53.4202934	0.00000578000	****
state	NR	SC	0	32.286713405	8.8961598	55.6772670	0.00010600000	***

state	DC	MD	0	2.300003515	0.5999902	4.0000169	0.00018000000	***
state	DC	VA	0	1.932897995	0.3937783	3.4720177	0.00105000000	**
state	OH	PA	0	-8.815786443	-17.4419364	-0.1896364	0.03770000000	*
state	DC	OH	0	7.892534122	-0.1617464	15.9468146	0.06400000000	ns
state	DE	OH	0	11.764418852	-0.3419381	23.8707758	0.07060000000	ns
state	NY	OH	0	7.901408238	-0.6498856	16.4527021	0.12100000000	ns
state	MD	PA	0	-3.223255835	-6.7487451	0.3022334	0.13500000000	ns
state	NC	PA	0	-5.820793405	-12.3864800	0.7448932	0.17800000000	ns
state	DC	NC	0	4.897541084	-0.8963532	10.6914354	0.26100000000	ns
state	PA	VA	0	2.856150316	-0.5946349	6.3069356	0.30300000000	ns
state	DE	NC	0	8.769425814	-1.9665723	19.5054239	0.33000000000	ns
state	NC	NY	0	-4.906415200	-11.3734395	1.5606091	0.49600000000	ns
state	OH	VA	0	-5.959636127	-13.9790869	2.0598147	0.54300000000	ns
state	MD	OH	0	5.592530607	-2.4593479	13.6444091	0.69000000000	ns
state	MD	NY	0	-2.308877630	-5.6470264	1.0292711	0.69800000000	ns
state	DE	TX	0	9.513164307	-4.5737938	23.6001224	0.74400000000	ns
state	DE	MD	0	6.171888245	-3.0249857	15.3687621	0.75500000000	ns
state	CA	OH	0	7.312523333	-4.1348027	18.7598494	0.83300000000	ns
state	CT	OH	0	7.302577397	-4.2254001	18.8305549	0.84400000000	ns
state	DE	VA	0	5.804782725	-3.3637141	14.9732795	0.84500000000	ns
state	CO	OH	0	10.246115217	-6.6048014	27.0970319	0.89200000000	ns
state	DE	NJ	0	6.288796389	-4.0872316	16.6648244	0.89600000000	ns
state	MA	OH	0	5.974777941	-4.0604273	16.0099831	0.91200000000	ns
state	NY	VA	0	1.941772111	-1.3173814	5.2009256	0.91200000000	ns
state	GA	OH	0	8.367847297	-5.7920761	22.5277707	0.91900000000	ns
state	NJ	OH	0	5.475622464	-3.9005289	14.8517739	0.92800000000	ns
state	PA	TX	0	6.564531897	-4.6733048	17.8023686	0.92800000000	ns
state	DE	FL	0	7.635214307	-5.6080962	20.8785248	0.93700000000	ns
state	IL	OH	0	6.631761268	-4.9808031	18.2443257	0.94300000000	ns
state	NJ	PA	0	-3.340163979	-9.2990685	2.6187405	0.95400000000	ns
state	OH	WV	0	-8.462228571	-24.1009664	7.1765092	0.96900000000	ns
state	DE	MA	0	5.789640911	-5.1855623	16.7648441	0.97800000000	ns
state	DC	TX	0	5.641279577	-5.1638093	16.4463684	0.98000000000	ns
state	AZ	DE	0	-12.100687034	-35.4309062	11.2295321	0.98200000000	ns
state	NC	VA	0	-2.964643089	-8.7100210	2.7807349	0.98300000000	ns

state	NY	TX	0	5.650153692	-5.5303265	16.8306339	0.98700000000	ns
state	NH	OH	0	9.092602632	-9.0838711	27.2690764	0.98900000000	ns
state	DC	NJ	0	2.416911659	-2.6791175	7.5129409	0.99500000000	ns
state	CO	NC	0	7.251122179	-8.6438823	23.1461267	0.99700000000	ns
state	DE	MI	0	6.946927676	-8.2961006	22.1899560	0.99700000000	ns
state	FL	PA	0	-4.686581897	-14.8468899	5.4737261	0.99700000000	ns
state	MD	NC	0	2.597537569	-3.1930171	8.3880922	0.99800000000	ns
state	AZ	PA	0	-9.152054624	-30.8809688	12.5768595	0.99900000000	ns
state	CA	NC	0	4.317530295	-5.6694137	14.3044743	0.99900000000	ns
state	CO	TX	0	7.994860672	-10.3308563	26.3205776	0.99900000000	ns
state	CT	NC	0	4.307584359	-5.7717034	14.3868722	0.99900000000	ns
state	DC	DE	0	-3.871884730	-13.0708617	5.3270922	0.99900000000	ns
state	DE	IL	0	5.132657585	-7.3012233	17.5665385	0.99900000000	ns
state	GA	NC	0	5.372854259	-7.6348822	18.3805907	0.99900000000	ns
state	NJ	NY	0	-2.425785774	-8.2758033	3.4242318	0.99900000000	ns
state	AZ	CA	0	-7.648791515	-30.6439327	15.3463497	1.00000000000	ns
state	AZ	CO	0	-10.582383399	-36.6915511	15.5267843	1.00000000000	ns
state	AZ	CT	0	-7.638845579	-30.6742425	15.3965514	1.00000000000	ns
state	AZ	DC	0	-8.228802304	-29.7370956	13.2794910	1.00000000000	ns
state	AZ	FL	0	-4.465472727	-27.9893070	19.0583615	1.00000000000	ns
state	AZ	GA	0	-8.704115479	-33.1630336	15.7548027	1.00000000000	ns
state	AZ	IL	0	-6.968029449	-30.0458738	16.1098149	1.00000000000	ns
state	AZ	IN	0	-4.626040404	-31.8831772	22.6310964	1.00000000000	ns
state	AZ	MA	0	-6.311046123	-28.6368292	16.0147369	1.00000000000	ns
state	AZ	MD	0	-5.928798789	-27.4361927	15.5785951	1.00000000000	ns
state	AZ	MI	0	-5.153759358	-29.8587268	19.5512081	1.00000000000	ns
state	AZ	MN	0	-5.920028708	-32.9037172	21.0636598	1.00000000000	ns
state	AZ	MO	0	-4.911288770	-32.4708337	22.6482562	1.00000000000	ns
state	AZ	NC	0	-3.331261220	-25.5404296	18.8779071	1.00000000000	ns
state	AZ	NH	0	-9.428870813	-36.4125593	17.5548176	1.00000000000	ns
state	AZ	NJ	0	-5.811890646	-27.8493011	16.2255198	1.00000000000	ns
state	AZ	NY	0	-8.237676419	-29.9369822	13.4616294	1.00000000000	ns
state	AZ	OH	0	-0.336268182	-23.2393113	22.5667749	1.00000000000	ns
state	AZ	RI	0	-7.690675325	-36.3868147	21.0054641	1.00000000000	ns
state	AZ	SC	0	-7.954545455	-38.3236848	22.4145939	1.00000000000	ns

state	AZ	TX	0	-2.587522727	-26.5964355	21.4213900	1.00000000000	ns
state	AZ	VA	0	-6.295904309	-27.7911791	15.1993704	1.00000000000	ns
state	AZ	WI	0	-7.994103896	-36.6902433	20.7020355	1.00000000000	ns
state	AZ	WV	0	-8.798496753	-34.1422409	16.5452474	1.00000000000	ns
state	CA	CO	0	-2.933591884	-19.9094727	14.0422889	1.00000000000	ns
state	CA	CT	0	0.009945936	-11.6999389	11.7198308	1.00000000000	ns
state	CA	DC	0	-0.580010789	-8.8925659	7.7325443	1.00000000000	ns
state	CA	DE	0	-4.451895519	-16.7315949	7.8278039	1.00000000000	ns
state	CA	FL	0	3.183318788	-9.4603622	15.8269998	1.00000000000	ns
state	CA	GA	0	-1.055323964	-15.3637330	13.2530851	1.00000000000	ns
state	CA	IL	0	0.680762066	-11.1124050	12.4739291	1.00000000000	ns
state	CA	IN	0	3.022751111	-15.6706541	21.7161563	1.00000000000	ns
state	CA	MA	0	1.337745392	-8.9059103	11.5814011	1.00000000000	ns
state	CA	MD	0	1.719992726	-6.5902350	10.0302205	1.00000000000	ns
state	CA	MI	0	2.495032157	-12.2300250	17.2200893	1.00000000000	ns
state	CA	MN	0	1.728762807	-16.5636218	20.0211474	1.00000000000	ns
state	CA	MO	0	2.737502745	-16.3941571	21.8691626	1.00000000000	ns
state	CA	NH	0	-1.780079298	-20.0724639	16.5123053	1.00000000000	ns
state	CA	NJ	0	1.836900870	-7.7620237	11.4358255	1.00000000000	ns
state	CA	NY	0	-0.588884904	-9.3838701	8.2061003	1.00000000000	ns
state	CA	PA	0	-1.503263109	-10.3710476	7.3645214	1.00000000000	ns
state	CA	RI	0	-0.041883810	-20.7773681	20.6936005	1.00000000000	ns
state	CA	SC	0	-0.305753939	-23.3008952	22.6893873	1.00000000000	ns
state	CA	TX	0	5.061268788	-8.4635153	18.5860529	1.00000000000	ns
state	CA	VA	0	1.352887206	-6.9259249	9.6316993	1.00000000000	ns
state	CA	WI	0	-0.345312381	-21.0807967	20.3901719	1.00000000000	ns
state	CA	WV	0	-1.149705238	-16.9230136	14.6236032	1.00000000000	ns
state	CO	CT	0	2.943537820	-14.0868328	19.9739084	1.00000000000	ns
state	CO	DC	0	2.353581095	-12.5464421	17.2536043	1.00000000000	ns
state	CO	DE	0	-1.518303635	-18.9453841	15.9087769	1.00000000000	ns
state	CO	FL	0	6.116910672	-11.5685293	23.8023506	1.00000000000	ns
state	CO	GA	0	1.878267920	-17.0331754	20.7897112	1.00000000000	ns
state	CO	IL	0	3.614353950	-13.4733875	20.7020954	1.00000000000	ns
state	CO	IN	0	5.956342995	-16.4569458	28.3696318	1.00000000000	ns
state	CO	MA	0	4.271337276	-11.7862030	20.3288775	1.00000000000	ns

state	CO	MD	0	4.653584610	-10.2451403	19.5523095	1.00000000000	ns
state	CO	MI	0	5.428624041	-13.7999855	24.6572336	1.00000000000	ns
state	CO	MN	0	4.662354691	-17.4175786	26.7422880	1.00000000000	ns
state	CO	MO	0	5.671094629	-17.1089960	28.4511852	1.00000000000	ns
state	CO	NH	0	1.153512586	-20.9264207	23.2334459	1.00000000000	ns
state	CO	NJ	0	4.770492754	-10.8836272	20.4246127	1.00000000000	ns
state	CO	NY	0	2.344706980	-12.8297414	17.5191553	1.00000000000	ns
state	CO	PA	0	1.430328775	-13.7864291	16.6470866	1.00000000000	ns
state	CO	RI	0	2.891708075	-21.2510430	27.0344591	1.00000000000	ns
state	CO	SC	0	2.627837945	-23.4813298	28.7370056	1.00000000000	ns
state	CO	VA	0	4.286479090	-10.5947456	19.1677037	1.00000000000	ns
state	CO	WI	0	2.588279503	-21.5544715	26.7310305	1.00000000000	ns
state	CO	WV	0	1.783886646	-18.2588022	21.8265755	1.00000000000	ns
state	CT	DC	0	-0.589956725	-9.0132319	7.8333184	1.00000000000	ns
state	CT	DE	0	-4.461841455	-16.8167599	7.8930769	1.00000000000	ns
state	CT	FL	0	3.173372852	-9.5433744	15.8901201	1.00000000000	ns
state	CT	GA	0	-1.065269900	-15.4382849	13.3077451	1.00000000000	ns
state	CT	IL	0	0.670816130	-11.2006531	12.5422854	1.00000000000	ns
state	CT	IN	0	3.012805175	-15.7300972	21.7557076	1.00000000000	ns
state	CT	MA	0	1.327799456	-9.0059062	11.6615051	1.00000000000	ns
state	CT	MD	0	1.710046790	-6.7109316	10.1310252	1.00000000000	ns
state	CT	MI	0	2.485086221	-12.3027567	17.2729292	1.00000000000	ns
state	CT	MN	0	1.718816871	-16.6241471	20.0617808	1.00000000000	ns
state	CT	MO	0	2.727556809	-16.4524693	21.9075829	1.00000000000	ns
state	CT	NH	0	-1.790025234	-20.1329892	16.5529387	1.00000000000	ns
state	CT	NJ	0	1.826954933	-7.8680100	11.5219199	1.00000000000	ns
state	CT	NY	0	-0.598830840	-9.4985362	8.3008746	1.00000000000	ns
state	CT	PA	0	-1.513209045	-10.4848641	7.4584460	1.00000000000	ns
state	CT	RI	0	-0.051829746	-20.8319477	20.7282882	1.00000000000	ns
state	CT	SC	0	-0.315699875	-23.3510968	22.7196971	1.00000000000	ns
state	CT	TX	0	5.051322852	-8.5417922	18.6444379	1.00000000000	ns
state	CT	VA	0	1.342941270	-7.0470361	9.7329187	1.00000000000	ns
state	CT	WI	0	-0.355258317	-21.1353763	20.4248596	1.00000000000	ns
state	CT	WV	0	-1.159651174	-16.9915888	14.6722865	1.00000000000	ns
state	DC	FL	0	3.763329577	-5.9161761	13.4428352	1.00000000000	ns

state	DC	GA	0	-0.475313175	-12.2464954	11.2958690	1.00000000000	ns
state	DC	IL	0	1.260772855	-7.2779009	9.7994467	1.00000000000	ns
state	DC	IN	0	3.602761900	-13.2279707	20.4334945	1.00000000000	ns
state	DC	MA	0	1.917756181	-4.3082090	8.1437213	1.00000000000	ns
state	DC	MI	0	3.075042946	-9.1992174	15.3493033	1.00000000000	ns
state	DC	MN	0	2.308773596	-14.0754107	18.6929579	1.00000000000	ns
state	DC	MO	0	3.317513534	-13.9986803	20.6337074	1.00000000000	ns
state	DC	NH	0	-1.200068509	-17.5842528	15.1841158	1.00000000000	ns
state	DC	NY	0	-0.008874115	-3.3528126	3.3350644	1.00000000000	ns
state	DC	PA	0	-0.923252320	-4.4542242	2.6077195	1.00000000000	ns
state	DC	RI	0	0.538126980	-18.5351651	19.6114190	1.00000000000	ns
state	DC	SC	0	0.274256850	-21.2340364	21.7825501	1.00000000000	ns
state	DC	WI	0	0.234698408	-18.8385937	19.3079905	1.00000000000	ns
state	DC	WV	0	-0.569694449	-14.0836657	12.9442768	1.00000000000	ns
state	DE	GA	0	3.396571555	-11.4443575	18.2375006	1.00000000000	ns
state	DE	IN	0	7.474646630	-11.6294368	26.5787300	1.00000000000	ns
state	DE	MN	0	6.180658326	-12.5312080	24.8925246	1.00000000000	ns
state	DE	MO	0	7.189398264	-12.3437278	26.7225243	1.00000000000	ns
state	DE	NH	0	2.671816221	-16.0400501	21.3836825	1.00000000000	ns
state	DE	NY	0	3.863010615	-5.7741243	13.5001455	1.00000000000	ns
state	DE	PA	0	2.948632410	-6.7549858	12.6522506	1.00000000000	ns
state	DE	RI	0	4.410011710	-16.6964545	25.5164779	1.00000000000	ns
state	DE	SC	0	4.146141580	-19.1840775	27.4763607	1.00000000000	ns
state	DE	WI	0	4.106583138	-16.9998830	25.2130493	1.00000000000	ns
state	DE	WV	0	3.302190281	-12.9557266	19.5601072	1.00000000000	ns
state	FL	GA	0	-4.238642752	-19.3821175	10.9048320	1.00000000000	ns
state	FL	IL	0	-2.502556722	-15.2960334	10.2909200	1.00000000000	ns
state	FL	IN	0	-0.160567677	-19.5006208	19.1794854	1.00000000000	ns
state	FL	MA	0	-1.845573396	-13.2265548	9.5354080	1.00000000000	ns
state	FL	MD	0	-1.463326062	-11.1408331	8.2141809	1.00000000000	ns
state	FL	MI	0	-0.688286631	-16.2260331	14.8494598	1.00000000000	ns
state	FL	MN	0	-1.454555981	-20.4072759	17.4981639	1.00000000000	ns
state	FL	MO	0	-0.445816043	-20.2097900	19.3181579	1.00000000000	ns
state	FL	NC	0	1.134211507	-10.0162731	12.2846961	1.00000000000	ns
state	FL	NH	0	-4.963398086	-23.9161180	13.9893218	1.00000000000	ns

state	FL	NJ	0	-1.346417918	-12.1507508	9.4579150	1.00000000000	ns
state	FL	NY	0	-3.772203692	-13.8690359	6.3246285	1.00000000000	ns
state	FL	OH	0	4.129204545	-8.3461925	16.6046016	1.00000000000	ns
state	FL	RI	0	-3.225202597	-24.5454879	18.0950827	1.00000000000	ns
state	FL	SC	0	-3.489072727	-27.0129070	20.0347615	1.00000000000	ns
state	FL	TX	0	1.877950000	-12.5273977	16.2832977	1.00000000000	ns
state	FL	VA	0	-1.830431582	-11.4809749	7.8201117	1.00000000000	ns
state	FL	WI	0	-3.528631169	-24.8489165	17.7916542	1.00000000000	ns
state	FL	WV	0	-4.333024026	-20.8675792	12.2015311	1.00000000000	ns
state	GA	IL	0	1.736086030	-12.7048609	16.1770329	1.00000000000	ns
state	GA	IN	0	4.078075075	-16.3891073	24.5452575	1.00000000000	ns
state	GA	MA	0	2.393069356	-10.8127869	15.5989256	1.00000000000	ns
state	GA	MD	0	2.775316690	-8.9942221	14.5448554	1.00000000000	ns
state	GA	MI	0	3.550356121	-13.3697345	20.4704467	1.00000000000	ns
state	GA	MN	0	2.784086771	-17.3174926	22.8856661	1.00000000000	ns
state	GA	MO	0	3.792826709	-17.0753923	24.6610458	1.00000000000	ns
state	GA	NH	0	-0.724755334	-20.8263347	19.3768240	1.00000000000	ns
state	GA	NJ	0	2.892224834	-9.8200335	15.6044831	1.00000000000	ns
state	GA	NY	0	0.466439060	-11.6502404	12.5831186	1.00000000000	ns
state	GA	PA	0	-0.447939145	-12.6175636	11.7216853	1.00000000000	ns
state	GA	RI	0	1.013440154	-21.3343219	23.3612022	1.00000000000	ns
state	GA	SC	0	0.749570025	-23.7093481	25.2084882	1.00000000000	ns
state	GA	TX	0	6.116592752	-9.7699406	22.0031261	1.00000000000	ns
state	GA	VA	0	2.408211170	-9.3391667	14.1555890	1.00000000000	ns
state	GA	WI	0	0.710011583	-21.6377504	23.0577736	1.00000000000	ns
state	GA	WV	0	-0.094381274	-17.9342079	17.7454454	1.00000000000	ns
state	IL	IN	0	2.341989045	-16.4530575	21.1370356	1.00000000000	ns
state	IL	MA	0	0.656983326	-9.7710011	11.0849678	1.00000000000	ns
state	IL	MD	0	1.039230661	-7.4971774	9.5756387	1.00000000000	ns
state	IL	MI	0	1.814270091	-13.0396077	16.6681479	1.00000000000	ns
state	IL	MN	0	1.048000741	-17.3482411	19.4442426	1.00000000000	ns
state	IL	MO	0	2.056740679	-17.1742444	21.2877258	1.00000000000	ns
state	IL	NC	0	3.636768230	-6.5391557	13.8126922	1.00000000000	ns
state	IL	NH	0	-2.460841364	-20.8570832	15.9354004	1.00000000000	ns
state	IL	NJ	0	1.156138804	-8.6392545	10.9515322	1.00000000000	ns

state	IL	NY	0	-1.269646970	-10.2786504	7.7393564	1.00000000000	ns
state	IL	PA	0	-2.184025175	-11.2641122	6.8960618	1.00000000000	ns
state	IL	RI	0	-0.722645875	-21.5498081	20.1045164	1.00000000000	ns
state	IL	SC	0	-0.986516005	-24.0643603	22.0913283	1.00000000000	ns
state	IL	TX	0	4.380506722	-9.2844178	18.0454312	1.00000000000	ns
state	IL	VA	0	0.672125141	-7.8337027	9.1779530	1.00000000000	ns
state	IL	WI	0	-1.026074447	-21.8532367	19.8010878	1.00000000000	ns
state	IL	WV	0	-1.830467304	-17.7241024	14.0631678	1.00000000000	ns
state	IN	MA	0	-1.685005719	-19.5485851	16.1785736	1.00000000000	ns
state	IN	MD	0	-1.302758385	-18.1323416	15.5268248	1.00000000000	ns
state	IN	MI	0	-0.527718954	-21.2883137	20.2328758	1.00000000000	ns
state	IN	MN	0	-1.293988304	-24.7201771	22.1322005	1.00000000000	ns
state	IN	MO	0	-0.285248366	-24.3724938	23.8019971	1.00000000000	ns
state	IN	NC	0	1.294779184	-16.4228402	19.0123986	1.00000000000	ns
state	IN	NH	0	-4.802830409	-28.2290192	18.6233584	1.00000000000	ns
state	IN	NJ	0	-1.185850242	-18.6876884	16.3159879	1.00000000000	ns
state	IN	NY	0	-3.611636015	-20.6857905	13.4625184	1.00000000000	ns
state	IN	OH	0	4.289772222	-14.2902240	22.8697685	1.00000000000	ns
state	IN	PA	0	-4.526014220	-21.6377817	12.5857533	1.00000000000	ns
state	IN	RI	0	-3.064634921	-28.4444556	22.3151857	1.00000000000	ns
state	IN	SC	0	-3.328505051	-30.5856418	23.9286317	1.00000000000	ns
state	IN	TX	0	2.038517677	-17.8887192	21.9657546	1.00000000000	ns
state	IN	VA	0	-1.669863905	-18.4839566	15.1442288	1.00000000000	ns
state	IN	WI	0	-3.368063492	-28.7478841	22.0117571	1.00000000000	ns
state	IN	WV	0	-4.172456349	-25.6892462	17.3443335	1.00000000000	ns
state	MA	MD	0	0.382247334	-5.8406101	6.6051047	1.00000000000	ns
state	MA	MI	0	1.157286765	-12.4988978	14.8134713	1.00000000000	ns
state	MA	MN	0	0.391017415	-17.0524743	17.8345092	1.00000000000	ns
state	MA	MO	0	1.399757353	-16.9219368	19.7214516	1.00000000000	ns
state	MA	NC	0	2.979784903	-5.3510686	11.3106384	1.00000000000	ns
state	MA	NH	0	-3.117824690	-20.5613164	14.3256671	1.00000000000	ns
state	MA	NJ	0	0.499155477	-7.3623598	8.3606708	1.00000000000	ns
state	MA	NY	0	-1.926630296	-8.7834396	4.9301790	1.00000000000	ns
state	MA	PA	0	-2.841008501	-9.7909489	4.1089319	1.00000000000	ns
state	MA	RI	0	-1.379629202	-21.3702365	18.6109781	1.00000000000	ns

state	MA	SC	0	-1.643499332	-23.9692824	20.6822837	1.00000000000	ns
state	MA	TX	0	3.723523396	-8.6289603	16.0760071	1.00000000000	ns
state	MA	VA	0	0.015141814	-6.1656994	6.1959831	1.00000000000	ns
state	MA	WI	0	-1.683057773	-21.6736650	18.3075495	1.00000000000	ns
state	MA	WV	0	-2.487450630	-17.2678879	12.2929867	1.00000000000	ns
state	MD	MI	0	0.775039431	-11.4976449	13.0477237	1.00000000000	ns
state	MD	MN	0	0.008770081	-16.3742335	16.3917737	1.00000000000	ns
state	MD	MO	0	1.017510019	-16.2975667	18.3325867	1.00000000000	ns
state	MD	NH	0	-3.500072024	-19.8830757	12.8829316	1.00000000000	ns
state	MD	NJ	0	0.116908143	-4.9753238	5.2091401	1.00000000000	ns
state	MD	RI	0	-1.761876536	-20.8341544	17.3104013	1.00000000000	ns
state	MD	SC	0	-2.025746666	-23.5331406	19.4816472	1.00000000000	ns
state	MD	TX	0	3.341276062	-7.4620224	14.1445745	1.00000000000	ns
state	MD	VA	0	-0.367105520	-1.8936054	1.1593944	1.00000000000	ns
state	MD	WI	0	-2.065305107	-21.1375830	17.0069727	1.00000000000	ns
state	MD	WV	0	-2.869697964	-16.3822377	10.6428418	1.00000000000	ns
state	MI	MN	0	-0.766269350	-21.1665201	19.6339814	1.00000000000	ns
state	MI	MO	0	0.242470588	-20.9135996	21.3985407	1.00000000000	ns
state	MI	NC	0	1.822498138	-11.6421944	15.2871907	1.00000000000	ns
state	MI	NH	0	-4.275111455	-24.6753622	16.1251393	1.00000000000	ns
state	MI	NJ	0	-0.658131287	-13.8375944	12.5213319	1.00000000000	ns
state	MI	NY	0	-3.083917061	-15.6898942	9.5220601	1.00000000000	ns
state	MI	OH	0	4.817491176	-9.7633239	19.3983063	1.00000000000	ns
state	MI	PA	0	-3.998295266	-16.6551708	8.6585802	1.00000000000	ns
state	MI	RI	0	-2.536915966	-25.1537063	20.0798744	1.00000000000	ns
state	MI	SC	0	-2.800786096	-27.5057535	21.9041813	1.00000000000	ns
state	MI	TX	0	2.566236631	-13.6965639	18.8290371	1.00000000000	ns
state	MI	VA	0	-1.142144950	-13.3935785	11.1092886	1.00000000000	ns
state	MI	WI	0	-2.840344538	-25.4571349	19.7764458	1.00000000000	ns
state	MI	WV	0	-3.644737395	-21.8204397	14.5309649	1.00000000000	ns
state	MN	MO	0	1.008739938	-22.7686302	24.7861101	1.00000000000	ns
state	MN	NC	0	2.588767488	-14.7052191	19.8827541	1.00000000000	ns
state	MN	NH	0	-3.508842105	-26.6162924	19.5986082	1.00000000000	ns
state	MN	NJ	0	0.108138063	-16.9647140	17.1809901	1.00000000000	ns
state	MN	NY	0	-2.317647711	-18.9517899	14.3164945	1.00000000000	ns

state	MN	OH	0	5.583760526	-12.5927132	23.7602343	1.00000000000	ns
state	MN	PA	0	-3.232025916	-19.9047739	13.4407221	1.00000000000	ns
state	MN	RI	0	-1.770646617	-26.8565636	23.3152704	1.00000000000	ns
state	MN	SC	0	-2.034516746	-29.0182052	24.9491717	1.00000000000	ns
state	MN	TX	0	3.332505981	-16.2190338	22.8840458	1.00000000000	ns
state	MN	VA	0	-0.375875601	-16.7429661	15.9912149	1.00000000000	ns
state	MN	WI	0	-2.074075188	-27.1599922	23.0118418	1.00000000000	ns
state	MN	WV	0	-2.878468045	-24.0477897	18.2908536	1.00000000000	ns
state	MO	NC	0	1.580027550	-16.5993852	19.7594403	1.00000000000	ns
state	MO	NH	0	-4.517582043	-28.2949522	19.2597881	1.00000000000	ns
state	MO	NJ	0	-0.900601876	-18.8697797	17.0685759	1.00000000000	ns
state	MO	NY	0	-3.326387649	-20.8792724	14.2264971	1.00000000000	ns
state	MO	OH	0	4.575020588	-14.4458435	23.5958847	1.00000000000	ns
state	MO	PA	0	-4.240765854	-21.8302399	13.3487082	1.00000000000	ns
state	MO	RI	0	-2.779386555	-28.4837112	22.9249381	1.00000000000	ns
state	MO	SC	0	-3.043256684	-30.6028016	24.5162882	1.00000000000	ns
state	MO	TX	0	2.323766043	-18.0151568	22.6626889	1.00000000000	ns
state	MO	VA	0	-1.384615539	-18.6846365	15.9154054	1.00000000000	ns
state	MO	WI	0	-3.082815126	-28.7871398	22.6215095	1.00000000000	ns
state	MO	WV	0	-3.887207983	-25.7858211	18.0114051	1.00000000000	ns
state	NC	NH	0	-6.097609594	-23.3915962	11.1963770	1.00000000000	ns
state	NC	NJ	0	-2.480629426	-10.0045906	5.0433317	1.00000000000	ns
state	NC	OH	0	2.994993038	-6.7780266	12.7680127	1.00000000000	ns
state	NC	RI	0	-4.359414105	-24.2196998	15.5008716	1.00000000000	ns
state	NC	SC	0	-4.623284235	-26.8324526	17.5858841	1.00000000000	ns
state	NC	TX	0	0.743738493	-11.3967073	12.8841842	1.00000000000	ns
state	NC	WI	0	-4.662842676	-24.5231284	15.1974430	1.00000000000	ns
state	NC	WV	0	-5.467235533	-20.0709302	9.1364591	1.00000000000	ns
state	NH	NJ	0	3.616980168	-13.4558719	20.6898322	1.00000000000	ns
state	NH	NY	0	1.191194394	-15.4429478	17.8253366	1.00000000000	ns
state	NH	PA	0	0.276816189	-16.3959318	16.9495642	1.00000000000	ns
state	NH	RI	0	1.738195489	-23.3477215	26.8241125	1.00000000000	ns
state	NH	SC	0	1.474325359	-25.5093631	28.4580138	1.00000000000	ns
state	NH	TX	0	6.841348086	-12.7101917	26.3928879	1.00000000000	ns

state	NH	VA	0	3.132966505	-13.2341240	19.5000570	1.00000000000	ns
state	NH	WI	0	1.434766917	-23.6511501	26.5206839	1.00000000000	ns
state	NH	WV	0	0.630374060	-20.5389476	21.7996958	1.00000000000	ns
state	NJ	RI	0	-1.878784679	-21.5468108	17.7892414	1.00000000000	ns
state	NJ	SC	0	-2.142654809	-24.1800653	19.8947557	1.00000000000	ns
state	NJ	TX	0	3.224367918	-8.5989449	15.0476807	1.00000000000	ns
state	NJ	VA	0	-0.484013663	-5.5248142	4.5567869	1.00000000000	ns
state	NJ	WI	0	-2.182213251	-21.8502394	17.4858129	1.00000000000	ns
state	NJ	WV	0	-2.986606108	-17.3277427	11.3545305	1.00000000000	ns
state	NY	PA	0	-0.914378205	-5.4664057	3.6376493	1.00000000000	ns
state	NY	RI	0	0.547001095	-18.7414323	19.8354345	1.00000000000	ns
state	NY	SC	0	0.283130965	-21.4161748	21.9824368	1.00000000000	ns
state	NY	WI	0	0.243572523	-19.0448609	19.5320059	1.00000000000	ns
state	NY	WV	0	-0.560820334	-14.3767752	13.2551346	1.00000000000	ns
state	OH	RI	0	-7.354407143	-27.9877096	13.2788954	1.00000000000	ns
state	OH	SC	0	-7.618277273	-30.5213203	15.2847658	1.00000000000	ns
state	OH	TX	0	-2.251254545	-15.6188514	11.1163423	1.00000000000	ns
state	OH	WI	0	-7.657835714	-28.2911382	12.9754668	1.00000000000	ns
state	PA	RI	0	1.461379300	-17.8603572	20.7831158	1.00000000000	ns
state	PA	SC	0	1.197509170	-20.5314050	22.9264233	1.00000000000	ns
state	PA	WI	0	1.157950728	-18.1637857	20.4796872	1.00000000000	ns
state	PA	WV	0	0.353557871	-13.5088534	14.2159692	1.00000000000	ns
state	RI	SC	0	-0.263870130	-28.9600095	28.4322693	1.00000000000	ns
state	RI	TX	0	5.103152597	-16.7511761	26.9574813	1.00000000000	ns
state	RI	VA	0	1.394771016	-17.6638393	20.4533813	1.00000000000	ns
state	RI	WI	0	-0.303428571	-27.2227935	26.6159363	1.00000000000	ns
state	RI	WV	0	-1.107821429	-24.4206753	22.2050324	1.00000000000	ns
state	SC	TX	0	5.367022727	-18.6418900	29.3759355	1.00000000000	ns
state	SC	VA	0	1.658641146	-19.8366336	23.1539159	1.00000000000	ns
state	SC	WI	0	-0.039558442	-28.7356979	28.6565810	1.00000000000	ns
state	SC	WV	0	-0.843951299	-26.1876954	24.4997928	1.00000000000	ns
state	TX	VA	0	-3.708381582	-14.4875328	7.0707697	1.00000000000	ns
state	TX	WI	0	-5.406581169	-27.2609099	16.4477475	1.00000000000	ns
state	TX	WV	0	-6.210974026	-23.4286577	11.0067096	1.00000000000	ns
state	VA	WI	0	-1.698199587	-20.7568099	17.3604107	1.00000000000	ns

state	VA	WV	0	-2.502592444	-15.9958343	10.9906494	1.00000000000	ns
state	WI	WV	0	-0.804392857	-24.1172467	22.5084610	1.00000000000	ns

We see that:

- Every pair of states are compared with an estimate, a 95% confidence interval, and an adjusted p-value.
- For example, the runners from the "CA" state have significantly higher mean run time than runners from the "NR" state. The difference is estimated to be 32.59 and can be as high as 44.99 and as low as 20.20.
- On the other hand, runners from "WI" state have statistically equivalent mean run time to runners from "WV" state.

To trust these results, we must test the assumptions of ANOVA on our data. The runners from different states are independent with no relation between them. Other tests will be described below.

4.4.3.4. Test for Outliers in the Run Time from Runners of Different States

We use the identify_outliers function with the argument, time, after the group_by function with the argument state to detect any outliers in the run time within the different states. Then, we use the select function to select the important columns to be viewed (state, time, is.outlier, is.extreme) instead of viewing all columns of the "run_filtered" data. Finally, we convert the results to a table as before.

```
run_filtered %>%
 group_by(state) %>%
 identify_outliers(time) %>% select(state, time, is.outlier, is.extreme) %>%

 flextable() %>%

 theme_box() %>%

 set_caption(caption = "Outlier test results for run time in runners from 28
states of Cherry Blossom Run data in 2009")
```

Table 4.47. *Outlier Test Results for the Run Time in Runners from 28 States of Cherry Blossom Run Data in 2009*

State	Time	is.outlier	is.extreme
DC	158.133	TRUE	FALSE
DE	141.183	TRUE	FALSE
MN	48.067	TRUE	FALSE
MO	155.883	TRUE	FALSE
PA	50.700	TRUE	FALSE
SC	79.617	TRUE	FALSE
SC	116.533	TRUE	FALSE
SC	132.983	TRUE	TRUE
VA	163.250	TRUE	FALSE
VA	169.617	TRUE	FALSE
WV	150.683	TRUE	FALSE
WV	150.667	TRUE	FALSE
WV	150.683	TRUE	FALSE

We have many outlying run time values in different states so a non-parametric alternative (Kruskal-Wallis test) should be used.

4.4.3.5. Test for Normality of the Run Time from Runners of Different States

As we saw in Chapter 1, normality can be checked using the QQ plot and Shapiro-Wilk test. For the ANOVA test, the normality assumption can be checked either by:

- Analyzing the ANOVA model residuals to check the normality for all groups together. The residuals are the difference between the actual run time and the predicted run time using the ANOVA test.
- Check normality for each group separately.

4.4.3.5.1. Analyzing the ANOVA Model Residuals Using QQ Plot

We will run the ANOVA test using the aov function then run the residuals function and finally the ggqqplot function.

```
ggqqplot(residuals(run_filtered %>% aov(formula = time ~ state)),

    title = "QQ plot of ANOVA model residuals of mean run time\n in runners from
```

```
28 states of Cherry Blossom Run data in 2009,"

    xlab = "Theoretical percentiles," ylab = "Sample percentiles")+

 theme(plot.title = element_text(hjust = 0.5))
```

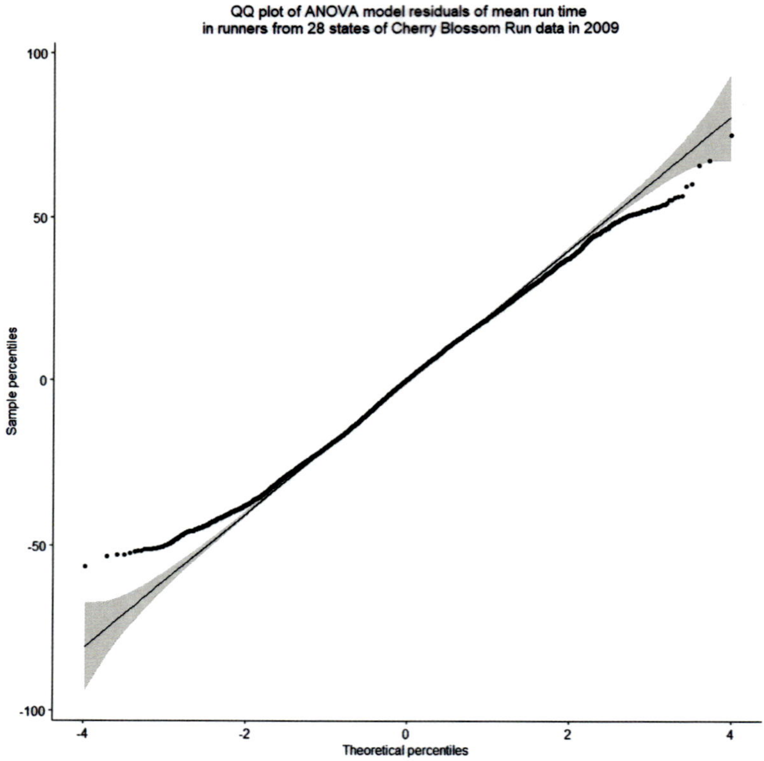

We see that not all data points (residuals) fall along the reference line or within the confidence band, so we can not assume the normality of this ANOVA model residuals and we should use the Kruskal-Wallis test.

4.4.3.5.2. Analyzing the ANOVA Model Residuals Using the Shapiro-Wilk Test

We will run the ANOVA test using the aov function then run the residuals function and finally the shapiro_test function.

```
shapiro_test(residuals(run_filtered %>% aov(formula = time ~ state)))
## Error in shapiro.test(data): sample size must be between 3 and 5000
```

The Shapiro test gives an error because it can handle a sample size of a maximum of 5000 but the residuals of this ANOVA test are 14877 in size (as the number of rows in "run_filtered" data). We can check that using the length function.

```
length(residuals(run_filtered %>% aov(formula = time ~ state)))

## [1] 14877
```

We have 14877 residual values. Alternatively, we can use the Anderson-Darling test for normality which can handle large sample sizes using the ad.test from the nortest package.

```
library(nortest)

ad.test(residuals(run_filtered %>% aov(formula = time ~ state)))
##
## Anderson-Darling normality test
##
## data: residuals(run_filtered %>% aov(formula = time ~ state))
## A = 5.7034, p-value = 4.82e-14
```

We see that the p-value is significant so the residuals from this ANOVA test are not normally distributed.

4.4.3.5.3. Check the Normality of Run Time in Each State Using the QQ Plot

We use the ggqqplot as done before.

```
ggqqplot(data = run_filtered, x = "time," facet.by = "state,"

    title = "QQ plot of run time in runners from 28 states of Cherry Blossom
Run data in 2009,"

    xlab = "Theoretical percentiles," ylab = "Sample percentiles")+

 theme(plot.title = element_text(hjust = 0.5))
```

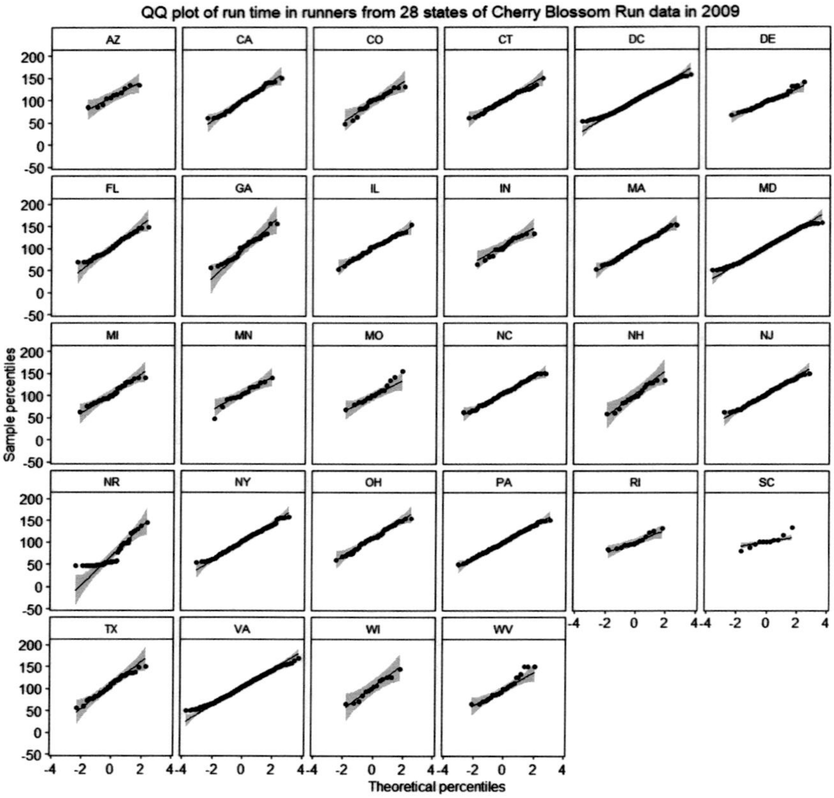

In some states like "SC" and "NR" states, not all data points fall along the reference line or within the confidence band, so we can not assume normality or run time in these states and we should use the Kruskal-Wallis test.

4.4.3.5.4. Check the Normality of Run Time in Each State Using the Shapiro-Wilk Test

We have seen in the "df" data frame that only 1 state "VA" has a count of more than 5000. So, all other states can be tested using the Shapiro-Wilk test and the "VA" state can be tested using the Anderson-Darling test.

To do the Shapiro-Wilk test for the run time of runners from all states except the "VA" state, we use the following functions:

- The filter function with the argument !state=="VA" to keep all states except the "VA" state.

- The group_by function with state argument split the original data frame into 27 different data frames, each containing a single state.
- The shapiro_test function with time argument to do the Shapiro test on the run time within each of the 27 data frames.
- The arrange function with "p" argument to arrange the states by their p-value in ascending order.

Then, we convert the result to a table as before.

```
run_filtered %>% filter(!state=="VA") %>% group_by(state) %>%

 shapiro_test(time) %>% arrange(p) %>%

 flextable() %>% theme_box() %>%

 set_caption(caption = "Shapiro Wilk test results of the run time of runners from
27 states of Cherry Blossom Run data in 2009")
```

Table 4.48. *Shapiro Wilk Test Results of the Run Time of Runners from 27 States of Cherry Blossom Run Data in 2009*

State	Variable	Statistic	p
NR	time	0.7916430	0.0000001010331
DC	time	0.9964880	0.0000003026398
MD	time	0.9976155	0.0000254297578
WV	time	0.9322716	0.0703558034419
NY	time	0.9950121	0.0901289298618
CO	time	0.9314712	0.1176689216068
MI	time	0.9541755	0.1636801110913
FL	time	0.9690047	0.1660520946277
DE	time	0.9718075	0.1711607928781
RI	time	0.9131650	0.1751648374851
GA	time	0.9600517	0.2027996095415
MN	time	0.9429599	0.2979244562344
OH	time	0.9818345	0.3143889157282
IN	time	0.9437351	0.3352867263881
CA	time	0.9817530	0.3534059875710
NJ	time	0.9923606	0.3555229987540
NH	time	0.9490626	0.3809120645476

SC	time	0.9282714	0.3936327687341
NC	time	0.9909337	0.4118030556767
PA	time	0.9966276	0.4494370300883
AZ	time	0.9369979	0.4858739931399
TX	time	0.9761737	0.4883669893670
MO	time	0.9597313	0.6264349115750
MA	time	0.9928759	0.7297291316348
WI	time	0.9619497	0.7550410155766
CT	time	0.9886693	0.7614992787130
IL	time	0.9914030	0.9131006409283

We see that only 3 states ("NR," "DC," and "MD") have significant p-values meaning that the run time of runners from these 3 states is not normally distributed and we should use the Kruskal-Wallis test.

To do the Anderson-Darling test for run time of runners from the "VA" state, we use the following functions:

- The filter function with the argument state=="VA" to keep only the "VA" state.
- The pull function with time argument extracts the time values from this data frame containing the "VA" state.

Then, we use the ad.test function as before.

```
ad.test(run_filtered %>% filter(state=="VA") %>% pull(time))
##
## Anderson-Darling normality test
##
## data: run_filtered %>% filter(state == "VA") %>% pull(time)
## A = 2.9814, p-value = 1.74e-07
```

We see that the p-value is significant meaning that the run time of runners from the "VA" state is not normally distributed and we should use the Kruskal-Wallis test.

4.4.3.6. Homogeneity of Variance of Run Time Across the Different States

We can test that using the levene_test function with the same formula as that of the ANOVA test.

```
run_filtered %>% levene_test(formula = time ~ state) %>% flextable() %>%
```

```
theme_box() %>%

set_caption(caption = "Levene's test results for homogeneity of variance of run time of runners from 28 states of Cherry Blossom Run data in 2009")
```

Table 4.49. *Levene's Test Results for Homogeneity of Variance of Run Time of Runners from 28 States of Cherry Blossom Run Data in 2009*

df1	df2	Statistic	p
27	14,849	2.597272	0.00001114296

The p-value is significant so we conclude that the variances of run time of runners from these 28 states are different. We can use the Welch one-way ANOVA test using the function welch_anova_test. This test does not require the assumption of equal variances across the different groups (states) but does require the normality assumption to be met.

4.4.3.7. Welch ANOVA Test

We use the welch_anova_test function using the same formula as that of the standard ANOVA test.

```
run_filtered %>% welch_anova_test(formula = time ~ state) %>% flextable() %>%

theme_box() %>%

set_caption(caption = "Welch ANOVA test results for the mean run time of runners from 28 states of Cherry Blossom Run data in 2009")
```

Table 4.50. *Welch ANOVA Test Results for the Mean Run Time of Runners from 28 States of Cherry Blossom Run Data in 2009*

.y.	n	Statistic	DFn	DFd	p	Method
time	14,877	5.32	27	297.6726	0.0000000000000495	Welch ANOVA

In the table above, we see that:

- The "DFn" is the degrees of freedom in the numerator and "DFd" is the degrees of freedom in the denominator (DFd).
- The obtained F-statistic value that corresponds to our sample results is 5.32.
- The p is the significant p-value, so we reject the null hypothesis

and conclude that at least one state run time mean is significantly different from another state's mean.

4.4.3.8. Post-Hoc Tests

A significant Welch ANOVA test is followed by Games Howell tests using the games_howell_test function to perform multiple pairwise tests between the different states with appropriate adjustment for the multiple testing. We will use the same formula of the ANOVA test with the games_howell_test function and arrange the adjusted p-values (p.adj) by using the arrange function.

```
run_filtered %>% games_howell_test(formula = time ~ state) %>%

  arrange(p.adj) %>% flextable() %>% theme_box() %>%

  set_caption(caption = "Games Howell tests of the mean run time
in runners from 28 states of Cherry Blossom Run data in 2009")
```

Table 4.51. *Games Howell Tests of the Mean Run Time in Runners from 28 States of Cherry Blossom Run Data in 2009*

.y.	Group 1	Group 2	Estimate	conf.low	conf.high	p.adj	p.adj. signif
time	NC	NR	-36.909997640	-52.17052437	-21.6494709	0.00000000000000	****
time	NR	OH	39.904990678	23.20088287	56.6090985	0.00000000000255	****
time	NJ	NR	-34.429368214	-49.45175929	-19.4069771	0.00000000002970	****
time	MD	NR	-34.312460071	-48.65153921	-19.9733809	0.00000000013700	****
time	NR	VA	33.945354551	19.62382760	48.2668815	0.00000000019200	****
time	MA	NR	-33.930212737	-49.53017052	-18.3302550	0.00000000062800	****
time	DC	NR	-32.012456556	-46.34647445	-17.6784387	0.00000000132000	****
time	NR	NY	32.003582440	17.38611844	46.6210464	0.00000000143000	****
time	FL	NR	-35.775786133	-53.61351043	-17.9380618	0.00000000327000	****
time	NR	PA	31.089204235	16.47227811	45.7061304	0.00000000382000	****
time	IL	NR	-33.273229410	-49.84871535	-16.6977435	0.00000000410000	****
time	CT	NR	-32.602413281	-48.76837801	-16.4364485	0.00000000490000	****
time	NR	TX	37.653736133	18.27947837	57.0279939	0.00000001390000	****
time	CA	NR	-32.592467345	-49.50489006	-15.6800446	0.00000001540000	****
time	MI	NR	-35.087499501	-54.43836057	-15.7366384	0.00000022200000	****
time	DE	NR	-28.140571826	-44.07210457	-12.2090391	0.00000046900000	****

time	GA	NR	-31.537143381	-53.08172423	-9.9925625	0.00008240000000	****
time	DC	MD	2.300003515	0.63085087	3.9691562	0.00011200000000	***
time	NR	RI	32.550583535	10.73318733	54.3679797	0.00018600000000	***
time	IN	NR	-35.615218456	-60.34769464	-10.8827423	0.00035300000000	***
time	MN	NR	-34.321230152	-58.63432152	-10.0081388	0.00044500000000	***
time	NR	WV	31.442762107	8.45006408	54.4354601	0.00048000000000	***
time	DC	VA	1.932897995	0.44269026	3.4231057	0.00050800000000	***
time	AZ	NR	-40.241258860	-67.44514532	-13.0373724	0.00068000000000	***
time	NR	SC	32.286713405	9.40338858	55.1700382	0.00077800000000	***
time	CO	NR	-29.658875461	-53.11401408	-6.2037368	0.00200000000000	**
time	MO	NR	-35.329970090	-62.70135520	-7.9585850	0.00300000000000	**
time	NH	NR	-30.812388046	-57.10514805	-4.5196280	0.00800000000000	**
time	NR	WI	32.247154964	0.93946191	63.5548480	0.03900000000000	*
time	DE	OH	11.764418852	0.04420093	23.4846368	0.04800000000000	*
time	DE	NC	8.769425814	-0.60443761	18.1432892	0.10200000000000	ns
time	MD	PA	-3.223255835	-6.69165920	0.2451475	0.11300000000000	ns
time	OH	PA	-8.815786443	-18.54407400	0.9125011	0.13500000000000	ns
time	NC	PA	-5.820793405	-12.35541704	0.7138302	0.16500000000000	ns
time	DC	OH	7.892534122	-1.38756734	17.1726356	0.22000000000000	ns
time	DC	NC	4.897541084	-0.91553064	10.7106128	0.25100000000000	ns
time	PA	VA	2.856150316	-0.53070064	6.2430013	0.26000000000000	ns
time	NY	OH	7.901408238	-1.82767199	17.6304885	0.30600000000000	ns
time	DE	MD	6.171888245	-1.53807287	13.8818494	0.31400000000000	ns
time	DE	VA	5.804782725	-1.87220730	13.4817727	0.42300000000000	ns
time	NC	NY	-4.906415200	-11.44211973	1.6292893	0.50000000000000	ns
time	DE	NJ	6.288796389	-2.66811103	15.2457038	0.61700000000000	ns
time	OH	VA	-5.959636127	-15.21973354	3.3004613	0.75500000000000	ns
time	MD	NY	-2.308877630	-5.77797399	1.1602187	0.76100000000000	ns
time	DE	TX	9.513164307	-6.02144730	25.0477759	0.81800000000000	ns
time	MD	OH	5.592530607	-3.69567077	14.8807320	0.85000000000000	ns
time	CT	OH	7.302577397	-4.74666434	19.3518191	0.86700000000000	ns
time	AZ	DE	-12.100687034	-37.88451797	13.6831439	0.87500000000000	ns
time	DE	MA	5.789640911	-4.16023886	15.7395207	0.90800000000000	ns
time	DE	FL	7.635214307	-5.77644578	21.0468744	0.91300000000000	ns
time	NY	VA	1.941772111	-1.44568643	5.3292306	0.93600000000000	ns

time	CA	OH	7.312523333	-5.77140521	20.3964519	0.93800000000000	ns
time	NJ	PA	-3.340163979	-9.21721532	2.5368874	0.93900000000000	ns
time	CO	OH	10.246115217	-11.05264209	31.5448725	0.96400000000000	ns
time	MA	OH	5.974777941	-5.24533605	17.1948919	0.96400000000000	ns
time	NJ	OH	5.475622464	-4.87993806	15.8311830	0.96400000000000	ns
time	IL	OH	6.631761268	-5.99265165	19.2561742	0.96800000000000	ns
time	DC	DE	-3.871884730	-11.57234304	3.8285736	0.96900000000000	ns
time	AZ	PA	-9.152054624	-34.74980956	16.4457003	0.97600000000000	ns
time	NC	VA	-2.964643089	-8.74429531	2.8150091	0.97700000000000	ns
time	PA	TX	6.564531897	-7.65598750	20.7850513	0.98500000000000	ns
time	DE	NY	3.863010615	-4.36380830	12.0898295	0.98900000000000	ns
time	AZ	DC	-8.228802304	-33.81900178	17.3613972	0.99000000000000	ns
time	AZ	NY	-8.237676419	-33.83544743	17.3600946	0.99100000000000	ns
time	DE	MI	6.946927676	-8.62026330	22.5141187	0.99100000000000	ns
time	DC	NJ	2.416911659	-2.63724608	7.4710694	0.99200000000000	ns
time	GA	OH	8.367847297	-10.58734885	27.3230434	0.99300000000000	ns
time	OH	SC	-7.618277273	-28.68595694	13.4494024	0.99400000000000	ns
time	DE	IL	5.132657585	-6.40075328	16.6660684	0.99600000000000	ns
time	OH	RI	-7.354407143	-26.98543932	12.2766250	0.99600000000000	ns
time	OH	WV	-8.462228571	-29.16621701	12.2417599	0.99600000000000	ns
time	CT	NC	4.307584359	-5.48000704	14.0951758	0.99700000000000	ns
time	DC	TX	5.641279577	-8.30111158	19.5836707	0.99700000000000	ns
time	MD	NC	2.597537569	-3.22903232	8.4241075	0.99700000000000	ns
time	NH	OH	9.092602632	-15.47103481	33.6562401	0.99700000000000	ns
time	AZ	CO	-10.582383399	-39.93861482	18.7738480	0.99800000000000	ns
time	NY	TX	5.650153692	-8.57089176	19.8711991	0.99800000000000	ns
time	AZ	CA	-7.648791515	-33.69201754	18.3944345	0.99900000000000	ns
time	AZ	CT	-7.638845579	-33.47533651	18.1976453	0.99900000000000	ns
time	CO	NC	7.251122179	-13.13775577	27.6400001	0.99900000000000	ns
time	CT	DE	-4.461841455	-15.35496919	6.4312863	0.99900000000000	ns
time	DE	IN	7.474646630	-14.96658624	29.9158795	0.99900000000000	ns
time	FL	PA	-4.686581897	-16.47485213	7.1016883	0.99900000000000	ns
time	NJ	NY	-2.425785774	-8.30397719	3.4524056	0.99900000000000	ns
time	AZ	FL	-4.465472727	-30.83458592	21.9036405	1.00000000000000	ns
time	AZ	GA	-8.704115479	-36.89755643	19.4893255	1.00000000000000	ns

time	AZ	IL	-6.968029449	-32.91204635	18.9759875	1.00000000000000	ns
time	AZ	IN	-4.626040404	-34.80829355	25.5562127	1.00000000000000	ns
time	AZ	MA	-6.311046123	-32.02474965	19.4026574	1.00000000000000	ns
time	AZ	MD	-5.928798789	-31.51902053	19.6614230	1.00000000000000	ns
time	AZ	MI	-5.153759358	-32.18477439	21.8772557	1.00000000000000	ns
time	AZ	MN	-5.920028708	-35.82614929	23.9860919	1.00000000000000	ns
time	AZ	MO	-4.911288770	-36.94924216	27.1266646	1.00000000000000	ns
time	AZ	NC	-3.331261220	-28.99059779	22.3280753	1.00000000000000	ns
time	AZ	NH	-9.428870813	-40.70071590	21.8429743	1.00000000000000	ns
time	AZ	NJ	-5.811890646	-31.44166676	19.8178855	1.00000000000000	ns
time	AZ	OH	-0.336268182	-26.31605763	25.6435213	1.00000000000000	ns
time	AZ	RI	-7.690675325	-36.03742567	20.6560750	1.00000000000000	ns
time	AZ	SC	-7.954545455	-36.91973419	21.0106433	1.00000000000000	ns
time	AZ	TX	-2.587522727	-29.62517413	24.4501287	1.00000000000000	ns
time	AZ	VA	-6.295904309	-31.88606673	19.2942581	1.00000000000000	ns
time	AZ	WI	-7.994103896	-43.00926587	27.0210581	1.00000000000000	ns
time	AZ	WV	-8.798496753	-37.86657407	20.2695806	1.00000000000000	ns
time	CA	CO	-2.933591884	-24.37101536	18.5038316	1.00000000000000	ns
time	CA	CT	0.009945936	-12.34752215	12.3674140	1.00000000000000	ns
time	CA	DC	-0.580010789	-10.27696364	9.1169421	1.00000000000000	ns
time	CA	DE	-4.451895519	-16.48994552	7.5861545	1.00000000000000	ns
time	CA	FL	3.183318788	-11.40226399	17.7689016	1.00000000000000	ns
time	CA	GA	-1.055323964	-20.18380860	18.0731607	1.00000000000000	ns
time	CA	IL	0.680762066	-12.23523397	13.5967581	1.00000000000000	ns
time	CA	IN	3.022751111	-19.94850189	25.9940041	1.00000000000000	ns
time	CA	MA	1.337745392	-10.21877388	12.8942647	1.00000000000000	ns
time	CA	MD	1.719992726	-7.98466378	11.4246492	1.00000000000000	ns
time	CA	MI	2.495032157	-14.03750894	19.0275733	1.00000000000000	ns
time	CA	MN	1.728762807	-20.74868647	24.2062121	1.00000000000000	ns
time	CA	MO	2.737502745	-23.16764184	28.6426473	1.00000000000000	ns
time	CA	NC	4.317530295	-6.75359491	15.3886555	1.00000000000000	ns
time	CA	NH	-1.780079298	-26.45132136	22.8911628	1.00000000000000	ns
time	CA	NJ	1.836900870	-8.88758159	12.5613833	1.00000000000000	ns
time	CA	NY	-0.588884904	-10.71371163	9.5359418	1.00000000000000	ns
time	CA	PA	-1.503263109	-11.62732698	8.6208008	1.00000000000000	ns

time	CA	RI	-0.041883810	-19.80668092	19.7229133	1.00000000000000	ns	
time	CA	SC	-0.305753939	-21.47509713	20.8635892	1.00000000000000	ns	
time	CA	TX	5.061268788	-11.46256594	21.5851035	1.00000000000000	ns	
time	CA	VA	1.352887206	-8.32504281	11.0308172	1.00000000000000	ns	
time	CA	WI	-0.345312381	-30.59885408	29.9082293	1.00000000000000	ns	
time	CA	WV	-1.149705238	-22.00333554	19.7039251	1.00000000000000	ns	
time	CO	CT	2.943537820	-18.00423559	23.8913112	1.00000000000000	ns	
time	CO	DC	2.353581095	-17.50851586	22.2156780	1.00000000000000	ns	
time	CO	DE	-1.518303635	-22.31691826	19.2803110	1.00000000000000	ns	
time	CO	FL	6.116910672	-15.95437053	28.1881919	1.00000000000000	ns	
time	CO	GA	1.878267920	-22.98029488	26.7368307	1.00000000000000	ns	
time	CO	IL	3.614353950	-17.59890218	24.8276101	1.00000000000000	ns	
time	CO	IN	5.956342995	-21.43969481	33.3523808	1.00000000000000	ns	
time	CO	MA	4.271337276	-16.32273828	24.8654128	1.00000000000000	ns	
time	CO	MD	4.653584610	-15.21124326	24.5184125	1.00000000000000	ns	
time	CO	MI	5.428624041	-17.72937847	28.5866265	1.00000000000000	ns	
time	CO	MN	4.662354691	-22.39186468	31.7165741	1.00000000000000	ns	
time	CO	MO	5.671094629	-23.97479201	35.3169813	1.00000000000000	ns	
time	CO	NH	1.153512586	-27.58294417	29.8899693	1.00000000000000	ns	
time	CO	NJ	4.770492754	-15.47814609	25.0191316	1.00000000000000	ns	
time	CO	NY	2.344706980	-17.67296283	22.3623768	1.00000000000000	ns	
time	CO	PA	1.430328775	-18.58703902	21.4476966	1.00000000000000	ns	
time	CO	RI	2.891708075	-22.08501550	27.8684316	1.00000000000000	ns	
time	CO	SC	2.627837945	-23.14521762	28.4008935	1.00000000000000	ns	
time	CO	TX	7.994860672	-15.18941005	31.1791314	1.00000000000000	ns	
time	CO	VA	4.286479090	-15.56888561	24.1418438	1.00000000000000	ns	
time	CO	WI	2.588279503	-30.49189771	35.6684567	1.00000000000000	ns	
time	CO	WV	1.783886646	-24.22671179	27.7944851	1.00000000000000	ns	
time	CT	DC	-0.589956725	-8.77659280	7.5966794	1.00000000000000	ns	
time	CT	FL	3.173372852	-10.51942716	16.8661729	1.00000000000000	ns	
time	CT	GA	-1.065269900	-19.57585354	17.4453137	1.00000000000000	ns	
time	CT	IL	0.670816130	-11.19606695	12.5376992	1.00000000000000	ns	
time	CT	IN	3.012805175	-19.55031694	25.5759273	1.00000000000000	ns	
time	CT	MA	1.327799456	-9.01286441	11.6684633	1.00000000000000	ns	
time	CT	MD	1.710046790	-6.48570038	9.9057940	1.00000000000000	ns	

time	CT	MI	2.485086221	-13.31069423	18.2808667	1.00000000000000	ns
time	CT	MN	1.718816871	-20.32779406	23.7654278	1.00000000000000	ns
time	CT	MO	2.727556809	-22.84525639	28.3003700	1.00000000000000	ns
time	CT	NH	-1.790025234	-26.08347076	22.5034203	1.00000000000000	ns
time	CT	NJ	1.826954933	-7.56143294	11.2153428	1.00000000000000	ns
time	CT	NY	-0.598830840	-9.28922023	8.0915586	1.00000000000000	ns
time	CT	PA	-1.513209045	-10.20273993	7.1763218	1.00000000000000	ns
time	CT	RI	-0.051829746	-19.35745586	19.2537964	1.00000000000000	ns
time	CT	SC	-0.315699875	-21.14866455	20.5172648	1.00000000000000	ns
time	CT	TX	5.051322852	-10.71878698	20.8214327	1.00000000000000	ns
time	CT	VA	1.342941270	-6.82119006	9.5070726	1.00000000000000	ns
time	CT	WI	-0.355258317	-30.38747696	29.6769603	1.00000000000000	ns
time	CT	WV	-1.159651174	-21.48212753	19.1628252	1.00000000000000	ns
time	DC	FL	3.763329577	-7.67375706	15.2004162	1.00000000000000	ns
time	DC	GA	-0.475313175	-17.53029553	16.5796692	1.00000000000000	ns
time	DC	IL	1.260772855	-7.79158182	10.3131275	1.00000000000000	ns
time	DC	IN	3.602761900	-18.10689321	25.3124170	1.00000000000000	ns
time	DC	MA	1.917756181	-4.83492727	8.6704396	1.00000000000000	ns
time	DC	MI	3.075042946	-10.97109523	17.1211811	1.00000000000000	ns
time	DC	MN	2.308773596	-18.82257349	23.4401207	1.00000000000000	ns
time	DC	MO	3.317513534	-21.56760588	28.2026329	1.00000000000000	ns
time	DC	NH	-1.200068509	-24.68625883	22.2861218	1.00000000000000	ns
time	DC	NY	-0.008874115	-3.45461898	3.4368707	1.00000000000000	ns
time	DC	PA	-0.923252320	-4.36832744	2.5218228	1.00000000000000	ns
time	DC	RI	0.538126980	-17.92776532	19.0040193	1.00000000000000	ns
time	DC	SC	0.274256850	-20.12360691	20.6721206	1.00000000000000	ns
time	DC	WI	0.234698408	-29.37749975	29.8468966	1.00000000000000	ns
time	DC	WV	-0.569694449	-19.67912264	18.5397337	1.00000000000000	ns
time	DE	GA	3.396571555	-14.92204117	21.7151843	1.00000000000000	ns
time	DE	MN	6.180658326	-15.73659914	28.0979158	1.00000000000000	ns
time	DE	MO	7.189398264	-18.28448128	32.6632778	1.00000000000000	ns
time	DE	NH	2.671816221	-21.50789879	26.8515312	1.00000000000000	ns
time	DE	PA	2.948632410	-5.27730919	11.1745740	1.00000000000000	ns
time	DE	RI	4.410011710	-14.76381503	23.5838384	1.00000000000000	ns
time	DE	SC	4.146141580	-16.59828140	24.8905646	1.00000000000000	ns

time	DE	WI	4.106583138	-25.86170473	34.0748710	1.00000000000000	ns
time	DE	WV	3.302190281	-16.85682052	23.4612011	1.00000000000000	ns
time	FL	GA	-4.238642752	-24.14545679	15.6681713	1.00000000000000	ns
time	FL	IL	-2.502556722	-16.68809672	11.6829833	1.00000000000000	ns
time	FL	IN	-0.160567677	-23.67418476	23.3530494	1.00000000000000	ns
time	FL	MA	-1.845573396	-14.84516853	11.1540217	1.00000000000000	ns
time	FL	MD	-1.463326062	-12.90670065	9.9800485	1.00000000000000	ns
time	FL	MI	-0.688286631	-18.14689339	16.7703201	1.00000000000000	ns
time	FL	MN	-1.454555981	-24.50052487	21.5914129	1.00000000000000	ns
time	FL	MO	-0.445816043	-26.79566930	25.9040372	1.00000000000000	ns
time	FL	NC	1.134211507	-11.44944618	13.7178692	1.00000000000000	ns
time	FL	NH	-4.963398086	-30.13256738	20.2057712	1.00000000000000	ns
time	FL	NJ	-1.346417918	-13.63648750	10.9436517	1.00000000000000	ns
time	FL	NY	-3.772203692	-15.56112039	8.0167130	1.00000000000000	ns
time	FL	OH	4.129204545	-10.20731676	18.4657259	1.00000000000000	ns
time	FL	RI	-3.225202597	-23.62353427	17.1731291	1.00000000000000	ns
time	FL	SC	-3.489072727	-25.16451232	18.1863669	1.00000000000000	ns
time	FL	TX	1.877950000	-15.58549319	19.3413932	1.00000000000000	ns
time	FL	VA	-1.830431582	-13.25199898	9.5911358	1.00000000000000	ns
time	FL	WI	-3.528631169	-34.09074029	27.0334780	1.00000000000000	ns
time	FL	WV	-4.333024026	-25.86496057	17.1989125	1.00000000000000	ns
time	GA	IL	1.736086030	-17.11167692	20.5838490	1.00000000000000	ns
time	GA	IN	4.078075075	-21.92574670	30.0818968	1.00000000000000	ns
time	GA	MA	2.393069356	-15.65903844	20.4451771	1.00000000000000	ns
time	GA	MD	2.775316690	-14.28355289	19.8341863	1.00000000000000	ns
time	GA	MI	3.550356121	-17.65237350	24.7530857	1.00000000000000	ns
time	GA	MN	2.784086771	-22.84056184	28.4087354	1.00000000000000	ns
time	GA	MO	3.792826709	-24.65909356	32.2447470	1.00000000000000	ns
time	GA	NC	5.372854259	-12.40734037	23.1530489	1.00000000000000	ns
time	GA	NH	-0.724755334	-28.18521105	26.7357004	1.00000000000000	ns
time	GA	NJ	2.892224834	-14.69913780	20.4835875	1.00000000000000	ns
time	GA	NY	0.466439060	-16.80758975	17.7404679	1.00000000000000	ns
time	GA	PA	-0.447939145	-17.72154630	16.8256680	1.00000000000000	ns
time	GA	RI	1.013440154	-22.30702977	24.3339101	1.00000000000000	ns
time	GA	SC	0.749570025	-23.48770427	24.9868443	1.00000000000000	ns

time	GA	TX	6.116592752	-15.11460940	27.3477949	1.00000000000000	ns
time	GA	VA	2.408211170	-14.63718159	19.4536039	1.00000000000000	ns
time	GA	WI	0.710011583	-31.42589310	32.8459163	1.00000000000000	ns
time	GA	WV	-0.094381274	-24.54706196	24.3582994	1.00000000000000	ns
time	IL	IN	2.341989045	-20.44120566	25.1251838	1.00000000000000	ns
time	IL	MA	0.656983326	-10.36659960	11.6805663	1.00000000000000	ns
time	IL	MD	1.039230661	-8.02133474	10.0997961	1.00000000000000	ns
time	IL	MI	1.814270091	-14.38511294	18.0136531	1.00000000000000	ns
time	IL	MN	1.048000741	-21.23128322	23.3272847	1.00000000000000	ns
time	IL	MO	2.056740679	-23.69479114	27.8082725	1.00000000000000	ns
time	IL	NC	3.636768230	-6.87483590	14.1483724	1.00000000000000	ns
time	IL	NH	-2.460841364	-26.95810528	22.0364225	1.00000000000000	ns
time	IL	NJ	1.156138804	-8.98853449	11.3008121	1.00000000000000	ns
time	IL	NY	-1.269646970	-10.77760440	8.2383105	1.00000000000000	ns
time	IL	PA	-2.184025175	-11.69118413	7.3231338	1.00000000000000	ns
time	IL	RI	-0.722645875	-20.27469799	18.8294062	1.00000000000000	ns
time	IL	SC	-0.986516005	-21.99657332	20.0235413	1.00000000000000	ns
time	IL	TX	4.380506722	-11.80303316	20.5640466	1.00000000000000	ns
time	IL	VA	0.672125141	-8.35995346	9.7042037	1.00000000000000	ns
time	IL	WI	-1.026074447	-31.17626053	29.1241116	1.00000000000000	ns
time	IL	WV	-1.830467304	-22.44169470	18.7807601	1.00000000000000	ns
time	IN	MA	-1.685005719	-23.96019204	20.5901806	1.00000000000000	ns
time	IN	MD	-1.302758385	-23.01442191	20.4089051	1.00000000000000	ns
time	IN	MI	-0.527718954	-24.99658799	23.9411501	1.00000000000000	ns
time	IN	MN	-1.293988304	-29.32605723	26.7380806	1.00000000000000	ns
time	IN	MO	-0.285248366	-30.75534294	30.1848462	1.00000000000000	ns
time	IN	NC	1.294779184	-20.81723981	23.4067982	1.00000000000000	ns
time	IN	NH	-4.802830409	-34.41452553	24.8088647	1.00000000000000	ns
time	IN	NJ	-1.185850242	-23.18816404	20.8164636	1.00000000000000	ns
time	IN	NY	-3.611636015	-25.43715079	18.2138788	1.00000000000000	ns
time	IN	OH	4.289772222	-18.56475877	27.1443032	1.00000000000000	ns
time	IN	PA	-4.526014220	-26.35130308	17.2992746	1.00000000000000	ns
time	IN	RI	-3.064634921	-29.17669894	23.0474291	1.00000000000000	ns
time	IN	SC	-3.328505051	-30.16922188	23.5122118	1.00000000000000	ns
time	IN	TX	2.038517677	-22.45291092	26.5299463	1.00000000000000	ns

time	IN	VA	-1.669863905	-23.37457197	20.0348442	1.00000000000000	ns
time	IN	WI	-3.368063492	-37.11221318	30.3760862	1.00000000000000	ns
time	IN	WV	-4.172456349	-31.23647191	22.8915592	1.00000000000000	ns
time	MA	MD	0.382247334	-6.38197560	7.1464703	1.00000000000000	ns
time	MA	MI	1.157286765	-14.08424514	16.3988187	1.00000000000000	ns
time	MA	MN	0.391017415	-21.34964972	22.1316846	1.00000000000000	ns
time	MA	MO	1.399757353	-23.94079294	26.7403076	1.00000000000000	ns
time	MA	NC	2.979784903	-5.70270210	11.6622719	1.00000000000000	ns
time	MA	NH	-3.117824690	-27.14365345	20.9080041	1.00000000000000	ns
time	MA	NJ	0.499155477	-7.71671604	8.7150270	1.00000000000000	ns
time	MA	NY	-1.926630296	-9.30559524	5.4523346	1.00000000000000	ns
time	MA	PA	-2.841008501	-10.21897071	4.5369537	1.00000000000000	ns
time	MA	RI	-1.379629202	-20.37052665	17.6112682	1.00000000000000	ns
time	MA	SC	-1.643499332	-22.26677792	18.9797793	1.00000000000000	ns
time	MA	TX	3.723523396	-11.47602680	18.9230736	1.00000000000000	ns
time	MA	VA	0.015141814	-6.70900044	6.7392841	1.00000000000000	ns
time	MA	WI	-1.683057773	-31.56622899	28.2001134	1.00000000000000	ns
time	MA	WV	-2.487450630	-22.42179170	17.4468904	1.00000000000000	ns
time	MD	MI	0.775039431	-13.27571307	14.8257919	1.00000000000000	ns
time	MD	MN	0.008770081	-21.12476996	21.1423101	1.00000000000000	ns
time	MD	MO	1.017510019	-23.86923000	25.9042500	1.00000000000000	ns
time	MD	NH	-3.500072024	-26.98823230	19.9880883	1.00000000000000	ns
time	MD	NJ	0.116908143	-4.95291983	5.1867361	1.00000000000000	ns
time	MD	RI	-1.761876536	-20.22923890	16.7054858	1.00000000000000	ns
time	MD	SC	-2.025746666	-22.42366399	18.3721707	1.00000000000000	ns
time	MD	TX	3.341276062	-10.60607198	17.2886241	1.00000000000000	ns
time	MD	VA	-0.367105520	-1.91104496	1.1768339	1.00000000000000	ns
time	MD	WI	-2.065305107	-31.67840009	27.5477899	1.00000000000000	ns
time	MD	WV	-2.869697964	-21.98227823	16.2428823	1.00000000000000	ns
time	MI	MN	-0.766269350	-24.80624778	23.2737091	1.00000000000000	ns
time	MI	MO	0.242470588	-26.89901635	27.3839575	1.00000000000000	ns
time	MI	NC	1.822498138	-13.09205898	16.7370553	1.00000000000000	ns
time	MI	NH	-4.275111455	-30.31639706	21.7661742	1.00000000000000	ns
time	MI	NJ	-0.658131287	-15.34556458	14.0293020	1.00000000000000	ns
time	MI	NY	-3.083917061	-17.39096475	11.2231306	1.00000000000000	ns

time	MI	OH	4.817491176	-11.50813621	21.1431186	1.00000000000000	ns
time	MI	PA	-3.998295266	-18.30485106	10.3082605	1.00000000000000	ns
time	MI	RI	-2.536915966	-24.07675664	19.0029247	1.00000000000000	ns
time	MI	SC	-2.800786096	-25.45121874	19.8496466	1.00000000000000	ns
time	MI	TX	2.566236631	-16.44060155	21.5730748	1.00000000000000	ns
time	MI	VA	-1.142144950	-15.17690252	12.8926126	1.00000000000000	ns
time	MI	WI	-2.840344538	-33.97661141	28.2959223	1.00000000000000	ns
time	MI	WV	-3.644737395	-26.32352476	19.0340500	1.00000000000000	ns
time	MN	MO	1.008739938	-29.18418983	31.2016697	1.00000000000000	ns
time	MN	NC	2.588767488	-18.97744387	24.1549788	1.00000000000000	ns
time	MN	NH	-3.508842105	-32.82677980	25.8090956	1.00000000000000	ns
time	MN	NJ	0.108138063	-21.34026038	21.5565365	1.00000000000000	ns
time	MN	NY	-2.317647711	-23.57507228	18.9397769	1.00000000000000	ns
time	MN	OH	5.583760526	-16.77079314	27.9383142	1.00000000000000	ns
time	MN	PA	-3.232025916	-24.48920500	18.0251532	1.00000000000000	ns
time	MN	RI	-1.770646617	-27.50848357	23.9671903	1.00000000000000	ns
time	MN	SC	-2.034516746	-28.52277341	24.4537399	1.00000000000000	ns
time	MN	TX	3.332505981	-20.73089744	27.3959094	1.00000000000000	ns
time	MN	VA	-0.375875601	-21.50181987	20.7500687	1.00000000000000	ns
time	MN	WI	-2.074075188	-35.59346559	31.4453152	1.00000000000000	ns
time	MN	WV	-2.878468045	-29.59194596	23.8350099	1.00000000000000	ns
time	MO	NC	1.580027550	-23.62901810	26.7890732	1.00000000000000	ns
time	MO	NH	-4.517582043	-36.11445575	27.0792917	1.00000000000000	ns
time	MO	NJ	-0.900601876	-26.02136777	24.2201640	1.00000000000000	ns
time	MO	NY	-3.326387649	-28.30488500	21.6521097	1.00000000000000	ns
time	MO	OH	4.575020588	-21.23493955	30.3849807	1.00000000000000	ns
time	MO	PA	-4.240765854	-29.21907982	20.7375481	1.00000000000000	ns
time	MO	RI	-2.779386555	-31.28432049	25.7255474	1.00000000000000	ns
time	MO	SC	-3.043256684	-32.15392395	26.0674106	1.00000000000000	ns
time	MO	TX	2.323766043	-24.84041698	29.4879491	1.00000000000000	ns
time	MO	VA	-1.384615539	-26.26574276	23.4965117	1.00000000000000	ns
time	MO	WI	-3.082815126	-38.39571157	32.2300813	1.00000000000000	ns
time	MO	WV	-3.887207983	-33.25171204	25.4772961	1.00000000000000	ns
time	NC	NH	-6.097609594	-29.96996068	17.7747415	1.00000000000000	ns
time	NC	NJ	-2.480629426	-9.95704972	4.9957909	1.00000000000000	ns

time	NC	OH	2.994993038	-7.72142128	13.7114074	1.00000000000000	ns
time	NC	RI	-4.359414105	-23.18305692	14.4642287	1.00000000000000	ns
time	NC	SC	-4.623284235	-25.15028750	15.9037190	1.00000000000000	ns
time	NC	TX	0.743738493	-14.11607473	15.6035517	1.00000000000000	ns
time	NC	WI	-4.662842676	-34.46449677	25.1388114	1.00000000000000	ns
time	NC	WV	-5.467235533	-25.17365224	14.2391812	1.00000000000000	ns
time	NH	NJ	3.616980168	-20.15142932	27.3853897	1.00000000000000	ns
time	NH	NY	1.191194394	-22.40778354	24.7901723	1.00000000000000	ns
time	NH	PA	0.276816189	-23.32194081	23.8755732	1.00000000000000	ns
time	NH	RI	1.738195489	-25.78008699	29.2564780	1.00000000000000	ns
time	NH	SC	1.474325359	-26.69487248	29.6435232	1.00000000000000	ns
time	NH	TX	6.841348086	-19.22508445	32.9077806	1.00000000000000	ns
time	NH	VA	3.132966505	-20.34836905	26.6143021	1.00000000000000	ns
time	NH	WI	1.434766917	-33.24417976	36.1137136	1.00000000000000	ns
time	NH	WV	0.630374060	-27.80606586	29.0668140	1.00000000000000	ns
time	NJ	RI	-1.878784679	-20.59522254	16.8376532	1.00000000000000	ns
time	NJ	SC	-2.142654809	-22.61585595	18.3305463	1.00000000000000	ns
time	NJ	TX	3.224367918	-11.39799566	17.8467315	1.00000000000000	ns
time	NJ	VA	-0.484013663	-5.49931968	4.5312923	1.00000000000000	ns
time	NJ	WI	-2.182213251	-31.93045032	27.5660238	1.00000000000000	ns
time	NJ	WV	-2.986606108	-22.53597700	16.5627648	1.00000000000000	ns
time	NY	PA	-0.914378205	-5.49935983	3.6706034	1.00000000000000	ns
time	NY	RI	0.547001095	-18.01024225	19.1042444	1.00000000000000	ns
time	NY	SC	0.283130965	-20.12983995	20.6961019	1.00000000000000	ns
time	NY	WI	0.243572523	-29.42124749	29.9083925	1.00000000000000	ns
time	NY	WV	-0.560820334	-19.84873358	18.7270929	1.00000000000000	ns
time	OH	TX	-2.251254545	-18.56415728	14.0616482	1.00000000000000	ns
time	OH	WI	-7.657835714	-37.84703930	22.5313679	1.00000000000000	ns
time	PA	RI	1.461379300	-17.09568780	20.0184464	1.00000000000000	ns
time	PA	SC	1.197509170	-19.21543030	21.6104486	1.00000000000000	ns
time	PA	WI	1.157950728	-28.50676515	30.8226666	1.00000000000000	ns
time	PA	WV	0.353557871	-18.93400935	19.6411251	1.00000000000000	ns
time	RI	SC	-0.263870130	-24.77337324	24.2456330	1.00000000000000	ns
time	RI	TX	5.103152597	-16.44733517	26.6536404	1.00000000000000	ns
time	RI	VA	1.394771016	-17.06751939	19.8570614	1.00000000000000	ns

time	RI	WI	-0.303428571	-32.47322553	31.8663684	1.00000000000000	ns
time	RI	WV	-1.107821429	-25.67597581	23.4603330	1.00000000000000	ns
time	SC	TX	5.367022727	-17.28750347	28.0215489	1.00000000000000	ns
time	SC	VA	1.658641146	-18.73912544	22.0564077	1.00000000000000	ns
time	SC	WI	-0.039558442	-32.67843301	32.5993161	1.00000000000000	ns
time	SC	WV	-0.843951299	-26.23340496	24.5455024	1.00000000000000	ns
time	TX	VA	-3.708381582	-17.63854243	10.2217793	1.00000000000000	ns
time	TX	WI	-5.406581169	-36.55959340	25.7464311	1.00000000000000	ns
time	TX	WV	-6.210974026	-28.91854690	16.4965988	1.00000000000000	ns
time	VA	WI	-1.698199587	-31.30819113	27.9117920	1.00000000000000	ns
time	VA	WV	-2.502592444	-21.60424710	16.5990622	1.00000000000000	ns
time	WI	WV	-0.804392857	-33.66115619	32.0523705	1.00000000000000	ns

We see that:

- Every pair of states are compared with an estimate, a 95% confidence interval, and an adjusted p-value.
- For example, the runners from the "NC" state have significantly higher mean run time than runners from the "NR" state with zero adjusted p-value. The difference is estimated to be 36.9 and can be as high as 52.17 and as low as 21.65.
- On the other hand, runners from "WI" state have statistically equivalent mean run time to runners from "WV" state with a 1.00 adjusted p-value.

4.4.4. Kruskal Wallis Test for More Than Two Samples

The Kruskal-Wallis test is a non-parametric alternative to the one-way ANOVA test. It can be viewed as an extension of the two-sample Wilcoxon test in case there are more than two groups to compare. It is used when the assumptions of a one-way ANOVA test are not met. The null hypothesis is that the medians of the continuous variable across the different groups are the same, while the alternative hypothesis is that at least one group's median differs from another group's median.

4.4.4.1. Kruskal Wallis Test of the Run Time from Runners of Different States

The null hypothesis is that all 28 states' median run time are equal, while the alternative hypothesis is that at least one state's median is different from another state's median.

To conduct this test, we use the kruskal_test function applied on the "run_filtered" data with the following argument, formula = time ~ state which is the same formula for the ANOVA test. This means that we want to compare the median run time across the different states of the "state" column.

Then, we convert the result to a table as before.

```
run_filtered %>% kruskal_test(formula = time ~ state) %>%

  flextable() %>% theme_box() %>%

 set_caption(caption = "Kruskal-Wallis test results of the median run time in runners from 28 states of Cherry Blossom Run data in 2009")
```

Table 4.52. *Kruskal-Wallis Test Results of the Median Run Time in Runners from 28 States of Cherry Blossom Run Data in 2009*

.y.	n	Statistic	df	p	Method
time	14,877	137.2318	27	0.000000000000000102	Kruskal-Wallis

In the table above, we see that:

- The "df" is the degrees of freedom and the obtained statistic value that corresponds to our sample results is 137.2318.
- The p is the very low p-value, so we reject the null hypothesis and conclude that at least one state run time median is significantly different from another state median.

4.4.4.2. Post-Hoc Test

A significant Kruskal-Wallis test is followed by Dunn's test to perform multiple pairwise tests between the different states with p-value adjustment. We will use the same formula of the ANOVA test with the dunn_test function and arrange the adjusted p-values (p.adj) by using the arrange function.

```
run_filtered %>% dunn_test(formula = time ~ state) %>%

 arrange(p.adj) %>%

  flextable() %>% theme_box() %>%

 set_caption(caption = "Dunn's test of the run time in runners from 28 states of Cherry Blossom Run data in 2009")
```

Table 4.53. *Dunn's Test of the Run Time in Runners from 28 States of Cherry Blossom Run Data in 2009*

.y.	Group 1	Group 2	n1	n2	statistic	p	p.adj	p.adj. signif
time	MD	NR	3,558	59	-8.945096060	0.0000000000000000003716264	0.0000000000000001404748	****
time	NR	VA	59	5,608	8.813077861	0.0000000000000000012175592	0.0000000000000004590198	****
time	NC	NR	158	59	-8.537742984	0.0000000000000000136868939	0.0000000000000051462721	****
time	NR	OH	59	80	8.373042892	0.0000000000000000561491565	0.0000000000000210559337	****
time	DC	NR	3,464	59	-8.070179042	0.0000000000000007019515580	0.0000000000002625298827	****
time	NJ	NR	207	59	-8.014131663	0.0000000000000011091783909	0.0000000000004137235398	****
time	NR	NY	59	522	7.757416452	0.0000000000000086676941849	0.0000000000032243822368	****
time	MA	NR	136	59	-7.473626139	0.0000000000000780145854416	0.0000000000289434111988	****
time	NR	PA	59	461	7.264532147	0.0000000000003743315950295	0.0000000001385026901609	****
time	NR	TX	59	44	6.748380648	0.0000000000149504305401209	0.0000000055167088693046	****
time	FL	NR	55	59	-6.471975399	0.0000000000967298736252015	0.0000000355965934940741	****
time	IL	NR	71	59	-6.456023187	0.0000000001074901467618103	0.0000000394488838615844	****
time	CA	NR	75	59	-6.287719493	0.0000000003221633390074665	0.0000001179117820767327	****
time	CT	NR	73	59	-6.283965127	0.0000000003300447704017191	0.0000001204663411966275	****
time	MI	NR	34	59	-5.487882343	0.0000000406780851009349864	0.0000148068229767403345	****
time	GA	NR	37	59	-5.058315291	0.0000004229766770399046842	0.0001535405337654853941	***
time	DC	MD	3,464	3,558	4.801602909	0.0000015740058321231468036	0.0005697901112285791133	***
time	IN	NR	18	59	-4.737039465	0.0000021686294630596223529	0.0007828752361645236347	***

time	MN	NR	19	59	-4.652571326	0.000003278212904513823 7618	0.00118015664562497657 12	**
time	AZ	NR	11	59	-4.522682082	0.0000061060919397939396030	0.0021920870063860242033	**
time	DE	NR	61	59	-4.446135457	0.0000087428831662758700527	0.0031299521735267616177	**
time	DC	VA	3,464	5,608	4.341804392	0.0000141317322330914423726	0.0050450284072136447611	**
time	CO	NR	23	59	-4.237345210	0.0000226178246644777784617	0.0080519455805540887661	**
time	NR	WV	59	28	4.111396291	0.0000393273519283836634321	0.0139612099345761998814	*
time	MO	NR	17	59	-4.105913920	0.0000402719441456345387739	0.0142562682275546269428	*
time	NH	NR	19	59	-3.935093761	0.0000831642228753435387538	0.0293569706749962702763	*
time	DE	OH	61	80	3.676976478	0.0002360147944412552603859	0.0830772076433218542579	ns
time	NR	WI	59	14	3.662232448	0.0002500268297352703809541	0.0877594172370799036065	ns
time	OH	PA	80	461	-3.570257288	0.0003566307663593387060168	0.1248207682257685413596	ns
time	NR	RI	59	14	3.500998969	0.0004635176361451277728815	0.1617676550146495972893	ns
time	MD	PA	3,558	461	-3.428434349	0.0006070733430841442849341	0.2112615233932822189633	ns
time	DC	OH	3,464	80	3.336543261	0.0008482722572811958721556	0.2943504732765749865031	ns
time	DE	NC	61	158	3.255668921	0.0011312558070570573158509	0.3914145092417418148045	ns
time	NC	PA	158	461	-3.234336612	0.0012192566086850079379311	0.4206435299963277585356	ns
time	NR	SC	59	11	3.127602694	0.0017623823928456302124329	0.6062595431388967393005	ns
time	NY	OH	522	80	3.093319976	0.0019793059916938414086185	0.6789019551509876126971	ns
time	PA	VA	461	5,608	3.073699344	0.0021142238487847071597148	0.7230645562843698304079	ns
time	DC	NC	3,464	158	2.987890370	0.0028091029800356884064960	0.9579041161921697522530	ns
time	AZ	CA	11	75	-1.211489992	0.2257076681175156085412681	1.0000000000000000000000	ns

time	AZ	CO	11	23	-1.210363078	0.2261396029926601991544288	1.0000000000000000000000	ns
time	AZ	CT	11	73	-1.191061396	0.2336294834950244092564020	1.0000000000000000000000	ns
time	AZ	DC	11	3,464	-1.409888222	0.1585726911047302956081495	1.0000000000000000000000	ns
time	AZ	DE	11	61	-2.055943989	0.0397879153886266448414410	1.0000000000000000000000	ns
time	AZ	FL	11	55	-0.824339032	0.4097469465479615102765365	1.0000000000000000000000	ns
time	AZ	GA	11	37	-1.236321264	0.2163391702479783296197979	1.0000000000000000000000	ns
time	AZ	IL	11	71	-1.074021471	0.2828130585111027772704517	1.0000000000000000000000	ns
time	AZ	IN	11	18	-0.548202466	0.5835528887538556919167831	1.0000000000000000000000	ns
time	AZ	MA	11	136	-1.021655454	0.3069440015782181618853031	1.0000000000000000000000	ns
time	AZ	MD	11	3,558	-1.030413098	0.3028161272193024000642936	1.0000000000000000000000	ns
time	AZ	MI	11	34	-0.875540030	0.3812801393781522496517766	1.0000000000000000000000	ns
time	AZ	MN	11	19	-0.681152295	0.4957751298339654333346971	1.0000000000000000000000	ns
time	AZ	MO	11	17	-0.917685015	0.3587837948977206092848746	1.0000000000000000000000	ns
time	AZ	NC	11	158	-0.585918761	0.5579301089142225666961394	1.0000000000000000000000	ns
time	AZ	NH	11	19	-1.180686621	0.2377272385073030402935501	1.0000000000000000000000	ns
time	AZ	NJ	11	207	-0.977955637	0.3280962658238202878102641	1.0000000000000000000000	ns
time	AZ	NY	11	522	-1.378049711	0.1681879405430833918089206	1.0000000000000000000000	ns
time	AZ	OH	11	80	-0.150671419	0.8802349200365144898938752	1.0000000000000000000000	ns
time	AZ	PA	11	461	-1.576167530	0.1149871993744154274885716	1.0000000000000000000000	ns
time	AZ	RI	11	14	-1.103315735	0.2698900759134375548775608	1.0000000000000000000000	ns
time	AZ	SC	11	11	-1.074501283	0.2825980698705294336114946	1.0000000000000000000000	ns

time	AZ	TX	11	44	-0.418639107	0.6754799047289292701634622	1.0000000000000000000000	ns
time	AZ	VA	11	5,608	-1.099857193	0.2713943483630942288264976	1.0000000000000000000000	ns
time	AZ	WI	11	14	-0.984351344	0.3249427927737382759687534	1.0000000000000000000000	ns
time	AZ	WV	11	28	-1.522656514	0.1278446629149252999901876	1.0000000000000000000000	ns
time	CA	CO	75	23	-0.220500437	0.8254814323576773471557999	1.0000000000000000000000	ns
time	CA	CT	75	73	0.036021826	0.9712649559178468949838248	1.0000000000000000000000	ns
time	CA	DC	75	3,464	-0.296648371	0.7667349778310329488917318	1.0000000000000000000000	ns
time	CA	DE	75	61	-1.637437507	0.1015390867085516068968332	1.0000000000000000000000	ns
time	CA	FL	75	55	0.669644286	0.5030845758967813496909116	1.0000000000000000000000	ns
time	CA	GA	75	37	-0.166384477	0.8678543894239751921304560	1.0000000000000000000000	ns
time	CA	IL	75	71	0.260513833	0.7944674461525296216279912	1.0000000000000000000000	ns
time	CA	IN	75	18	0.690936386	0.4896055185434402545752164	1.0000000000000000000000	ns
time	CA	MA	75	136	0.492902689	0.6220813471491442037120123	1.0000000000000000000000	ns
time	CA	MD	75	3,558	0.685526708	0.4930116128689396304274339	1.0000000000000000000000	ns
time	CA	MI	75	34	0.422965797	0.6723202156968539622283743	1.0000000000000000000000	ns
time	CA	MN	75	19	0.518160006	0.6043466365312328836267852	1.0000000000000000000000	ns
time	CA	MO	75	17	0.134196513	0.8932471834397305299191316	1.0000000000000000000000	ns
time	CA	NC	75	158	1.486502280	0.1371463142124494383189415	1.0000000000000000000000	ns
time	CA	NH	75	19	-0.218719242	0.8268687592905317185199010	1.0000000000000000000000	ns
time	CA	NJ	75	207	0.657029189	0.5111621481133367117521971	1.0000000000000000000000	ns
time	CA	NY	75	522	-0.232443670	0.8161934334805560631309618	1.0000000000000000000000	ns

time	CA	OH	75	80	2.132161633	0.0329935613524310472621792	1.0000000000000000000000	ns
time	CA	PA	75	461	-0.720588720	0.4711625957780212758940763	1.0000000000000000000000	ns
time	CA	RI	75	14	-0.183382198	0.8544981427416559194298884	1.0000000000000000000000	ns
time	CA	SC	75	11	-0.207578452	0.8355581310385016280406489	1.0000000000000000000000	ns
time	CA	TX	75	44	1.316643101	0.1879582841931299042048664	1.0000000000000000000000	ns
time	CA	VA	75	5,608	0.509330428	0.6105206332345853859067120	1.0000000000000000000000	ns
time	CA	WI	75	14	-0.018745641	0.9850440183597811705240588	1.0000000000000000000000	ns
time	CA	WV	75	28	-0.680354009	0.4962803342971349729317865	1.0000000000000000000000	ns
time	CO	CT	23	73	0.244563120	0.8067947227503116103264347	1.0000000000000000000000	ns
time	CO	DC	23	3,464	0.085723572	0.9316861634755890797521261	1.0000000000000000000000	ns
time	CO	DE	23	61	-0.939001297	0.3477300784665616761870410	1.0000000000000000000000	ns
time	CO	FL	23	55	0.690396048	0.4899451614148668809889386	1.0000000000000000000000	ns
time	CO	GA	23	37	0.072045902	0.9425653785650360827474969	1.0000000000000000000000	ns
time	CO	IL	23	71	0.398851558	0.6900025847000352818838564	1.0000000000000000000000	ns
time	CO	IN	23	18	0.743270794	0.4573177502042244935154258	1.0000000000000000000000	ns
time	CO	MA	23	136	0.547550522	0.5840005707415185653985645	1.0000000000000000000000	ns
time	CO	MD	23	3,558	0.633616117	0.5263313803553398839696342	1.0000000000000000000000	ns
time	CO	MI	23	34	0.518570240	0.6040604669283768934917589	1.0000000000000000000000	ns
time	CO	MN	23	19	0.598804856	0.5493030238700915557359394	1.0000000000000000000000	ns
time	CO	MO	23	17	0.277022216	0.7817630476645323067685922	1.0000000000000000000000	ns
time	CO	NC	23	158	1.169474608	0.2422124658080064274479071	1.0000000000000000000000	ns

time	CO	NH	23	19	-0.011671564	0.9906876507183377533749535	1.0000000000000000000000	ns
time	CO	NJ	23	207	0.642001135	0.5208724459826228336822851	1.0000000000000000000000	ns
time	CO	NY	23	522	0.111954679	0.9108593411965596464696659	1.0000000000000000000000	ns
time	CO	OH	23	80	1.670576097	0.0948054370469179757963119	1.0000000000000000000000	ns
time	CO	PA	23	461	-0.173942200	0.8619108870613768624835416	1.0000000000000000000000	ns
time	CO	RI	23	14	-0.002457448	0.9980392420056104496595140	1.0000000000000000000000	ns
time	CO	SC	23	11	-0.039453830	0.9685285628842341676403294	1.0000000000000000000000	ns
time	CO	TX	23	44	1.175970513	0.2396066592326999977746738	1.0000000000000000000000	ns
time	CO	VA	23	5,608	0.534891463	0.5927249119331432503088308	1.0000000000000000000000	ns
time	CO	WI	23	14	0.138943950	0.8894944407981594247658563	1.0000000000000000000000	ns
time	CO	WV	23	28	-0.348668012	0.7273385616810745801785743	1.0000000000000000000000	ns
time	CT	DC	73	3,464	-0.342825956	0.7317293978689876077226018	1.0000000000000000000000	ns
time	CT	DE	73	61	-1.661609660	0.0965910652875941605488563	1.0000000000000000000000	ns
time	CT	FL	73	55	0.632626970	0.5269772703494555177172742	1.0000000000000000000000	ns
time	CT	GA	73	37	-0.194984043	0.8454054396610518606891560	1.0000000000000000000000	ns
time	CT	IL	73	71	0.223264002	0.8233300422911505878076355	1.0000000000000000000000	ns
time	CT	IN	73	18	0.666606599	0.5050234531377714164435133	1.0000000000000000000000	ns
time	CT	MA	73	136	0.447788444	0.6543058842127853491632550	1.0000000000000000000000	ns
time	CT	MD	73	3,558	0.626420279	0.5310393114863680708026550	1.0000000000000000000000	ns
time	CT	MI	73	34	0.392645777	0.6945811238965272638168358	1.0000000000000000000000	ns
time	CT	MN	73	19	0.493735402	0.6214930596254870653893931	1.0000000000000000000000	ns

time	CT	MO	73	17	0.111865886	0.9109297461609376922453407	1.0000000000000000000000	ns
time	CT	NC	73	158	1.431034007	0.1524204690344274915059231	1.0000000000000000000000	ns
time	CT	NH	73	19	-0.241111956	0.8094683465208050154870989	1.0000000000000000000000	ns
time	CT	NJ	73	207	0.607012222	0.5438428013965057594703012	1.0000000000000000000000	ns
time	CT	NY	73	522	-0.277104686	0.7816997240358658505243739	1.0000000000000000000000	ns
time	CT	OH	73	80	2.080654472	0.0374655441606706260393445	1.0000000000000000000000	ns
time	CT	PA	73	461	-0.759262020	0.4476958322790670075086439	1.0000000000000000000000	ns
time	CT	RI	73	14	-0.203287110	0.8389106297263828615484726	1.0000000000000000000000	ns
time	CT	SC	73	11	-0.225527142	0.8215692127548388512536803	1.0000000000000000000000	ns
time	CT	TX	73	44	1.278993239	0.2008994368396512519847619	1.0000000000000000000000	ns
time	CT	VA	73	5,608	0.452306278	0.6510483539678031394970503	1.0000000000000000000000	ns
time	CT	WI	73	14	-0.039004176	0.9688870592025382588730054	1.0000000000000000000000	ns
time	CT	WV	73	28	-0.704477575	0.4811354107946112512728121	1.0000000000000000000000	ns
time	DC	DE	3,464	61	-1.917749601	0.0551427691261530059096962	1.0000000000000000000000	ns
time	DC	FL	3,464	55	1.129466222	0.2587012111333296671134008	1.0000000000000000000000	ns
time	DC	GA	3,464	37	0.007238761	0.9942243547273740267300468	1.0000000000000000000000	ns
time	DC	IL	3,464	71	0.648600617	0.5165965568684620645711902	1.0000000000000000000000	ns
time	DC	IN	3,464	18	0.913915049	0.3607614854237571333506196	1.0000000000000000000000	ns
time	DC	MA	3,464	136	1.207046810	0.2274141173866393861313639	1.0000000000000000000000	ns
time	DC	MI	3,464	34	0.708319783	0.4787466942928567115167482	1.0000000000000000000000	ns
time	DC	MN	3,464	19	0.729013286	0.4659935352381407991373408	1.0000000000000000000000	ns

time	DC	MO	3,464	17	0.290670572	0.7713032807207454988329687	1.0000000000000000000000	ns
time	DC	NH	3,464	19	-0.093687335	0.9253575313914620403821232	1.0000000000000000000000	ns
time	DC	NJ	3,464	207	1.721473568	0.0851649245842755892033082	1.0000000000000000000000	ns
time	DC	NY	3,464	522	0.126069092	0.8996772334734559617430705	1.0000000000000000000000	ns
time	DC	PA	3,464	461	-1.111342631	0.2664208960964759564937765	1.0000000000000000000000	ns
time	DC	RI	3,464	14	-0.070077717	0.9441318022257751962911243	1.0000000000000000000000	ns
time	DC	SC	3,464	11	-0.107279078	0.9145675818693427272521035	1.0000000000000000000000	ns
time	DC	TX	3,464	44	1.876265885	0.0606187789965979204054314	1.0000000000000000000000	ns
time	DC	WI	3,464	14	0.108906526	0.9132766302186394735684871	1.0000000000000000000000	ns
time	DC	WV	3,464	28	-0.611628332	0.5407836887100798684002712	1.0000000000000000000000	ns
time	DE	FL	61	55	2.157618294	0.0309575211650547979513881	1.0000000000000000000000	ns
time	DE	GA	61	37	1.194436221	0.2323073754584894790031768	1.0000000000000000000000	ns
time	DE	IL	61	71	1.864222736	0.0622904318317489963385825	1.0000000000000000000000	ns
time	DE	IN	61	18	1.728593488	0.0838818758849513707032131	1.0000000000000000000000	ns
time	DE	MA	61	136	2.292109331	0.0218993350863987724930215	1.0000000000000000000000	ns
time	DE	MD	61	3,558	2.805749395	0.0050199717456045284472155	1.0000000000000000000000	ns
time	DE	MI	61	34	1.727703663	0.0840413665272123217020450	1.0000000000000000000000	ns
time	DE	MN	61	19	1.581115534	0.1138516235761971306938989	1.0000000000000000000000	ns
time	DE	MO	61	17	1.160830186	0.2457109645837548816960094	1.0000000000000000000000	ns
time	DE	NH	61	19	0.860755608	0.3893726592235692840482386	1.0000000000000000000000	ns
time	DE	NJ	61	207	2.545676811	0.0109066114058086593291419	1.0000000000000000000000	ns

time	DE	NY	61	522	1.874302049	0.0608888052281111799568514	1.0000000000000000000000	ns
time	DE	PA	61	461	1.413618564	0.1574739276711676350117841	1.0000000000000000000000	ns
time	DE	RI	61	14	0.772498887	0.4398190058267939517300249	1.0000000000000000000000	ns
time	DE	SC	61	11	0.657256772	0.5110158267756688132976706	1.0000000000000000000000	ns
time	DE	TX	61	44	2.691464946	0.0071138973910465242572743	1.0000000000000000000000	ns
time	DE	VA	61	5,608	2.652985731	0.0079783243526783138160896	1.0000000000000000000000	ns
time	DE	WI	61	14	0.934241678	0.3501792411384527792250765	1.0000000000000000000000	ns
time	DE	WV	61	28	0.576691760	0.564147699926713364885700	1.0000000000000000000000	ns
time	FL	GA	55	37	-0.716312873	0.4737981799492498313775002	1.0000000000000000000000	ns
time	FL	IL	55	71	-0.421659075	0.6732738802598668970134099	1.0000000000000000000000	ns
time	FL	IN	55	18	0.230050305	0.8180526801922496371588522	1.0000000000000000000000	ns
time	FL	MA	55	136	-0.300294251	0.7639527177090008613902228	1.0000000000000000000000	ns
time	FL	MD	55	3,558	-0.286218926	0.7747104488068903282993460	1.0000000000000000000000	ns
time	FL	MI	55	34	-0.144073222	0.8854426497963847619843136	1.0000000000000000000000	ns
time	FL	MN	55	19	0.053375632	0.9574326205540204526300840	1.0000000000000000000000	ns
time	FL	MO	55	17	-0.298490916	0.7653285082607976796964522	1.0000000000000000000000	ns
time	FL	NC	55	158	0.572068976	0.5672752461391830092196642	1.0000000000000000000000	ns
time	FL	NH	55	19	-0.657829867	0.5106474604448988374727492	1.0000000000000000000000	ns
time	FL	NJ	55	207	-0.199919338	0.8415436661659880801522604	1.0000000000000000000000	ns
time	FL	NY	55	522	-1.041030208	0.2978615285631868725424454	1.0000000000000000000000	ns
time	FL	OH	55	80	1.277777428	0.2013279152827606166553664	1.0000000000000000000000	ns

time	FL	PA	55	461	-1.462238567	0.1436758465072802692930054	1.000000000000000000000	ns
time	FL	RI	55	14	-0.575474823	0.5649702136285247311420221	1.000000000000000000000	ns
time	FL	SC	55	11	-0.562836160	0.5735464546965141074963412	1.000000000000000000000	ns
time	FL	TX	55	44	0.648408158	0.5167209954547480332820442	1.000000000000000000000	ns
time	FL	VA	55	5,608	-0.440401924	0.6596460317547883089872585	1.000000000000000000000	ns
time	FL	WI	55	14	-0.415354135	0.6778826771128005912459003	1.000000000000000000000	ns
time	FL	WV	55	28	-1.161095786	0.2456029482822560117138977	1.000000000000000000000	ns
time	GA	IL	37	71	0.377605454	0.7057237121222375009210737	1.000000000000000000000	ns
time	GA	IN	37	18	0.747374538	0.4548375105381510241642218	1.000000000000000000000	ns
time	GA	MA	37	136	0.562615740	0.5736965717011284215942624	1.000000000000000000000	ns
time	GA	MD	37	3,558	0.686312385	0.4925161405740029474387143	1.000000000000000000000	ns
time	GA	MI	37	34	0.508797080	0.6108944662176173379108945	1.000000000000000000000	ns
time	GA	MN	37	19	0.589957588	0.5552190839518653664441672	1.000000000000000000000	ns
time	GA	MO	37	17	0.237111714	0.8125701250060605174141415	1.000000000000000000000	ns
time	GA	NC	37	158	1.324312822	0.1853991739941362737464914	1.000000000000000000000	ns
time	GA	NH	37	19	-0.080600599	0.9357595898442416793017173	1.000000000000000000000	ns
time	GA	NJ	37	207	0.683393194	0.4943584196784506779032142	1.000000000000000000000	ns
time	GA	NY	37	522	0.027759958	0.9778536023853020564544636	1.000000000000000000000	ns
time	GA	OH	37	80	1.891835554	0.0585128945480799383949133	1.000000000000000000000	ns
time	GA	PA	37	461	-0.329453743	0.7418127518847825729864098	1.000000000000000000000	ns
time	GA	RI	37	14	-0.063622547	0.9492707781054730009628884	1.000000000000000000000	ns

time	GA	SC	37	11	-0.097821115	0.9220743401504951641811658	1.0000000000000000000000	ns
time	GA	TX	37	44	1.270762498	0.2038131539642039080639790	1.0000000000000000000000	ns
time	GA	VA	37	5,608	0.561601756	0.5743873834200121653026372	1.0000000000000000000000	ns
time	GA	WI	37	14	0.089136317	0.9289735751701346799791281	1.0000000000000000000000	ns
time	GA	WV	37	28	-0.468095157	0.6397165427972244522436540	1.0000000000000000000000	ns
time	IL	IN	71	18	0.523737498	0.6004611305273568344631485	1.0000000000000000000000	ns
time	IL	MA	71	136	0.189570887	0.8496454021164198122662015	1.0000000000000000000000	ns
time	IL	MD	71	3,558	0.307459516	0.7584936328886493495105015	1.0000000000000000000000	ns
time	IL	MI	71	34	0.212463870	0.8317451616156292804049599	1.0000000000000000000000	ns
time	IL	MN	71	19	0.348228677	0.7276684525385994639634646	1.0000000000000000000000	ns
time	IL	MO	71	17	-0.026253524	0.9790551245842780136996453	1.0000000000000000000000	ns
time	IL	NC	71	158	1.156979152	0.2472808780104581993786184	1.0000000000000000000000	ns
time	IL	NH	71	19	-0.384490470	0.7006149582475011960980282	1.0000000000000000000000	ns
time	IL	NJ	71	207	0.330205266	0.7412448678388932066241068	1.0000000000000000000000	ns
time	IL	NY	71	522	-0.567945374	0.5700720607879454782107587	1.0000000000000000000000	ns
time	IL	OH	71	80	1.837257090	0.0661719512508237017733848	1.0000000000000000000000	ns
time	IL	PA	71	461	-1.042094493	0.2973678713487160063522197	1.0000000000000000000000	ns
time	IL	RI	71	14	-0.330088265	0.7413332697076675525948986	1.0000000000000000000000	ns
time	IL	SC	71	11	-0.339961518	0.7338855082134658758263868	1.0000000000000000000000	ns
time	IL	TX	71	44	1.078310419	0.2808952488143112158347492	1.0000000000000000000000	ns
time	IL	VA	71	5,608	0.134539253	0.8929761735329517780002107	1.0000000000000000000000	ns

time	IL	WI	71	14	-0.166176413	0.86801812130346578388889530	1.0000000000000000000000	ns
time	IL	WV	71	28	-0.868505959	0.38511741136477228852896681	1.0000000000000000000000	ns
time	IN	MA	18	136	-0.440383658	0.65965925915125112055648806	1.0000000000000000000000	ns
time	IN	MD	18	3,558	-0.428951252	0.66795870125334233513569877	1.0000000000000000000000	ns
time	IN	MI	18	34	-0.322137125	0.74734881403843167468892226	1.0000000000000000000000	ns
time	IN	MN	18	19	-0.146740545	0.88333681445692213696219114	1.0000000000000000000000	ns
time	IN	MO	18	17	-0.429627863	0.66746636544164839044412293	1.0000000000000000000000	ns
time	IN	NC	18	158	0.108911991	0.91327229561866718476892240	1.0000000000000000000000	ns
time	IN	NH	18	19	-0.722134124	0.47021201972068749075361889	1.0000000000000000000000	ns
time	IN	NJ	18	207	-0.377627775	0.70570712848080230372715996	1.0000000000000000000000	ns
time	IN	NY	18	522	-0.876195218	0.38092391590527041600466887	1.0000000000000000000000	ns
time	IN	OH	18	80	0.618492892	0.53625048156039922808702116	1.0000000000000000000000	ns
time	IN	PA	18	461	-1.128228238	0.25922354121554652683911197	1.0000000000000000000000	ns
time	IN	RI	18	14	-0.658730917	0.51006857560397289574893388	1.0000000000000000000000	ns
time	IN	SC	18	11	-0.648976809	0.51635336632135830914336334	1.0000000000000000000000	ns
time	IN	TX	18	44	0.245461016	0.80609948937745479202732221	1.0000000000000000000000	ns
time	IN	VA	18	5,608	-0.517381644	0.60488977083780692822756446	1.0000000000000000000000	ns
time	IN	WI	18	14	-0.524221742	0.60012432042918240071571174	1.0000000000000000000000	ns
time	IN	WV	18	28	-1.099020237	0.27175923874363827614786226	1.0000000000000000000000	ns
time	MA	MD	136	3,558	0.104093280	0.91709532391192760680809222	1.0000000000000000000000	ns

time	MA	MI	136	34	0.086339643	0.9311964253067255281592907	1.0000000000000000000000	ns
time	MA	MN	136	19	0.253920302	0.7995571298602562881896461	1.0000000000000000000000	ns
time	MA	MO	136	17	-0.135452724	0.8922539404549933994559296	1.0000000000000000000000	ns
time	MA	NC	136	158	1.175928687	0.2396233741740958766985869	1.0000000000000000000000	ns
time	MA	NH	136	19	-0.518819399	0.6038866884528246714580746	1.0000000000000000000000	ns
time	MA	NJ	136	207	0.159975293	0.8729005367693151162811205	1.0000000000000000000000	ns
time	MA	NY	136	522	-1.034513832	0.3008960137149039870685385	1.0000000000000000000000	ns
time	MA	OH	136	80	1.929051138	0.0537245140699724871291565	1.0000000000000000000000	ns
time	MA	PA	136	461	-1.645935115	0.0997771184100271768535606	1.0000000000000000000000	ns
time	MA	RI	136	14	-0.442790156	0.6579175240012624659158291	1.0000000000000000000000	ns
time	MA	SC	136	11	-0.439958644	0.6599670607740885097669548	1.0000000000000000000000	ns
time	MA	TX	136	44	1.032843963	0.3016769260975674660230084	1.0000000000000000000000	ns
time	MA	VA	136	5,608	-0.134686283	0.8928599185670064164455084	1.0000000000000000000000	ns
time	MA	WI	136	14	-0.272019019	0.7856073958886315988792148	1.0000000000000000000000	ns
time	MA	WV	136	28	-1.067665232	0.2856715471432274000562757	1.0000000000000000000000	ns
time	MD	MI	3,558	34	0.043292279	0.9654685462601101386681535	1.0000000000000000000000	ns
time	MD	MN	3,558	19	0.230818423	0.8174558682838415357707618	1.0000000000000000000000	ns
time	MD	MO	3,558	17	-0.180737347	0.8565737430915393302299776	1.0000000000000000000000	ns
time	MD	NC	3,558	158	1.579940521	0.1141204882759454669605148	1.0000000000000000000000	ns
time	MD	NH	3,558	19	-0.591941488	0.5538897705792922288026148	1.0000000000000000000000	ns
time	MD	NJ	3,558	207	0.119768813	0.9046662874164186352032857	1.0000000000000000000000	ns

time	MD	NY	3,558	522	-2.319016386	0.0203941478816860762013352	1.000000000000000000000	ns
time	MD	OH	3,558	80	2.323764130	0.0201381392199158348876864	1.000000000000000000000	ns
time	MD	RI	3,558	14	-0.498073792	0.6184320319713265678984726	1.000000000000000000000	ns
time	MD	SC	3,558	11	-0.486817646	0.6263875643033864903941321	1.000000000000000000000	ns
time	MD	TX	3,558	44	1.120993802	0.2622905007485855644056016	1.000000000000000000000	ns
time	MD	VA	3,558	5,608	-0.969690313	0.3322008803123850939620354	1.000000000000000000000	ns
time	MD	WI	3,558	14	-0.319080031	0.7496658259298814019899737	1.000000000000000000000	ns
time	MD	WV	3,558	28	-1.215783040	0.2240675811095888259050213	1.000000000000000000000	ns
time	MI	MN	34	19	0.159320914	0.8734160443660889949768489	1.000000000000000000000	ns
time	MI	MO	34	17	-0.173037500	0.8626219513598052390790372	1.000000000000000000000	ns
time	MI	NC	34	158	0.640001208	0.5221718140530042795433019	1.000000000000000000000	ns
time	MI	NH	34	19	-0.501419916	0.6160756261664277477763108	1.000000000000000000000	ns
time	MI	NJ	34	207	0.005962163	0.9952429104258295744500629	1.000000000000000000000	ns
time	MI	NY	34	522	-0.656239026	0.5116703424286844770207949	1.000000000000000000000	ns
time	MI	OH	34	80	1.246799563	0.2124710009611904260040660	1.000000000000000000000	ns
time	MI	PA	34	461	-0.996945969	0.3187907368172905875347567	1.000000000000000000000	ns
time	MI	RI	34	14	-0.443507415	0.6573987569002464059764179	1.000000000000000000000	ns
time	MI	SC	34	11	-0.445314950	0.6560921653208289239245232	1.000000000000000000000	ns
time	MI	TX	34	44	0.712000257	0.4764646169987240553744812	1.000000000000000000000	ns
time	MI	VA	34	5,608	-0.164188511	0.8695827449933810626703234	1.000000000000000000000	ns
time	MI	WI	34	14	-0.292565628	0.7698541893972414840163765	1.000000000000000000000	ns

time	MI	WV	34	28	-0.933093471	0.3507717096400561063163082	1.0000000000000000000000	ns
time	MN	MO	19	17	-0.290653678	0.7713162025852493552946498	1.0000000000000000000000	ns
time	MN	NC	19	158	0.310352554	0.7562928702906408506834168	1.0000000000000000000000	ns
time	MN	NH	19	19	-0.583330417	0.5596708898693214528918816	1.0000000000000000000000	ns
time	MN	NJ	19	207	-0.185769108	0.8526258313580474812454213	1.0000000000000000000000	ns
time	MN	NY	19	522	-0.692715056	0.4884883887257038259654962	1.0000000000000000000000	ns
time	MN	OH	19	80	0.821345633	0.4114494216139490401218382	1.0000000000000000000000	ns
time	MN	PA	19	461	-0.951757181	0.3412201426055108122170623	1.0000000000000000000000	ns
time	MN	RI	19	14	-0.529416597	0.5965164874644479642284978	1.0000000000000000000000	ns
time	MN	SC	19	11	-0.528159001	0.5973889831590791787974126	1.0000000000000000000000	ns
time	MN	TX	19	44	0.425998752	0.6701087555648967963861651	1.0000000000000000000000	ns
time	MN	VA	19	5,608	-0.321482381	0.7478448621214109914845380	1.0000000000000000000000	ns
time	MN	WI	19	14	-0.393331528	0.6940746351687968607180323	1.0000000000000000000000	ns
time	MN	WV	19	28	-0.954674695	0.3397422305911517170784464	1.0000000000000000000000	ns
time	MO	NC	17	158	0.675391069	0.4994273381643767883986129	1.0000000000000000000000	ns
time	MO	NH	17	19	-0.276241589	0.7823625158190059547536066	1.0000000000000000000000	ns
time	MO	NJ	17	207	0.208099204	0.8351515083841132280895181	1.0000000000000000000000	ns
time	MO	NY	17	522	-0.262734061	0.7927555622341253549478779	1.0000000000000000000000	ns
time	MO	OH	17	80	1.148220569	0.2508775198719174204242677	1.0000000000000000000000	ns
time	MO	PA	17	461	-0.509249308	0.6105774848232852214380273	1.0000000000000000000000	ns
time	MO	RI	17	14	-0.247815137	0.8042774428090798677359885	1.0000000000000000000000	ns

time	MO	SC	17	11	-0.266357731	0.7899637157596428593819837	1.0000000000000000000000	ns
time	MO	TX	17	44	0.749297874	0.4536776891124618127371093	1.0000000000000000000000	ns
time	MO	VA	17	5,608	0.095332188	0.9240509767680334940465059	1.0000000000000000000000	ns
time	MO	WI	17	14	-0.115004071	0.9084418952109845069031735	1.0000000000000000000000	ns
time	MO	WV	17	28	-0.607291229	0.5436576583450627442317682	1.0000000000000000000000	ns
time	NC	NH	158	19	-1.089772528	0.2758133582781480686030307	1.0000000000000000000000	ns
time	NC	NJ	158	207	-1.134886426	0.2564229079661229371289721	1.0000000000000000000000	ns
time	NC	NY	158	522	-2.611704079	0.0090092198837892281670925	1.0000000000000000000000	ns
time	NC	OH	158	80	0.978401227	0.3278759214924938381052755	1.0000000000000000000000	ns
time	NC	RI	158	14	-0.938966036	0.3477481827337715603043478	1.0000000000000000000000	ns
time	NC	SC	158	11	-0.883369901	0.3770364474036217439234520	1.0000000000000000000000	ns
time	NC	TX	158	44	0.243953037	0.8072671919143297181165053	1.0000000000000000000000	ns
time	NC	VA	158	5,608	-1.850002603	0.0643131743545954925878050	1.0000000000000000000000	ns
time	NC	WI	158	14	-0.767074312	0.4430373341456543823113634	1.0000000000000000000000	ns
time	NC	WV	158	28	-1.751409443	0.0798754076460685413785257	1.0000000000000000000000	ns
time	NH	NJ	19	207	0.603746235	0.5460123699804677599445313	1.0000000000000000000000	ns
time	NH	NY	19	522	0.117623009	0.9063663733151506862739666	1.0000000000000000000000	ns
time	NH	OH	19	80	1.562923940	0.1180704859583324994876108	1.0000000000000000000000	ns
time	NH	PA	19	461	-0.143295454	0.8860568459544991837262273	1.0000000000000000000000	ns
time	NH	RI	19	14	0.007907935	0.9936904467362797088725301	1.0000000000000000000000	ns

time	NH	SC	19	11	-0.028624675	0.9771639321628966534660776	1.0000000000000000000000	ns
time	NH	TX	19	44	1.115421619	0.2646697894818696439322991	1.0000000000000000000000	ns
time	NH	VA	19	5,608	0.502077469	0.6156130286203639334630111	1.0000000000000000000000	ns
time	NH	WI	19	14	0.143993004	0.8855059942417535800984751	1.0000000000000000000000	ns
time	NH	WV	19	28	-0.317938251	0.7505317765962128406798115	1.0000000000000000000000	ns
time	NJ	NY	207	522	-1.427536274	0.1534253770970118169181262	1.0000000000000000000000	ns
time	NJ	OH	207	80	1.930512320	0.0535433901977151530116039	1.0000000000000000000000	ns
time	NJ	PA	207	461	-2.130727067	0.0331116338738655716089632	1.0000000000000000000000	ns
time	NJ	RI	207	14	-0.513996284	0.6072545887234515049613037	1.0000000000000000000000	ns
time	NJ	SC	207	11	-0.502784547	0.6151157595063618810371509	1.0000000000000000000000	ns
time	NJ	TX	207	44	0.972700310	0.3307022712586032420212234	1.0000000000000000000000	ns
time	NJ	VA	207	5,608	-0.414641033	0.6784047052602060201564882	1.0000000000000000000000	ns
time	NJ	WI	207	14	-0.340424278	0.7335370383178305697668975	1.0000000000000000000000	ns
time	NJ	WV	207	28	-1.188065334	0.2348076706441336314323820	1.0000000000000000000000	ns
time	NY	PA	522	461	-0.954670610	0.3397442971777428488699968	1.0000000000000000000000	ns
time	NY	RI	522	14	-0.091152040	0.9273717824584456481673556	1.0000000000000000000000	ns
time	NY	SC	522	11	-0.125762418	0.8999199914303124270276157	1.0000000000000000000000	ns
time	NY	TX	522	44	1.775563482	0.0758048935497009357398213	1.0000000000000000000000	ns
time	NY	VA	522	5,608	1.921047769	0.0547256854987331481376955	1.0000000000000000000000	ns
time	NY	WI	522	14	0.085835830	0.9315969232029582824949898	1.0000000000000000000000	ns
time	NY	WV	522	28	-0.628772678	0.5294978895524626860691342	1.0000000000000000000000	ns

time	OH	RI	80	14	-1.367210516	0.1715593302603491410174286	1.0000000000000000000000	ns
time	OH	SC	80	11	-1.274103409	0.2026267704513991241288551	1.0000000000000000000000	ns
time	OH	TX	80	44	-0.493748865	0.6214835506559988065333755	1.0000000000000000000000	ns
time	OH	VA	80	5,608	-2.517740809	0.0118110200783294507637100	1.0000000000000000000000	ns
time	OH	WI	80	14	-1.201758633	0.2294570571466031105867245	1.0000000000000000000000	ns
time	OH	WV	80	28	-2.246919381	0.0246451798742392119700995	1.0000000000000000000000	ns
time	PA	RI	461	14	0.133916886	0.8934682971970184794940906	1.0000000000000000000000	ns
time	PA	SC	461	11	0.074404531	0.9406885033695894238192636	1.0000000000000000000000	ns
time	PA	TX	461	44	2.153202590	0.0313027602340191501983924	1.0000000000000000000000	ns
time	PA	WI	461	14	0.310599699	0.7561049557190898662284440	1.0000000000000000000000	ns
time	PA	WV	461	28	-0.313178424	0.7541451097702147610135626	1.0000000000000000000000	ns
time	RI	SC	14	11	-0.033829537	0.9730130822282493374686396	1.0000000000000000000000	ns
time	RI	TX	14	44	0.988812453	0.3227549102746907760952411	1.0000000000000000000000	ns
time	RI	VA	14	5,608	0.420763605	0.6739277101924044943714875	1.0000000000000000000000	ns
time	RI	WI	14	14	0.126816467	0.8990856622605168935180586	1.0000000000000000000000	ns
time	RI	WV	14	28	-0.297214359	0.7663028602683994439104254	1.0000000000000000000000	ns
time	SC	TX	11	44	0.940509455	0.3469563019858150076935033	1.0000000000000000000000	ns
time	SC	VA	11	5,608	0.418228973	0.6757797140739913999141208	1.0000000000000000000000	ns
time	SC	WI	11	14	0.152793928	0.8785607861937638762839242	1.0000000000000000000000	ns
time	SC	WV	11	28	-0.235093038	0.8141365221060015144871613	1.0000000000000000000000	ns
time	TX	VA	44	5,608	-1.260828655	0.2073705871741013118114694	1.0000000000000000000000	ns

time	TX	WI	44	14	-0.832604555	0.4050677893209727598033965	1.0000000000000000000000	ns
time	TX	WV	44	28	-1.657525358	0.0974133063510279617602805	1.0000000000000000000000	ns
time	VA	WI	5,608	14	-0.241641482	0.8090579766293215513428549	1.0000000000000000000000	ns
time	VA	WV	5,608	28	-1.107820099	0.2679395179884538902292945	1.0000000000000000000000	ns
time	WI	WV	14	28	-0.443649401	0.6572960831173089157886125	1.0000000000000000000000	ns

We see that:

- Every pair of states is compared with sample size, statistics, p-value, adjusted p-value, and adjusted p-value significance symbol.
- For example, the runners from the “MD” state have significantly higher run time than runners from the “NR” state with a significant adjusted p-value.
- On the other hand, runners from the “WI” state have statistically equivalent run time to runners from the “WV” state with an adjusted p-value of 1.00.

CHAPTER 5

BIVARIATE ANALYSIS FOR CATEGORICAL-CATEGORICAL DATA

Contents

5.1. DATA USED IN THIS CHAPTER

5.1.1. American Community Survey of 2012

The results from the US Census American Community Survey performed in 2012 are stored under the name "acs12." The data is part of the openintro package and its source is https://www.census.gov/programs-surveys/acs.

To load this data into our R session, we will load the openintro package using the library function. Then, we will load the "acs12" data using the data function. We will also load the tidyverse package because it contains many packages for efficient data analysis.

```
library(tidyverse)
```

```
library(openintro)
```

```
data("acs12")
```

To see the data structure, we will use the glimpse function from the dplyr package.

```
glimpse(acs12)
## Rows: 2,000
## Columns: 13
## $ income      <int> 60000, 0, NA, 0, 0, 1700, NA, NA, NA, 45000, NA, 8600, 0,…
## $ employment  <fct> not in labor force, not in labor force, NA, not in labor …
## $ hrs_work    <int> 40, NA, NA, NA, NA, 40, NA, NA, NA, 84, NA, 23, NA, NA, N…
## $ race        <fct> white, white, white, white, white, other, white, other, a…
## $ age         <int> 68, 88, 12, 17, 77, 35, 11, 7, 6, 27, 8, 69, 69, 17, 10, …
## $ gender      <fct> female, male, female, male, female, female, male, male, m…
## $ citizen     <fct> yes, yes, yes, yes, yes, yes, yes, yes, yes, yes, yes, ye…
## $ time_to_work <int> NA, NA, NA, NA, NA, 15, NA, NA, NA, 40, NA, 5, NA, NA, NA…
## $ lang        <fct> english, english, english, other, other, other, english, …
## $ married     <fct> no, no, no, no, no, yes, no, no, no, yes, no, no, yes, no…
## $ edu         <fct> college, hs or lower, hs or lower, hs or lower, hs or low…
## $ disability  <fct> no, yes, no, no, yes, yes, no, yes, no, no, no, no, yes, …
## $ birth_qrtr  <fct> jul thru sep, jan thru mar, oct thru dec, oct thru dec, j…
```

We see that the "acs12" data contains 2000 rows and 13 columns:

1. income: the annual income. It is a numeric column.
2. employment: the employment status. It is a factor column.
3. hrs_work: the hours worked per week. It is an integer column.

4. race: the respondent's race. It is a factor column.
5. age: the respondent's age in years. It is an integer column.
6. gender: the respondent's gender. It is a factor column.
7. citizen: whether the person is a U.S. citizen. It is a factor column.
8. time_to_work: the travel time to work in minutes. It is an integer column.
9. lang: the language spoken at home. It is a factor column.
10. married: whether the person is married. It is a factor column.
11. edu: the respondent's education level. It is a factor column.
12. disability: whether the person is dizabled. It is a factor column.
13. birth_qrtr: the quarter of the year that the respondent was born.□ It is a factor column.

5.1.2. The Minneapolis Police Use of Force Data

The Minneapolis police use of force data from 2016 through August 2021 is stored in the "mn_police_use_of_force" data frame which is part of the openintro package of R. The data source is https://opendata.minneapolismn.gov/search?groupIds=79606f50581f4a33b14a19e61c4891f7. To load this data into our R session, we will use the data function as before followed by the glimpse function to get the data structure.

```
data("mn_police_use_of_force")

glimpse(mn_police_use_of_force)
## Rows: 12,925
## Columns: 13
## $ response_datetime <chr> "2016/01/01 00:47:36," "2016/01/01 02:19:34," "2016/…
## $ problem          <chr> "Assault in Progress ," "Fight ," "Fight ," "Fight "…
## $ is_911_call      <chr> "Yes," "No," "No," "No," "No," "No," "No," "No," "No…
## $ primary_offense  <chr> "DASLT1," "DISCON," "DISCON," "PRIORI," "PRIORI," "P…
## $ subject_injury   <chr> "," "," "," "," "," "," "," "," "," "No," "No," "Yes…
## $ force_type       <chr> "Bodily Force," "Chemical Irritant," "Chemical Irrit…
## $ force_type_action <chr> "Body Weight to Pin," "Personal Mace," "Personal Mac…
## $ race             <chr> "Black," "Black," "White," "Black," "Black," "Black"…
## $ sex              <chr> "Male," "Female," "Female," "Male," "Male," "Male," …
## $ age              <int> 20, 27, 23, 20, 20, 20, 20, 20, 20, 18, 18, 21, 21, …
## $ type_resistance  <chr> "Tensed," "Verbal Non-Compliance," "Verbal Non-Compl…
## $ precinct         <chr> "1," "1," "1," "1," "1," "1," "1," "1," "1," "1," "1…
## $ neighborhood     <chr> "Downtown East," "Downtown West," "Downtown West," "…
```

The data contains 12925 observations (rows) on the following 13 columns:

1. response_datetime: the datetime of police response. It is a character column.
2. problem: the problem that required police response. It is a character column.
3. is_911_call: whether the response was initiated by a call to 911. It is a character column.
4. primary_offense: the offense of the subject. It is a character column.
5. subject_injury: Whether the subject was injured. It is a character column.
6. force_type: the type of police force used. It is a character column.
7. force_type_action: the detail of the police force used. It is a character column.
8. race: the race of the subject. It is a character column.
9. sex: the gender of the subject. It is a character column.
10. age: the age of the subject. It is an integer column.
11. type_resistance: the resistance to police by the subject. It is a character column.
12. precinct: the precinct where the response occurred. It is a character column.
13. neighborhood: the neighborhood where the response occurred. It is a character column.

5.2. SUMMARY STATISTICS

As we saw in Chapter 2, the category sample size and proportion are the only measures that are used to describe categorical data. To look at the relation between 2 categorical variables, we can see how the counts or proportions of 1 categorical variable change under the different levels of the other categorical variable.

5.2.1. The Count

5.2.1.1. The Count of Different Employment Statuses in the 2 Genders

To get these counts from the American Community Survey data, we use the count function, applied to "acs12" data, with the arguments gender, and employment to get the the count of different employment statuses in males and females. Then, we convert the result to a table as before.

```
library(flextable)

acs12 %>% count(gender, employment) %>%

 flextable() %>% theme_box() %>%

 set_caption(caption = "The count of different employment statuses in males and females of the American Community Survey data")
```

Table 5.1. The Count of Different Employment Statuses in Males and Females of the American Community Survey Data

Gender	Employment	n
male	not in labor force	283
male	unemployed	59
male	employed	470
male		219
female	not in labor force	373
female	unemployed	47
female	employed	373
female		176

We see that:

- There are 283 males not in labor force compared to 373 females.
- There are 59 unemployed males compared to 47 females.
- There are 470 employed males compared to 373 females. So males are more employed than females.
- There are 219 males with missing employment status compared to 176 females.

5.2.1.2. The Count of Different Employment Statuses in the Different Races

To get these counts, we use the count function with the arguments race, and employment to get the the count of different employment statuses in the different races.

```
acs12 %>% count(race, employment) %>%

 flextable() %>% theme_box() %>%

  set_caption(caption = "The count of different employment statuses in the different races of the American Community Survey data")
```

Table 5.2. *The Count of Different Employment Statuses in the Different Races of the American Community Survey Data*

Race	Employment	n
white	not in labor force	520
white	unemployed	72
white	employed	670
white		293
black	not in labor force	66
black	unemployed	20
black	employed	76
black		44
asian	not in labor force	31
asian	unemployed	3
asian	employed	39
asian		14
other	not in labor force	39
other	unemployed	11
other	employed	58
other		44

We see that:

- There are 520 Whites not in labor force compared to 66 Blacks, 31 Asians, and 39 other races.
- There are 72 unemployed Whites compared to 20 Blacks, 3 Asians, and 11 other races.
- There are 670 employed Whites compared to 76 Blacks, 39 Asians, and 58 other races. So Whites are more employed than other races.
- There are 293 Whites with missing employment status compared to 44 Blacks, 14 Asians, and 44 other races.

5.2.1.3. The Count of Force Types in the Different Races

To get these counts from the Minneapolis police use of force data, we use the count function, applied on "mn_police_use_of_force" data, with the arguments race, force_type to get the count of different force types applied on the different races. Then, we convert the result to a table as before.

```
mn_police_use_of_force %>% count(race, force_type) %>%

 flextable() %>% theme_box() %>%

 set_caption(caption = "The count of different force types applied on different
races from the Minneapolis police use of force data")
```

Table 5.3. The Count of Different Force Types Applied on Different Races from the Minneapolis Police Use of Force Data

Race	force_type	n
Asian	Bodily Force	78
Asian	Chemical Irritant	32
Asian	Gun Point Display	1
Asian	Improvised Weapon	1
Asian	Taser	17
Black	Baton	2
Black	Bodily Force	5,519
Black	Chemical Irritant	1,033
Black	Firearm	2
Black	Gun Point Display	76
Black	Improvised Weapon	83
Black	Less Lethal	23
Black	Less Lethal Projectile	3
Black	Maximal Restraint Technique	104
Black	Police K9 Bite	48
Black	Taser	755

Native American	Bodily Force	616
Native American	Chemical Irritant	18
Native American	Gun Point Display	8
Native American	Improvised Weapon	10
Native American	Less Lethal	6
Native American	Maximal Restraint Technique	14
Native American	Police K9 Bite	8
Native American	Taser	104
Other/Mixed Race	Bodily Force	137
Other/Mixed Race	Chemical Irritant	50
Other/Mixed Race	Gun Point Display	3
Other/Mixed Race	Improvised Weapon	1
Other/Mixed Race	Police K9 Bite	2
Other/Mixed Race	Taser	12
Pacific Islander	Bodily Force	5
Pacific Islander	Chemical Irritant	1
White	Baton	1
White	Bodily Force	2,454
White	Chemical Irritant	191
White	Gun Point Display	16
White	Improvised Weapon	47
White	Less Lethal	27
White	Maximal Restraint Technique	42
White	Police K9 Bite	17
White	Taser	334

	Baton	1
	Bodily Force	621
	Chemical Irritant	268
	Improvised Weapon	6
	Less Lethal	31
	Maximal Restraint Technique	10
	Police K9 Bite	2
	Taser	85

We see that:

- The "Bodily Force" type was applied to 78 Asians compared to 5519 Blacks, 616 Native Americans, 137 Other/Mixed Races, 5 Pacific Islanders, and 2454 Whites. So "Bodily Force" was applied more to Blacks than to other races.
- The "Chemical Irritant" force type was applied to 32 Asians compared to 1033 Blacks, 18 Native Americans, 50 Other/Mixed Races, 1 Pacific Islander, and 191 Whites. So "Chemical Irritant" was applied more to Blacks than to other races and so on.

5.2.1.4. The Count of Force Types in the Different Neighborhoods

To get these counts from the Minneapolis police use of force data, we use the count function with the arguments neighborhood, and force_type to get the count of different force types applied in the different neighborhoods. Then, we convert the result to a table as before.

```
mn_police_use_of_force %>% count(neighborhood,force_type) %>%

 flextable() %>%

 theme_box() %>%

  set_caption(caption = "The count of different force types applied in the different neighborhoods from the Minneapolis police use of force data")
```

Table 5.4. The Count of Different Force Types Applied in the Different Neighborhoods from the Minneapolis Police Use of Force Data

Neighborhood	force_type	n
	Bodily Force	3
	Chemical Irritant	1
Armatage	Bodily Force	19
Armatage	Chemical Irritant	1
Armatage	Maximal Restraint Technique	1
Armatage	Police K9 Bite	1
Armatage	Taser	6
Audubon Park	Bodily Force	89
Audubon Park	Chemical Irritant	3
Audubon Park	Taser	6
Bancroft	Bodily Force	23
Bancroft	Chemical Irritant	4
Bancroft	Improvised Weapon	2
Bancroft	Taser	1
Beltrami	Bodily Force	10
Beltrami	Less Lethal	1
Bottineau	Bodily Force	7
Bottineau	Chemical Irritant	1
Bottineau	Police K9 Bite	1
Bottineau	Taser	1
Bryant	Bodily Force	22
Bryant	Police K9 Bite	2
Bryant	Taser	1
Bryn – Mawr	Bodily Force	15
Bryn – Mawr	Taser	3
CARAG	Bodily Force	154
CARAG	Chemical Irritant	4
CARAG	Gun Point Display	1
CARAG	Improvised Weapon	3
CARAG	Police K9 Bite	1

CARAG	Taser	12
Camden Industrial	Bodily Force	3
Cedar – Isles – Dean	Bodily Force	4
Cedar – Isles – Dean	Chemical Irritant	2
Cedar Riverside	Bodily Force	136
Cedar Riverside	Chemical Irritant	31
Cedar Riverside	Gun Point Display	3
Cedar Riverside	Improvised Weapon	1
Cedar Riverside	Less Lethal	3
Cedar Riverside	Maximal Restraint Technique	4
Cedar Riverside	Police K9 Bite	3
Cedar Riverside	Taser	24
Central	Bodily Force	122
Central	Chemical Irritant	10
Central	Gun Point Display	2
Central	Police K9 Bite	1
Central	Taser	23
Cleveland	Bodily Force	86
Cleveland	Chemical Irritant	1
Cleveland	Gun Point Display	1
Cleveland	Improvised Weapon	1
Cleveland	Maximal Restraint Technique	2
Cleveland	Police K9 Bite	2
Cleveland	Taser	4
Columbia Park	Bodily Force	31
Columbia Park	Less Lethal	1
Columbia Park	Maximal Restraint Technique	5
Columbia Park	Police K9 Bite	1
Columbia Park	Taser	2
Como	Bodily Force	105
Como	Chemical Irritant	2

Como	Gun Point Display	4
Como	Improvised Weapon	2
Como	Maximal Restraint Technique	2
Como	Taser	15
Cooper	Bodily Force	8
Cooper	Chemical Irritant	1
Cooper	Police K9 Bite	2
Corcoran	Bodily Force	76
Corcoran	Chemical Irritant	2
Corcoran	Firearm	1
Corcoran	Gun Point Display	1
Corcoran	Improvised Weapon	1
Corcoran	Less Lethal	1
Corcoran	Maximal Restraint Technique	1
Corcoran	Taser	6
Diamond Lake	Bodily Force	27
Diamond Lake	Chemical Irritant	1
Diamond Lake	Improvised Weapon	1
Diamond Lake	Taser	3
Downtown East	Bodily Force	102
Downtown East	Chemical Irritant	3
Downtown East	Maximal Restraint Technique	2
Downtown East	Taser	24
Downtown West	Bodily Force	1,688
Downtown West	Chemical Irritant	999
Downtown West	Gun Point Display	8
Downtown West	Improvised Weapon	17
Downtown West	Less Lethal	7
Downtown West	Maximal Restraint Technique	19
Downtown West	Taser	190

ECCO	Bodily Force	20
ECCO	Chemical Irritant	2
ECCO	Taser	3
East Harriet	Bodily Force	15
East Harriet	Gun Point Display	1
East Harriet	Improvised Weapon	1
East Harriet	Taser	4
East Isles	Bodily Force	51
East Isles	Chemical Irritant	4
East Isles	Improvised Weapon	3
East Isles	Taser	6
East Phillips	Baton	1
East Phillips	Bodily Force	231
East Phillips	Chemical Irritant	16
East Phillips	Gun Point Display	6
East Phillips	Improvised Weapon	1
East Phillips	Maximal Restraint Technique	4
East Phillips	Police K9 Bite	2
East Phillips	Taser	31
Elliot Park	Baton	1
Elliot Park	Bodily Force	215
Elliot Park	Chemical Irritant	11
Elliot Park	Gun Point Display	1
Elliot Park	Improvised Weapon	2
Elliot Park	Less Lethal	3
Elliot Park	Maximal Restraint Technique	3
Elliot Park	Taser	47
Ericsson	Bodily Force	14
Ericsson	Improvised Weapon	1
Ericsson	Taser	1
Field	Bodily Force	10
Field	Taser	6

Folwell	Bodily Force	273
Folwell	Chemical Irritant	16
Folwell	Gun Point Display	6
Folwell	Improvised Weapon	10
Folwell	Maximal Restraint Technique	3
Folwell	Police K9 Bite	6
Folwell	Taser	31
Fulton	Bodily Force	15
Fulton	Improvised Weapon	1
Fulton	Taser	4
Hale	Bodily Force	1
Hale	Taser	1
Harrison	Bodily Force	130
Harrison	Chemical Irritant	8
Harrison	Gun Point Display	3
Harrison	Improvised Weapon	2
Harrison	Maximal Restraint Technique	3
Harrison	Police K9 Bite	1
Harrison	Taser	8
Hawthorne	Bodily Force	403
Hawthorne	Chemical Irritant	49
Hawthorne	Gun Point Display	5
Hawthorne	Improvised Weapon	6
Hawthorne	Less Lethal	2
Hawthorne	Maximal Restraint Technique	3
Hawthorne	Police K9 Bite	2
Hawthorne	Taser	32
Hiawatha	Bodily Force	39
Hiawatha	Police K9 Bite	1
Hiawatha	Taser	7
Holland	Bodily Force	112

Holland	Chemical Irritant	4
Holland	Gun Point Display	1
Holland	Less Lethal	5
Holland	Maximal Restraint Technique	1
Holland	Police K9 Bite	1
Holland	Taser	21
Howe	Bodily Force	29
Howe	Gun Point Display	1
Howe	Improvised Weapon	1
Howe	Police K9 Bite	2
Howe	Taser	9
Jordan	Bodily Force	383
Jordan	Chemical Irritant	15
Jordan	Gun Point Display	7
Jordan	Improvised Weapon	13
Jordan	Less Lethal Projectile	2
Jordan	Maximal Restraint Technique	7
Jordan	Police K9 Bite	4
Jordan	Taser	48
Keewaydin	Bodily Force	18
Keewaydin	Chemical Irritant	1
Keewaydin	Maximal Restraint Technique	1
Kenny	Bodily Force	1
Kenwood	Bodily Force	17
Kenwood	Chemical Irritant	2
Kenwood	Improvised Weapon	1
Kenwood	Maximal Restraint Technique	2
Kenwood	Taser	1
King Field	Bodily Force	72
King Field	Improvised Weapon	4

King Field	Maximal Restraint Technique	7
King Field	Police K9 Bite	1
King Field	Taser	3
Lind – Bohanon	Bodily Force	111
Lind – Bohanon	Chemical Irritant	5
Lind – Bohanon	Gun Point Display	2
Lind – Bohanon	Improvised Weapon	2
Lind – Bohanon	Less Lethal Projectile	1
Lind – Bohanon	Maximal Restraint Technique	4
Lind – Bohanon	Police K9 Bite	1
Lind – Bohanon	Taser	16
Linden Hills	Bodily Force	22
Linden Hills	Chemical Irritant	1
Linden Hills	Improvised Weapon	1
Linden Hills	Less Lethal	1
Linden Hills	Taser	1
Logan Park	Bodily Force	20
Logan Park	Chemical Irritant	1
Logan Park	Maximal Restraint Technique	3
Logan Park	Police K9 Bite	1
Logan Park	Taser	3
Longfellow	Bodily Force	99
Longfellow	Chemical Irritant	30
Longfellow	Gun Point Display	2
Longfellow	Less Lethal	21
Longfellow	Maximal Restraint Technique	1
Longfellow	Police K9 Bite	1
Longfellow	Taser	16
Loring Park	Bodily Force	287
Loring Park	Chemical Irritant	23
Loring Park	Gun Point Display	3

Loring Park	Improvised Weapon	4
Loring Park	Less Lethal	6
Loring Park	Maximal Restraint Technique	9
Loring Park	Police K9 Bite	2
Loring Park	Taser	80
Lowry Hill	Bodily Force	34
Lowry Hill	Chemical Irritant	7
Lowry Hill	Gun Point Display	1
Lowry Hill	Maximal Restraint Technique	2
Lowry Hill	Police K9 Bite	1
Lowry Hill	Taser	5
Lowry Hill East	Bodily Force	367
Lowry Hill East	Chemical Irritant	126
Lowry Hill East	Improvised Weapon	14
Lowry Hill East	Less Lethal	3
Lowry Hill East	Police K9 Bite	1
Lowry Hill East	Taser	43
Lyndale	Bodily Force	194
Lyndale	Chemical Irritant	6
Lyndale	Gun Point Display	2
Lyndale	Improvised Weapon	2
Lyndale	Less Lethal	4
Lyndale	Maximal Restraint Technique	5
Lyndale	Police K9 Bite	1
Lyndale	Taser	32
Lynnhurst	Bodily Force	17
Lynnhurst	Police K9 Bite	1
Lynnhurst	Taser	4
Marcy Holmes	Bodily Force	246
Marcy Holmes	Chemical Irritant	24
Marcy Holmes	Gun Point Display	2

Marcy Holmes	Less Lethal	5
Marcy Holmes	Maximal Restraint Technique	5
Marcy Holmes	Taser	28
Marshall Terrace	Bodily Force	21
Marshall Terrace	Maximal Restraint Technique	1
Marshall Terrace	Police K9 Bite	1
Marshall Terrace	Taser	4
McKinley	Bodily Force	143
McKinley	Gun Point Display	1
McKinley	Improvised Weapon	4
McKinley	Maximal Restraint Technique	2
McKinley	Police K9 Bite	4
McKinley	Taser	9
Mid – City Industrial	Bodily Force	25
Mid – City Industrial	Chemical Irritant	2
Mid – City Industrial	Maximal Restraint Technique	1
Mid – City Industrial	Taser	4
Midtown Phillips	Bodily Force	128
Midtown Phillips	Chemical Irritant	3
Midtown Phillips	Gun Point Display	1
Midtown Phillips	Improvised Weapon	4
Midtown Phillips	Police K9 Bite	3
Midtown Phillips	Taser	8
Minnehaha	Bodily Force	10
Morris Park	Bodily Force	6
Morris Park	Maximal Restraint Technique	1
Morris Park	Police K9 Bite	2
Morris Park	Taser	3
Near – North	Bodily Force	462
Near – North	Chemical Irritant	33

Near – North	Gun Point Display	6
Near – North	Improvised Weapon	6
Near – North	Less Lethal	1
Near – North	Maximal Restraint Technique	4
Near – North	Police K9 Bite	2
Near – North	Taser	48
Nicollet Island – East Bank	Baton	1
Nicollet Island – East Bank	Bodily Force	64
Nicollet Island – East Bank	Chemical Irritant	7
Nicollet Island – East Bank	Gun Point Display	2
Nicollet Island – East Bank	Improvised Weapon	1
Nicollet Island – East Bank	Less Lethal	1
Nicollet Island – East Bank	Maximal Restraint Technique	6
Nicollet Island – East Bank	Police K9 Bite	1
Nicollet Island – East Bank	Taser	23
North Loop	Bodily Force	253
North Loop	Chemical Irritant	27
North Loop	Improvised Weapon	1
North Loop	Less Lethal	2
North Loop	Maximal Restraint Technique	10
North Loop	Taser	30
Northeast Park	Bodily Force	52
Northeast Park	Chemical Irritant	2
Northeast Park	Less Lethal	2
Northeast Park	Police K9 Bite	1

Northeast Park	Taser	6
Northrop	Bodily Force	22
Northrop	Improvised Weapon	2
Northrop	Taser	2
Page	Bodily Force	4
Page	Taser	1
Phillips West	Bodily Force	113
Phillips West	Chemical Irritant	11
Phillips West	Gun Point Display	2
Phillips West	Improvised Weapon	1
Phillips West	Less Lethal	1
Phillips West	Taser	19
Powderhorn Park	Bodily Force	124
Powderhorn Park	Chemical Irritant	14
Powderhorn Park	Gun Point Display	2
Powderhorn Park	Improvised Weapon	1
Powderhorn Park	Less Lethal	1
Powderhorn Park	Maximal Restraint Technique	3
Powderhorn Park	Police K9 Bite	4
Powderhorn Park	Taser	22
Prospect Park – East River Road	Bodily Force	94
Prospect Park – East River Road	Chemical Irritant	3
Prospect Park – East River Road	Improvised Weapon	1
Prospect Park – East River Road	Less Lethal	4
Prospect Park – East River Road	Maximal Restraint Technique	7
Prospect Park – East River Road	Taser	31
Regina	Bodily Force	20
Regina	Taser	2

Seward	Bodily Force	88
Seward	Chemical Irritant	3
Seward	Less Lethal	2
Seward	Maximal Restraint Technique	3
Seward	Police K9 Bite	1
Seward	Taser	19
Sheridan	Bodily Force	26
Sheridan	Maximal Restraint Technique	2
Sheridan	Taser	7
Shingle Creek	Bodily Force	42
Shingle Creek	Maximal Restraint Technique	1
Shingle Creek	Taser	5
St. Anthony East	Bodily Force	24
St. Anthony East	Chemical Irritant	1
St. Anthony East	Gun Point Display	2
St. Anthony East	Police K9 Bite	1
St. Anthony East	Taser	4
St. Anthony West	Bodily Force	32
St. Anthony West	Improvised Weapon	1
St. Anthony West	Maximal Restraint Technique	4
St. Anthony West	Taser	10
Standish	Bodily Force	28
Standish	Chemical Irritant	9
Standish	Gun Point Display	1
Standish	Improvised Weapon	1
Standish	Less Lethal	1
Standish	Maximal Restraint Technique	2
Standish	Police K9 Bite	2
Standish	Taser	10

Steven's Square – Loring Heights	Bodily Force	174
Steven's Square – Loring Heights	Chemical Irritant	1
Steven's Square – Loring Heights	Improvised Weapon	10
Steven's Square – Loring Heights	Less Lethal	1
Steven's Square – Loring Heights	Maximal Restraint Technique	3
Steven's Square – Loring Heights	Police K9 Bite	1
Steven's Square – Loring Heights	Taser	35
Sumner – Glenwood	Bodily Force	31
Sumner – Glenwood	Gun Point Display	2
Sumner – Glenwood	Maximal Restraint Technique	2
Sumner – Glenwood	Taser	5
Tangletown	Bodily Force	37
Tangletown	Chemical Irritant	1
Tangletown	Less Lethal	1
Tangletown	Taser	4
University of Minnesota	Bodily Force	32
University of Minnesota	Chemical Irritant	8
University of Minnesota	Gun Point Display	2
University of Minnesota	Maximal Restraint Technique	2
University of Minnesota	Taser	8
Ventura Village	Bodily Force	155
Ventura Village	Chemical Irritant	5
Ventura Village	Gun Point Display	2
Ventura Village	Improvised Weapon	2

Ventura Village	Less Lethal	1
Ventura Village	Maximal Restraint Technique	4
Ventura Village	Police K9 Bite	2
Ventura Village	Taser	27
Victory	Bodily Force	39
Victory	Chemical Irritant	6
Victory	Police K9 Bite	2
Victory	Taser	6
Waite Park	Bodily Force	59
Waite Park	Chemical Irritant	2
Waite Park	Gun Point Display	1
Waite Park	Maximal Restraint Technique	5
Waite Park	Police K9 Bite	1
Waite Park	Taser	5
Webber – Camden	Bodily Force	163
Webber – Camden	Chemical Irritant	16
Webber – Camden	Gun Point Display	5
Webber – Camden	Improvised Weapon	2
Webber – Camden	Maximal Restraint Technique	3
Webber – Camden	Police K9 Bite	1
Webber – Camden	Taser	19
Wenonah	Bodily Force	33
Wenonah	Firearm	1
Wenonah	Less Lethal	1
Wenonah	Taser	7
West Calhoun	Bodily Force	12
West Calhoun	Taser	1
Whittier	Bodily Force	384
Whittier	Chemical Irritant	17
Whittier	Gun Point Display	6
Whittier	Improvised Weapon	12

Whittier	Less Lethal	2
Whittier	Maximal Restraint Technique	3
Whittier	Police K9 Bite	1
Whittier	Taser	45
Willard – Hay	Baton	1
Willard – Hay	Bodily Force	256
Willard – Hay	Chemical Irritant	2
Willard – Hay	Gun Point Display	4
Willard – Hay	Improvised Weapon	2
Willard – Hay	Police K9 Bite	3
Willard – Hay	Taser	32
Windom	Bodily Force	54
Windom	Gun Point Display	1
Windom	Less Lethal	2
Windom	Maximal Restraint Technique	2
Windom	Taser	21
Windom Park	Bodily Force	44
Windom Park	Chemical Irritant	3
Windom Park	Gun Point Display	1
Windom Park	Less Lethal	1
Windom Park	Police K9 Bite	1
Windom Park	Taser	13

We see that:

- The "Bodily Force" type was applied 1688 times in "Downtown West" compared to 10 times in "Beltrami" and 1 time only in "Hale." So "Bodily Force" was applied more in "Downtown West" than in other neighborhoods.
- The "Chemical Irritant" force type was applied 999 times in "Downtown West" but never applied in "Beltrami" and "Hale." So "Chemical Irritant" was applied more in "Downtown West" than in other neighborhoods.

5.2.2. The Proportion

When examining the relation between 2 categorical variables, the proportion or percentage is preferred over counts because this allows comparison between the different levels of one categorical variable if they have different sample sizes.

5.2.2.1. The Proportion of Different Employment Statuses in the 2 Genders

To get these proportions, we use the following functions:

- The count function with the arguments gender, and employment to get the count of different employment statuses in males and females.
- The drop_na function deletes any rows that contain missings in the gender or employment status.
- The group_by function with the gender argument to split the count results into two, one for males and one for females.
- The mutate function creates a new column "proportion" by dividing the count over the sum of counts for each gender. The sum of proportions will be 1 or 100% for each gender.
- The arrange function with the argument desc(proportion) to arrange the proportions in descending order. Then we convert the result to a table as before.

```
acs12 %>% count(gender, employment) %>% drop_na() %>%

 group_by(gender) %>% mutate(proportion = n/sum(n)) %>%

 arrange(desc(proportion)) %>%

 flextable() %>% theme_box() %>%

 set_caption(caption = "The count and proportion of different employment statuses in males and females of the American Community Survey data")
```

Table 5.5. The Count and Proportion of Different Employment Statuses in Males and Females of the American Community Survey Data

Gender	Employment	n	Proportion
male	employed	470	0.5788177
female	not in labor force	373	0.4703657

Gender	Employment	n	Proportion
female	employed	373	0.4703657
male	not in labor force	283	0.3485222
male	unemployed	59	0.0726601
female	unemployed	47	0.0592686

We see that:

- The percentage of employed males is 57.9% compared to 47% of females. So males are more employed than females.
- The percentage of females not in labor force is 47% compared to 34.9% of males. So females are more likely to not be in the labor force than males.
- The percentage of unemployed males is 7.3% compared to 5.9% of females. So males are more unemployed than females.

5.2.2.2. The Proportion of Different Employment Statuses in the Different Races

We use the same functions as above but group by race instead to get the proportions of employment statuses in each race.

```
acs12 %>% count(race, employment) %>% drop_na() %>%

 group_by(race) %>% mutate(proportion = n/sum(n)) %>%

 arrange(desc(proportion)) %>%

 flextable() %>% theme_box() %>%

 set_caption(caption = "The count and proportion of different employment statuses
in the different races of the American Community Survey data")
```

Table 5.6. The Count and Proportion of Different Employment Statuses in the Different Races of the American Community Survey Data

Race	Employment	n	Proportion
other	employed	58	0.53703704
asian	employed	39	0.53424658
white	employed	670	0.53090333

Race	Employment	n	Proportion
black	employed	76	0.46913580
asian	not in labor force	31	0.42465753
white	not in labor force	520	0.41204437
black	not in labor force	66	0.40740741
other	not in labor force	39	0.36111111
black	unemployed	20	0.12345679
other	unemployed	11	0.10185185
white	unemployed	72	0.05705230
asian	unemployed	3	0.04109589

We see that:

- The percentage of employed other races is 53.7% compared to 53.4% Asians, 53% Whites, and 46.9% Blacks. So Blacks are less employed than other races.
- The percentage of Asians not in labor force is 42.5% compared to 41.2% Whites, 40.7% Blacks, and 36% other races. So other races are less likely to not be in the labor force than other races.
- The percentage of unemployed Blacks is 12.3% compared to 10% of other races, 5.7% of Whites, and 4.1% of Asians. So Blacks are more unemployed than other races.

5.2.2.3. The Proportion of Force Types in the Different Races

We use the same functions as above but group by race instead to get the proportions of the different force types used in each race.

```
mn_police_use_of_force %>% count(race, force_type) %>% drop_na() %>%

 group_by(race) %>% mutate(proportion = n/sum(n)) %>%

 arrange(desc(proportion)) %>%



 flextable() %>% theme_box() %>%

 set_caption(caption = "The count and proportion of different force types applied on different races from the Minneapolis police use of force data")
```

Table 5.7. The Count and Proportion of Different Force Types Applied on Different Races from the Minneapolis Police Use of Force Data

Race	force_type	n	Proportion
Pacific Islander	Bodily Force	5	0.8333333333
Native American	Bodily Force	616	0.7857142857
White	Bodily Force	2,454	0.7842761266
Black	Bodily Force	5,519	0.7216265690
Other/Mixed Race	Bodily Force	137	0.6682926829
Asian	Bodily Force	78	0.6046511628
Asian	Chemical Irritant	32	0.2480620155
Other/Mixed Race	Chemical Irritant	50	0.2439024390
Pacific Islander	Chemical Irritant	1	0.1666666667
Black	Chemical Irritant	1,033	0.1350679916
Native American	Taser	104	0.1326530612
Asian	Taser	17	0.1317829457
White	Taser	334	0.1067433685
Black	Taser	755	0.0987186192
White	Chemical Irritant	191	0.0610418664
Other/Mixed Race	Taser	12	0.0585365854
Native American	Chemical Irritant	18	0.0229591837
Native American	Maximal Restraint Technique	14	0.0178571429
White	Improvised Weapon	47	0.0150207734
Other/Mixed Race	Gun Point Display	3	0.0146341463
Black	Maximal Restraint Technique	104	0.0135983264

Race	force_type	n	Proportion
White	Maximal Restraint Technique	42	0.0134228188
Native American	Improvised Weapon	10	0.0127551020
Black	Improvised Weapon	83	0.0108525105
Native American	Gun Point Display	8	0.0102040816
Native American	Police K9 Bite	8	0.0102040816
Black	Gun Point Display	76	0.0099372385
Other/Mixed Race	Police K9 Bite	2	0.0097560976
White	Less Lethal	27	0.0086289549
Asian	Gun Point Display	1	0.0077519380
Asian	Improvised Weapon	1	0.0077519380
Native American	Less Lethal	6	0.0076530612
Black	Police K9 Bite	48	0.0062761506
White	Police K9 Bite	17	0.0054330457
White	Gun Point Display	16	0.0051134548
Other/Mixed Race	Improvised Weapon	1	0.0048780488
Black	Less Lethal	23	0.0030073222
Black	Less Lethal Projectile	3	0.0003922594
White	Baton	1	0.0003195909
Black	Baton	2	0.0002615063
Black	Firearm	2	0.0002615063

We see that:

- The “Bodily Force” type was applied mostly to Pacific Islanders (83.3%) compared to 78.6% on Native Americans, 78.4% on Whites, 72.2% on Blacks, 66.8% on Other/Mixed Races, and 60.5% on Asians. So “Bodily Force” was applied less frequently to Asians and more frequently to Pacific Islanders than to other races.
- The “Chemical Irritant” force type was applied to Asians 24.8% of the time compared to 24.4% on Other/Mixed Races, 16.7% on Pacific

Islanders, 13.5% on Blacks, 6.1% on Whites, and 2.3% on Native Americans. So "Chemical Irritant" was applied less frequently to Native Americans and more frequently to Asians than to other races.

5.2.2.4. The Proportion of Force Types in the Different Neighborhoods

We use the same functions as above but group by neighborhood instead to get the proportions of the different force types used in each neighborhood. We also filter out when the neighborhood is an empty space by using the filter function with the argument !neighborhood=="."

```
mn_police_use_of_force %>% count(neighborhood,force_type) %>%

 filter(!neighborhood=="") %>%

 drop_na() %>%

 group_by(neighborhood) %>% mutate(proportion = n/sum(n)) %>%

 arrange(desc(proportion)) %>%

 flextable() %>%

 theme_box() %>%

 set_caption(caption = "The count and proportion of different force types applied
in the different neighborhoods from the Minneapolis police use of force data")
```

Table 5.8. The Count and Proportion of Different Force Types applied in the Different Neighborhoods from the Minneapolis Police use of Force Data

Neighborhood	**force_type**	**n**	**Proportion**
Camden Industrial	Bodily Force	3	1.000000000
Kenny	Bodily Force	1	1.000000000
Minnehaha	Bodily Force	10	1.000000000
West Calhoun	Bodily Force	12	0.923076923
Beltrami	Bodily Force	10	0.909090909
Regina	Bodily Force	20	0.909090909
Audubon Park	Bodily Force	89	0.908163265
Keewaydin	Bodily Force	18	0.900000000

Cleveland	Bodily Force	86	0.886597938
Bryant	Bodily Force	22	0.880000000
CARAG	Bodily Force	154	0.880000000
McKinley	Bodily Force	143	0.877300613
Ericsson	Bodily Force	14	0.875000000
Shingle Creek	Bodily Force	42	0.875000000
Midtown Phillips	Bodily Force	128	0.870748299
Tangletown	Bodily Force	37	0.860465116
Corcoran	Bodily Force	76	0.853932584
Willard – Hay	Bodily Force	256	0.853333333
Linden Hills	Bodily Force	22	0.846153846
Northrop	Bodily Force	22	0.846153846
Diamond Lake	Bodily Force	27	0.843750000
Harrison	Bodily Force	130	0.838709677
Bryn – Mawr	Bodily Force	15	0.833333333
Hiawatha	Bodily Force	39	0.829787234
King Field	Bodily Force	72	0.827586207
Northeast Park	Bodily Force	52	0.825396825
Near – North	Bodily Force	462	0.822064057
Whittier	Bodily Force	384	0.817021277
Waite Park	Bodily Force	59	0.808219178
Como	Bodily Force	105	0.807692308
Hawthorne	Bodily Force	403	0.802788845
ECCO	Bodily Force	20	0.800000000
Page	Bodily Force	4	0.800000000
Jordan	Bodily Force	383	0.799582463
East Isles	Bodily Force	51	0.796875000
Marcy Holmes	Bodily Force	246	0.793548387
Folwell	Bodily Force	273	0.791304348
East Phillips	Bodily Force	231	0.791095890
Lyndale	Bodily Force	194	0.788617886
Wenonah	Bodily Force	33	0.785714286
North Loop	Bodily Force	253	0.783281734

Ventura Village	Bodily Force	155	0.782828283
Lind – Bohanon	Bodily Force	111	0.781690141
Mid – City Industrial	Bodily Force	25	0.781250000
Webber – Camden	Bodily Force	163	0.779904306
Downtown East	Bodily Force	102	0.778625954
Marshall Terrace	Bodily Force	21	0.777777778
Columbia Park	Bodily Force	31	0.775000000
Sumner – Glenwood	Bodily Force	31	0.775000000
Steven's Square – Loring Heights	Bodily Force	174	0.773333333
Lynnhurst	Bodily Force	17	0.772727273
Holland	Bodily Force	112	0.772413793
Central	Bodily Force	122	0.772151899
Phillips West	Bodily Force	113	0.768707483
Bancroft	Bodily Force	23	0.766666667
Elliot Park	Bodily Force	215	0.759717314
Seward	Bodily Force	88	0.758620690
Fulton	Bodily Force	15	0.750000000
St. Anthony East	Bodily Force	24	0.750000000
Sheridan	Bodily Force	26	0.742857143
Kenwood	Bodily Force	17	0.739130435
Victory	Bodily Force	39	0.735849057
Cooper	Bodily Force	8	0.727272727
Powderhorn Park	Bodily Force	124	0.725146199
East Harriet	Bodily Force	15	0.714285714
Logan Park	Bodily Force	20	0.714285714
Bottineau	Bodily Force	7	0.700000000
Windom Park	Bodily Force	44	0.698412698
Loring Park	Bodily Force	287	0.693236715
Howe	Bodily Force	29	0.690476190
St. Anthony West	Bodily Force	32	0.680851064
Lowry Hill	Bodily Force	34	0.680000000

Armatage	Bodily Force	19	0.678571429
Windom	Bodily Force	54	0.675000000
Prospect Park – East River Road	Bodily Force	94	0.671428571
Cedar – Isles – Dean	Bodily Force	4	0.666666667
Cedar Riverside	Bodily Force	136	0.663414634
Lowry Hill East	Bodily Force	367	0.662454874
Field	Bodily Force	10	0.625000000
University of Minnesota	Bodily Force	32	0.615384615
Nicollet Island – East Bank	Bodily Force	64	0.603773585
Longfellow	Bodily Force	99	0.582352941
Downtown West	Bodily Force	1,688	0.576502732
Standish	Bodily Force	28	0.518518519
Hale	Bodily Force	1	0.500000000
Hale	Taser	1	0.500000000
Morris Park	Bodily Force	6	0.500000000
Field	Taser	6	0.375000000
Downtown West	Chemical Irritant	999	0.341188525
Cedar – Isles – Dean	Chemical Irritant	2	0.333333333
Windom	Taser	21	0.262500000
Morris Park	Taser	3	0.250000000
Lowry Hill East	Chemical Irritant	126	0.227436823
Prospect Park – East River Road	Taser	31	0.221428571
Nicollet Island – East Bank	Taser	23	0.216981132
Armatage	Taser	6	0.214285714
Howe	Taser	9	0.214285714
St. Anthony West	Taser	10	0.212765957
Windom Park	Taser	13	0.206349206
Fulton	Taser	4	0.200000000

Page	Taser	1	0.200000000
Sheridan	Taser	7	0.200000000
Loring Park	Taser	80	0.193236715
East Harriet	Taser	4	0.190476190
Standish	Taser	10	0.185185185
Downtown East	Taser	24	0.183206107
Cooper	Police K9 Bite	2	0.181818182
Lynnhurst	Taser	4	0.181818182
Longfellow	Chemical Irritant	30	0.176470588
Bryn – Mawr	Taser	3	0.166666667
Morris Park	Police K9 Bite	2	0.166666667
Standish	Chemical Irritant	9	0.166666667
Wenonah	Taser	7	0.166666667
Elliot Park	Taser	47	0.166077739
Seward	Taser	19	0.163793103
Steven's Square – Loring Heights	Taser	35	0.155555556
University of Minnesota	Chemical Irritant	8	0.153846154
University of Minnesota	Taser	8	0.153846154
Cedar Riverside	Chemical Irritant	31	0.151219512
Hiawatha	Taser	7	0.148936170
Marshall Terrace	Taser	4	0.148148148
Central	Taser	23	0.145569620
Holland	Taser	21	0.144827586
Lowry Hill	Chemical Irritant	7	0.140000000
Ventura Village	Taser	27	0.136363636
Bancroft	Chemical Irritant	4	0.133333333
Lyndale	Taser	32	0.130081301
Phillips West	Taser	19	0.129251701
Powderhorn Park	Taser	22	0.128654971
Columbia Park	Maximal Restraint Technique	5	0.125000000

Mid – City Industrial	Taser	4	0.125000000
St. Anthony East	Taser	4	0.125000000
Sumner – Glenwood	Taser	5	0.125000000
Longfellow	Less Lethal	21	0.123529412
ECCO	Taser	3	0.120000000
Cedar Riverside	Taser	24	0.117073171
Como	Taser	15	0.115384615
Victory	Chemical Irritant	6	0.113207547
Victory	Taser	6	0.113207547
Lind – Bohanon	Taser	16	0.112676056
Logan Park	Maximal Restraint Technique	3	0.107142857
Logan Park	Taser	3	0.107142857
Willard – Hay	Taser	32	0.106666667
East Phillips	Taser	31	0.106164384
Shingle Creek	Taser	5	0.104166667
Jordan	Taser	48	0.100208768
Bottineau	Chemical Irritant	1	0.100000000
Bottineau	Police K9 Bite	1	0.100000000
Bottineau	Taser	1	0.100000000
Lowry Hill	Taser	5	0.100000000
Hawthorne	Chemical Irritant	49	0.097609562
Whittier	Taser	45	0.095744681
Northeast Park	Taser	6	0.095238095
Longfellow	Taser	16	0.094117647
Diamond Lake	Taser	3	0.093750000
East Isles	Taser	6	0.093750000
Tangletown	Taser	4	0.093023256
North Loop	Taser	30	0.092879257
Beltrami	Less Lethal	1	0.090909091
Cooper	Chemical Irritant	1	0.090909091

Regina	Taser	2	0.090909091
Webber – Camden	Taser	19	0.090909091
Marcy Holmes	Taser	28	0.090322581
Folwell	Taser	31	0.089855072
Kenwood	Chemical Irritant	2	0.086956522
Kenwood	Maximal Restraint Technique	2	0.086956522
Near – North	Taser	48	0.085409253
St. Anthony West	Maximal Restraint Technique	4	0.085106383
North Loop	Chemical Irritant	27	0.083591331
Morris Park	Maximal Restraint Technique	1	0.083333333
Powderhorn Park	Chemical Irritant	14	0.081871345
King Field	Maximal Restraint Technique	7	0.080459770
Bryant	Police K9 Bite	2	0.080000000
ECCO	Chemical Irritant	2	0.080000000
Lowry Hill East	Taser	43	0.077617329
Marcy Holmes	Chemical Irritant	24	0.077419355
Northrop	Improvised Weapon	2	0.076923077
Northrop	Taser	2	0.076923077
West Calhoun	Taser	1	0.076923077
Webber – Camden	Chemical Irritant	16	0.076555024
Phillips West	Chemical Irritant	11	0.074829932
CARAG	Taser	12	0.068571429
Waite Park	Maximal Restraint Technique	5	0.068493151
Waite Park	Taser	5	0.068493151
Corcoran	Taser	6	0.067415730
Bancroft	Improvised Weapon	2	0.066666667
Nicollet Island – East Bank	Chemical Irritant	7	0.066037736
Downtown West	Taser	190	0.064890710

Hawthorne	Taser	32	0.063745020
Central	Chemical Irritant	10	0.063291139
East Isles	Chemical Irritant	4	0.062500000
Ericsson	Improvised Weapon	1	0.062500000
Ericsson	Taser	1	0.062500000
Mid – City Industrial	Chemical Irritant	2	0.062500000
St. Anthony East	Gun Point Display	2	0.062500000
Audubon Park	Taser	6	0.061224490
Near – North	Chemical Irritant	33	0.058718861
Sheridan	Maximal Restraint Technique	2	0.057142857
Nicollet Island – East Bank	Maximal Restraint Technique	6	0.056603774
Loring Park	Chemical Irritant	23	0.055555556
McKinley	Taser	9	0.055214724
East Phillips	Chemical Irritant	16	0.054794521
Midtown Phillips	Taser	8	0.054421769
Harrison	Chemical Irritant	8	0.051612903
Harrison	Taser	8	0.051612903
Columbia Park	Taser	2	0.050000000
Fulton	Improvised Weapon	1	0.050000000
Keewaydin	Chemical Irritant	1	0.050000000
Keewaydin	Maximal Restraint Technique	1	0.050000000
Prospect Park – East River Road	Maximal Restraint Technique	7	0.050000000
Sumner – Glenwood	Gun Point Display	2	0.050000000
Sumner – Glenwood	Maximal Restraint Technique	2	0.050000000
East Harriet	Gun Point Display	1	0.047619048
East Harriet	Improvised Weapon	1	0.047619048
Howe	Police K9 Bite	2	0.047619048
Windom Park	Chemical Irritant	3	0.047619048

East Isles	Improvised Weapon	3	0.046875000
Folwell	Chemical Irritant	16	0.046376812
King Field	Improvised Weapon	4	0.045977011
Lynnhurst	Police K9 Bite	1	0.045454545
Steven's Square – Loring Heights	Improvised Weapon	10	0.044444444
Kenwood	Improvised Weapon	1	0.043478261
Kenwood	Taser	1	0.043478261
Cleveland	Taser	4	0.041237113
Bryant	Taser	1	0.040000000
Lowry Hill	Maximal Restraint Tech-nique	2	0.040000000
Elliot Park	Chemical Irritant	11	0.038869258
Linden Hills	Chemical Irritant	1	0.038461538
Linden Hills	Improvised Weapon	1	0.038461538
Linden Hills	Less Lethal	1	0.038461538
Linden Hills	Taser	1	0.038461538
University of Minnesota	Gun Point Display	2	0.038461538
University of Minnesota	Maximal Restraint Tech-nique	2	0.038461538
Victory	Police K9 Bite	2	0.037735849
Marshall Terrace	Maximal Restraint Tech-nique	1	0.037037037
Marshall Terrace	Police K9 Bite	1	0.037037037
Standish	Maximal Restraint Tech-nique	2	0.037037037
Standish	Police K9 Bite	2	0.037037037
Whittier	Chemical Irritant	17	0.036170213
Armatage	Chemical Irritant	1	0.035714286
Armatage	Maximal Restraint Tech-nique	1	0.035714286
Armatage	Police K9 Bite	1	0.035714286
Logan Park	Chemical Irritant	1	0.035714286
Logan Park	Police K9 Bite	1	0.035714286

Lind – Bohanon	Chemical Irritant	5	0.035211268
Holland	Less Lethal	5	0.034482759
King Field	Taser	3	0.034482759
Bancroft	Taser	1	0.033333333
Northeast Park	Chemical Irritant	2	0.031746032
Northeast Park	Less Lethal	2	0.031746032
Jordan	Chemical Irritant	15	0.031315240
Diamond Lake	Chemical Irritant	1	0.031250000
Diamond Lake	Improvised Weapon	1	0.031250000
Mid – City Industrial	Maximal Restraint Technique	1	0.031250000
St. Anthony East	Chemical Irritant	1	0.031250000
St. Anthony East	Police K9 Bite	1	0.031250000
North Loop	Maximal Restraint Technique	10	0.030959752
Como	Gun Point Display	4	0.030769231
Audubon Park	Chemical Irritant	3	0.030612245
Folwell	Improvised Weapon	10	0.028985507
Prospect Park – East River Road	Less Lethal	4	0.028571429
Lind – Bohanon	Maximal Restraint Technique	4	0.028169014
Holland	Chemical Irritant	4	0.027586207
Waite Park	Chemical Irritant	2	0.027397260
Midtown Phillips	Improvised Weapon	4	0.027210884
Jordan	Improvised Weapon	13	0.027139875
Seward	Chemical Irritant	3	0.025862069
Seward	Maximal Restraint Technique	3	0.025862069
Whittier	Improvised Weapon	12	0.025531915
Lowry Hill East	Improvised Weapon	14	0.025270758
Ventura Village	Chemical Irritant	5	0.025252525
Columbia Park	Less Lethal	1	0.025000000
Columbia Park	Police K9 Bite	1	0.025000000
Windom	Less Lethal	2	0.025000000

Windom	Maximal Restraint Technique	2	0.025000000
McKinley	Improvised Weapon	4	0.024539877
McKinley	Police K9 Bite	4	0.024539877
Lyndale	Chemical Irritant	6	0.024390244
Webber – Camden	Gun Point Display	5	0.023923445
Howe	Gun Point Display	1	0.023809524
Howe	Improvised Weapon	1	0.023809524
Wenonah	Firearm	1	0.023809524
Wenonah	Less Lethal	1	0.023809524
Powderhorn Park	Police K9 Bite	4	0.023391813
Tangletown	Chemical Irritant	1	0.023255814
Tangletown	Less Lethal	1	0.023255814
Downtown East	Chemical Irritant	3	0.022900763
CARAG	Chemical Irritant	4	0.022857143
Corcoran	Chemical Irritant	2	0.022471910
Loring Park	Maximal Restraint Technique	9	0.021739130
Prospect Park – East River Road	Chemical Irritant	3	0.021428571
Hiawatha	Police K9 Bite	1	0.021276596
St. Anthony West	Improvised Weapon	1	0.021276596
Shingle Creek	Maximal Restraint Technique	1	0.020833333
Cleveland	Maximal Restraint Technique	2	0.020618557
Cleveland	Police K9 Bite	2	0.020618557
East Phillips	Gun Point Display	6	0.020547945
Midtown Phillips	Chemical Irritant	3	0.020408163
Midtown Phillips	Police K9 Bite	3	0.020408163
Lyndale	Maximal Restraint Technique	5	0.020325203
Ventura Village	Maximal Restraint Technique	4	0.020202020
Lowry Hill	Gun Point Display	1	0.020000000

Lowry Hill	Police K9 Bite	1	0.020000000
Cedar Riverside	Maximal Restraint Technique	4	0.019512195
Harrison	Gun Point Display	3	0.019354839
Harrison	Maximal Restraint Technique	3	0.019354839
Nicollet Island – East Bank	Gun Point Display	2	0.018867925
Standish	Gun Point Display	1	0.018518519
Standish	Improvised Weapon	1	0.018518519
Standish	Less Lethal	1	0.018518519
Powderhorn Park	Maximal Restraint Technique	3	0.017543860
Folwell	Gun Point Display	6	0.017391304
Folwell	Police K9 Bite	6	0.017391304
Seward	Less Lethal	2	0.017241379
CARAG	Improvised Weapon	3	0.017142857
Lyndale	Less Lethal	4	0.016260163
Marcy Holmes	Less Lethal	5	0.016129032
Marcy Holmes	Maximal Restraint Technique	5	0.016129032
Northeast Park	Police K9 Bite	1	0.015873016
Windom Park	Gun Point Display	1	0.015873016
Windom Park	Less Lethal	1	0.015873016
Windom Park	Police K9 Bite	1	0.015873016
Como	Chemical Irritant	2	0.015384615
Como	Improvised Weapon	2	0.015384615
Como	Maximal Restraint Technique	2	0.015384615
Downtown East	Maximal Restraint Technique	2	0.015267176
Cedar Riverside	Gun Point Display	3	0.014634146
Cedar Riverside	Less Lethal	3	0.014634146
Cedar Riverside	Police K9 Bite	3	0.014634146
Jordan	Gun Point Display	7	0.014613779

Jordan	Maximal Restraint Technique	7	0.014613779
Loring Park	Less Lethal	6	0.014492754
Webber – Camden	Maximal Restraint Technique	3	0.014354067
Lind – Bohanon	Gun Point Display	2	0.014084507
Lind – Bohanon	Improvised Weapon	2	0.014084507
East Phillips	Maximal Restraint Technique	4	0.013698630
Waite Park	Gun Point Display	1	0.013698630
Waite Park	Police K9 Bite	1	0.013698630
Phillips West	Gun Point Display	2	0.013605442
Steven's Square – Loring Heights	Maximal Restraint Technique	3	0.013333333
Willard – Hay	Gun Point Display	4	0.013333333
Harrison	Improvised Weapon	2	0.012903226
Whittier	Gun Point Display	6	0.012765957
Central	Gun Point Display	2	0.012658228
Windom	Gun Point Display	1	0.012500000
McKinley	Maximal Restraint Technique	2	0.012269939
Hawthorne	Improvised Weapon	6	0.011952191
Longfellow	Gun Point Display	2	0.011764706
Powderhorn Park	Gun Point Display	2	0.011695906
King Field	Police K9 Bite	1	0.011494253
Corcoran	Firearm	1	0.011235955
Corcoran	Gun Point Display	1	0.011235955
Corcoran	Improvised Weapon	1	0.011235955
Corcoran	Less Lethal	1	0.011235955
Corcoran	Maximal Restraint Technique	1	0.011235955
Near – North	Gun Point Display	6	0.010676157
Near – North	Improvised Weapon	6	0.010676157
Elliot Park	Less Lethal	3	0.010600707
Elliot Park	Maximal Restraint Technique	3	0.010600707

Cleveland	Chemical Irritant	1	0.010309278
Cleveland	Gun Point Display	1	0.010309278
Cleveland	Improvised Weapon	1	0.010309278
Ventura Village	Gun Point Display	2	0.010101010
Ventura Village	Improvised Weapon	2	0.010101010
Ventura Village	Police K9 Bite	2	0.010101010
Willard – Hay	Police K9 Bite	3	0.010000000
Hawthorne	Gun Point Display	5	0.009960159
Loring Park	Improvised Weapon	4	0.009661836
Webber – Camden	Improvised Weapon	2	0.009569378
Nicollet Island – East Bank	Baton	1	0.009433962
Nicollet Island – East Bank	Improvised Weapon	1	0.009433962
Nicollet Island – East Bank	Less Lethal	1	0.009433962
Nicollet Island – East Bank	Police K9 Bite	1	0.009433962
Folwell	Maximal Restraint Technique	3	0.008695652
Seward	Police K9 Bite	1	0.008620690
Jordan	Police K9 Bite	4	0.008350731
Lyndale	Gun Point Display	2	0.008130081
Lyndale	Improvised Weapon	2	0.008130081
Loring Park	Gun Point Display	3	0.007246377
Prospect Park – East River Road	Improvised Weapon	1	0.007142857
Near – North	Maximal Restraint Technique	4	0.007117438
Elliot Park	Improvised Weapon	2	0.007067138
Lind – Bohanon	Less Lethal Projectile	1	0.007042254
Lind – Bohanon	Police K9 Bite	1	0.007042254
Holland	Gun Point Display	1	0.006896552
Holland	Maximal Restraint Technique	1	0.006896552

Holland	Police K9 Bite	1	0.006896552
East Phillips	Police K9 Bite	2	0.006849315
Midtown Phillips	Gun Point Display	1	0.006802721
Phillips West	Improvised Weapon	1	0.006802721
Phillips West	Less Lethal	1	0.006802721
Willard – Hay	Chemical Irritant	2	0.006666667
Willard – Hay	Improvised Weapon	2	0.006666667
Downtown West	Maximal Restraint Tech-nique	19	0.006489071
Harrison	Police K9 Bite	1	0.006451613
Marcy Holmes	Gun Point Display	2	0.006451613
Whittier	Maximal Restraint Tech-nique	3	0.006382979
Central	Police K9 Bite	1	0.006329114
North Loop	Less Lethal	2	0.006191950
McKinley	Gun Point Display	1	0.006134969
Hawthorne	Maximal Restraint Tech-nique	3	0.005976096
Longfellow	Maximal Restraint Tech-nique	1	0.005882353
Longfellow	Police K9 Bite	1	0.005882353
Powderhorn Park	Improvised Weapon	1	0.005847953
Powderhorn Park	Less Lethal	1	0.005847953
Downtown West	Improvised Weapon	17	0.005806011
CARAG	Gun Point Display	1	0.005714286
CARAG	Police K9 Bite	1	0.005714286
Lowry Hill East	Less Lethal	3	0.005415162
Ventura Village	Less Lethal	1	0.005050505
Cedar Riverside	Improvised Weapon	1	0.004878049
Loring Park	Police K9 Bite	2	0.004830918
Webber – Camden	Police K9 Bite	1	0.004784689
Steven's Square – Loring Heights	Chemical Irritant	1	0.004444444
Steven's Square – Loring Heights	Less Lethal	1	0.004444444

Steven's Square – Loring Heights	Police K9 Bite	1	0.004444444
Whittier	Less Lethal	2	0.004255319
Jordan	Less Lethal Projectile	2	0.004175365
Lyndale	Police K9 Bite	1	0.004065041
Hawthorne	Less Lethal	2	0.003984064
Hawthorne	Police K9 Bite	2	0.003984064
Near – North	Police K9 Bite	2	0.003558719
Elliot Park	Baton	1	0.003533569
Elliot Park	Gun Point Display	1	0.003533569
East Phillips	Baton	1	0.003424658
East Phillips	Improvised Weapon	1	0.003424658
Willard – Hay	Baton	1	0.003333333
North Loop	Improvised Weapon	1	0.003095975
Downtown West	Gun Point Display	8	0.002732240
Downtown West	Less Lethal	7	0.002390710
Whittier	Police K9 Bite	1	0.002127660
Lowry Hill East	Police K9 Bite	1	0.001805054
Near – North	Less Lethal	1	0.001779359

We see that:

- The "Bodily Force" type was applied at all times in "Camden Industrial," "Kenny," and "Minnehaha" with a percentage of 100%, but they have sample sizes of 3,1, and 10 respectively for this force type.
- The "Bodily Force" type was applied less frequently in "Hale," "Morris Park," "Standish," and "Downtown West" with a percentage of 50%,50%,51.9%, and 57.7% but they have sample sizes of 1,6,28 and 1688 respectively for this force type.
- The "Chemical Irritant" force type was applied mostly in "Downtown West," "Cedar – Isles – Dean," and "Lowry Hill East" with a percentage of 34.1%,33.3%, and 22.7% respectively, but they have sample sizes of 999,2, and 126 respectively for this force type.
- The "Chemical Irritant" type was applied less frequently in "Steven's Square – Loring Heights," "Willard – Hay," "Cleveland," and "Como" with a percentage of 0.44%,0.67%,1%, and 1.5% respectively, but they have sample sizes of 1,2,1,2 respectively for this force type.

5.2.2.5. The Proportion of Force Types in the 10 Most Frequent Neighborhoods

Instead of looking at the 86 different neighborhoods, we can look at the 10 most frequent neighborhoods using the fct_lump_n function with the argument n=10 within the mutate function. We can see the result of this function by using the count function with the argument neighborhood after these functions.

```
mn_police_use_of_force %>%

 mutate(neighborhood= fct_lump_n(neighborhood, n=10)) %>%

 count(neighborhood) %>%

 flextable() %>%

 theme_box() %>%

 set_caption(caption = "The count of the 10 most frequent neighborhoods from the Minneapolis police use of force data")
```

Table 5.9. The Count of the 10 Most Frequent Neighborhoods from the Minneapolis Police use of Force Data

Neighborhood	**n**
Downtown West	2,928
Folwell	345
Hawthorne	502
Jordan	479
Loring Park	414
Lowry Hill East	554
Marcy Holmes	310
Near – North	562
North Loop	323
Whittier	470
Other	6,038

So the 10 most frequent neighborhoods are "Downtown West," "Folwell," "Hawthorne," "Jordan," "Loring Park," "Lowry Hill East," "Marcy Holmes,"

"Near – North," "North Loop," "Whittier." All other less frequent neighborhoods were lumped in the "Other" category with a frequency of 6038.

So we use the mutate and fct_lump_n functions before all previous functions to get the proportions of the different force types used in these 11 neighborhoods (with the extra one for the "Other" category).

```
mn_police_use_of_force %>%

 mutate(neighborhood= fct_lump_n(neighborhood, n=10)) %>%

 count(neighborhood,force_type) %>%

 filter(!neighborhood=="") %>%

 drop_na() %>%

 group_by(neighborhood) %>% mutate(proportion = n/sum(n)) %>%

 arrange(desc(proportion)) %>%

 flextable() %>%

 theme_box() %>%

 set_caption(caption = "The count and proportion of different force types applied
in 11 neighborhoods from the Minneapolis police use of force data")
```

Table 5.10. The Count and Proportion of Different Force Types Applied in 11 Neighborhoods from the Minneapolis Police Use of Force Data

Neighborhood	force_type	n	Proportion
Near – North	Bodily Force	462	0.8220640569
Whittier	Bodily Force	384	0.8170212766
Hawthorne	Bodily Force	403	0.8027888446
Jordan	Bodily Force	383	0.7995824635
Marcy Holmes	Bodily Force	246	0.7935483871
Folwell	Bodily Force	273	0.7913043478
North Loop	Bodily Force	253	0.7832817337
Other	Bodily Force	4,684	0.7757535608
Loring Park	Bodily Force	287	0.6932367150

Lowry Hill East	Bodily Force	367	0.6624548736
Downtown West	Bodily Force	1,688	0.5765027322
Downtown West	Chemical Irritant	999	0.3411885246
Lowry Hill East	Chemical Irritant	126	0.2274368231
Loring Park	Taser	80	0.1932367150
Other	Taser	732	0.1212321961
Jordan	Taser	48	0.1002087683
Hawthorne	Chemical Irritant	49	0.0976095618
Whittier	Taser	45	0.0957446809
North Loop	Taser	30	0.0928792570
Marcy Holmes	Taser	28	0.0903225806
Folwell	Taser	31	0.0898550725
Near – North	Taser	48	0.0854092527
North Loop	Chemical Irritant	27	0.0835913313
Lowry Hill East	Taser	43	0.0776173285
Marcy Holmes	Chemical Irritant	24	0.0774193548
Downtown West	Taser	190	0.0648907104
Hawthorne	Taser	32	0.0637450199
Near – North	Chemical Irritant	33	0.0587188612
Loring Park	Chemical Irritant	23	0.0555555556
Folwell	Chemical Irritant	16	0.0463768116
Other	Chemical Irritant	264	0.0437230871
Whittier	Chemical Irritant	17	0.0361702128
Jordan	Chemical Irritant	15	0.0313152401
North Loop	Maximal Restraint Technique	10	0.0309597523
Folwell	Improvised Weapon	10	0.0289855072
Jordan	Improvised Weapon	13	0.0271398747
Whittier	Improvised Weapon	12	0.0255319149
Lowry Hill East	Improvised Weapon	14	0.0252707581

Loring Park	Maximal Restraint Technique	9	0.0217391304
Other	Maximal Restraint Technique	107	0.0177210997
Folwell	Gun Point Display	6	0.0173913043
Folwell	Police K9 Bite	6	0.0173913043
Marcy Holmes	Less Lethal	5	0.0161290323
Marcy Holmes	Maximal Restraint Technique	5	0.0161290323
Jordan	Gun Point Display	7	0.0146137787
Jordan	Maximal Restraint Technique	7	0.0146137787
Loring Park	Less Lethal	6	0.0144927536
Whittier	Gun Point Display	6	0.0127659574
Hawthorne	Improvised Weapon	6	0.0119521912
Other	Improvised Weapon	65	0.0107651540
Near – North	Gun Point Display	6	0.0106761566
Near – North	Improvised Weapon	6	0.0106761566
Other	Gun Point Display	61	0.0101026830
Hawthorne	Gun Point Display	5	0.0099601594
Other	Less Lethal	59	0.0097714475
Other	Police K9 Bite	59	0.0097714475
Loring Park	Improvised Weapon	4	0.0096618357
Folwell	Maximal Restraint Technique	3	0.0086956522
Jordan	Police K9 Bite	4	0.0083507307
Loring Park	Gun Point Display	3	0.0072463768
Near – North	Maximal Restraint Technique	4	0.0071174377
Downtown West	Maximal Restraint Technique	19	0.0064890710
Marcy Holmes	Gun Point Display	2	0.0064516129

Whittier	Maximal Restraint Technique	3	0.0063829787
North Loop	Less Lethal	2	0.0061919505
Hawthorne	Maximal Restraint Technique	3	0.0059760956
Downtown West	Improvised Weapon	17	0.0058060109
Lowry Hill East	Less Lethal	3	0.0054151625
Loring Park	Police K9 Bite	2	0.0048309179
Whittier	Less Lethal	2	0.0042553191
Jordan	Less Lethal Pro-jectile	2	0.0041753653
Hawthorne	Less Lethal	2	0.0039840637
Hawthorne	Police K9 Bite	2	0.0039840637
Near – North	Police K9 Bite	2	0.0035587189
North Loop	Improvised Weapon	1	0.0030959752
Downtown West	Gun Point Display	8	0.0027322404
Downtown West	Less Lethal	7	0.0023907104
Whittier	Police K9 Bite	1	0.0021276596
Lowry Hill East	Police K9 Bite	1	0.0018050542
Near – North	Less Lethal	1	0.0017793594
Other	Baton	4	0.0006624710
Other	Firearm	2	0.0003312355
Other	Less Lethal Pro-jectile	1	0.0001656178

We see that:

- The "Bodily Force" type was applied most frequently in "Near – North," "Whittier," and "Hawthorne" with a percentage of 82.2%,81.7%, and 80.3% respectively.
- The "Bodily Force" type was applied less frequently in "Loring Park," "Lowry Hill East," and "Downtown West" with a percentage of 69.3%,66.2%, and 57.7% respectively.
- The "Chemical Irritant" force type was applied mostly in "Downtown West," "Lowry Hill East," and "Hawthorne" with a percentage of 34.1%, 22.7%, and 9.8% respectively.

- The "Chemical Irritant" type was applied less frequently in "Other," "Whittier," and "Jordan" with a percentage of 4.4%, 3.6%, and 3.1% respectively.

5.3. SUMMARY PLOTS

5.3.1. Stacked Bar Plot

In the stacked bar plot, each bar of one categorical variable has a height equal to the number of rows or observations at each level of the other categorical variable.

5.3.1.1. Bar Plot of the Count of Different Employment Statuses in the 2 Genders

To draw this plot, we use the following functions:

- The count function, applied on "acs12" data, with the arguments gender, and employment to get the number of rows for each gender and employment status.
- The ggplot function with the argument, aes(x = gender, fill = employment, y = n), to plot the gender on the x-axis, n or count on the y-axis, and different fill color for each employment status.
- The geom_col function to plot the bar plot with the arguments, position = "stack" to plot a stacked bar plot, and color = "Black" so the bar plot with its compartments has a black border.
- The labs function to add a title, x-axis title, y-axis title, and legend title.
- The theme_classic and theme functions as described before.

```
acs12 %>% count(gender, employment) %>%

 ggplot(aes(x = gender, fill = employment, y = n)) +

 geom_col(position = "stack," color = "Black")+


 labs(title = "Stacked bar plot of different employment statuses in males and females \nof the American Community Survey data,"

    y = "Count," x = "Gender," fill = "Employment")+
```

```
theme_classic()+
theme(plot.title = element_text(hjust = 0.5))
```

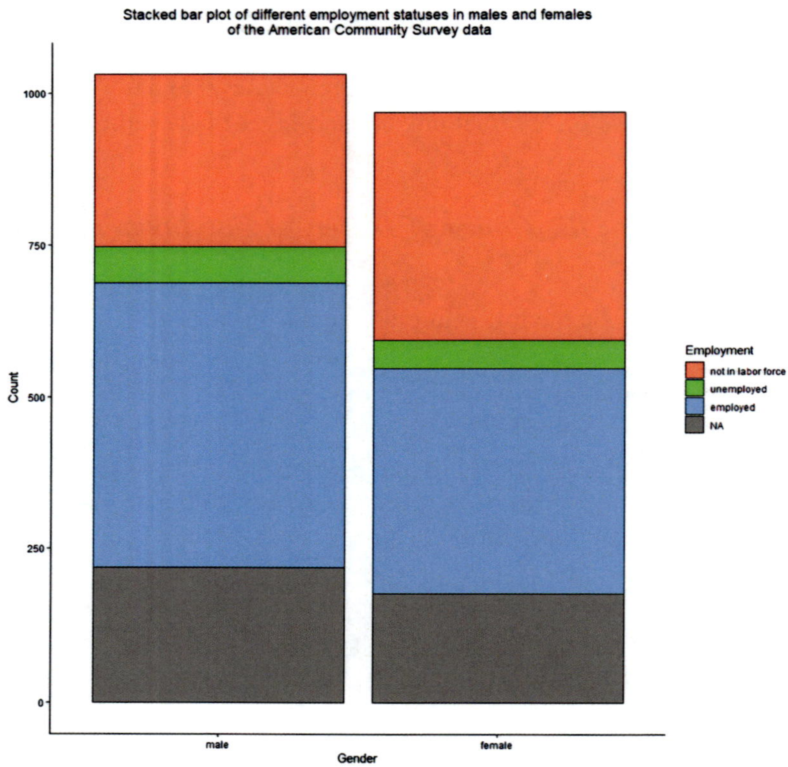

We see that:

- There are 2 bars one for males and one for females. The height of a male's bar is higher than that of a female so there is a higher count of males in our data than females.
- Each bar is divided into 4 compartments, 3 for the employment statuses and 1 for the NA or missing values.
- The largest compartment in males was for the employed compartment which is larger than the employed compartment in females, so we have a higher count of employed males than employed females in our data.

- The not in labor force compartment in females is larger than that of males, so we have a higher count of females not in the labor force than males not in the labor force in our data.
- The unemployed compartment in males is larger than that of females, so we have a higher count of unemployed males than unemployed females in our data.
- The missing "NA" compartment in males is larger than that of females, so we have a higher count of missing employment status in males than that of females in our data.

To create a more informative plot, we can:

- Delete the missing "NA" compartment using the drop_na function after the count function.
- Add a count label to each compartment by using the geom_text function with the arguments:
- aes(label = n) to plot a count label.
- position = position_stack(vjust = 0.5) to vertically justify this count label to be in the middle of each compartment.
- fontface = "bold" so the count labels will have bold fonts.

```
acs12 %>% count(gender, employment) %>% drop_na() %>%

 ggplot(aes(x = gender, fill = employment, y = n)) +

 geom_col(position = "stack," color = "Black")+

 geom_text(aes(label = n),

      position = position_stack(vjust = 0.5),

       fontface = "bold")+

 labs(title = "Stacked bar plot of different employment statuses in males and females with count labels\nof the American Community Survey data,"

    y = "Count," x = "Gender," fill = "Employment")+

 theme_classic()+

 theme(plot.title = element_text(hjust = 0.5))
```

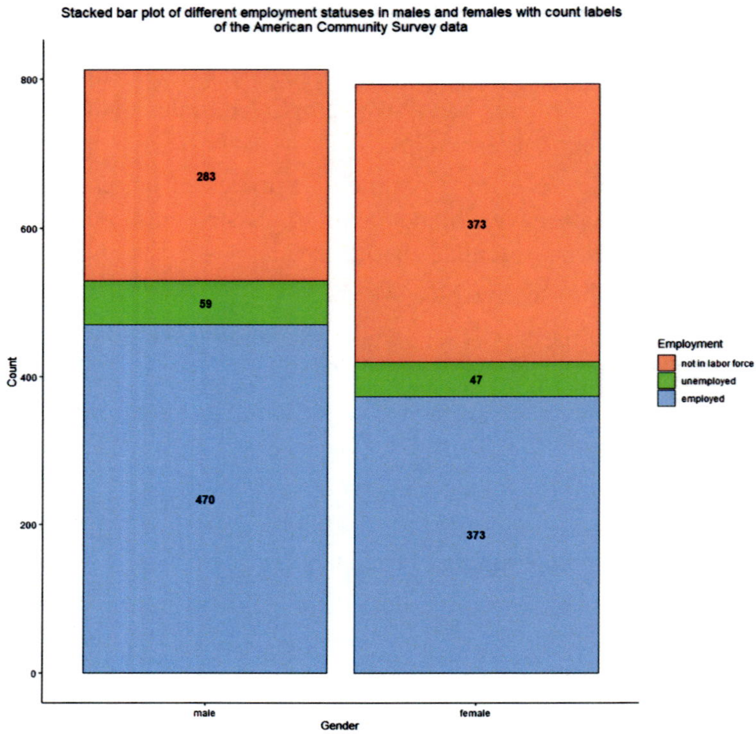

We see that the count of employed and unemployed males is higher than that of employed and unemployed females. However, the count of females not in the labor force is higher than that of males.

5.3.1.2. Bar Plot of the Count of Different Employment Statuses in the Different Races

We can use the same functions as above to get these counts as a stacked bar plot.

```
acs12 %>% count(race, employment) %>% drop_na() %>%

 ggplot(aes(x = race, fill = employment, y = n)) +

 geom_col(position = "stack," color = "Black")+

 geom_text(aes(label = n),
```

```
    position = position_stack(vjust = 0.5),
     fontface = "bold")+
labs(title = "Stacked bar plot of different employment statuses in the different
races with count labels\nof the American Community Survey data,"
   y = "Count," x = "Race," fill = "Employment")+
theme_classic()+
theme(plot.title = element_text(hjust = 0.5))
```

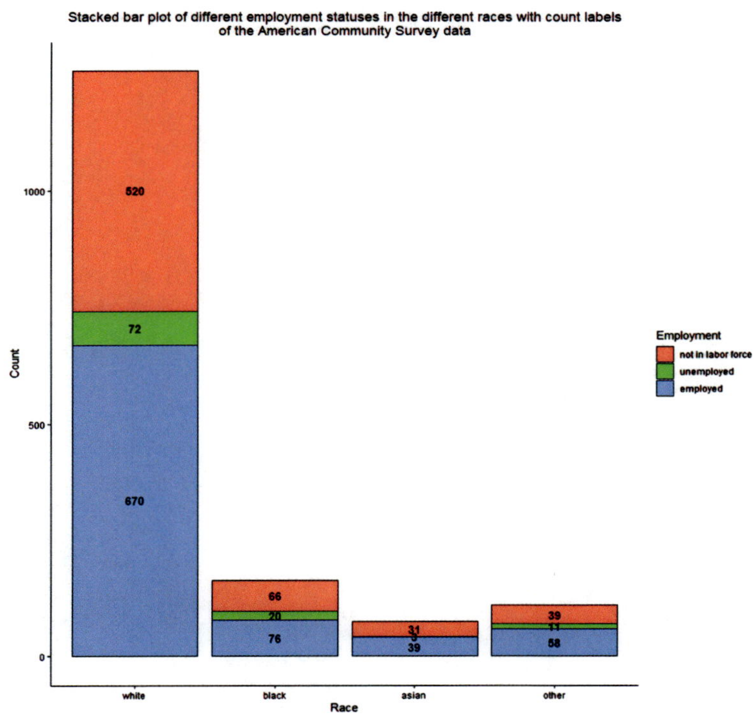

We see that:

- The longest bar was for Whites so Whites have the highest count in our data, and Asians have the lowest count.
- The counts of different employment statuses become crowded in the low-frequency races as Blacks, Asians, and others.

5.3.1.3. Bar Plot of the Count of Different Force Types in the Different Races

We can use the same functions to draw a bar plot of different force types applied to the different races. However, because we have 11 different force types, the count labels will be very crowded for each bar. So we can neglect the count labels by avoiding using the geom_text function.

```
mn_police_use_of_force %>% count(race, force_type) %>% drop_na() %>%

 ggplot(aes(x = race, fill = force_type, y = n)) +

 geom_col(position = "stack," color = "Black")+
 labs(title = "Stacked bar plot of different force types applied on different races\nfrom the Minneapolis police use of force data,"
    y = "Count," x = "Race," fill = "Force type")+
 theme_classic()+
 theme(plot.title = element_text(hjust = 0.5))
```

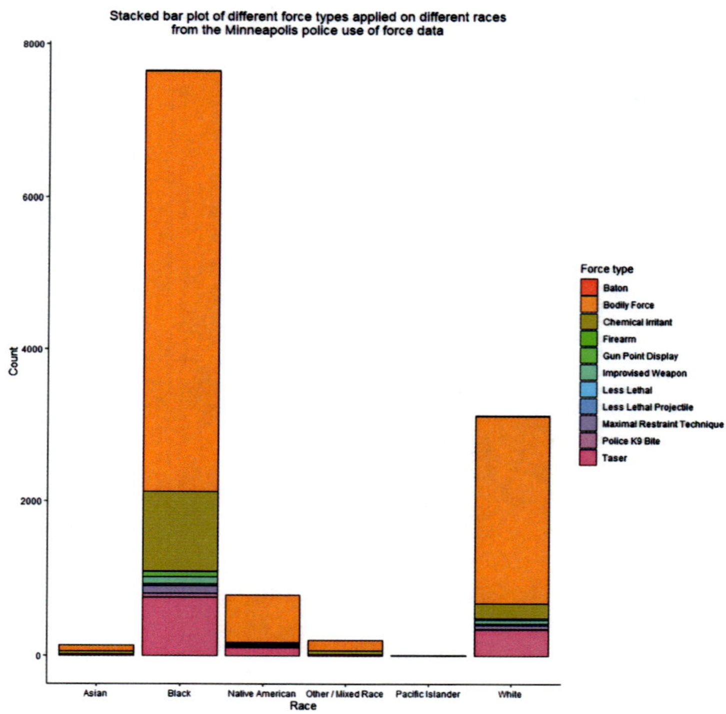

We see that:

- Blacks have the longest bar so the highest count in the Minneapolis police use of force data was for the Blacks and the lowest count was for the Pacific Islanders with the shortest bar.
- Only the "Bodily force" type, "Chemical Irritant" and "Taser" force types are seen clearly while other force types are difficult to discern due to low counts.
- The "Bodily force" type was more frequently applied to Blacks, followed by Whites, Native Americans, Other/Mixed Races, and Asians.

5.3.1.4. Bar Plot of the Count of Different Force Types in the Different Neighborhoods

To avoid crowding seen before, we will use the fct_lump_n function to focus on the 5 most frequent neighborhoods and the 3 most frequent force types. So the neighborhoods will have 6 levels (5 most frequent neighborhoods+ other category), while the force type will have 4 levels (3 most frequent force types and other category).

```
mn_police_use_of_force %>%

 mutate(neighborhood= fct_lump_n(neighborhood, n=5)) %>%

 mutate(force_type = fct_lump_n(force_type,n = 3)) %>%

 count(neighborhood,force_type) %>%

 filter(!neighborhood==“”) %>%

 drop_na() %>%

 ggplot(aes(x = neighborhood, fill = force_type, y = n)) +

 geom_col(position = “stack,” color = “Black”)+


 labs(title = “Stacked bar plot of 4 force types applied in 6 neighborhoods\n
from the Minneapolis police use of force data,”

   y = “Count,” x = “Neighborhood,” fill = “Force type”)+
```

```
theme_classic()+
theme(plot.title = element_text(hjust = 0.5))
```

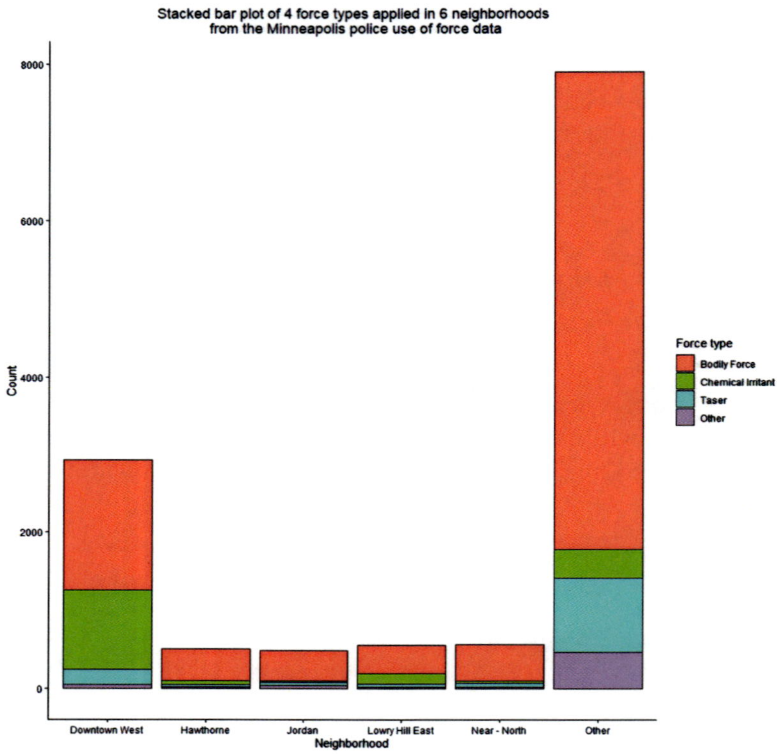

We see that:

- The "Other" neighborhood has the longest bar which is expected because it contains the counts of 81 different neighborhoods.
- The "Bodily Force" type is applied most frequently in the "other" neighborhood followed by the "Downtown West" then other neighborhoods.
- The "Chemical Irritant" type is applied most frequently in the "Downtown West" neighborhood followed by the "Other" then other neighborhoods.
- The "Taser" type is applied most frequently in the "other" neighborhood followed by the "Downtown West" and then other neighborhoods.

5.3.2. Grouped Bar Plot

In a grouped bar plot, the different bars of one categorical variable are dodged side-by-side at each level of the other categorical variable.

5.3.2.1. Grouped Bar Plot of the Count of Different Employment Statuses in the 2 Genders

To draw this plot, we use the same functions as that in section 5.3.1.1. except that we use the argument position = "dodge" instead of "stack" within the geom_col function.

```
acs12 %>% count(gender, employment) %>%
  ggplot(aes(x = gender, fill = employment, y = n)) +
  geom_col(position = "dodge," color = "Black")+
  labs(title = "Grouped bar plot of different employment statuses in males and
females \nof the American Community Survey data,"
     y = "Count," x = "Gender," fill = "Employment")+
  theme_classic()+
  theme(plot.title = element_text(hjust = 0.5))
```

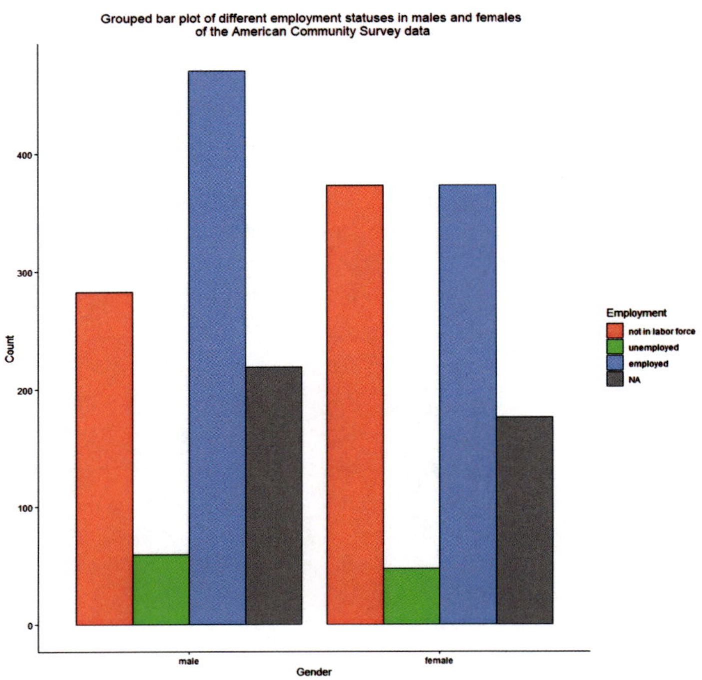

We see that:

- Each gender has 4 bars, 3 for the employment statuses and 1 for the NA or missing values.
- The tallest bar in males was for the employed status which is taller than that in females, so we have a higher count of employed males than employed females in our data.
- The not in labor force bar for females is taller than that of males, so we have a higher count of females not in the labor force than males not in the labor force in our data.
- The unemployed bar in males is taller than that of females, so we have a higher count of unemployed males than unemployed females in our data.
- The missing "NA" bar in males is taller than that of females, so we have a higher count of missing employment status in males than that of females in our data.

To create a more informative plot, we can:

- Delete the missing "NA" compartment using the drop_na function after the count function.
- Add a count label to each compartment by using the geom_label function (draws a rectangle behind the text, making it easier to read) with the arguments:
- aes(label = n) to plot a count label.
- position = position_dodge(width = 0.9) to align narrow geom (text of count) with wider geom (the wide position of each gender with 3 bars).

```
acs12 %>% count(gender, employment) %>% drop_na() %>%
 ggplot(aes(x = gender, fill = employment, y = n)) +
 geom_col(position = "dodge," color = "Black")+
 geom_label(aes(label = n),

      position = position_dodge(width = 0.9))+

 labs(title = "Grouped bar plot of different employment statuses in males and
females with count labels\nof the American Community Survey data,"

    y = "Count," x = "Gender," fill = "Employment")+
 theme_classic()+

 theme(plot.title = element_text(hjust = 0.5))
```

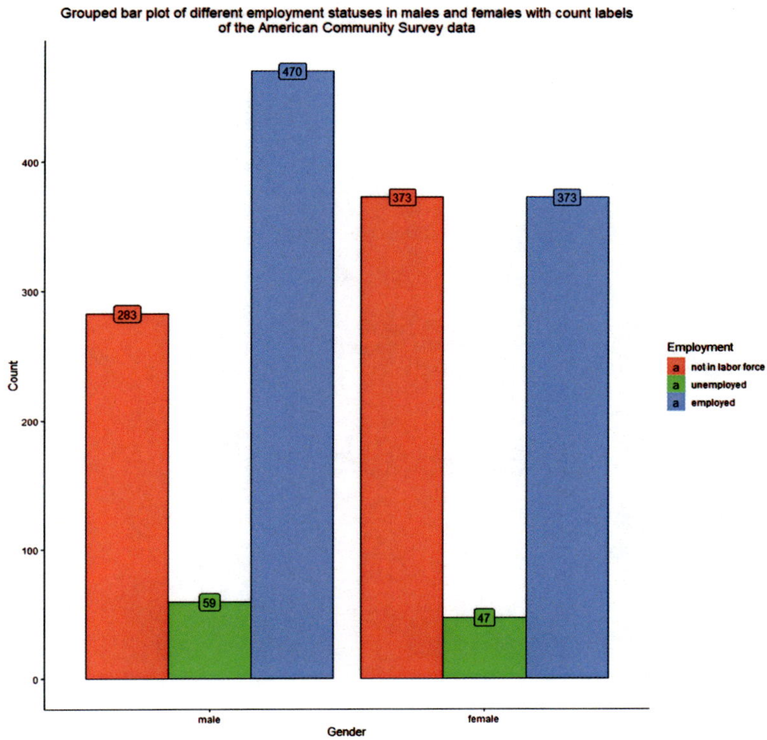

We see that the count of employed and unemployed males is higher than that of employed and unemployed females. However, the count of females not in the labor force is higher than that of males.

5.3.2.2. Grouped Bar Plot of the Count of Different Employment Statuses in the Different Races

We can use the same functions as above to get these counts as a grouped bar plot.

```
acs12 %>% count(race, employment) %>% drop_na() %>%

 ggplot(aes(x = race, fill = employment, y = n)) +

 geom_col(position = "dodge," color = "Black")+

 geom_label(aes(label = n),
```

```
    position = position_dodge(width = 0.9))+

 labs(title = "Grouped bar plot of different employment statuses in the different
races with count labels\nof the American Community Survey data,"

   y = "Count," x = "Race," fill = "Employment")+

 theme_classic()+

 theme(plot.title = element_text(hjust = 0.5))
```

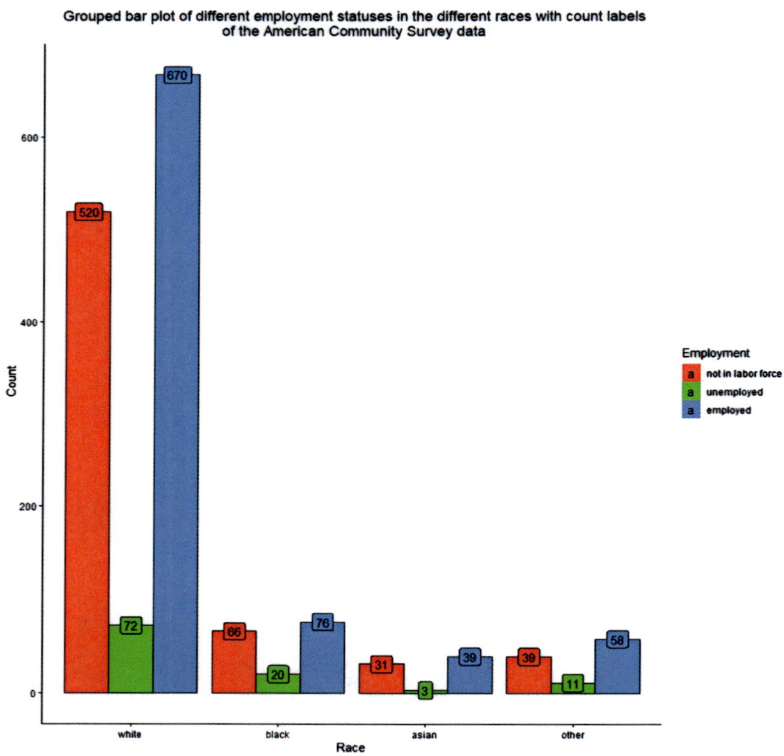

We see that:

- The 3 bars of Whites that correspond to "employed," "unemployed," and "not in labor force" statuses are taller than that of other races, so

Whites have the highest count of all employment statuses than any other race in our data.

- On the other hand, Asians have the lowest count of all employment statuses than any other race in our data.

5.3.2.3. Grouped Bar Plot of the Count of Different Force Types in the Different Races

We can use the same functions to draw a bar plot of different force types applied to the different races. However, because we have 11 different force types, the count labels will be very crowded for each race. We can solve that by using the geom_label_repel function from the ggrepel package, so the text labels repel away from each other and away from the data points. For reproducibility, we use the argument seed = 123 to add the counts at the same random positions.

```
library(ggrepel)

mn_police_use_of_force %>% count(race, force_type) %>% drop_na() %>%

 ggplot(aes(x = race, fill = force_type, y = n)) +

 geom_col(position = "dodge," color = "Black")+

 geom_label_repel(aes(label = n),

          position = position_dodge(width = 0.9),

          seed = 123)+

 labs(title = "Grouped bar plot of different force types applied on different races\nfrom the Minneapolis police use of force data,"

    y = "Count," x = "Race," fill = "Force type")+

 theme_classic()+

 theme(plot.title = element_text(hjust = 0.5))
```

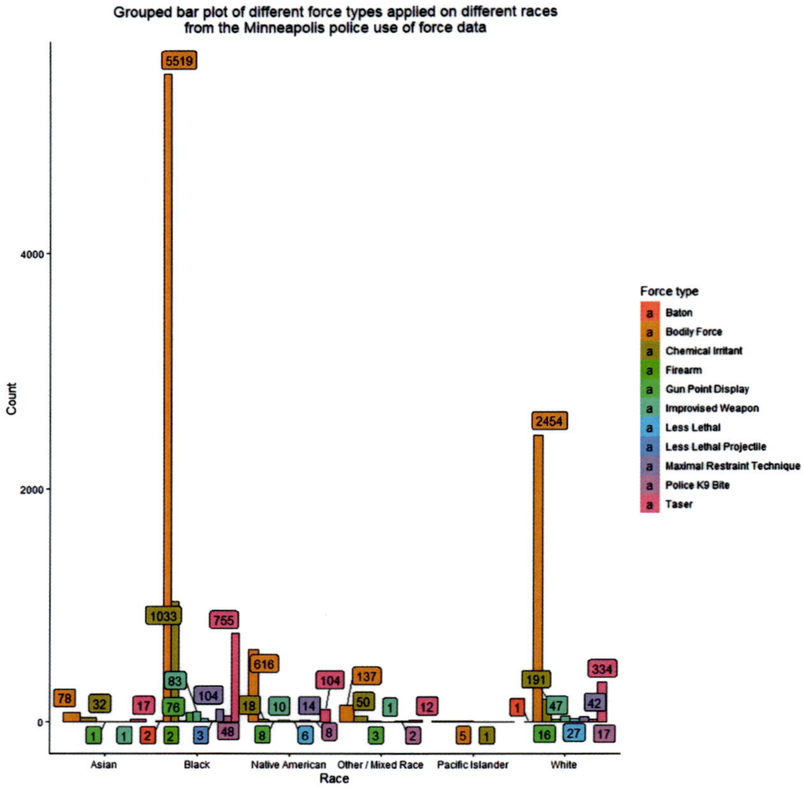

We see that:

- The "Bodily Force" type mostly applied to Blacks (5519) followed by Whites (2454), Native Americans (616), Other/Mixed Race (137), Asians (78), and Pacific Islanders (5).
- The "Chemical Irritant" was more frequently applied to Blacks (1033), followed by Whites (191), Other/Mixed Races (50), Asians (32), Native Americans (18), and Pacific Islanders (1).

5.3.2.4. Grouped Bar Plot of the Count of Different Force Types in the Different Neighborhoods

To avoid crowding seen before, we will use the fct_lump_n function to focus on the 5 most frequent neighborhoods. So the neighborhoods will have 6 levels (5 most frequent neighborhoods+ other category).

```
mn_police_use_of_force %>%

 mutate(neighborhood= fct_lump_n(neighborhood, n=5)) %>%

 count(neighborhood,force_type) %>%

 filter(!neighborhood=="") %>%

 drop_na() %>%

 ggplot(aes(x = neighborhood, fill = force_type, y = n)) +

 geom_col(position = "dodge," color = "Black")+

 geom_label_repel(aes(label = n),

          position = position_dodge(width = 0.9),

          seed = 123)+


  labs(title = "Grouped bar plot of different force types applied in 6 neighborhoods\n from the Minneapolis police use of force data,"

    y = "Count," x = "Neighborhood," fill = "Force type")+

 theme_classic()+

 theme(plot.title = element_text(hjust = 0.5))
```

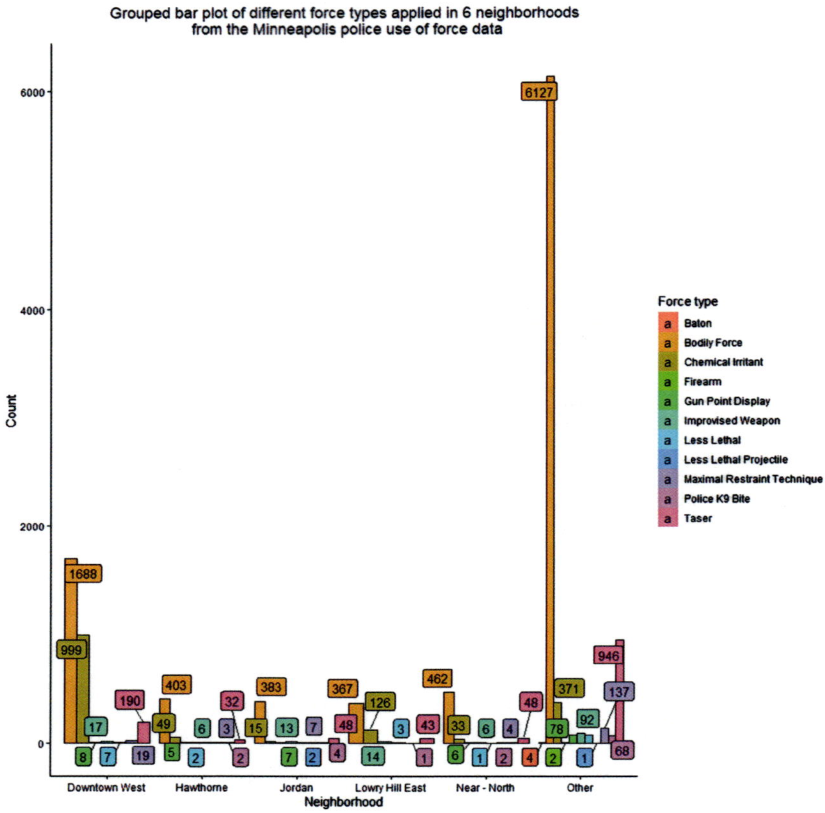

We see that:

- The "Bodily Force" type is applied most frequently in the "other" neighborhood (6127) followed by the "Downtown West" (1688) then other neighborhoods.
- The "Chemical Irritant" type is applied most frequently in the "Downtown West" neighborhood (999) followed by the "Other" (371) then other neighborhoods.
- The "Taser" type is applied most frequently in the "other" neighborhood (946) followed by the "Downtown West" (190) then other neighborhoods.

5.3.3. Percent Stacked Bar Plot

A percent stacked bar plot is a stacked bar plot where each bar of one categorical variable represents 100 percent and is filled with the different levels of another categorical variable. This allows comparison between different levels of one categorical variable if they have different sample sizes.

5.3.3.1. Percent Stacked Bar Plot of Different Employment Statuses in the 2 Genders

To draw this plot, we use the following functions:

- The count function, applied on "acs12" data, with the arguments gender, and employment to get the number of rows for each gender and employment status.
- The drop_na function deletes any rows that contain missings in the gender or employment status.
- The group_by function with the gender argument to split the count results into two, one for males and one for females.
- The mutate function creates a new column "proportion" by dividing the count over the sum of counts for each gender. The sum of proportions will be 1 or 100% for each gender.
- The ungroup function removes the grouping effect.
- The ggplot function with the argument, aes(x = gender, fill = employment, y = proportion), to plot the gender on the x-axis, proportion on the y-axis, and different fill color for each employment status.
- The geom_col function to plot the bar plot with the arguments, position = "fill" to plot a percent stacked bar plot, and color = "Black" so the bar plot with its compartments has a black border.
- The geom_text function to add a percentage label to each compartment using the arguments:

++ aes(label = percent(proportion)) to convert the proportion to a percentage label using the percent function from the scales package.

++ position = position_fill(vjust = 0.5) to vertically justify this percentage label to be in the middle of each compartment.

- The labs function to add a title, x-axis title, y-axis title, and legend title.

- The scale_y_continuous function with the argument labels = percent to convert the proportion label to percentage labels.
- The theme_classic and theme functions as described before.

```
library(scales)

acs12 %>% count(gender, employment) %>% drop_na() %>%

 group_by(gender) %>% mutate(proportion = n/sum(n)) %>%

 ungroup() %>%

 ggplot(aes(x = gender, fill = employment, y = proportion)) +

 geom_col(position = "fill," color = "Black")+

 geom_text(aes(label = percent(proportion)),

      position = position_fill(vjust = 0.5))+


 labs(title = "Percent stacked bar plot of different employment statuses in males
and females\n of the American Community Survey data,"

    y = "Percentage," x = "Gender," fill = "Employment")+

 scale_y_continuous(labels = percent)+

 theme_classic()+


 theme(plot.title = element_text(hjust = 0.5))
```

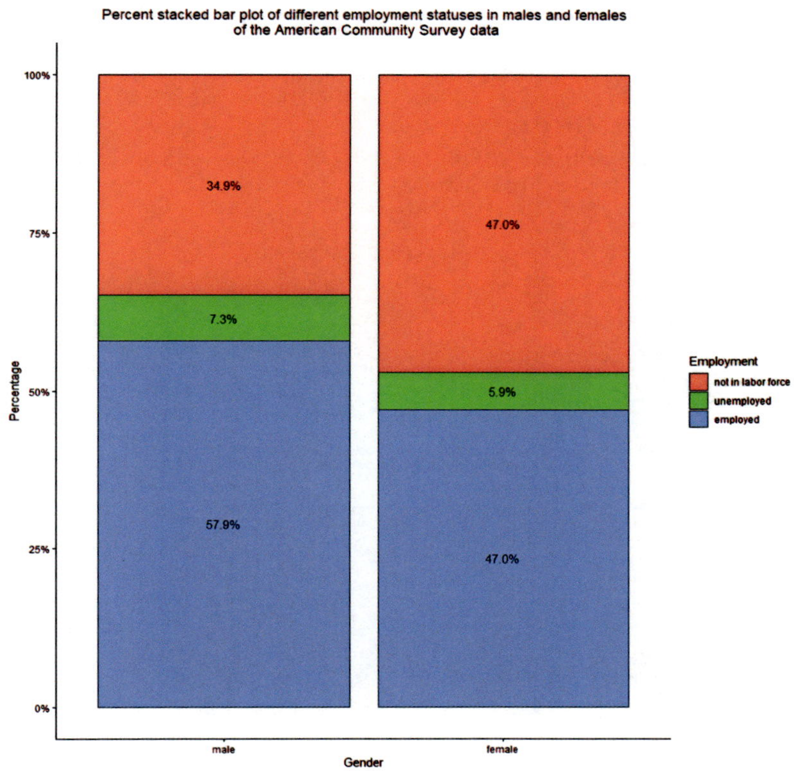

We see that:

- There are 2 bars one for males and one for females. The height of each bar is 100%.
- Males have a higher percentage of employed and unemployed statuses but a lower percentage of "not in labor force" than females.

5.3.3.2. Percent Stacked Bar Plot of Different Employment Statuses in the Different Races

To create this plot, we will use the same functions as above and modify them accordingly to include race instead of gender.

```
acs12 %>% count(race, employment) %>% drop_na() %>%
 group_by(race) %>% mutate(proportion = n/sum(n)) %>%
 ungroup() %>%
```

```
ggplot(aes(x = race, fill = employment, y = proportion)) +
geom_col(position = "fill," color = "Black")+
geom_text(aes(label = percent(proportion)),

     position = position_fill(vjust = 0.5))+
labs(title = "Percent stacked bar plot of different employment statuses in the different races\n of the American Community Survey data,"

   y = "Percentage," x = "Race," fill = "Employment")+
scale_y_continuous(labels = percent)+
theme_classic()+
theme(plot.title = element_text(hjust = 0.5))
```

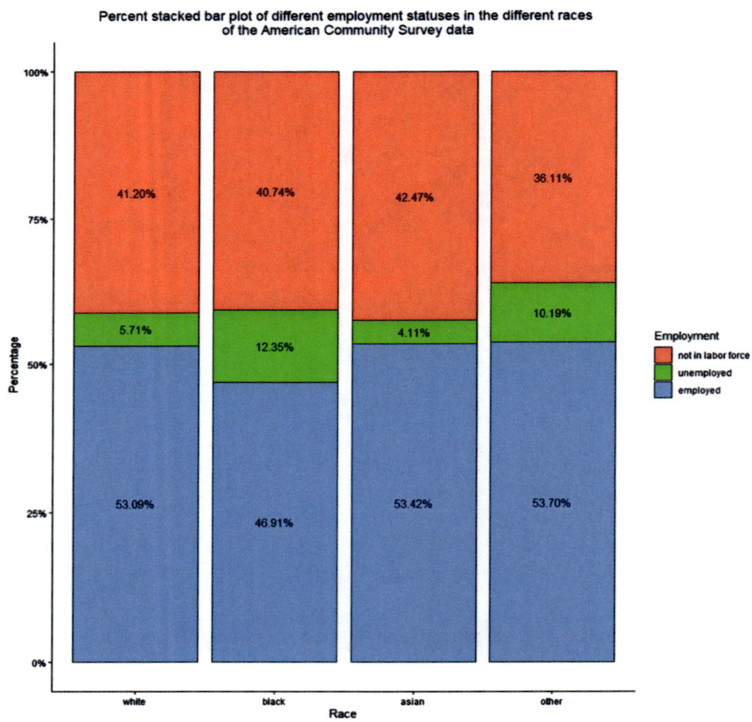

We see that:

- The highest percentage of employed was found in Other races (53.7%) and the lowest percentage was found in Blacks (46.91%).
- The highest percentage of unemployed was found in Blacks (12.35%)

and the lowest percentage was found in Asians (4.11%).

- The highest percentage of "not in labor force" was found in Asians (42.47%) and the lowest percentage was found in other races (36.11%).

5.3.3.3. Percent Stacked Bar Plot of Different Force Types in the Different Races

we use the same above functions applied on the "mn_police_use_of_force" data and modify them accordingly.

```
mn_police_use_of_force %>% count(race, force_type) %>% drop_na() %>%

 group_by(race) %>% mutate(proportion = n/sum(n)) %>%

 ungroup() %>%

 ggplot(aes(x = race, fill = force_type, y = proportion)) +

 geom_col(position = "fill," color = "Black")+

 geom_text(aes(label = percent(proportion)),

      position = position_fill(vjust = 0.5))+


 labs(title = "Percent stacked bar plot of different force types applied on different races \nfrom the Minneapolis police use of force data,"


  y = "Percentage," x = "Race," fill = "Force type")+


scale_y_continuous(labels = percent)+


theme_classic()+


theme(plot.title = element_text(hjust = 0.5))
```

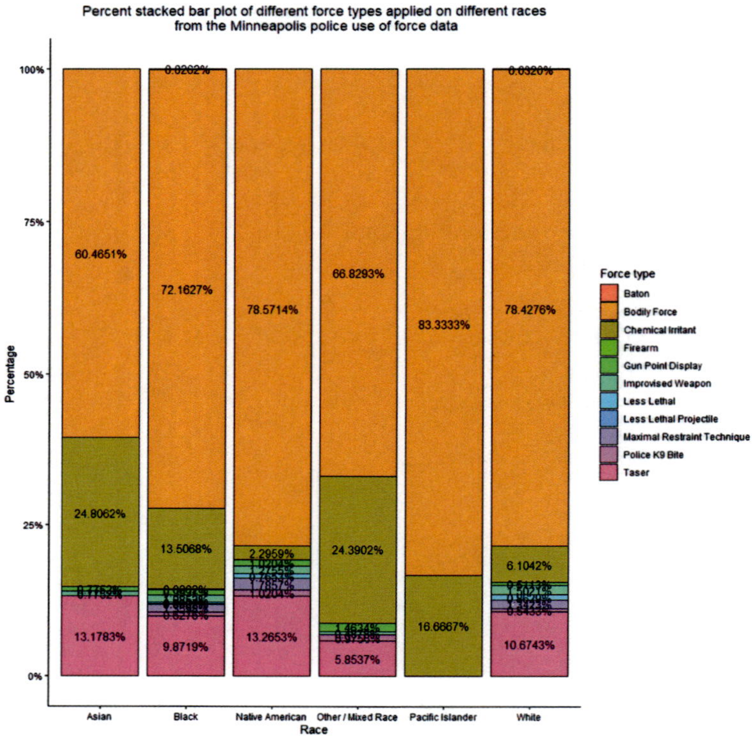

We see that the percentage labels are crowded due to the 11 different levels of force types. Instead, we can focus on the 3 most frequent force types using the fct_lump_n as done before.

```
mn_police_use_of_force %>%
 mutate(force_type = fct_lump_n(force_type, n = 3)) %>%

 count(race, force_type) %>% drop_na() %>%
 group_by(race) %>% mutate(proportion = n/sum(n)) %>%

 ungroup() %>%
  ggplot(aes(x = race, fill = force_type, y = proportion)) +

 geom_col(position = “fill,” color = “Black”)+

 geom_text(aes(label = percent(proportion)),
```

```
    position = position_fill(vjust = 0.5))+
  labs(title = "Percent stacked bar plot of 4 force types applied on different
races \nfrom the Minneapolis police use of force data,"

   y = "Percentage," x = "Race," fill = "Force type")+
  scale_y_continuous(labels = percent)+
  theme_classic()+
  theme(plot.title = element_text(hjust = 0.5))
```

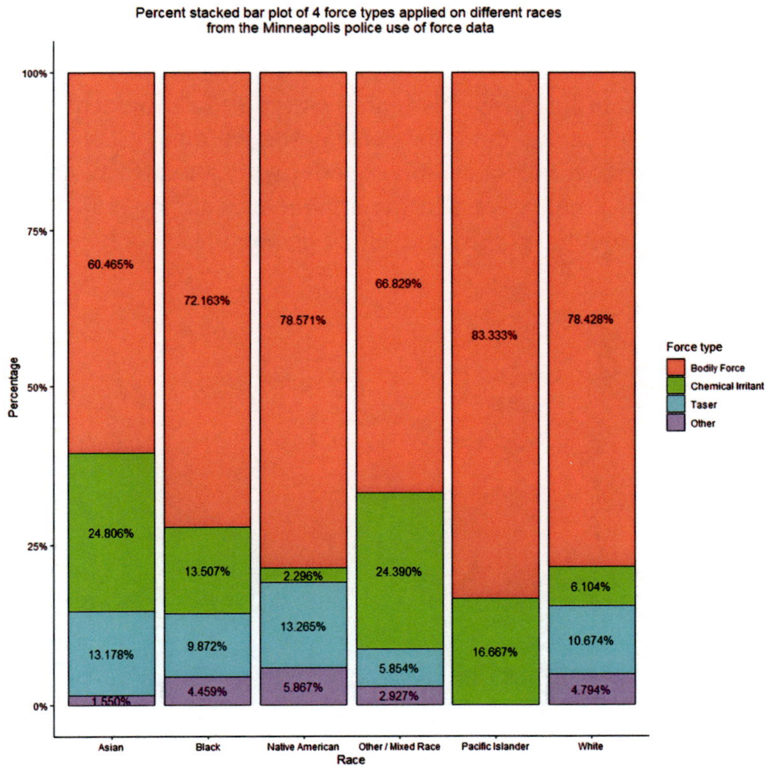

We see that:

- The other force type includes all force types except "Bodily Force," "Chemical Irritant," and "Taser."
- The highest percentage of "Bodily Force" was applied to Pacific Islanders (83.3%) and the lowest percentage was applied to Asians (60.465%).
- The highest percentage of "Chemical Irritant" was applied to Asians

(24.8%) and the lowest percentage was applied to Native Americans (2.3%).

- The highest percentage of "Taser" was applied to Native Americans (13.3%) and the lowest percentage was applied to Pacific Islanders (0%), so the compartment of "Taser" disappeared from the Pacific Islander bar.

5.3.3.4. Percent Stacked Bar Plot of Different Force Types in the Different Neighborhoods

we use the same above functions applied on the "mn_police_use_of_force" data and modify them accordingly. We also focus on the 3 most frequent force types and the 20 most frequent neighborhoods using the fct_lump_n as done before. In addition, we plot the different neighborhoods on the y-axis to avoid crowding them on the x-axis. Finally, we add the argument accuracy = 0.1 inside the percent function to plot the percentage with 1 decimal place only.

```
mn_police_use_of_force %>%

 mutate(force_type = fct_lump_n(force_type, n = 3),

 neighborhood= fct_lump_n(neighborhood, n=20)) %>%

count(neighborhood,force_type) %>%

 filter(!neighborhood=="“") %>%

 drop_na() %>%

 group_by(neighborhood) %>% mutate(proportion = n/sum(n)) %>%

 ungroup() %>%

  ggplot(aes(x = proportion, fill = force_type, y = neighborhood)) +

 geom_col(position = "fill," color = "Black")+

 geom_text(aes(label = percent(proportion, accuracy = 0.1)),

      position = position_fill(vjust = 0.5))+
```

```
labs(title = "Percent stacked bar plot of 4 force types applied in 21 neighborhoods \nfrom the Minneapolis police use of force data,"

   y = "Neighborhood," x = "Percentage," fill = "Force type")+

scale_x_continuous(labels = percent)+

theme_classic()+

theme(plot.title = element_text(hjust = 0.5))
```

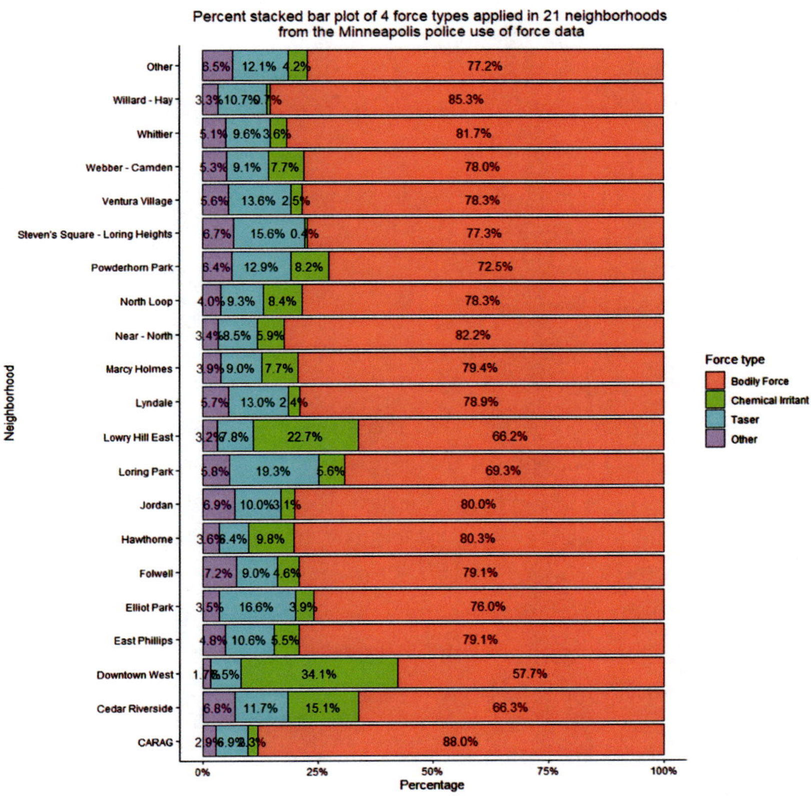

We see that:

- The other neighborhood includes all neighborhoods except the 20 listed neighborhoods.

- The highest percentage of "Bodily Force" was applied in the "CARAG" neighborhood (88%) and the lowest percentage was applied in "Downtown West" (57.7%).
- The highest percentage of "Chemical Irritant" was applied in "Downtown West" (34.1%) and the lowest percentage was applied in "Steven's Square – Loring Heights" (0.4%).
- The highest percentage of "Taser" was applied in "Loring Park" (19.3%) and the lowest percentage was applied in "Hawthorne" (6.4%).

5.3.4. Line Plot

The line plot can show the relation between 2 categorical variables by plotting the count or percentage of one categorical variable at each level of the other categorical variable.

5.3.4.1. Line Plot for the Count of Different Employment Statuses in the 2 Genders

To draw this plot, we use the following functions:

- The count function, applied on "acs12" data, with the arguments gender, and employment to get the number of rows for each gender and employment status.
- The drop_na function deletes any rows that contain missings in the gender or employment status.
- The group_by function with the gender argument to split the count results into two, one for males and one for females.
- The mutate function creates a new column "proportion" by dividing the count over the sum of counts for each gender. The sum of proportions will be 1 or 100% for each gender.
- The ungroup function removes the grouping effect.
- The ggplot function with the argument, aes(x = gender, color = employment, y = n, group = employment), to plot the gender on the x-axis, n or count on the y-axis, and a different color for each employment status.
- The geom_line function with the argument aes(group = employment) plots a different line for each employment status.
- The geom_point function to plot a point for each count value.
- The geom_label_repel function with the argument aes(label = n) adds a count label to each point and the seed argument for reproducibility.
- The labs, theme_classic, and theme functions as described before.

```
acs12 %>% count(gender, employment) %>% drop_na() %>%
 group_by(gender) %>% mutate(proportion = n/sum(n)) %>%
 ungroup() %>%

 ggplot(aes(x = gender, color = employment, y = n)) +

 geom_line(aes(group = employment))+ geom_point()+

 geom_label_repel(aes(label = n), seed = 123)+
 labs(title = "Line plot of the count of different employment statuses in males
and females\n of the American Community Survey data,"

   y = "Count," x = "Gender," color = "Employment")+
 theme_classic()+
 theme(plot.title = element_text(hjust = 0.5))
```

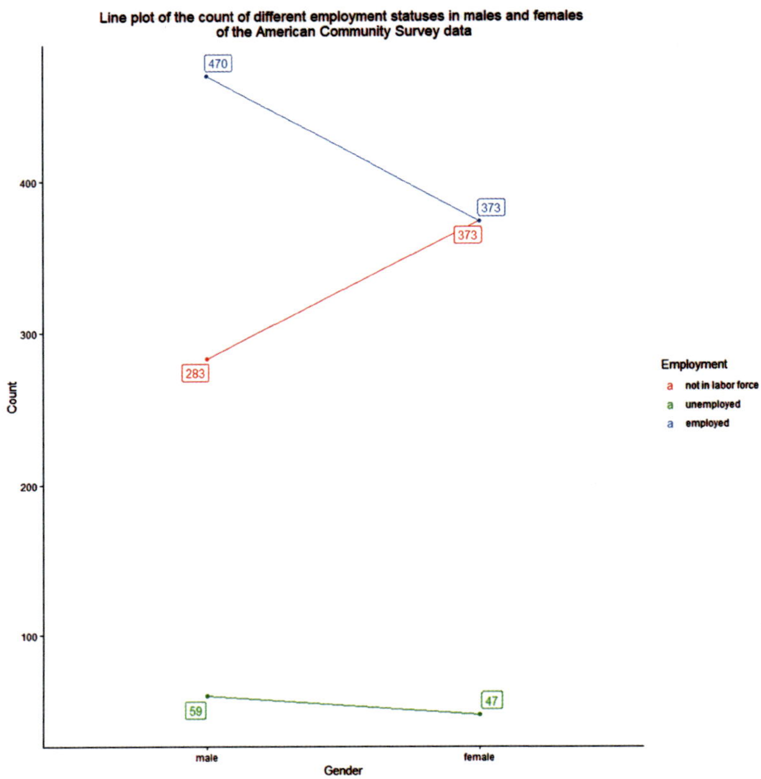

We see that:

- There are 3 lines for the 3 different employment statuses.
- Males have a higher count of employed and unemployed statuses but a lower count of "not in labor force" than females.
- The count of "not in labor force" and "employed" is equal in females.

5.3.4.2. Line Plot for the Percentage of Different Employment Statuses in the 2 Genders

We use the same functions as above except that:

- We plot the proportion on the y-axis.
- Convert the labels to percentages using the percent function. Also, we do that for the y-axis text.

```
acs12 %>% count(gender, employment) %>% drop_na() %>%

 group_by(gender) %>% mutate(proportion = n/sum(n)) %>%

 ungroup() %>%

 ggplot(aes(x = gender, color = employment, y = proportion)) +

 geom_line(aes(group = employment))+ geom_point()+

 geom_label_repel(aes(label = percent(proportion, accuracy = 0.1)),

         seed = 123)+

 scale_y_continuous(labels = percent)+


 labs(title = "Line plot of the percentage of different employment statuses in
males and females\n of the American Community Survey data,"

    y = "Percentage," x = "Gender," color = "Employment")+

 theme_classic()+

 theme(plot.title = element_text(hjust = 0.5))
```

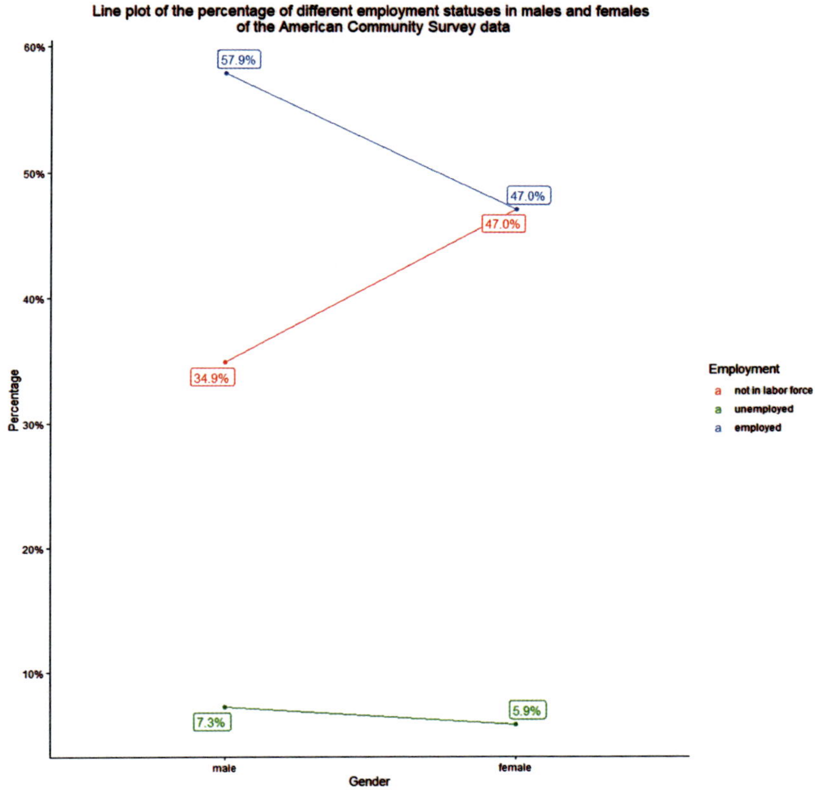

We see that:

- The sum of the percentage for each gender is 100%.
- Males have a higher percentage of employed and unemployed statuses but a lower percentage of "not in labor force" than females.
- The percentage of "not in labor force" and "employed" is equal in females.

5.3.4.3. Line Plot for the Count of Different Employment Statuses in the Different Races

We use the same functions as above and modify them accordingly.

```
acs12 %>% count(race, employment) %>% drop_na() %>%
```

```
group_by(race) %>% mutate(proportion = n/sum(n)) %>%

ungroup() %>%

ggplot(aes(x = race, color = employment, y = n)) +

geom_line(aes(group = employment))+ geom_point()+

geom_label_repel(aes(label = n), seed = 123)+
labs(title = "Line plot of the count of different employment statuses in the different races \nof the American Community Survey data,"

   y = "Count," x = "Race," color = "Employment")+
theme_classic()+
theme(plot.title = element_text(hjust = 0.5))
```

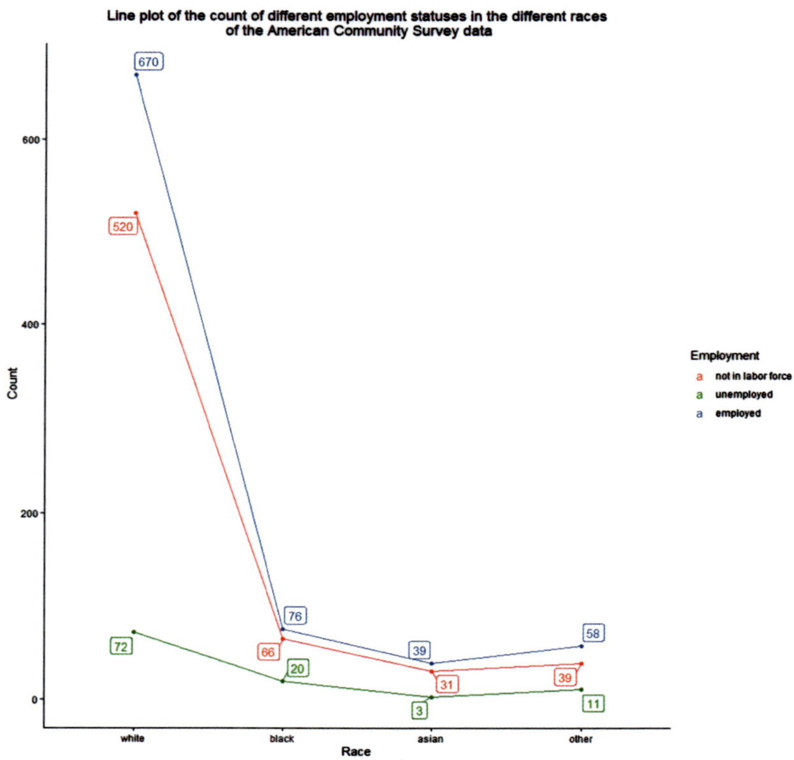

We see that:

- The count of different employment statuses is higher in Whites than in other races.

5.3.4.4. Line Plot For The Percentage of Different Employment Statuses in the Different Races

We use the same functions as above.

```
acs12 %>% count(race, employment) %>% drop_na() %>%

 group_by(race) %>% mutate(proportion = n/sum(n)) %>%

 ungroup() %>%

 ggplot(aes(x = race, color = employment, y = proportion)) +

 geom_line(aes(group = employment))+ geom_point()+

 geom_label_repel(aes(label = percent(proportion, accuracy = 0.1)),

        seed = 123)+

 scale_y_continuous(labels = percent)+


 labs(title = "Line plot of the percentage of different employment statuses in the different races\n of the American Community Survey data,"

    y = "Percentage," x = "Race," color = "Employment")+

 theme_classic()+

 theme(plot.title = element_text(hjust = 0.5))
```

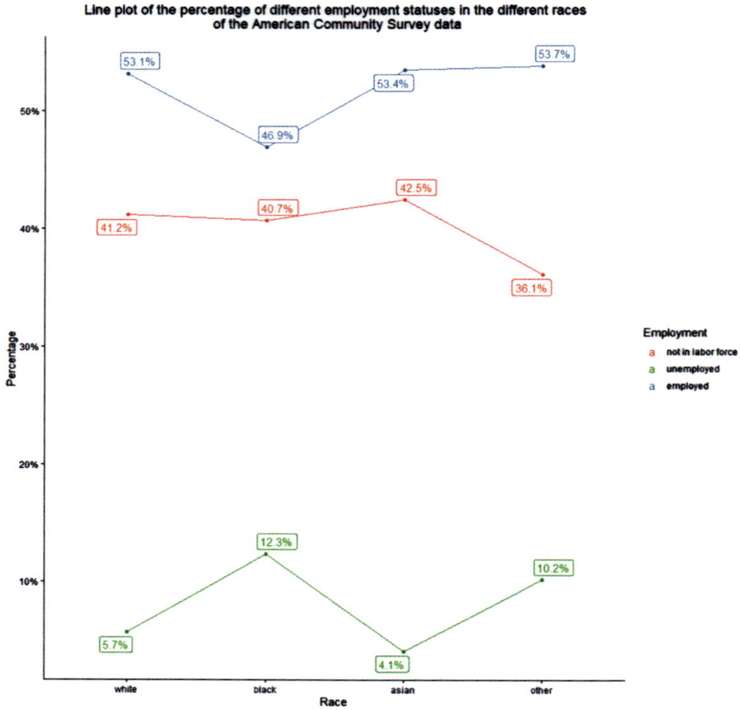

We see that:

- The sum of the percentage for each race is 100%.
- The highest percentage of employed was found in Other races (53.7%) and the lowest percentage was found in Blacks (46.9%).
- The highest percentage of unemployed was found in Blacks (12.3%) and the lowest percentage was found in Asians (4.1%).
- The highest percentage of "not in labor force" was found in Asians (42.5%) and the lowest percentage was found in other races (36.1%).

5.3.4.5. Line Plot for the Count of Different Force Types Applied on Different Races

We use the same functions as above but use the "mn_police_use_of_force" data.

```
mn_police_use_of_force %>% count(race, force_type) %>% drop_na() %>%
 group_by(race) %>% mutate(proportion = n/sum(n)) %>%
```

```
ungroup() %>%

ggplot(aes(x = race, color = force_type, y = n)) +

geom_line(aes(group = force_type))+ geom_point()+

geom_label_repel(aes(label = n),

        seed = 123)+
 labs(title = "Line plot of the count of different force types applied on
different races\n from the Minneapolis police use of force data,"

   y = "Count," x = "Race," color = "Force type")+

theme_classic()+

theme(plot.title = element_text(hjust = 0.5))
```

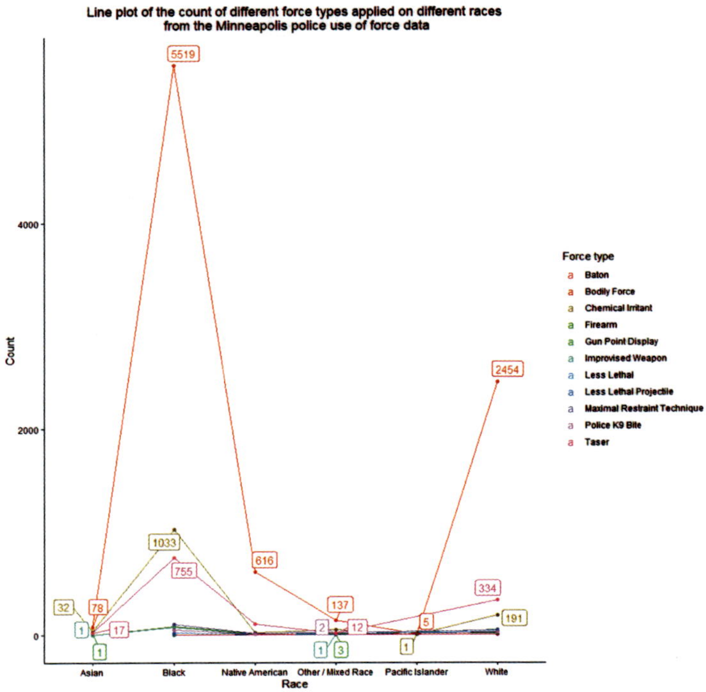

We see that:

- The "Bodily Force" type has a higher count in all races than other force types.
- Some points are not labeled due to crowding.

Instead, we can focus on the 3 most frequent force types using the fct_lump_n function.

```
mn_police_use_of_force %>%
 mutate(force_type = fct_lump_n(force_type,n = 3)) %>%

 count(race, force_type) %>% drop_na() %>%

 group_by(race) %>% mutate(proportion = n/sum(n)) %>%

 ungroup() %>%

 ggplot(aes(x = race, color = force_type, y = n)) +

 geom_line(aes(group = force_type))+ geom_point()+

 geom_label_repel(aes(label = n),

         seed = 123)+

 labs(title = "Line plot of the count of 4 force types applied on different races\n from the Minneapolis police use of force data,"

   y = "Count," x = "Race," color = "Force type")+

 theme_classic()+

 theme(plot.title = element_text(hjust = 0.5))
```

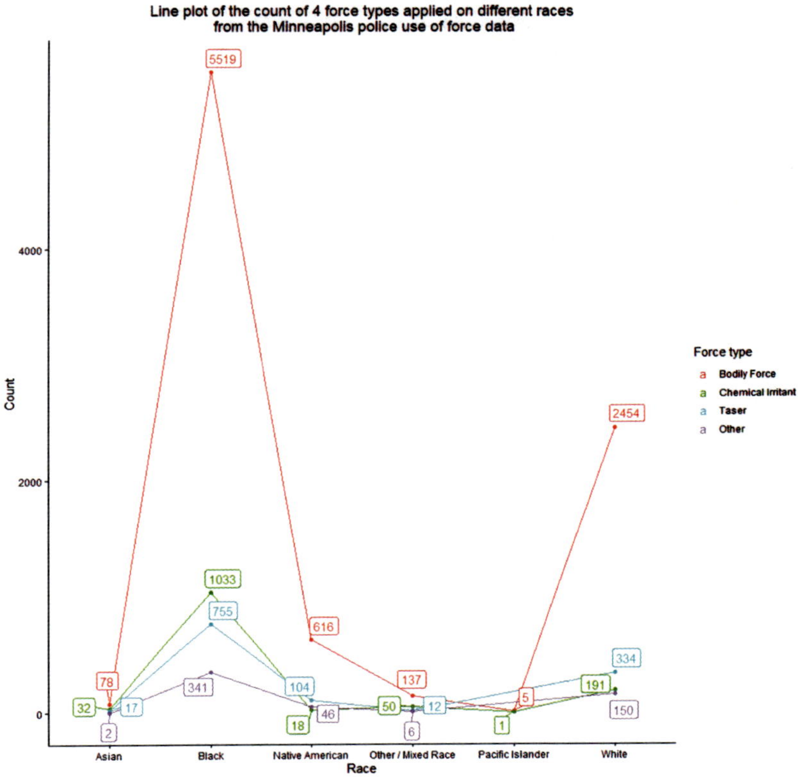

We see that

- The "Bodily Force" type has a higher count than the other force types in all races.
- The count of 4 force types is higher in Blacks than in other races.

5.3.4.6. Line Plot for the Proportion of Different Force Types Applied on Different Races

We again focus on the 3 most frequent force types.

```
mn_police_use_of_force %>%
 mutate(force_type = fct_lump_n(force_type,n = 3)) %>%

 count(race, force_type) %>% drop_na() %>%
 group_by(race) %>% mutate(proportion = n/sum(n)) %>%
```

```
ungroup() %>%
ggplot(aes(x = race, color = force_type, y = proportion)) +
geom_line(aes(group = force_type))+ geom_point()+

geom_label_repel(aes(label = percent(proportion, accuracy = 0.1)),

        seed = 123)+
scale_y_continuous(labels = percent)+

labs(title = "Line plot of the proportion of 4 force types applied on different races\n from the Minneapolis police use of force data,"

   y = "Percentage," x = "Race," color = "Force type")+
theme_classic()+
theme(plot.title = element_text(hjust = 0.5))
```

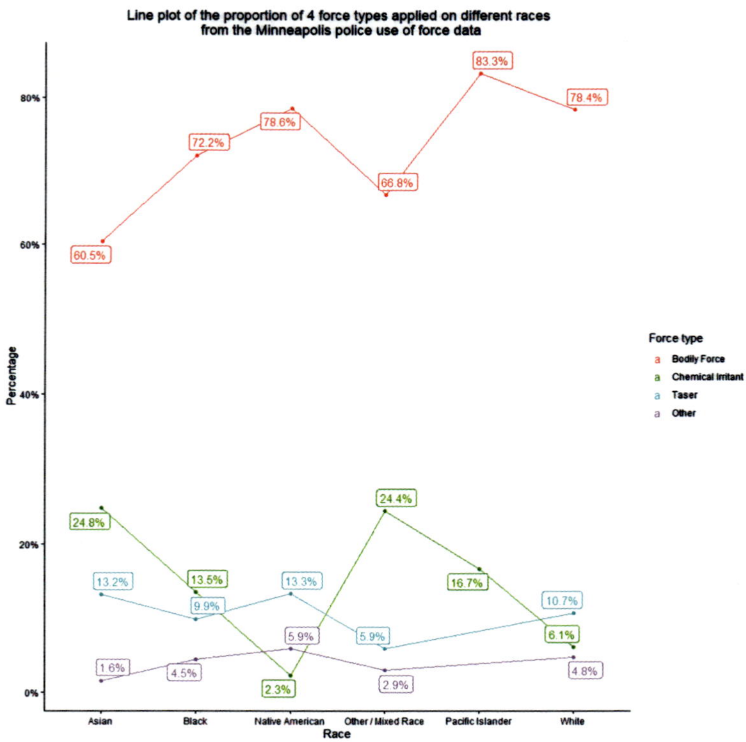

We see that:

- The sum of the percentage for each race is 100%.
- The highest percentage of "Bodily Force" was applied to Pacific Islanders (83.3%) and the lowest percentage was applied to Asians (60.5%).
- The highest percentage of "Chemical Irritant" was applied to Asians (24.8%) and the lowest percentage was applied to Native Americans (2.3%).
- The highest percentage of "Taser" was applied to Native Americans (13.3%) and the lowest percentage was applied to Pacific Islanders (0%), so the point of "Taser" disappeared from the Pacific Islanders.

5.3.4.7. Line Plot for the Count of Different Force Types Applied in Different Neighborhoods

We will focus on the 3 most frequent force types and the 20 most frequent neighborhoods using the fct_lump_n as done before. In addition, we plot the different neighborhoods on the y-axis to avoid crowding them on the x-axis. We also plot a separate black line for each neighborhood by using the arguments aes(group = neighborhood) and color = "black."

```
mn_police_use_of_force %>%

 mutate(force_type = fct_lump_n(force_type, n = 3),

 neighborhood= fct_lump_n(neighborhood, n=20)) %>%

count(neighborhood,force_type) %>%

 filter(!neighborhood=="") %>%

 drop_na() %>%

 group_by(neighborhood) %>% mutate(proportion = n/sum(n)) %>%

 ungroup() %>%

  ggplot(aes(x = n, color = force_type, y = neighborhood)) +

 geom_line(aes(group = neighborhood), color = "black")+ geom_point()+
```

```
geom_label_repel(aes(label = n),

        seed = 123)+

labs(title = "Line plot of the count of 4 force types applied in 21 neighborhoods \nfrom the Minneapolis police use of force data,"

   y = "Neighborhood," x = "Count," color = "Force type")+

theme_classic()+

theme(plot.title = element_text(hjust = 0.5))
```

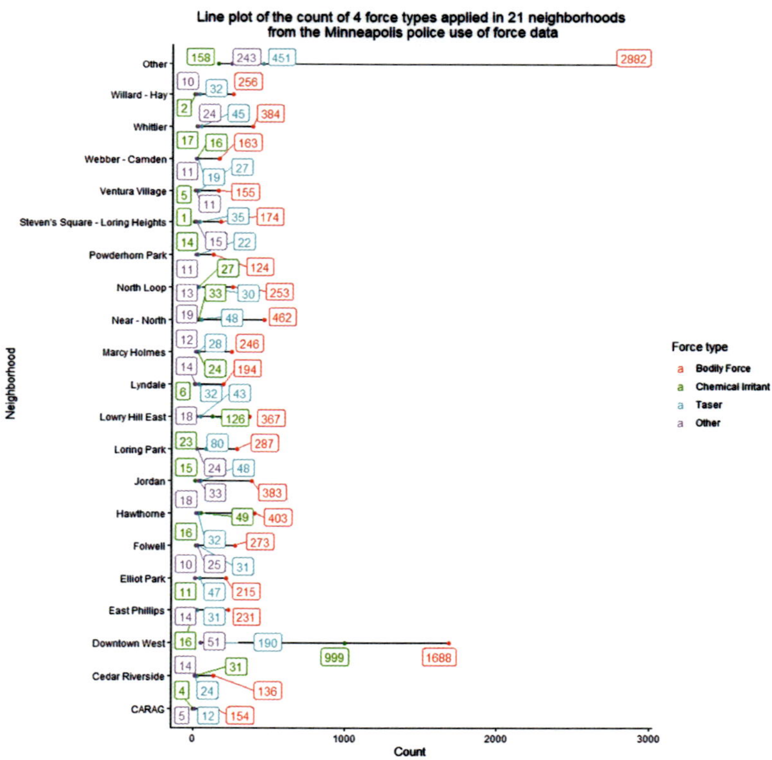

We see that:

- The "Bodily Force" type is applied most frequently in the "other" neighborhood (2882) followed by the "Downtown West" (1688) then other neighborhoods.
- The "Chemical Irritant" type is applied most frequently in the "Downtown West" neighborhood (999) followed by the "Other" (158) then other neighborhoods.
- The "Taser" type is applied most frequently in the "other" neighborhood (451) followed by the "Downtown West" (190) then other neighborhoods.

5.3.4.8. Line Plot for the Proportion of Different Force Types Applied in Different Neighborhoods

```
mn_police_use_of_force %>%

 mutate(force_type = fct_lump_n(force_type, n = 3),

 neighborhood= fct_lump_n(neighborhood, n=20)) %>%

count(neighborhood,force_type) %>%

 filter(!neighborhood==“”) %>%

 drop_na() %>%

 group_by(neighborhood) %>% mutate(proportion = n/sum(n)) %>%

 ungroup() %>%

  ggplot(aes(x = proportion, color = force_type, y = neighborhood)) +

 geom_line(aes(group = neighborhood), color = “black”)+ geom_point()+

 geom_label_repel(aes(label = percent(proportion, accuracy = 0.1)),

         seed = 123)+

 scale_x_continuous(labels = percent)+
```

```
labs(title = "Line plot of the proportion of 4 force types applied in 21 neighborhoods \nfrom the Minneapolis police use of force data,"

  y = "Neighborhood," x = "Percentage," color = "Force type")+

theme_classic()+

theme(plot.title = element_text(hjust = 0.5))
```

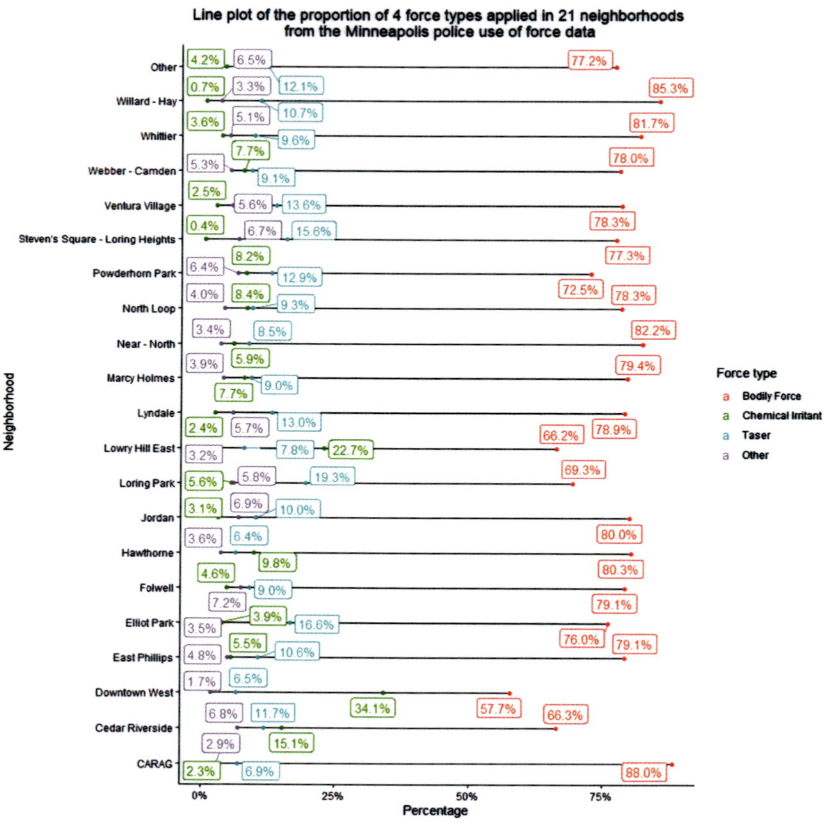

We see that:

- The sum of percentages for each neighborhood is 100%.
- The highest percentage of "Bodily Force" was applied in the "CARAG" neighborhood (88%) and the lowest percentage was applied in "Downtown West" (57.7%).

- The highest percentage of "Chemical Irritant" was applied in "Downtown West" (34.1%) and the lowest percentage was applied in "Steven's Square – Loring Heights" (0.4%).
- The highest percentage of "Taser" was applied in "Loring Park" (19.3%) and the lowest percentage was applied in "Hawthorne" (6.4%).

5.4. STATISTICAL TESTS

5.4.1. Chi-square Test

The Chi-square test uses the contingency table of data to calculate an expected table. The expected table contains the theoretical data values that would be expected when there is no relation between 2 categorical variables.

The contingency table is a table with R rows and C columns. It displays the relationship between two categorical variables, where the variable in the rows has R categories and the variable in the columns has C categories.

The null hypothesis is that the proportions of one categorical variable are the same at the different levels of the other categorical variable. The alternative hypothesis is that at least, two proportions are different from each other.

5.4.1.1. Assumptions of the Test

- Unpaired data meaning that all data observations are independent.
- The normal approximation to the binomial distribution is valid. The normal approximation can be shown to be approximately true if no expected value in the expected table is less than 5 (sometimes known as "the rule of five").

In case of an expected value less than 5, the Fisher exact test is a suitable alternative. It is not important to assign which categorical variable to columns or rows. The chi-square test requires a matrix of columns and rows. Although the hypothesis testing for the chi-square test compares proportions, but chi-square test uses the actual count to test that.

5.4.1.2. Chi-square Test of the Different Employment Statuses in the 2 Genders

The null hypothesis is that the proportions of employment statuses are the same in the 2 genders. The alternative hypothesis is that at least, two employment statuses are different from each other.

To conduct this test, we must have a matrix of columns and rows for the count of employment statuses in each gender. To do that, we use the following functions:

- The count function with the arguments gender, and employment to get the count of employment statuses in each gender.
- The drop_na function to delete rows that have missings in the gender or employment columns.
- The pivot_wider function with the argument, names_from = "gender," to convert the gender column to 2 columns for the males and females, and the argument, values_from = "n," to fill these 2 columns by the count or n.

Then, we convert the result to a table as before.

```
acs12 %>% count(gender, employment) %>% drop_na() %>%

 pivot_wider(names_from = "gender," values_from = "n") %>%

 flextable() %>% theme_box() %>%

 set_caption(caption = "Matrix of the count of different employment statuses in males and females of the American Community Survey data")
```

Table 5.11. Matrix of the Count of Different Employment Statuses in Males and Females of the American Community Survey Data

Employment	Male	female
not in labor force	283	373
unemployed	59	47
employed	470	373

Then, to conduct a chi-square test on this matrix with counts, we convert the employment column to row names using the column_to_rownames function (as it is a character column and not a count column). Then, we use the chisq_test function from the rstatix package. So, we first load the rstatix package into our R session.

```
library(rstatix)

acs12 %>% count(gender, employment) %>% drop_na() %>%

 pivot_wider(names_from = "gender," values_from = "n") %>%
```

```
column_to_rownames("employment") %>% chisq_test() %>%

flextable() %>% theme_box() %>%

set_caption(caption = "Chi-square test results of different employment statuses
in males and females of the American Community Survey data")
```

Table 5.12. *Chi-square Test Results of Different Employment Statuses in Males and Females of the American Community Survey Data*

n	statistic	p	df	method	p.signif
1,605	24.64591	0.00000445	2	Chi-square test	****

We see that:

- The table contains the statistic = 24.6 which corresponds to our sample results and the p-value = 0.00000445.
- The p_value is the probability of our sample results under the null hypothesis (the employment status proportions are the same in the 2 genders). Since this probability is too low, we reject the null hypothesis and conclude that the employment status proportions are different in the 2 genders or the gender proportions are different in the different employment statuses.

To get a closer look at the Chi-square test results, we can use the chisq_descriptives function after the chisq_test function.

```
acs12 %>% count(gender, employment) %>% drop_na() %>%

pivot_wider(names_from = "gender," values_from = "n") %>%

column_to_rownames("employment") %>% chisq_test() %>%

chisq_descriptives() %>%

flextable() %>% theme_box() %>%

set_caption(caption = "Chi-square descriptive statistics of different employment
statuses in males and females of the American Community Survey data")
```

Table 5.13. Chi-square Descriptive Statistics of Different Employment Statuses in Males and Females of the American Community Survey Data

Var1	Var2	Observed	Prop	row.prop	col.prop	Expected	resid	std.resid
not in labor force	male	283	0.17632399	0.4314024	0.3485222	331.88287	-2.6832692	-4.964432
unemployed	male	59	0.03676012	0.5566038	0.0726601	53.62741	0.7336517	1.080009
employed	male	470	0.29283489	0.5575326	0.5788177	426.48972	2.1068693	4.350093
not in labor force	female	373	0.23239875	0.5685976	0.4703657	324.11713	2.7152240	4.964432
unemployed	female	47	0.02928349	0.4433962	0.0592686	52.37259	-0.7423887	-1.080009
employed	female	373	0.23239875	0.4424674	0.4703657	416.51028	-2.1319598	-4.350093

We see that:

- The Var1 and Var2 are the levels of 2 categorical variables.
- The observed is the observed or actual count.
- The prop is the proportion of each count to all data. The sum of this column is 1 or 100%.
- The row.prop is the proportion of each count within each row. The sum of the 2 proportions for each level of employment status is 1 or 100%.
- The col.prop is the proportion of each count within each column. The sum of the 3 proportions for each level of gender (male or female) is 1 or 100%.
- The expected column is the expected values if there is no relation between gender and employment status. We see that all expected values are greater than 5 so the normal approximation to the binomial distribution is valid.
- The resid column contains the Pearson residuals and the std.resid column contains the standardized residuals.

A significant Chi-square test can be followed by a pairwise proportion test using the pairwise_prop_test function to find which groups are different in their proportions.

```
acs12 %>% count(gender, employment) %>% drop_na() %>%

 pivot_wider(names_from = "gender," values_from = "n") %>%

 column_to_rownames("employment") %>% pairwise_prop_test() %>%

 flextable() %>% theme_box() %>%

 set_caption(caption = "Pairwise proportion test results of different employment statuses in males and females of the American Community Survey data")
```

Table 5.14. Pairwise Proportion Test Results of Different Employment Statuses in Males and Females of the American Community Survey Data

Group1	Group2	p	p.adj	p.adj. signif
not in labor force	unemployed	0.02150000	0.04300000	*
not in labor force	employed	0.00000164	0.00000492	****
unemployed	employed	1.00000000	1.00000000	ns

We conclude that:

- The "not in labor force" had significantly different gender proportions than the "unemployed" status. For example, the male proportion in "not in labor force" is 0.431 compared to 0.557 in "unemployed" status.
- The "not in labor force" had significantly different gender proportions than the "employed" status. For example, the male proportion in "not in labor force" is 0.431 compared to 0.558 in "employed" status.
- The "unemployed" had statistically equivalent gender proportions to the "employed" status. For example, the male proportion in "unemployed" is 0.557 compared to 0.558 in "employed" status.

5.4.1.3. Chi-square Test of the Different Employment Statuses in the Different Races

The null hypothesis is that the proportions of employment statuses are the same in the different races. The alternative hypothesis is that at least, two employment statuses are different from each other.

To conduct this test, we must have a matrix of columns and rows for the count of employment statuses in each race. To do that, we use the same above functions.

```
acs12 %>% count(race, employment) %>% drop_na() %>%

 pivot_wider(names_from = "race," values_from = "n") %>%

 flextable() %>% theme_box() %>%

 set_caption(caption = "Matrix of the count of different employment statuses in the different races of the American Community Survey data")
```

Table 5.15. Matrix of the Count of Different Employment Statuses in the Different Races of the American Community Survey Data

Employment	White	Black	Asian	Other
not in labor force	520	66	31	39
unemployed	72	20	3	11
employed	670	76	39	58

Then, to conduct a chi-square test on this matrix with counts, we convert the employment column to row names using the column_to_rownames function. Then, we use the chisq_test function.

```
acs12 %>% count(race, employment) %>% drop_na() %>%

 pivot_wider(names_from = "race," values_from = "n") %>%

 column_to_rownames("employment") %>% chisq_test() %>%

 flextable() %>% theme_box() %>%

 set_caption(caption = "Chi-square test results of different employment statuses in the different races of the American Community Survey data")
```

Table 5.16. Chi-square Test Results of Different Employment Statuses in the Different Races of the American Community Survey Data

n	Statistic	p	df	Method	p.signif
1,605	14.18197	0.0277	6	Chi-square test	*

We see a warning saying that the Chi-squared approximation may be incorrect. To get a closer look at the Chi-square test results, we can use the chisq_descriptives function after the chisq_test function.

```
acs12 %>% count(race, employment) %>% drop_na() %>%

 pivot_wider(names_from = "race," values_from = "n") %>%

 column_to_rownames("employment") %>% chisq_test() %>%

 chisq_descriptives() %>%

 flextable() %>% theme_box() %>%

 set_caption(caption = "Chi-square descriptive statistics of different employment statuses in the different races of the American Community Survey data")
```

Table 5.17. *Chi-square Descriptive Statistics of Different Employment Statuses in the Different Races of the American Community Survey Data*

Var1	Var2	Observed	prop	row.prop	col.prop	expected	resid	std.resid
not in labor force	white	520	0.323987539	0.79268293	0.41204437	515.808100	0.1845724	0.5192323
unemployed	white	72	0.044859813	0.67924528	0.05705230	83.347040	-1.2429038	-2.7820484
employed	white	670	0.417445483	0.79478055	0.53090333	662.844860	0.2779151	0.8724945
not in labor force	black	66	0.041121495	0.10060976	0.40740741	66.213084	-0.0261866	-0.0359160
unemployed	black	20	0.012461059	0.18867925	0.12345679	10.699065	2.8435029	3.1030925
employed	black	76	0.047352025	0.09015421	0.46913580	85.087850	-0.9852068	-1.5079668
not in labor force	asian	31	0.019314642	0.04725610	0.42465753	29.836760	0.2129578	0.2834693
unemployed	asian	3	0.001869159	0.02830189	0.04109589	4.821184	-0.8294246	-0.8784596
employed	asian	39	0.024299065	0.04626335	0.53424658	38.342056	0.1062554	0.1578408
not in labor force	other	39	0.024299065	0.05945122	0.36111111	44.142056	-0.7739458	-1.0421772
unemployed	other	11	0.006853583	0.10377358	0.10185185	7.132710	1.4480362	1.5514677
employed	other	58	0.036137072	0.06880190	0.53703704	56.725234	0.1692554	0.2543485

We have 1 expected value smaller than 5 for the unemployed and Asian race (4.82) so the Chi-square test is not suitable in this case and Fisher exact test should be used.

5.4.1.4. Chi-square Test of the Different Force Types Applied on the Different Races

The null hypothesis is that the proportions of force types are the same in the different races. The alternative hypothesis is that at least, two force types are different from each other.

To conduct this test, we must have a matrix of columns and rows for the count of force types in each race. To do that, we use the same above functions. We use the additional argument values_fill = 0 to fill zero values when a certain force type is not applied to a specific race.

```
mn_police_use_of_force %>% count(race, force_type) %>% drop_na() %>%
 pivot_wider(names_from = "race," values_from = "n," values_fill = 0) %>%
 flextable() %>% theme_box() %>%
 set_caption(caption = "Matrix of the count of different force types applied on the different races from the Minneapolis police use of force data")
```

Table 5.18. *Matrix of the Count of Different Force Types Applied on the Different Races from the Minneapolis Police use of Force Data*

force_type	Asian	Black	Native American	Other/ Mixed Race	Pacific Islander	White
Bodily Force	78	5,519	616	137	5	2,454
Chemical Irritant	32	1,033	18	50	1	191
Gun Point Display	1	76	8	3	0	16
Improvised Weapon	1	83	10	1	0	47
Taser	17	755	104	12	0	334
Baton	0	2	0	0	0	1
Firearm	0	2	0	0	0	0
Less Lethal	0	23	6	0	0	27

force_ type	Asian	Black	Native American	Other/ Mixed Race	Pacific Islander	White
Less Lethal Projectile	0	3	0	0	0	0
Maximal Restraint Technique	0	104	14	0	0	42
Police K9 Bite	0	48	8	2	0	17

For example, the Firearm force type was not applied to all races except Blacks in 2 cases, so we filled 0 values for all races except Black.

Then, to conduct a chi-square test on this matrix with counts, we convert the force type column to row names using the column_to_rownames function. Then, we use the chisq_test function.

```
mn_police_use_of_force %>% count(race, force_type) %>% drop_na() %>%

 pivot_wider(names_from = "race," values_from = "n," values_fill = 0) %>%

 column_to_rownames("force_type") %>% chisq_test() %>%

 flextable() %>% theme_box() %>%

 set_caption(caption = "Chi-square test results of different force types applied on the different races from the Minneapolis police use of force data")
```

Table 5.19. Chi-square Test Results of Different Force Types Applied on the Different Races from the Minneapolis Police use of Force Data

n	statistic	p	df	method	p.signif
11,901	293.5087	0.0000000000000000000000000000000000353	50	Chi-square test	****

Again, we see a warning saying that the Chi-square test is not suitable in this case and Fisher exact test should be used.

5.4.1.5. Chi-square Test of the Different Force Types Applied in the Different Neighborhoods

The null hypothesis is that the proportions of force types are the same in the different neighborhoods. The alternative hypothesis is that at least, two force types are different from each other.

To conduct this test, we must have a matrix of columns and rows for the count of force types in each neighborhood. To do that, we use the same above functions. We use the additional argument values_fill = 0 to fill zero values when a certain force type is not applied in a specific neighborhood.

```
mn_police_use_of_force %>% count(neighborhood, force_type) %>%

 filter(!neighborhood=="") %>%

 drop_na() %>%

 pivot_wider(names_from = "force_type," values_from = "n,"

        values_fill = 0) %>%

 flextable() %>% theme_box() %>%

 set_caption(caption = "Matrix of the count of different force types applied in
different neighborhoods from the Minneapolis police use of force data")
```

Table 5.20. Matrix of the Count of Different Force Types Applied in Different Neighborhoods from the Minneapolis Police Use of Force Data

Neighborhood	Bodily Force	Chemical Irritant	Maximal Restraint Technique	Police K9 Bite	Taser	Improvised Weapon	Less Lethal	Gun Point Display	Firearm	Baton	Less Lethal Projectile
Armatage	19	1	1	1	6	0	0	0	0	0	0
Audubon Park	89	3	0	0	6	0	0	0	0	0	0
Bancroft	23	4	0	0	1	2	0	0	0	0	0
Beltrami	10	0	0	0	0	0	1	0	0	0	0
Bottineau	7	1	0	1	1	0	0	0	0	0	0
Bryant	22	0	0	2	1	0	0	0	0	0	0
Bryn – Mawr	15	0	0	0	3	0	0	0	0	0	0
CARAG	154	4	0	1	12	3	0	1	0	0	0
Camden Industrial	3	0	0	0	0	0	0	0	0	0	0
Cedar – Isles – Dean	4	2	0	0	0	0	0	0	0	0	0
Cedar Riverside	136	31	4	3	24	1	3	3	0	0	0
Central	122	10	0	1	23	0	0	2	0	0	0
Cleveland	86	1	2	2	4	1	0	1	0	0	0
Columbia Park	31	0	5	1	2	0	1	0	0	0	0
Como	105	2	2	0	15	2	0	4	0	0	0
Cooper	8	1	0	2	0	0	0	0	0	0	0

Corcoran	76	2	1	0	6	1	1	1	1	0	0
Diamond Lake	27	1	0	0	3	1	0	0	0	0	0
Downtown East	102	3	2	0	24	0	0	0	0	0	0
Downtown West	1,688	999	19	0	190	17	7	8	0	0	0
ECCO	20	2	0	0	3	0	0	0	0	0	0
East Harriet	15	0	0	0	4	1	0	1	0	0	0
East Isles	51	4	0	0	6	3	0	0	0	0	0
East Phillips	231	16	4	2	31	1	0	6	0	1	0
Elliot Park	215	11	3	0	47	2	3	1	0	1	0
Ericsson	14	0	0	0	1	1	0	0	0	0	0
Field	10	0	0	0	6	0	0	0	0	0	0
Folwell	273	16	3	6	31	10	0	6	0	0	0
Fulton	15	0	0	0	4	1	0	0	0	0	0
Hale	1	0	0	0	1	0	0	0	0	0	0
Harrison	130	8	3	1	8	2	0	3	0	0	0
Hawthorne	403	49	3	2	32	6	2	5	0	0	0
Hiawatha	39	0	0	1	7	0	0	0	0	0	0
Holland	112	4	1	1	21	0	5	1	0	0	0
Howe	29	0	0	2	9	1	0	1	0	0	0
Jordan	383	15	7	4	48	13	0	7	0	0	2
Keewaydin	18	1	1	0	0	0	0	0	0	0	0

Kenny	1	0	0	0	0	0	0	0	0	0	0
Kenwood	17	2	2	0	1	1	0	0	0	0	0
King Field	72	0	7	1	3	4	0	0	0	0	0
Lind – Bohanon	111	5	4	1	16	2	0	2	0	0	1
Linden Hills	22	1	0	0	1	1	1	0	0	0	0
Logan Park	20	1	3	1	3	0	0	0	0	0	0
Longfellow	99	30	1	1	16	0	21	2	0	0	0
Loring Park	287	23	9	2	80	4	6	3	0	0	0
Lowry Hill	34	7	2	1	5	0	0	1	0	0	0
Lowry Hill East	367	126	0	1	43	14	3	0	0	0	0
Lyndale	194	6	5	1	32	2	4	2	0	0	0
Lynnhurst	17	0	0	1	4	0	0	0	0	0	0
Marcy Holmes	246	24	5	0	28	0	5	2	0	0	0
Marshall Terrace	21	0	1	1	4	0	0	0	0	0	0
McKinley	143	0	2	4	9	4	0	1	0	0	0
Mid – City Industrial	25	2	1	0	4	0	0	0	0	0	0
Midtown Phillips	128	3	0	3	8	4	0	1	0	0	0
Minnehaha	10	0	0	0	0	0	0	0	0	0	0
Morris Park	6	0	1	2	3	0	0	0	0	0	0

Near – North	462	33	4	2	48	6	1	6	0	0	0
Nicollet Island – East Bank	64	7	6	1	23	1	1	2	0	1	0
North Loop	253	27	10	0	30	1	2	0	0	0	0
Northeast Park	52	2	0	1	6	0	2	0	0	0	0
Northrop	22	0	0	0	2	2	0	0	0	0	0
Page	4	0	0	0	1	0	0	0	0	0	0
Phillips West	113	11	0	0	19	1	1	2	0	0	0
Powderhorn Park	124	14	3	4	22	1	1	2	0	0	0
Prospect Park – East River Road	94	3	7	0	31	1	4	0	0	0	0
Regina	20	0	0	0	2	0	0	0	0	0	0
Seward	88	3	3	1	19	0	2	0	0	0	0
Sheridan	26	0	2	0	7	0	0	0	0	0	0
Shingle Creek	42	0	1	0	5	0	0	0	0	0	0
St. Anthony East	24	1	0	1	4	0	0	2	0	0	0
St. Anthony West	32	0	4	0	10	1	0	0	0	0	0
Standish	28	9	2	2	10	1	1	1	0	0	0
Steven's Square – Loring Heights	174	1	3	1	35	10	1	0	0	0	0

Sumner – Glenwood	31	0	2	0	5	0	0	2	0	0	0
Tangletown	37	1	0	0	4	0	1	0	0	0	0
University of Minnesota	32	8	2	0	8	0	0	2	0	0	0
Ventura Village	155	5	4	2	27	2	1	2	0	0	0
Victory	39	6	0	2	6	0	0	0	0	0	0
Waite Park	59	2	5	1	5	0	0	1	0	0	0
Webber – Camden	163	16	3	1	19	2	0	5	0	0	0
Wenonah	33	0	0	0	7	0	1	0	1	0	0
West Calhoun	12	0	0	0	1	0	0	0	0	0	0
Whittier	384	17	3	1	45	12	2	6	0	0	0
Willard – Hay	256	2	0	3	32	2	0	4	0	1	0
Windom	54	0	2	0	21	0	2	1	0	0	0
Windom Park	44	3	0	1	13	0	1	1	0	0	0

Then, to conduct a chi-square test on this matrix with counts, we convert the neighborhood column to row names using the column_to_rownames function. Then, we use the chisq_test function.

```
mn_police_use_of_force %>% count(neighborhood, force_type) %>%

filter(!neighborhood=="“") %>%

drop_na() %>%

pivot_wider(names_from = "force_type," values_from = "n,"

        values_fill = 0) %>%

column_to_rownames("neighborhood") %>% chisq_test() %>%

flextable() %>% theme_box() %>%

set_caption(caption = "Chi-square test results of different force types applied in different neighborhoods from the Minneapolis police use of force data")
```

Table 5.21. Chi-square Test Results of Different Force Types Applied in Different Neighborhoods from the Minneapolis Police Use of Force Data

n	Statistic	p	df	method	p.signif
12,921	3,791.092	0	850	Chi-square test	****

Again, we see a warning saying that the Chi-square test is not suitable in this case and Fisher exact test should be used.

5.4.2. Fisher Exact Test

The Fisher exact test is used when the expected value in any cell of the contingency table is less than 5. For tables in which the use of the Chi-square test is suitable, the two tests give very similar results although the p-value will be different as the Fisher exact test uses the hypergeometric distribution to calculate its p-value. Also, the Fisher test uses the same matrix formula as the Chi-square test. The Fisher test also needs unpaired data meaning that all data observations are independent.

5.4.2.1. Fisher Test of the Different Employment Statuses in the Two Genders

The null hypothesis is that the proportions of employment statuses are the same in the 2 genders. The alternative hypothesis is that at least, two employment statuses are different from each other.

To conduct this test, we must have a matrix of columns and rows for the count of employment statuses in each gender as done before. Then, we use the fisher_test function from the rstatix package.

```
acs12 %>% count(gender, employment) %>% drop_na() %>%

 pivot_wider(names_from = "gender," values_from = "n") %>%

 column_to_rownames("employment") %>% fisher_test() %>%

 flextable() %>% theme_box() %>%

 set_caption(caption = "Fisher test results of different employment statuses in males and females of the American Community Survey data")
```

Table 5.22. Fisher Test Results of Different Employment Statuses in Males and Females of the American Community Survey Data

n	p	p.signif
1,605	0.00000437	****

We see that:

- The table contains the p-value which is very low.
- The p_value is too low, so we reject the null hypothesis and conclude that the employment status proportions are different in the two genders or the gender proportions are different in the different employment statuses.

A significant Fisher test can be followed by a pairwise Fisher test using the pairwiseNominalIndependence function, from the rcompanion package, to find which groups (employment statuses) in the rows are different in their proportions.

The pairwiseNominalIndependence function requires a matrix data class so we convert the last data frame to a matrix using the as.matrix function. The pairwiseNominalIndependence function uses the arguments:

- compare = "row" to find which employment statuses in the rows are different in their proportions.
- fisher = TRUE to do a pairwise Fisher test.
- gtest = FALSE, chisq = FALSE so do not do pairwise Chi-square or G-tests.

```
library(rcompanion)

acs12 %>% count(gender, employment) %>% drop_na() %>%

 pivot_wider(names_from = "gender," values_from = "n") %>%

 column_to_rownames("employment") %>% as.matrix() %>%

 pairwiseNominalIndependence(compare = "row," fisher = TRUE, gtest = FALSE,
chisq = FALSE) %>%

 flextable() %>% theme_box() %>%

 set_caption(caption = "Pairwise Fisher test results of different employment
statuses in males and females of the American Community Survey data")
```

Table 5.23. Pairwise Fisher test Results of Different Employment Statuses in Males and Females of the American Community Survey Data

Comparison	p.Fisher	p.adj. Fisher
not in labor force : unemployed	0.02030000	0.03040000
not in labor force : employed	0.00000128	0.00000384
unemployed : employed	1.00000000	1.00000000

We conclude that based on the adjusted p-values from the pairwise Fisher test "p.adj.Fisher":

- The "not in labor force" had significantly different gender proportions than the "unemployed" status. For example, the male proportion in "not in labor force" is 0.431 compared to 0.557 in "unemployed" status.
- The "not in labor force" had significantly different gender proportions than the "employed" status. For example, the male proportion in "not in labor force" is 0.431 compared to 0.558 in "employed" status.

- The "unemployed" had statistically equivalent gender proportions to the "employed" status. For example, the male proportion in "unemployed" is 0.557 compared to 0.558 in "employed" status.

5.4.2.2. Fisher Test of the Different Employment Statuses in the Different Races

The null hypothesis is that the proportions of employment statuses are the same in the different races. The alternative hypothesis is that at least, two employment statuses are different from each other.

To conduct this test, we must have a matrix of columns and rows for the count of employment statuses in the different races as done before. Then, we use the fisher_test function from the rstatix package. Because we have a larger than 2X2 table, we use the argument simulate.p.value = TRUE.

```
set.seed(123)

acs12 %>% count(race, employment) %>% drop_na() %>%

 pivot_wider(names_from = "race," values_from = "n") %>%

 column_to_rownames("employment") %>%

 fisher_test(simulate.p.value = T) %>%

 flextable() %>% theme_box() %>%

 set_caption(caption = "Fisher test results of different employment statuses in the different races of the American Community Survey data")
```

Table 5.24. Fisher Test Results of Different Employment Statuses in the Different Races of the American Community Survey Data

n	p	p.signif
1,605	0.0435	*

We see that:

- The table contains the p-value which is lower than the cut-off value of 0.05.
- The p_value is significant, so we reject the null hypothesis and conclude that the employment status proportions are different in the different races or the race proportions are different in the different

employment statuses.

A significant Fisher test can be followed by a pairwise Fisher test using the pairwiseNominalIndependence function to find which employment statuses in the rows are different in their proportions.

```
acs12 %>% count(race, employment) %>% drop_na() %>%

 pivot_wider(names_from = "race," values_from = "n") %>%

 column_to_rownames("employment") %>% as.matrix() %>%

 pairwiseNominalIndependence(compare = "row," fisher = TRUE,

               gtest = FALSE, chisq = FALSE) %>%
 flextable() %>% theme_box() %>%

 set_caption(caption = "Pairwise Fisher test results of comparing different employment statuses in their proportions of different races of the American Community Survey data")
```

Table 5.25. Pairwise Fisher Test Results of Comparing Different Employment Statuses in Their Proportions of Different Races of the American Community Survey Data

Comparison	p.Fisher	p.adj. Fisher
not in labor force : unemployed	0.01320	0.0198
not in labor force : employed	0.81700	0.8170
unemployed : employed	0.00737	0.0198

We conclude that based on the adjusted p-values from the pairwise Fisher test "p.adj.Fisher":

- The "not in labor force" had significantly different race proportions than the "unemployed" status. For example, the White proportion in "not in labor force" is 0.79 compared to 0.68 in "unemployed" status.
- The "not in labor force" had statistically equivalent race proportions to the "employed" status. For example, the White proportion in "not in labor force" is 0.79 compared to 0.79 in "employed" status.
- The "unemployed" had significantly different race proportions than the "employed" status. For example, the White proportion in "unemployed" status is 0.68 compared to 0.79 in "employed" status.

We can also use the pairwiseNominalIndependence function to find which races in the columns are different in their proportions.

```
acs12 %>% count(race, employment) %>% drop_na() %>%

 pivot_wider(names_from = "race," values_from = "n") %>%

 column_to_rownames("employment") %>% as.matrix() %>%

 pairwiseNominalIndependence(compare = "column," fisher = TRUE,

              gtest = FALSE, chisq = FALSE) %>%

 flextable() %>% theme_box() %>%

  set_caption(caption = "Pairwise Fisher test results of comparing different races in their proportions of different employment statuses of the American Community Survey data")
```

Table 5.26. Pairwise Fisher Test Results of Comparing Different Races in their Proportions of Different Employment Statuses of the American Community Survey Data

Comparison	p.Fisher	p.adj.Fisher
white : black	0.00804	0.0482
white : asian	0.94000	0.9400
white : other	0.14600	0.2920
black : asian	0.13000	0.2920
black : other	0.53700	0.6440
asian : other	0.29500	0.4420

We conclude that based on the adjusted p-values from the pairwise Fisher test "p.adj.Fisher":

- Only the White race had significantly different employment status proportions than the Black race. For example, the unemployed proportion in White is 0.057 compared to 0.123 in Black.
- All other race comparisons (white : asian, white : other, black : asian, black : other, and asian : other) had statistically equivalent employment status proportions to each other.

5.4.2.3. Fisher Test of the Different Force Types Applied on the Different Races

The null hypothesis is that the proportions of force types are the same in the different races. The alternative hypothesis is that at least, two force types are different from each other.

To conduct this test, we must have a matrix of columns and rows for the count of force types in the different races as done before. Then, we use the fisher_test function from the rstatix package. Because we have a larger than 2X2 table, we use the argument simulate.p.value = TRUE.

```
set.seed(123)

mn_police_use_of_force %>% count(race, force_type) %>% drop_na() %>%

 pivot_wider(names_from = "race," values_from = "n," values_fill = 0) %>%

 column_to_rownames("force_type") %>%

 fisher_test(simulate.p.value = T) %>%

 flextable() %>% theme_box() %>%

 set_caption(caption = "Fisher test results of different force types applied on the different races from the Minneapolis police use of force data")
```

Table 5.27. Fisher Test Results of Different Force Types Applied on the Different Races from the Minneapolis Police Use of Force Data

n	p	p.signif
11,901	0.0005	***

We see that:

- The Table 5.27 contains the p-value which is lower than the cut-off value of 0.05.
- The p_value is significant, so we reject the null hypothesis and conclude that the force type proportions are different in the different races or the race proportions are different in the different force types.

A significant Fisher test can be followed by a pairwise Fisher test using the pairwiseNominalIndependence function to find which force types in the rows are different in their proportions. However, due to the many zeros in many force types, we must group them to focus on the 5 most frequent types using the fct_lump_n function as before. We also use the argument simulate.p.value = TRUE because of the large cell counts.

```
set.seed(123)

mn_police_use_of_force %>%

 mutate(force_type = fct_lump_n(force_type, n=5)) %>%

 count(race, force_type) %>% drop_na() %>%

 pivot_wider(names_from = "race," values_from = "n," values_fill = 0) %>%

 column_to_rownames("force_type") %>% as.matrix() %>%

 pairwiseNominalIndependence(compare = "row," fisher = TRUE,

              gtest = FALSE, chisq = FALSE,

              simulate.p.value = TRUE) %>%

 flextable() %>% theme_box() %>%

 set_caption(caption = "Pairwise Fisher test results of comparing different force types in their proportions of different races of the Minneapolis police use of force data")
```

Table 5.28. Pairwise Fisher Test Results of Comparing Different Force Types in Their Proportions of Different Races of the Minneapolis Police Use of Force Data

Comparison	p.Fisher	p.adj. Fisher
Bodily Force : Chemical Irritant	0.0005	0.0015
Bodily Force : Improvised Weapon	0.7030	0.7110
Bodily Force : Taser	0.1040	0.2600
Bodily Force : Other	0.5600	0.6460
Bodily Force : Maximal Restraint Technique	0.4100	0.6120
Chemical Irritant : Improvised Weapon	0.0005	0.0015

Comparison	p.Fisher	p.adj. Fisher
Chemical Irritant : Taser	0.0005	0.0015
Chemical Irritant : Other	0.0005	0.0015
Chemical Irritant : Maximal Restraint Technique	0.0005	0.0015
Improvised Weapon : Taser	0.7110	0.7110
Improvised Weapon : Other	0.3940	0.6120
Improvised Weapon : Maximal Restraint Technique	0.3280	0.6120
Taser : Other	0.4190	0.6120
Taser : Maximal Restraint Technique	0.5080	0.6350
Other : Maximal Restraint Technique	0.4490	0.6120

We conclude that based on the adjusted p-values "p.adj.Fisher":

- The "Bodily Force" type had significantly different race proportions than the "Chemical Irritant" force type.
- The "Chemical Irritant" force type had significantly different race proportions than the "Improvised Weapon," "Taser," "Other," and "Maximal Restraint Technique" force types.
- All other pairwise force-type comparisons are statistically equivalent.

We can also use the pairwiseNominalIndependence function to find which races in the columns are different in their proportions of different force types.

```
set.seed(123)

mn_police_use_of_force %>%

 mutate(force_type = fct_lump_n(force_type, n=5)) %>%

 count(race, force_type) %>% drop_na() %>%

 pivot_wider(names_from = "race," values_from = "n," values_fill = 0) %>%

 column_to_rownames("force_type") %>% as.matrix() %>%

 pairwiseNominalIndependence(compare = "column," fisher = TRUE,
```

```
            gtest = FALSE, chisq = FALSE,

            simulate.p.value = TRUE) %>%

flextable() %>% theme_box() %>%

 set_caption(caption = "Pairwise Fisher test results of comparing different races in their proportions of different force types of of the Minneapolis police use of force data")
```

Table 5.29. Pairwise Fisher Test results of Comparing Different Races in Their Proportions of Different Force Types of the Minneapolis Police Use of Force Data

Comparison	p.Fisher	p.adj.Fisher
Asian : Black	0.0045	0.00750
Asian : Native American	0.0005	0.00107
Asian : Other/Mixed Race	0.1170	0.17600
Asian : Pacific Islander	0.7430	0.85700
Asian : White	0.0005	0.00107
Black : Native American	0.0005	0.00107
Black : Other/Mixed Race	0.0010	0.00188
Black : Pacific Islander	1.0000	1.00000
Black : White	0.0005	0.00107
Native American : Other/Mixed Race	0.0005	0.00107
Native American : Pacific Islander	0.3950	0.53900
Native American : White	0.0005	0.00107
Other/Mixed Race : Pacific Islander	1.0000	1.00000
Other/Mixed Race : White	0.0005	0.00107
Pacific Islander : White	0.5810	0.72600

We conclude that based on the adjusted p-values "p.adj.Fisher":

- The Asian race had significantly different force-type proportions than the Black, Native American, and White races.
- The Black race had significantly different force-type proportions than the Native American, Other/Mixed, and White races.

- The Native American race had significantly different force type proportions than the Other/Mixed and White races.
- The Other/Mixed race had significantly different force type proportions than the White race.

5.4.2.4. Fisher Test of the Different Force Types Applied in the Different Neighborhoods

The null hypothesis is that the proportions of force types are the same in the different neighborhoods. The alternative hypothesis is that at least, two force types are different from each other.

To conduct this test, we must have a matrix of columns and rows for the count of force types in the different races as done before. Then, we use the fisher_test function from the rstatix package. Because we have a larger than 2X2 table, we use the argument simulate.p.value = TRUE.

```
set.seed(123)

mn_police_use_of_force %>% count(neighborhood, force_type) %>%

 filter(!neighborhood=="") %>%

 drop_na() %>%

 pivot_wider(names_from = "force_type," values_from = "n,"

       values_fill = 0) %>%

 column_to_rownames("neighborhood") %>%

 fisher_test(simulate.p.value = T) %>%

 flextable() %>% theme_box() %>%

 set_caption(caption = "Fisher test results of different force types applied
in the different neighborhoods from the Minneapolis police use of force data")
```

Table 5.30. Fisher Test Results of Different Force Types Applied in the Different Neighborhoods from the Minneapolis Police Use of Force Data

n	p	p.signif
12,921	0.0005	***

We see that:

- The Table 5.30 contains the p-value which is lower than the cut-off value of 0.05.
- The p_value is significant, so we reject the null hypothesis and conclude that the force type proportions are different in the different neighborhoods or that the neighborhood proportions are different in the different force types.

A significant Fisher test can be followed by a pairwise Fisher test using the pairwiseNominalIndependence function to find which force types in the columns are different in their proportions. However, due to the many zeros in many force types, we must group them to focus on the 5 most frequent types using the fct_lump_n function as before. We also use the argument simulate.p.value = TRUE because of the large cell counts.

```
set.seed(123)

mn_police_use_of_force %>%

 mutate(force_type = fct_lump_n(force_type, n=5)) %>%

 count(neighborhood, force_type) %>%

 filter(!neighborhood=="") %>%

 drop_na() %>%

 pivot_wider(names_from = "force_type," values_from = "n,"

        values_fill = 0) %>%

 column_to_rownames("neighborhood") %>% as.matrix() %>%

 pairwiseNominalIndependence(compare = "column," fisher = TRUE,

                gtest = FALSE, chisq = FALSE,
```

```
            simulate.p.value = TRUE) %>%

flextable() %>% theme_box() %>%

 set_caption(caption = "Pairwise Fisher test results of comparing different
force types in their proportions of different neighborhoods of the Minneapolis
police use of force data")
```

Table 5.31. Pairwise Fisher Test Results of Comparing Different Force Types in Their Proportions of Different Neighborhoods of the Minneapolis Police Use of Force Data

Comparison	p.Fisher	p.adj.Fisher
Bodily Force : Chemical Irritant	0.0005	0.000536
Bodily Force : Maximal Restraint Technique	0.0005	0.000536
Bodily Force : Taser	0.0005	0.000536
Bodily Force : Other	0.0005	0.000536
Bodily Force : Improvised Weapon	0.0030	0.003000
Chemical Irritant : Maximal Restraint Technique	0.0005	0.000536
Chemical Irritant : Taser	0.0005	0.000536
Chemical Irritant : Other	0.0005	0.000536
Chemical Irritant : Improvised Weapon	0.0005	0.000536
Maximal Restraint Technique : Taser	0.0005	0.000536
Maximal Restraint Technique : Other	0.0005	0.000536
Maximal Restraint Technique : Improvised Weapon	0.0005	0.000536
Taser : Other	0.0005	0.000536
Taser : Improvised Weapon	0.0005	0.000536
Other : Improvised Weapon	0.0005	0.000536

We conclude that based on the adjusted p-values "p.adj.Fisher":

- All force types ("Bodily Force," "Chemical Irritant," "Maximal Restraint Technique, "Taser," "Improvised Weapon," and "Other") have different neighborhood proportions than each other.

We can also use the pairwiseNominalIndependence function to find which neighborhoods in the rows are different in their proportions of different force types. However, due to many zeros in many neighborhoods, we must group them to focus on the 20 most frequent neighborhoods using the fct_lump_n function as before. We also use the argument simulate.p.value = TRUE because of the large cell counts.

```
set.seed(123)

mn_police_use_of_force %>%

 mutate(neighborhood = fct_lump_n(neighborhood, n=20)) %>%

 count(neighborhood, force_type) %>%

 filter(!neighborhood==““) %>%

 drop_na() %>%

 pivot_wider(names_from = “force_type,” values_from = “n,”

        values_fill = 0) %>%

 column_to_rownames(“neighborhood”) %>% as.matrix() %>%

 pairwiseNominalIndependence(compare = “row,” fisher = TRUE,

                gtest = FALSE, chisq = FALSE,

                simulate.p.value = TRUE) %>%

 flextable() %>% theme_box() %>%

 set_caption(caption = “Pairwise Fisher test results of comparing different neighborhoods in their proportions of different force types of the Minneapolis police use of force data”)
```

Table 5.32. Pairwise Fisher Test Results of Comparing Different Neighborhoods in Their Proportions of Different Force Types of the Minneapolis Police Use of Force Data

Comparison	p.Fisher	p.adj. Fisher
CARAG : Cedar Riverside	0.0005	0.00135
CARAG : Downtown West	0.0005	0.00135
CARAG : East Phillips	0.0720	0.09630
CARAG : Elliot Park	0.0070	0.01300
CARAG : Folwell	0.3430	0.38900
CARAG : Hawthorne	0.0355	0.05320
CARAG : Jordan	0.4910	0.52600
CARAG : Loring Park	0.0005	0.00135
CARAG : Lowry Hill East	0.0005	0.00135
CARAG : Lyndale	0.0615	0.08550
CARAG : Marcy Holmes	0.0030	0.00624
CARAG : Near – North	0.3930	0.43400
CARAG : North Loop	0.0005	0.00135
CARAG : Powderhorn Park	0.0010	0.00247
CARAG : Steven's Square – Loring Heights	0.0025	0.00530
CARAG : Ventura Village	0.1340	0.16500
CARAG : Webber – Camden	0.0430	0.06310
CARAG : Whittier	0.6910	0.71100
CARAG : Willard – Hay	0.3510	0.39600
CARAG : Other	0.0630	0.08700
Cedar Riverside : Downtown West	0.0005	0.00135
Cedar Riverside : East Phillips	0.0035	0.00700
Cedar Riverside : Elliot Park	0.0005	0.00135
Cedar Riverside : Folwell	0.0005	0.00135
Cedar Riverside : Hawthorne	0.0020	0.00442
Cedar Riverside : Jordan	0.0005	0.00135
Cedar Riverside : Loring Park	0.0020	0.00442
Cedar Riverside : Lowry Hill East	0.0005	0.00135
Cedar Riverside : Lyndale	0.0005	0.00135

Cedar Riverside : Marcy Holmes	0.0115	0.02060
Cedar Riverside : Near – North	0.0005	0.00135
Cedar Riverside : North Loop	0.0040	0.00778
Cedar Riverside : Powderhorn Park	0.5500	0.58000
Cedar Riverside : Steven's Square – Loring Heights	0.0005	0.00135
Cedar Riverside : Ventura Village	0.0010	0.00247
Cedar Riverside : Webber – Camden	0.0550	0.07800
Cedar Riverside : Whittier	0.0005	0.00135
Cedar Riverside : Willard – Hay	0.0005	0.00135
Cedar Riverside : Other	0.0005	0.00135
Downtown West : East Phillips	0.0005	0.00135
Downtown West : Elliot Park	0.0005	0.00135
Downtown West : Folwell	0.0005	0.00135
Downtown West : Hawthorne	0.0005	0.00135
Downtown West : Jordan	0.0005	0.00135
Downtown West : Loring Park	0.0005	0.00135
Downtown West : Lowry Hill East	0.0005	0.00135
Downtown West : Lyndale	0.0005	0.00135
Downtown West : Marcy Holmes	0.0005	0.00135
Downtown West : Near – North	0.0005	0.00135
Downtown West : North Loop	0.0005	0.00135
Downtown West : Powderhorn Park	0.0005	0.00135
Downtown West : Steven's Square – Loring Heights	0.0005	0.00135
Downtown West : Ventura Village	0.0005	0.00135
Downtown West : Webber – Camden	0.0005	0.00135
Downtown West : Whittier	0.0005	0.00135
Downtown West : Willard – Hay	0.0005	0.00135
Downtown West : Other	0.0005	0.00135
East Phillips : Elliot Park	0.0635	0.08720
East Phillips : Folwell	0.1580	0.18900
East Phillips : Hawthorne	0.0255	0.03940
East Phillips : Jordan	0.1250	0.15600

East Phillips : Loring Park	0.0035	0.00700
East Phillips : Lowry Hill East	0.0005	0.00135
East Phillips : Lyndale	0.1360	0.16600
East Phillips : Marcy Holmes	0.0855	0.11200
East Phillips : Near – North	0.4470	0.48400
East Phillips : North Loop	0.0205	0.03210
East Phillips : Powderhorn Park	0.4180	0.46000
East Phillips : Steven's Square – Loring Heights	0.0010	0.00247
East Phillips : Ventura Village	0.4450	0.48400
East Phillips : Webber – Camden	0.9310	0.94000
East Phillips : Whittier	0.0750	0.09970
East Phillips : Willard – Hay	0.0035	0.00700
East Phillips : Other	0.0910	0.11900
Elliot Park : Folwell	0.0005	0.00135
Elliot Park : Hawthorne	0.0005	0.00135
Elliot Park : Jordan	0.0025	0.00530
Elliot Park : Loring Park	0.5660	0.59400
Elliot Park : Lowry Hill East	0.0005	0.00135
Elliot Park : Lyndale	0.6990	0.71600
Elliot Park : Marcy Holmes	0.0195	0.03080
Elliot Park : Near – North	0.0080	0.01470
Elliot Park : North Loop	0.0035	0.00700
Elliot Park : Powderhorn Park	0.0480	0.07000
Elliot Park : Steven's Square – Loring Heights	0.0085	0.01550
Elliot Park : Ventura Village	0.5810	0.60400
Elliot Park : Webber – Camden	0.0165	0.02670
Elliot Park : Whittier	0.0245	0.03810
Elliot Park : Willard – Hay	0.0010	0.00247
Elliot Park : Other	0.1320	0.16300
Folwell : Hawthorne	0.0070	0.01300
Folwell : Jordan	0.7150	0.72900
Folwell : Loring Park	0.0005	0.00135
Folwell : Lowry Hill East	0.0005	0.00135

Folwell : Lyndale	0.0150	0.02500
Folwell : Marcy Holmes	0.0010	0.00247
Folwell : Near – North	0.1230	0.15500
Folwell : North Loop	0.0005	0.00135
Folwell : Powderhorn Park	0.1100	0.14000
Folwell : Steven's Square – Loring Heights	0.0015	0.00354
Folwell : Ventura Village	0.1860	0.21900
Folwell : Webber – Camden	0.3610	0.40300
Folwell : Whittier	0.3540	0.39800
Folwell : Willard – Hay	0.0030	0.00624
Folwell : Other	0.0130	0.02280
Hawthorne : Jordan	0.0010	0.00247
Hawthorne : Loring Park	0.0005	0.00135
Hawthorne : Lowry Hill East	0.0005	0.00135
Hawthorne : Lyndale	0.0005	0.00135
Hawthorne : Marcy Holmes	0.0550	0.07800
Hawthorne : Near – North	0.3390	0.38700
Hawthorne : North Loop	0.0145	0.02460
Hawthorne : Powderhorn Park	0.0160	0.02650
Hawthorne : Steven's Square – Loring Heights	0.0005	0.00135
Hawthorne: Ventura Village	0.0020	0.00442
Hawthorne: Webber – Camden	0.4390	0.48000
Hawthorne : Whittier	0.0020	0.00442
Hawthorne : Willard – Hay	0.0005	0.00135
Hawthorne : Other	0.0005	0.00135
Jordan : Loring Park	0.0005	0.00135
Jordan : Lowry Hill East	0.0005	0.00135
Jordan : Lyndale	0.0800	0.10600
Jordan : Marcy Holmes	0.0005	0.00135
Jordan : Near – North	0.0500	0.07190
Jordan : North Loop	0.0005	0.00135
Jordan : Powderhorn Park	0.0195	0.03080
Jordan : Steven's Square – Loring Heights	0.0195	0.03080

Jordan : Ventura Village	0.5290	0.56300
Jordan : Webber – Camden	0.1540	0.18500
Jordan : Whittier	0.5720	0.59800
Jordan : Willard – Hay	0.0145	0.02460
Jordan : Other	0.0020	0.00442
Loring Park : Lowry Hill East	0.0005	0.00135
Loring Park : Lyndale	0.1870	0.21900
Loring Park : Marcy Holmes	0.0020	0.00442
Loring Park : Near – North	0.0005	0.00135
Loring Park : North Loop	0.0015	0.00354
Loring Park : Powderhorn Park	0.1830	0.21700
Loring Park : Steven's Square – Loring Heights	0.0010	0.00247
Loring Park : Ventura Village	0.2370	0.27500
Loring Park : Webber – Camden	0.0025	0.00530
Loring Park : Whittier	0.0005	0.00135
Loring Park : Willard – Hay	0.0005	0.00135
Loring Park : Other	0.0135	0.02320
Lowry Hill East : Lyndale	0.0005	0.00135
Lowry Hill East : Marcy Holmes	0.0005	0.00135
Lowry Hill East : Near – North	0.0005	0.00135
Lowry Hill East : North Loop	0.0005	0.00135
Lowry Hill East : Powderhorn Park	0.0005	0.00135
Lowry Hill East : Steven's Square – Loring Heights	0.0005	0.00135
Lowry Hill East : Ventura Village	0.0005	0.00135
Lowry Hill East : Webber – Camden	0.0005	0.00135
Lowry Hill East : Whittier	0.0005	0.00135
Lowry Hill East : Willard – Hay	0.0005	0.00135
Lowry Hill East : Other	0.0005	0.00135
Lyndale : Marcy Holmes	0.0420	0.06210
Lyndale : Near – North	0.0125	0.02210
Lyndale : North Loop	0.0120	0.02140
Lyndale : Powderhorn Park	0.0925	0.12000
Lyndale : Steven's Square – Loring Heights	0.0485	0.07020

Lyndale : Ventura Village	0.9650	0.96500
Lyndale : Webber – Camden	0.0400	0.05960
Lyndale : Whittier	0.1030	0.13200
Lyndale : Willard – Hay	0.0150	0.02500
Lyndale : Other	0.8980	0.91100
Marcy Holmes : Near – North	0.0595	0.08330
Marcy Holmes : North Loop	0.4500	0.48500
Marcy Holmes : Powderhorn Park	0.0710	0.09560
Marcy Holmes : Steven's Square – Loring Heights	0.0005	0.00135
Marcy Holmes : Ventura Village	0.0165	0.02670
Marcy Holmes : Webber – Camden	0.1480	0.17900
Marcy Holmes : Whittier	0.0025	0.00530
Marcy Holmes : Willard – Hay	0.0005	0.00135
Marcy Holmes : Other	0.0315	0.04790
Near – North : North Loop	0.0135	0.02320
Near – North : Powderhorn Park	0.0335	0.05060
Near – North : Steven's Square – Loring Heights	0.0005	0.00135
Near – North : Ventura Village	0.0645	0.08800
Near – North : Webber – Camden	0.6660	0.68900
Near – North : Whittier	0.3910	0.43400
Near – North : Willard – Hay	0.0015	0.00354
Near – North : Other	0.0040	0.00778
North Loop : Powderhorn Park	0.0300	0.04600
North Loop : Steven's Square – Loring Heights	0.0005	0.00135
North Loop : Ventura Village	0.0055	0.01050
North Loop : Webber – Camden	0.0575	0.08100
North Loop : Whittier	0.0005	0.00135
North Loop : Willard – Hay	0.0005	0.00135
North Loop : Other	0.0105	0.01900
Powderhorn Park : Steven's Square – Loring Heights	0.0005	0.00135
Powderhorn Park : Ventura Village	0.2950	0.34000
Powderhorn Park : Webber – Camden	0.5310	0.56300

Powderhorn Park : Whittier	0.0040	0.00778
Powderhorn Park : Willard – Hay	0.0005	0.00135
Powderhorn Park : Other	0.3240	0.37200
Steven's Square – Loring Heights : Ventura Village	0.1000	0.12900
Steven's Square – Loring Heights : Webber – Camden	0.0005	0.00135
Steven's Square – Loring Heights : Whittier	0.0070	0.01300
Steven's Square – Loring Heights : Willard – Hay	0.0015	0.00354
Steven's Square – Loring Heights : Other	0.0005	0.00135
Ventura Village : Webber – Camden	0.1470	0.17800
Ventura Village : Whittier	0.2230	0.26000
Ventura Village : Willard – Hay	0.0660	0.08940
Ventura Village : Other	0.9500	0.95500
Webber – Camden : Whittier	0.1290	0.16000
Webber – Camden : Willard – Hay	0.0005	0.00135
Webber – Camden : Other	0.1120	0.14200
Whittier : Willard – Hay	0.0165	0.02670
Whittier : Other	0.0055	0.01050
Willard – Hay : Other	0.0005	0.00135

We conclude that based on the adjusted p-values "p.adj.Fisher":

- The "CARAG" neighborhood had significantly different force type proportions than the "Cedar Riverside," "Downtown West," "Elliot Park," "Loring Park," "Lowry Hill East." "Marcy Holmes," "North Loop," "Powderhorn Park," and "Steven's Square – Loring Heights" neighborhoods, while has statistically equivalent proportions to all other neighborhoods.
- Other neighborhoods can be noted similarly based on their adjusted p-values.

BIBLIOGRAPHY

1. Çetinkaya-Rundel, M., Diez, D., Bray, A., Kim, A., Baumer, B., Ismay, C., Paterno, N., & Barr, C., (2022). *openintro: Data Sets and Supplemental Functions from 'OpenIntro' Textbooks and Labs*. R package version 2.4.0. https://CRAN.R-project.org/package=openintro (accessed on 02 April 2024).
2. Gohel, D., (2022). *Flextable: Functions for Tabular Reporting*. R package version 0.7.0. https://CRAN.R-project.org/package=flextable (accessed on 02 April 2024).
3. Gross, J., & Ligges, U., (2015). *nortest: Tests for Normality*. R package version 1.0-4, https://CRAN.R-project.org/package=nortest (accessed on 02 April 2024).
4. Kassambara, A., (2020). *ggpubr: 'ggplot2' Based Publication Ready Plots*. R package version 0.4.0. https://CRAN.R-project.org/package=ggpubr (accessed on 02 April 2024).
5. Kassambara, A., (2022). *rstatix: Pipe-Friendly Framework for Basic Statistical Tests*. R package version 0.7.1. https://CRAN.R-project.org/package=rstatix (accessed on 02 April 2024).
6. Mangiafico, S., (2022). *rcompanion: Functions to Support Extension Education Program Evaluation.* R package version 2.4.18. https://CRAN.R-project.org/package=rcompanion (accessed on 02 April 2024).
7. R Core Team, (2022). *R: A Language and Environment for Statistical Computing*. R Foundation for Statistical Computing, Vienna, Austria. https://www.R-project.org/ (accessed on 02 April 2024).
8. Slowikowski, K., (2021). *ggrepel: Automatically Position Non-Overlapping Text Labels with 'ggplot2.'* R package version 0.9.1. https://

CRAN.R-project.org/package=ggrepel (accessed on 02 April 2024).

9. Wickham, et al., (2019). Welcome to the tidyverse. *Journal of Open Source Software*, *4*(43), 1686. https://doi.org/10.21105/joss.01686.
10. Wickham, H., & Seidel, D., (2022). *Scales: Scale Functions for Visualization*. R package version 1.2.0. https://CRAN.R-project.org/package=scales (accessed on 02 April 2024).
11. Wickham, H., (2016). *ggplot2: Elegant Graphics for Data Analysis*. Springer-Verlag New York.
12. Wickham, H., (2021). *forcats: Tools for Working with Categorical Variables (Factors)*. R package version 0.5.1. https://CRAN.R-project.org/package=forcats (accessed on 02 April 2024).
13. Wickham, H., (2022). *stringr: Simple, Consistent Wrappers for Common String Operations*. R package version 1.5.0. https://CRAN.R-project.org/package=stringr (accessed on 02 April 2024).
14. Wickham, H., François, R., Henry, L., Müller, K., & Vaughan, D., (2023). *dplyr: A Grammar of Data Manipulation*. R package version 1.1.2. https://CRAN.R-project.org/package=dplyr (accessed on 02 April 2024).
15. Wickham, H., Hester, J., & Bryan, J., (2022). *readr: Read Rectangular Text Data*. R package version 2.1.2. https://CRAN.R-project.org/package=readr (accessed on 02 April 2024).
16. Wickham, H., Vaughan, D., & Girlich, M., (2023). *tidyr: Tidy Messy Data*. R package version 1.3.0. https://CRAN.R-project.org/package=tidyr (accessed on 02 April 2024).
17. Wilkins, D., (2021). *treemapify: Draw Treemaps in 'ggplot2.'* R package version 2.5.5. https://CRAN.R-project.org/package=treemapify (accessed on 02 April 2024).

INDEX

D

E

F

N

O

P

Printed in the United States
by Baker & Taylor Publisher Services